Twenty-seventh Edition

Rugg's

Recommendations
on the
Colleges

*Compiled and Edited by the College Staff of
Rugg's Recommendations*

by Frederick E. Rugg

Rugg's Recommendations • Fallbrook, California

Copyright © 2010
Frederick E. Rugg

Copies of this book may be ordered from:
Rugg's Recommendations
P.O. Box 417
Fallbrook, CA 92088
760-728-4558 or 760-728-4467

Price: $25.95

ISBN 13: 978-1-883062-76-7
ISBN 10: 1-883062-76-4

LC# 89-062896

Prior Editions: ©1980, 1982, 1984, 1986, 1988, 1989, 1990, 1991,1992, 1993, 1994, 1995, 1996, 1997, 1998, 1999, 2000, 2001, 2002, 2003, 2004, 2005, 2006, 2007, 2008, 2009, 2010
by Rugg's Recommendations

Notice of Copyright

To
Barbara, Betsie, and Sue

TABLE OF CONTENTS

TABLE OF CONTENTS continues next page

TABLE OF CONTENTS, continued

**SECTION THREE - Avg. SAT-1, New SAT-1
& ACT Totals / Recommended Majors 205**

SOME NOTES FROM THE AUTHOR

WHY THIS BOOK?

As a secondary school college counselor, I heard the following question from a student or parent almost daily: "Can you please give us a list of quality colleges where one can major in psychology (or engineering or business or whatever)?"

For many years I pulled out the college handbooks and came up with a list of hundreds of colleges for each category and spent too much time with the student sifting through the multitude of schools, trying to narrow down the huge list.

I thought about a way out of this dilemma for a long time. People from Harvard would find an easy solution. They might tell the parents and student not to worry about a college major—just go to a fine liberal arts college (like Harvard) and everything will fall into place. After all, it's not the major and professors that count, it's the wonderful student body that makes a great college great. Right?

Well...over the years, I had trouble convincing parents of the merits of that argument. I guess they realize that all good universities are not good in every field.

Today, there's just so much pressure on young people to line up their careers and pick their occupations in life early. Career education seems to start in kindergarten these days. I've noticed that many parents pick right up on it and give Johnny the business if he hasn't chosen his career by the sophomore year of high school or earlier. No matter what I told Johnny and his parents, they still wanted a list of "the quality colleges with a good psychology (or whatever) department."

This book lists the quality departments at quality colleges and it will make the school counselor's job easier. For example, a public school counselor can use it constantly in January when juniors (and sometimes sophomores) line up outside his/her office, asking for a list of colleges to "go with" their PSAT scores. Probably a prep school counselor, a junior and community college transfer counselor, or a librarian might even find more use of this guide for college majors. Since this book is for the aid of the counselor, it is, then, also a guide for students and their parents in the college admissions process.

WHY THESE 1115 COLLEGES?

From our experience in the college admissions process, we have chosen 1115 quality four-year colleges (out of over 2000 that offer bachelor degrees) to study. We began with the 280 colleges that have survived the careful screening process involved in the granting of a Phi Beta Kappa chapter. The Phi Beta Kappa schools are listed in Appendix A. These colleges received chapters for superior undergraduate performance in the liberal arts and sciences.

To this list were added 835 colleges—schools that our staff felt are as good (or better) as several of the Phi Beta Kappa colleges or have excellent specialized programs. We should also note that, in general, the more well-respected the college, the more departments and majors were included. Berkeley is listed under 40 departments while some others only under one. The typical school in the study was noted with 9 departments. A departmental page averages 190 recommended colleges.

HOW IT'S DONE

Over the years, college students have been surveyed - the number well into five figures. If you want a straight answer, the young folks seldom waver. We also receive monthly evaluations from secondary school counselors around the country. Some colleges submit to us departments at their schools that they consider "hidden gems". They also send us departments they consider their "strongholds". Weekly, a variety of college personnel lobby for a certain program at their university. Also, almost every week we get "tipped off" on a great department at a college at workshops I present around the U.S.A. on the college admissions process. Almost every year since 1977 I've added 300 departments to my list. This year the number is over 600.

What can eliminate a department or stop its consideration? No balance. For example, too many professors from the same alma mater in a department, or too many professors in a department graduating from that very college. If the average college in America gives out 6% of it's degrees in, say, the field of Psychology, and the department in question is at a 3% level, this sets up a "red flag", too. So departments are entered based on the numbers.

But we are always also looking for "college departments that are student oriented." We do not want students to enter a college department where the professors are always away in Washington D.C., doing their own thing. We have a top initial researcher who spends all of her time on the Internet (departmental Web sites) comparing departments and loves to check out department sizes, quality of courses offered, events in their departments, learning outside the classroom, internships, diversity within the department, etc.

HOW DO YOU USE THIS BOOK?

If you know what you want to major in at college—great!—just look it up. In most cases, you will find each departmental section organized into three groups of colleges:

Group I—Most Selective Colleges

Colleges here are among the 100 most selective colleges in America. They accept very few students with high school averages below 80 (top prep schools can, of course, lower this figure significantly) and College Board scores below 1800 (New SAT-1) and 27 (on the American College Test).

Group II—Very Selective Colleges

Many of the students at these colleges have "B" averages (80-90), and College Board scores between 1650 and 1800 (New SAT-1) and ACTs between 24 and 26.

Group III—Selective Colleges

Although these colleges are, in general, easier to get into than Group I and II colleges, please keep in mind that they are, in our opinion at least, among the top 1100 colleges in the country. Many students at these colleges have College Board scores just under 1650 (New SAT-1), or just under 24 on the ACTs.

Now that we have an idea of the group breakdown, a student may need help deciding from which group(s) to select his/her colleges. The guidance counselor can help here—having knowledge of colleges and a student's grade point average, class rank, board scores, etc. Most students will want to start with a group of 8 to 10 colleges from the departmental major page. This "major page" is a starting point. Schools can be added to the student's list by his/her counselor—from the counselor's own knowledge of the student, and knowledge of other colleges that might "fit" the student. Schools can be eliminated from a student's list after reviewing the college catalogs (see Appendix F—The Get Going Form), checking out undesirable features (city vs. rural setting, etc.), visiting the colleges, and other personal preferences. If the student does not have a major in mind, he or she should go to a typical liberal arts (e.g., English or Math) page to get started. I've also included a letter code system for the college's enrollment figure. The enrollment letter appears beside each college name with the following code:

XL = Extra Large Enrollment (over 20,000 students)
L = Large Enrollment (from 8,000 to 20,000 students)
M = Medium Enrollment (from 3,000 to 8,000 students)
R = Moderate Enrollment (from 1,000 to 3,000 students)
S = Small Enrollment (under 1,000 students)

SOME PARTING SHOTS

I don't care to go into the argument of "Picking a college because it has a great Mathematics Department" vs. "Picking a school because the school overall is great (Yeah Harvard!) and you'll probably change your major anyway." The fact of the matter is that parents, career educators, and other educators are telling 16-year-olds (and younger) to have a career and a major all mapped out and I bet will continue to do so. I'm sure high school counselors will continue to be asked to help Suzy find a list of quality schools with "excellent majors in mathematics." Personally, I see nothing wrong with a high school senior, who loves mathematics, trying to pick a quality school where the math department at that institution is ranked by its students as one of the top majors at that school and is generally recognized as being top notch by college counselors. If Suzy changes her mind after a year or two, she's at least given it a good shot with a premier math department. And chances are excellent that if she changes her major, it was because another outstanding department at that school helped her grow and reassess her career goals. She'll probably stay with that department for her new major. No harm done.

A few other comments on this book and some random thoughts...

1. Some state universities, like Penn State, are very competitive for out-of-staters. A university such as this may be in Group II for in-staters, but, in reality, is a Group I school for "outsiders."

2. In general, a college that is competitive is that way for all majors—but there are some departments that are exceptions. For example, engineering is a tough major and must be considered "Group II" at a "Group III" school.

3. A knowledgeable observer of the college scene will note that some competitive "alternative" colleges do not appear in this work, e.g., Hampshire College (MA), St. John's (MD). The jury is not unanimous on these progressive schools, and they are not included in this book except under "Miscellaneous Majors Pages."

4. A few majors in this book, such as engineering, have not been broken down into subdivisions (Civil, Electrical, Mechanical, etc.). Students will have to research these majors more fully. Well, what's wrong with that? Good to have the youngsters doing some hard work and research on the college admissions process. Foreign Languages, however, is broken down.

5. Every year a few more colleges close their doors. Today, colleges are under pressure to compete and "Be Hot." We need a college guide to weed things out a bit, a consumer-oriented handbook. We hope this helps.

6. Don't overlook the good small liberal arts college. Too many large universities are too impersonal. But some kids love a big school. Some thrive in the anonymity of a huge lecture hall.

7. Keep in mind that weak departments at Harvard, Yale, Stanford, Princeton, etc. might be equal to or better than the strongest departments at many colleges and universities.

8. This book is an aid for counselors, parents, and kids—nothing more. It is not a guide for the colleges to compare themselves one with the other.

9. Do not be surprised if you discover that the best of the more expensive schools are actually least expensive—because they have financial aid, the part-time jobs, etc. They're able to meet a student's financial need in many cases.

10. Students should discuss with their counselors the socioeconomic factors of the colleges they are considering. Will the college of your choice have several students enrolled with your socioeconomic background? And, please get in your college visits.

11. When you visit a college, seek out the students who attend and ask them the following question: "When you sign up for classes, do you get 100% of your choices, or only 4 out of 10 courses, or...?" Also, does the faculty seem to be there, to like to talk to you, to meet and greet you? Or are they not to be found?

12. Most states have a "flagship" university, the leader of the system (e.g., The University of North Carolina at Chapel Hill). In this book it is listed as just "No. Carolina." The other members of the University system are listed as follows: No. Carolina (Asheville), No. Carolina (Charlotte), No. Carolina (Greensboro), No. Carolina (Pembroke), No. Carolina (Wilmington).

13. Some colleges do a great job with private school youngsters, others do a fantastic job with public school youngsters. Some colleges are outstanding with both groups. A very fine college with an outstanding record with public school youngsters is Virginia's Roanoke College.

14. A tip for the high school senior: Don't ease up in your senior year. Take a tough course load with courses such as Physics. College admissions people aren't stupid. The first thing they look at when they review your high school record is the quality of your high school courses.

15. To parents and counselors: Hang tough. The pieces will finally fit.

16. Keep in mind that a starter list of colleges to consider for your daughter #1 may be a terrible list for your daughter #2.

17. I received a phone call from a community college instructor in the Mid-West. He also consults with companies recruiting college graduates, and has found my lists to be the best. He said to me on the phone, "The true test of any college guidebook or college list is, 'Does the information work?' So if the best information comes from college janitors, you go after college janitors."

18. I give an apology now to many of the top secondary prep schools in the country. Many of you may not be happy with my emphasis on adding departments to the Cal States, the Mass States, Connecticut States, Pennsylvania States, Michigan and Illinois States, etc. But the public school counselors and parents need these recommendations and they are over 90% of my customer base.

19. Some more thoughts on the college visit. I have never known someone to visit two college campuses, and then to report that both the colleges are equal, and that the visitor has no favorite of the two. NEVER. So visit. If you can't visit during the school year, visit during the college's vacation(s). If you cannot do that, please have the student visit the college's website, the department page in question, e-mail professors, e-mail or write admission and/or financial aid. Again, have the student do it.

20. This book is not perfect. It has never claimed to be perfect. Our study is not scientific. It has never claimed to be. But it is a good place to start and represents tens of thousands of contacts. I'll repeat that. We have never claimed to be perfect. There is no expert in the field. There never will be. The field is too big. We've even moved to many parts of the country to try to put together "the big picture." We do our best.

Frederick E. Rugg

San Diego County, California
January, 2010 (27th Edition)

SOME NOTES ON THE TWENTY-SEVENTH EDITION

The twenty-seventh edition contains over 800 entry changes since the twenty-sixth edition. All 100 plus majors have been revised. Firefighting, Robotics Technology and Sign Language Interpretation - these three majors have been added.

The "Average SAT-1/Average New SAT/ACT Total/Recommended majors" pages are included mainly because of counselors' requests. School counselors wanted average score comparisons and an index of colleges showing recommended majors. In all cases, SAT Total Scores are noted and the equivalent ACT score is provided. These scores are the best estimate by our staff for the entering fall class of 2010. Especially young counselors tell us this section is a quick ready reference—a marker for them. And if you're looking for schools that do not require SAT's, please see "www.fairtest.org" for the latest list.

As in the past, when a state university is noted like Wisconsin, we mean the flagship at Madison, if no other city follows in parenthesis.

Finally, in the middle of the book, you will find every college's website.

Frederick E. Rugg

San Diego County, California
January, 2010 (27th Edition)

ACKNOWLEDGMENTS

I would like to thank the following for their help in the preparation of this guidebook: Phi Beta Kappa Office, Bureau of Educational Statistics, our Research Aides, a variety of college personnel, and especially the great number of secondary counselors who've filled out questionnaires and tip me off on quality departments to look at. I am independent of the colleges and these people are, too.

A "Thank You" also goes to the counselors and students I've worked with who have contributed each in their own way. At last count, I've worked 25,000 hours in five secondary school guidance cubicles with 30 counselors, and conducted over 600 workshops with over 8000 counselors. Of course I've learned from them. Together we've probably done the college admissions process a million times. Also I thank the counselors and students and university officials in the United States and abroad for their help, suggestions, and, yes, their complaints. I appreciate, too, those departments who have sent us vitae on their professors. College PR officers who write always get a reading. And the same goes for anyone who e-mails me. Eighty percent of college personnel who write me and tip me off on a great major at their school find it in the next year's book!

I am also grateful to George Gibbs, Ed Wall, Reg Alexander, Arvin R. Anderson, Howard Ahlskog, Hy Kleinman, Michele M. Charles, Gary Metras, Edward Field, Betty Rossie, Horacio Rodrigues, A.P. Stevens, Madeline Field, Cyrus Benson, John Barker, Fred Ames, Matthew Jagielski, Gilbert Field, Jeff Sheehan, Charles Doebler, Joan Girard, Mrs. Fran Fisher, Ralph Strycharz, Dennis Gurn, John DeBonville, Sammy Edwards, Eric Goodhart, Kevin L. Miller, Gloria Broecker, Hoover Sutton, Francona, J.R., Rebecca Lou, Cousin Leonard, Dave Congalton, Steve Stassen, Dwayne Copeland, Dianne Pelletier, Sarah Rudinski, Art Northrop, Roger Dexter, Carl Schulkin, Peter Frederick Stassen, Tom Strong, who always made us look good, and to all the secretaries I've worked with over the years.

And finally, a special thanks to my wife, Barbara, for her patience and industry, and daughters, Betsie and Susan.

Inquiries and comments about this guide should be addressed to:

Rugg's Recommendations
P.O. Box 417
Fallbrook, CA 92088

SECTION ONE
RECOMMENDED UNDERGRADUATE PROGRAMS

AGRICULTURE

Author's Note: *Students in the schools of Agriculture, in general, tend to have median college test scores below the University's overall median.*

GROUP I
Most Selective

Cornell (NY)	L	Maryland, U. of	XL
Florida, U. of	XL	Pennsylvania State	XL
Illinois, U. of (Urbana-Champaign)	XL	Rutgers (NJ)	L
Iowa State	XL		

GROUP II
Very Selective

Auburn (AL)	L	Minnesota, U. of	XL
California, U. of (Davis)	XL	Missouri, U. of	XL
California, U. of (Riverside)	L	New Hampshire, U. of	L
Cal. Poly. State U. (San Luis Obispo)	L	North Carolina State	L
Clemson (SC)	L	Puerto Rico, U. of (Mayaguez)	L
Connecticut, U. of	XL	Purdue (IN)	XL
Hawaii, U. of	L	Texas A&M	XL
Kansas State	L	Vermont, U. of	M
Maine, U. of	L	Virginia Tech	L
Michigan State	XL	Wisconsin, U. of	XL

GROUP III
Selective

Arizona, U. of	XL	Northwest Missouri State (MO)	M
Arkansas, U. of	L	Ohio State	XL
Berea (KY)	R	Oklahoma State	L
Cal. Poly. State U. (Pomona)	L	Oregon State	L
California State U. (Chico)	L	Ozarks, College of the (MO)	R
California State U. (Fresno)	L	Tarleton State (TX)	M
Colorado State	L	Tennessee, U. of	XL
Delaware Valley (PA)	R	Tennessee, U. of (Martin)	M
Dordt (IA)	R	Texas State U. (San Marcos)	L
Georgia, U. of	XL	Texas Tech U.	L
Idaho, U. of	L	Tuskegee University (AL)	M
Kentucky, U. of	L	Utah State	L
Louisiana State	XL	Washington State	L
Mississippi State	L	Western Illinois	L
Montana State	L	Western Kentucky	L
Murray State (KY)	M	Wilmington (OH)	S
Nebraska, U. of	L	Wisconsin, U. of (Platteville)	M
Nevada, U. of (Reno)	L	Wisconsin, U. of (River Falls)	M
New Mexico State U.	L	Wyoming, U. of	L
North Dakota State	L		

AMERICAN STUDIES

GROUP I
Most Selective

American U. (DC)	M
Amherst (MA)	R
Bard (NY)	R
Bates (ME)	R
▲ Barnard (NY)	R
Brandeis (MA)	M
Brown (RI)	M
Buffalo (SUNY) (NY)	L
California, U. of (San Diego)	L
Carleton (MN)	R
Case Western Reserve (OH)	M
Chicago, U. of (IL)	M
Emory (GA)	M
Franklin & Marshall (PA)	R
George Washington (DC)	M
Georgetown (DC)	M
Harvard (MA)	M
Johns Hopkins (MD)	M
Kalamazoo (MI)	R
Lehigh (PA)	M
Maryland, U. of	XL
Maryland, U. of (Baltimore County)	M
Michigan, U. of	XL
Minnesota, U. of	XL
Muhlenberg (PA)	R
North Carolina, U. of	L
Northwestern (IL)	M
Pennsylvania, U. of	L
Pomona (CA)	R
Reed (OR)	R
Rutgers (NJ)	L
Sarah Lawrence (NY)	R
▲ Smith (MA)	R
St. Olaf (MN)	R
South, U. of the (TN)	R
Stanford (CA)	M
Trinity (CT)	R
Tufts (MA)	M
Tulane (LA)	M
Virginia, U. of	L
Wake Forest (NC)	M
Wesleyan (CT)	R
Willamette (OR)	R
William & Mary (VA)	R
Williams (MA)	R
Yale (CT)	M

GROUP II
Very Selective

Alabama, U. of	L
Arizona, U. of	XL
Bowling Green (OH)	L
California State U. (Fresno)	L
California State U. (Fullerton)	L
California, U. of (Santa Cruz)	M
DePaul (IL)	L
Eastern Connecticut	M
Florida State	L
Fredonia (SUNY)(NY)	M
George Mason (VA)	L
Hawaii, U. of	L
Hillsdale (MI)	R
Hobart & Wm. Smith (NY)	R
Iowa, U. of	XL
Kansas, U. of	L
Knox (IL)	R
La Salle (PA)	M
Lebanon Valley (PA)	R
Loyola Marymount (CA)	M
Manhattanville (NY)	R
Mary Washington (VA)	M
Massachusetts, U. of (Boston)	M
New Mexico, U. of	L
▲ Pine Manor (MA)	S
Queens (CUNY)(NY)	L
Queens (NC)	R
Ramapo (NJ)	M
Randolph College (VA)	S
Rider (NJ)	R
Skidmore (NY)	R
South Florida, U. of	L
Texas, U. of	XL
Wagner (NY)	R
Washington College (MD)	S
Washington State	XL
Wells (NY)	S
▲ Wesleyan College (GA)	S
Western Connecticut	M
Wyoming, U. of	L

Enrollment Code
■ *Men Only* ▲ *Women Only* | S = Small (less than 1000 students) R = Moderate (1000-3000 students) M = Medium (3000-8000 students) L = Large (8000-20,000 students) XL = Extra Large (over 20,000 students)

ANTHROPOLOGY

GROUP I
Most Selective

American (DC)	M	Lawrence (WI)	R
Albany (SUNY) (NY)	L	Macalester (MN)	R
▲Barnard (NY)	R	MIT (MA)	M
Binghamton (SUNY)(NY)	L	Michigan, U. of	XL
Boston U. (MA)	L	New College (FL)	S
Bowdoin (ME)	R	New York U.	L
Brandeis (MA)	R	North Carolina, U. of	L
▲Bryn Mawr (PA)	S	Northwestern (IL)	M
Buffalo (SUNY) (NY)	L	Notre Dame (IN)	M
California, U. of (Berkeley)	XL	Pennsylvania, U. of	L
California, U. of (Los Angeles)	XL	Pitzer (CA)	S
Case Western Reserve (OH)	M	Pomona (CA)	R
Chicago, U. of (IL)	M	Princeton (NJ)	M
Colorado College	R	Reed (OR)	R
Columbia (NY)	M	Rice (TX)	M
Connecticut College	R	Rutgers (NJ)	L
Dartmouth (NH)	M	Sarah Lawrence (NY)	R
Duke (NC)	M	Skidmore (NY)	R
Emory (GA)	M	▲Smith (MA)	R
Florida, U. of	XL	Southern Methodist (TX)	M
Georgetown (DC)	M	South, U. of the (TN)	R
Grinnell (IA)	R	Stanford (CA)	M
Harvard (MA)	M	Tulane (LA)	M
Illinois, U. of (Urbana-Champaign)	XL	Vanderbilt (TN)	M
Johns Hopkins (MD)	M	Virginia, U. of	L
Kalamazoo (MI)	R	Washington U. (MO)	M
Kansas State	L	William & Mary (VA)	R
Kenyon (OH)	R	Yale (CT)	M
Lafayette (PA)	R		

GROUP II
Very Selective

Alabama, U. of	L	Grand Valley (MI)	L
Arizona, U. of	XL	Hamline (MN)	R
Arizona State	XL	Hofstra (NY)	M
Beloit (WI)	R	Hunter (CUNY)(NY)	L
Brown (RI)	M	Indiana (PA)	L
California State U. (Chico)	L	Iowa, U. of	XL
California, U. of (Irvine)	L	Ithaca (NY)	M
California, U. of (Santa Cruz)	M	James Madision (VA)	L
California, U. of (Davis)	XL	Kansas, U. of	L
City College (CUNY)(NY)	L	Knox (IL)	R
Colorado State	L	Loyola (IL)	M
Colorado, U. of	L	Luther (IA)	R
Earlham (IN)	R	Maine, U. of	L
Elon (NC)	R	Maryland, U. of	XL
George Mason (VA)	L	Massachusetts, U. of	L
George Washington (DC)	M		

GROUP II continues next page

ANTHROPOLOGY, continued

GROUP II, continued

Michigan State	XL	Stony Brook (SUNY)(NY)	L
Nevada, U. of (Las Vegas)	L	▲ Sweet Briar (VA)	S
Oklahoma, U. of	XL	Syracuse (NY)	L
Oregon, U. of	L	Texas A&M	XL
Pacific Lutheran (WA)	R	Towson (MD)	L
Pittsburgh, U. of (PA)	L	Tulsa, U. of (OK)	M
Rhode Island, U. of	L	Washington State	L
Ripon (WI)	R	Washington, U. of	XL
St. Mary's College of Maryland	R	Western Washington U.	R
Santa Clara (CA)	M	William Paterson (NJ)	M
Sonoma State (CA)	M	Wisconsin, U. of	XL
South Florida, U. of	L	Wisconsin, U. of (Milwaukee)	L

GROUP III
Selective

Alaska, U. of (Fairbanks)	M	Mercyhurst (PA)	R
Arkansas, U. of	L	Minnesota State U. (Moorhead)	M
Ball State (IN)	L	New Mexico State U.	L
California State U. (Fullerton)	L	New Mexico, U. of	L
California State U. (Long Beach)	L	Pittsburgh, U. of (Greensburg)	R
California State U. (Sacramento)	M	Plattsburgh (SUNY)(NY)	M
Central Washington	L	Potsdam (SUNY)(NY)	M
Colorado, U. of (Colorado Springs)	M	Queens (CUNY) (NY)	L
Fort Lewis (CO)	M	San Jose State (CA)	L
Hawaii, U. of	L	Tennessee, U. of	XL
Humboldt State (CA)	M	Texas State U. (San Marcos)	L
Louisiana State	Xl	Western Connecticut	M
Massachusetts, U. of (Boston)	M	Wyoming, U. of	L

Enrollment Code

■ *Men Only*   S = Small (less than 1000 students)   R = Moderate (1000-3000 students)   M = Medium (3000-8000 students)
▲ *Women Only*   L = Large (8000-20,000 students)   XL = Extra Large (over 20,000 students)

ARCHITECTURE

GROUP I
Most Selective

▲Barnard (NY) .... R
Buffalo (SUNY) (NY) L
California, U. of (Berkeley) XL
Carnegie Mellon (PA) .... M
Columbia (NY) .... M
Cooper Union (NY) .... S
Cornell (NY) L
Florida, U. of XL
Georgia Inst. of Tech. L
Illinois Inst. of Tech. .... R
Illinois, U. of (Urbana-Champaign) XL
Lehigh (PA) .... M
Maryland, U. of XL
Miami, U. of (FL) L

Miami U. (OH) L
Michigan, U. of XL
Minnesota, U. of XL
MIT (MA) .... M
New Jersey Inst. of Tech .... M
Notre Dame (IN) .... M
Princeton (NJ) .... M
Rensselaer (NY) .... M
Rice (TX) .... M
Temple (PA) XL
Tulane (LA) .... M
Virginia, U. of L
Washington U. (MO) .... M
Yale (CT) .... M

GROUP II
Very Selective

Arizona State XL
Arizona, U. of XL
Auburn (AL) L
Boston Arch. Center (MA) .... S
California College of Art & Crafts .... S
Cal. Poly. State U. (San Luis Obispo) L
Catholic U. (DC) .... M
Cincinnati, U. of (OH) L
Clemson (SC) L
Detroit Mercy, U. of (MI) .... M
Drexel (PA) .... M
Drury (MO) .... R
Florida International L
Kentucky, U. of L
Houston, U. of (TX) L
Illinois, U. of (Chicago) L
Iowa State XL
Kansas State L
Kansas, U. of L
Kentucky, U. of L
Milwaukee Sch. of Engineering (WI) .... R
Montana State L
Nebraska, U. of L

North Carolina State L
Northeastern (MA) L
Ohio State XL
Oklahoma, U. of XL
Oklahoma State L
Oregon, U. of L
Parsons (NY) .... R
Pennsylvania State XL
Rhode Island School of Design (RI) .... R
Sch. of the Art Institute of Chicago (IL) .. S
Southern California, U. of L
Syracuse (NY) L
Tennessee, U. of XL
Texas A&M XL
Texas Tech U. L
Texas, U. of (Austin) XL
Utah, U. of L
Virginia Tech. L
Washington State L
Washington, U. of XL
West Virginia U. L

Landscape Architecture

Enrollment Code

■ *Men Only*   S = Small (less than 1000 students)   R = Moderate (1000-3000 students)   M = Medium (3000-8000 students)
▲ *Women Only*   L = Large (8000-20,000 students)   XL = Extra Large (over 20,000 students)

| ARCHITECTURE, continued |

Andrews (MI)	R	Nevada, U. of (Las Vegas)	L
Arkansas, U. of	L	New York Institute of Tech	M
Ball State (IN)	L	North Carolina (Charlotte)	L
Cal. Poly. State U. (Pomona)	L	North Dakota State	L
City College (CUNY) (NY)	L	Norwich (VT)	R
Florida A&M	M	Philadelphia U. (PA)	R
Howard (DC)	M	Pratt Inst. (NY)	R
Idaho, U. of	L	Roger Williams (RI)	M
Keene State (NH)	R	Southern Polytechnic (GA)	R
Kent State (OH)	L	Texas, U. of (Arlington)	L
Louisiana-Lafayette	L	Texas, U. of (San Antonio)	L
Louisiana State	XL	Tuskegee University (AL)	M
Marywood (PA)	R	Wisconsin, U. of (Milwaukee)	L
Mississippi State	L	π Woodbury (CA)	S
Morgan State (MD)	M		

π *Also, Interior Architecture*

ART (STUDIO)

GROUP I
Most Selective

Albany (SUNY)(NY)	L	Michigan, U. of	XL
American U. (DC)	M	Middlebury (VT)	R
Bard (NY)	R	New Jersey, College of	M
Bates (ME)	R	New York U.	L
Binghamton (SUNY)(NY)	L	Pennsylvania, U. of	L
Boston College (MA)	L	Pepperdine (CA)	R
Boston U. (MA)	L	R.I. School of Design	R
Brown (RI)	M	Rhodes (TN)	R
▲Bryn Mawr (PA)	S	Rochester, U. of (NY)	M
Buffalo (SUNY)(NY)	L	Rutgers (NJ)	L
Carnegie Mellon (PA)	M	Sarah Lawrence (NY)	R
Centre (KY)	R	▲Scripps (CA)	S
Chicago, U. of (IL)	M	Skidmore (NY)	R
Colby (ME)	R	▲Smith (MA)	R
Colgate (NY)	R	Southwestern (TX)	R
Colorado College	R	Stanford (CA)	M
Connecticut College	R	St. Olaf (MN)	R
Cooper Union (NY)	S	Texas, U. of	XL
Cornell (NY)	L	Trinity (TX)	R
Cornish (WA)	S	Tulane (LA)	M
Dallas, U. of (TX)	R	Vassar (NY)	R
Dartmouth (NH)	M	Virginia, U. of	L
DePauw (IN)	R	Washington & Lee (VA)	R
Drew (NJ)	R	Washington U. (MO)	M
Florida, U. of	XL	▲Wellesley (MA)	R
Furman (SC)	R	Wesleyan (CT)	R
Harvard (MA)	M	Wheaton (IL)	R
Haverford (PA)	S	Whitman (WA)	R
Kenyon (OH)	R	Williams (MA)	R
Lafayette (PA)	R	Wisconsin, U. of (Madison)	XL
Lawrence (WI)	R	Yale (CT)	M
Macalester (MN)	R		

ART (STUDIO), continued

GROUP II
Very Selective

Adelphi (NY) .... R	Elmira (NY) .... R
▲Agnes Scott (GA) .... S	Florida International L
Alabama, U. of L	Florida State L
Alaska, U. of (Anchorage) .... M	Fredonia (SUNY)(NY) .... M
Albright (PA) .... R	Gordon (MA) .... R
Alfred (NY) .... R	Guilford (NC) .... R
Allegheny (PA) .... R	Hamline (MN) .... R
Alma (MI) .... R	Hobart & William Smith (NY) .... R
Arizona, U. of XL	Hofstra (NY) .... M
Art Center College of Design (CA) .... R	▲Hollins (VA) .... S
Art Institute of Chicago (IL) .... R	Hood (MD) .... S
Asbury (KY) .... R	Houghton (NY) .... S
Auburn (AL) L	Houston, U. of (TX) L
Augustana (IL) .... R	Hunter (CUNY) (NY) L
Belmont (TN) .... R	Idaho, College of .... S
Bennington (VT) .... S	Illinois, U. of (Chicago) L
Berea (KY) .... R	Indiana (PA) L
Birmingham-Southern (AL) .... R	Iowa State XL
Bowling Green (OH) L	Iowa, U. of XL
Bradley (IL) .... M	James Madison (VA) L
Brigham Young (UT) XL	Juniata (PA) .... R
Butler (IN) .... R	Kansas, U. of L
California College of Arts & Crafts ...... S	Kansas State L
California Institute of the Arts .... S	Knox (IL) .... R
California, U. of (Davis) XL	Lake Forest (IL) .... R
California, U. of (Irvine) L	Lebanon Valley (PA) .... R
California, U. of (Santa Barbara) L	Lewis & Clark (OR) .... R
Carroll (WI) .... R	Lindenwood (MO) .... M
Centenary (LA) .... S	Longwood (VA) .... R
Cincinnati, U. of (OH) L	Loras (IA) .... R
Clarke (IA) .... S	Louisville (KY) L
Cleveland Institute of Art (OH) .... S	Loyola (IL) .... M
Coastal Carolina (SC) .... M	Loyola (LA) .... R
Coe (IA) .... R	Loyola Marymount (CA) .... M
Colorado State L	Manhattanville (NY) .... S
Connecticut, U. of XL	Marietta (OH) .... R
▲Converse (SC) .... S	Maryland Institute–College of Art .... S
Cornell (IA) .... R	Maryland, U. of (Baltimore County) .... M
Creighton (NE) .... M	Mass. College of Art .... R
Dana (NE) .... S	Messiah (PA) .... R
Delaware, U. of L	▲Mills (CA) .... S
Denison (OH) .... R	Minnesota, U. of (Morris) .... R
Denver, U. of (CO) .... M	Mississippi State L
Drake (IA) .... M	Missouri, U. of (Kansas City) .... M
East Carolina (NC) L	

GROUP II continues next page

ART (STUDIO), continued

•• ———————————— GROUP II, continued ———————————— ••

Montana State	L	Salisbury (MD)	M
Moore College of Art (PA)	S	San Diego State (CA)	XL
Moravian (PA)	R	San Francisco Art Institute (CA)	S
Morningside (IA)	S	Sch. of the Art Institute of Chicago	S
Mount Mercy (IA)	S	Seattle Pacific (WA)	R
Muhlenberg (PA)	R	Shepherd (WV)	M
Nazareth (NY)	R	▲Simmons (MA)	R
North Dakota, U. of	M	Southern Methodist (TX)	M
North Texas	L	Syracuse (NY)	L
Ohio State	XL	Temple (PA)	L
Ohio U.	L	Tennessee, U. of	XL
Oregon, U. of	L	Tulsa, U. of (OK)	R
Otis Art Institute (CA)	R	Utah, U. of	L
Pacific, U. of the (CA)	M	Warren Wilson (NC)	S
Pacific U. (OR)	R	Washington & Jefferson (PA)	R
Parsons School of Design (NY)	R	Washington, U. of	XL
Portland State (OR)	M	▲Wesleyan Col. (GA)	S
Pratt Institute (NY)	R	Western Washington U.	L
Principia (IL)	S	Westminster (UT)	R
Puget Sound (WA)	R	Westmont (CA)	R
Purchase (SUNY)(NY)	R	West Virginia, U. of	L
Randolph College (VA)	S	Wheaton (MA)	R
Redlands, U. of (CA)	R	Whitworth (WA)	R
▲Rosemont (PA)	R	William Paterson (NJ)	M
Rowan (NJ)	M	Wisconsin Lutheran	S
▲St. Mary's College (IN)	R	Wisconsin, U. of (Steven's Point)	L
St. Rose (NY)	R	Wittenberg (OH)	R

Enrollment Code

■ *Men Only*   S = Small (less than 1000 students)   R = Moderate (1000-3000 students)   M = Medium (3000-8000 students)

▲ *Women Only*   L = Large (8000-20,000 students)   XL = Extra Large (over 20,000 students)

ART (STUDIO), continued

GROUP III
Selective

Abilene Christian (TX)	M	Fort Hays (KS)	M
Adrian (MI)	R	Fort Lewis (CO)	M
Akron, U. of (OH)	L	Frostburg (MD)	M
▲ Alverno (WI)	R	George Fox (OR)	R
Anna Maria (MA)	S	Georgia Southern	L
Aquinas (MI)	R	Goucher (MD)	R
Arcadia (PA)	R	Grand Valley (MI)	L
Arizona State	XL	Greensboro College (NC)	S
Arts, U. of the (PA)	R	Hastings (NE)	R
Ball State (IN)	L	Hawaii, U. of	L
Belhaven (MS)	R	Henderson State (AR)	M
Berea (WV)	R	Humboldt State (CA)	M
Bethany (KS)	S	Huntington (IN)	S
Bloomsburg (PA)	M	Indiana State	L
Boise State (ID)	L	Jacksonville (FL)	R
Brescia (KY)	S	Johnson State (VT)	R
Briar Cliff (IA)	R	Judson (AL)	S
California College of Arts & Crafts	S	Kansas City Art institute (MO)	S
California State U. (Channel Islands)	R	Kean (NJ)	M
California State U. (East Bay)	M	Keene State (NH)	R
California State U. (Fresno)	L	Kent State (OH)	L
California State U. (Long Beach)	L	Kutztown (PA)	M
California State U. (Los Angeles)	L	Lambuth (TN)	S
California State U. (Monterey Bay)	R	Lesley (MA)	S
California State U. (Northridge)	L	Lewis-Clark State (ID)	R
California State U. (San Bernardino)	M	Lock Haven (PA)	M
California State U. (San Jose)	L	Long Island U. (C.W.Post)(NY)	M
Case Western Reserve (OH)	M	Louisiana-Lafayette	L
Castleton State (VT)	R	Louisiana State	XL
▲ Cedar Crest (PA)	S	Lycoming (PA)	R
▲ Chatham (PA)	S	▲ Mary Baldwin (VA)	S
Chowan (NC)	S	Marymount Manhattan (NY)	R
Coker (SC)	S	Maryville (St. Louis) (MO)	R
Colorado, U. of (Denver)	M	Marywood (PA)	R
Columbia (MO)	R	Massachusetts, U. of (Dartmouth)	M
Culver-Stockton (MO)	S	Massachusetts, U. of (Lowell)	M
Dordt (IA)	R	McPherson (KS)	S
East Tennessee	L	Memphis College of Art (TN)	S
Eastern Illinois	L	Memphis, U. of (TN)	L
Edgewood (WI)	S	▲ Meredith (NC)	R
Edinboro (PA)	M	Mercyhurst (PA)	R
Emmanuel (MA)	S	Midwestern State U. (TX)	M
Emporia State (KS)	M	Millersville (PA)	M
Endicott (MA)	R	Millikin (IL)	R
Fairleigh Dickinson (NJ)	M		
Fontbonne (MO)	R		

GROUP III continues next page

ART (STUDIO), continued

••• ▬▬▬▬▬▬▬▬▬▬ GROUP III, continued ▬▬▬▬▬▬▬▬▬▬ •••

Minnesota, U. of (Duluth)	M	St. Edward's (TX)	M
Minnesota State U. (Moorhead)	M	St. Francis (IN)	R
Mississippi College	R	▲ Salem College (NC)	S
Missouri Southern State	M	Salem State (MA)	M
Monmouth (NJ)	R	San Jose State (CA)	L
Montana State (Billings)	R	Santa Fe, College of (NM)	S
Montclair State (NJ)	M	Schreiner (TX)	S
Montevallo (AL)	R	Seton Hill (PA)	S
Montserrat (MA)	S	Shawnee State (OH)	R
Mount St. Joseph (OH)	R	Siena Heights (MI)	S
Mount St. Mary's (CA)	R	Silver Lake (WI)	S
Murray State (KY)	M	South Dakota, U. of	M
Museum of Fine Arts, School of (MA)	R	Southeastern Louisiana	L
Nebraska, U. of (Kearney)	M	Southern Maine	M
Nevada, U. of (Las Vegas)	L	Southern Oregon State U.	M
New Mexico, U. of	L	Texas A&M (Corpus Christi)	M
Nicholls State (LA)	M	Texas Tech. U.	L
North Carolina (Asheville)	R	Texas, U. of (El Paso)	L
North Carolina (Greensboro)	M	Texas, U. of (San Antonio)	L
North Carolina, U. of (Pembroke)	R	Texas, U. of (Tyler)	R
Northern Arizona	XL	Towson (MD)	L
Northern Illinois U.	L	Union University (TN)	R
Northern Iowa	L	Virginia Commonwealth U.	L
Northern Michigan	M	Viterbo (WI)	R
Northwestern (MN)	R	Visual Arts, School of (NY)	R
Old Dominion (VA)	L	Wayne State (MI)	L
Otterbein (OH)	R	Wayne State (NE)	R
Ozarks, College of the (MO)	R	Weber State (UT)	L
Pennsylvania Acad. of the Fine Arts	S	West Chester (PA)	M
Peru State (NE)	R	West Virginia Wesleyan	R
▲ Pine Manor (MA)	S	Western Carolina (NC)	M
Plattsburgh (SUNY)(NY)	M	Western Connecticut	M
Plymouth State (NH)	M	Western Michigan	L
Potsdam (SUNY)(NY)	M	Westmont (CA)	R
Roanoke (VA)	R	Wingate (NC)	R
Rockford (IL)	S	Winthrop (SC)	M
Rocky Mountain (MT)	S	Wisconsin, U. of (Green Bay)	M
Roger Williams (RI)	M	Wisconsin, U. of (Superior)	M
St. Andrew's (NC)	S	Youngstown State (OH)	L

Enrollment Code

■ *Men Only*
▲ *Women Only*

S = Small (less than 1000 students)	R = Moderate (1000-3000 students)	M = Medium (3000-8000 students)
L = Large (8000-20,000 students)	XL = Extra Large (over 20,000 students)	

ART HISTORY

• ━━━━━━━━━━━━━━ **GROUP I** ━━━━━━━━━━━━━━ •
Most Selective

Albany (SUNY)(NY)	L	Northwestern (IL)	M
Bard (NY)	R	Oberlin (OH)	R
▲Barnard (NY)	R	Pennsylvania, U. of	L
Binghamton (SUNY)(NY)	L	Pittsburgh, U. of (PA)	L
Boston College (MA)	L	Pomona (CA)	R
Boston U. (MA)	L	Princeton (NJ)	M
Bowdoin (ME)	R	Reed (OR)	R
Brown (RI)	M	Rochester, U. of (NY)	M
▲Bryn Mawr (PA)	S	Rutgers (NJ)	L
California, U. of (Los Angeles)	XL	Sarah Lawrence (NY)	R
Case Western Reserve U. (OH)	M	▲Scripps (CA)	S
Chicago, U. of (IL)	M	Skidmore (NY)	R
Colgate (NY)	R	▲Smith (MA)	R
Colorado College	R	Stanford (CA)	M
Columbia (NY)	M	Swarthmore (PA)	R
Connecticut College	R	Syracuse (NY)	L
Cornell (NY)	L	Trinity (CT)	R
Emory (GA)	M	Trinity (TX)	R
Georgetown (DC)	M	Vanderbilt (TN)	M
George Washington (DC)	M	Vassar (NY)	R
Harvard (MA)	M	Washington U. (MO)	M
Johns Hopkins (MD)	M	▲Wellesley (MA)	R
Lawrence (WI)	R	Wesleyan (CT)	R
Michigan, U. of	XL	Willamette (OR)	R
Middlebury (VT)	R	Williams (MA)	R
▲Mount Holyoke (MA)	R	Wisconsin, U. of	XL
New York U.	L	Yale (CT)	M
North Carolina, U. of	L		

ART HISTORY continues next page

■ *Men Only*	**Enrollment Code**
▲ *Women Only*	S = Small (less than 1000 students) R = Moderate (1000-3000 students) M = Medium (3000-8000 students)
	L = Large (8000-20,000 students) XL = Extra Large (over 20,000 students)

ART HISTORY, continued

GROUP II
Very Selective

Alfred (NY) .... R	Manhattanville (NY) .... S
Art Institute of Chicago (IL) .... R	Massachusetts, U. of (Lowell) .... M
California State U. (Northridge) L	McDaniel (MD) .... R
California, U. of (Riverside) L	▲ Mills (CA) .... S
California, U. of (Santa Barbara) L	Moore College of Art (PA) .... S
California, U. of (Santa Cruz) .... M	Minnesota, U. of XL
City College (CUNY)(NY) L	Missouri, U. of XL
Clarke (IA) .... S	Missouri, U. of (Kansas City) .... M
College of Charleston (SC) L	New Paltz (SUNY)(NY) .... M
Colorado State L	Oakland (MI) .... M
Columbia College Chicago (IL) .... M	Ohio U. L
Delaware, U. of L	Oregon, U. of L
Denison (OH) .... R	Queens (CUNY)(NY) L
Denver, U. of (CO) .... M	Radford (VA) .... M
East Carolina L	▲ Rosemont (PA) .... S
Eastern Connecticut .... M	St. Bonaventure (NY) .... R
Edinboro (PA) .... M	▲ Salem College (NC) .... S
Florida State L	San Diego State U. (CA) XL
George Mason (VA) L	Sonoma State (CA) .... M
Georgia, U. of XL	Southern Methodist (TX) .... M
▲ Hollins (VA) .... S	Stony Brook (SUNY)(NY) L
Hunter (CUNY) (NY) L	▲ Sweet Briar (VA) .... S
Illinois, U. of (Chicago) L	Utah, U. of L
Indiana (PA) L	Washington, U. of XL
Juniata (PA) .... R	Wayne State (MI) L
Kansas, U. of L	Wheaton (MA) .... R
Lake Forest (IL) .... R	Wooster (OH) .... R
Lebanon Valley (PA) .... R	

ASTRONOMY

GROUP I
Most Selective

Amherst (MA) .... R	▲Mount Holyoke (MA) .... R
▲Barnard (NY) .... R	Northwestern (IL) .... M
Boston U. L	Pennsylvania, U. of L
Brigham Young (UT) XL	Pennsylvania State XL
▲Bryn Mawr (PA) .... S	Union (NY) .... R
California Inst. of Tech. .... S	Vassar (NY) .... R
Case Western Reserve U. (OH) .... M	Villanova (PA) .... M
Cornell (NY) L	Virginia, U. of L
# Franklin & Marshall (PA) .... R	▲Wellesley (MA) .... R
Harvard (MA) .... M	Wesleyan (CT) .... R
Haverford (PA) .... S	Whitman (WA) .... R
Illinois, U. of (Urbana-Champaign) XL	Williams (MA) .... R
Michigan, U. of XL	Wisconsin, U. of XL
MIT (MA) .... M	

GROUP II
Very Selective

Arizona, U. of XL	Minnesota, U. of XL
Colorado, U. of L	Minnesota State U. (Mankato) L
Drake (IA) .... M	North Carolina State L
Earlham (IN) .... R	Ohio State U. XL
Florida Inst. of Tech. .... R	Oklahoma, U. of XL
Florida, U. of XL	Pittsburgh, U. of (PA) L
Georgia, U. of XL	San Diego State XL
Hawaii, U. of L	San Francisco State U. L
Indiana U. XL	Southern California L
Iowa, U. of XL	Stony Brook (SUNY) (NY) L
Kansas, U. of L	Texas, U. of (Austin) XL
Maryland, U. of XL	Washington, U. of XL
Massachusetts, U. of L	Wheaton (MA) .... R

GROUP III
Selective

Benedictine (KS) .... R	Nebraska, U. of L
Georgia State L	Northern Arizona XL
Hawaii, U. of (Hilo) .... R	Western Connecticut .... M
Louisiana State XL	Wisconsin, U. of (La Crosse) L
Lycoming (PA) .... R	Wyoming, U. of L
Montana, U. of .... M	

 # Also Astrophysics

BIOCHEMISTRY (Molecular Biology)

GROUP I
Most Selective

▲Barnard (NY) .... R
Binghamton (SUNY) (NY) L
Bowdoin (ME) .... R
Brandeis (MA) .... R
Brown (RI) .... M
California, U. of (Berkeley) XL
California, U. of (Los Angeles) XL
California, U. of (San Diego) L
Case Western Reserve (OH) .... M
Chicago, U. of (IL) .... M
Clarkson (NY) .... M
Columbia (NY) .... M
Connecticut College .... R
Cornell (NY) L
Dallas, U. of (TX) .... R
DePauw (IL) .... R
Geneseo (SUNY) (NY) .... M
Georgetown (DC) .... M
Georgia, U. of XL
Harvard (MA) .... M

Iowa, U. of XL
Kenyon (OH) .... M
Lehigh (PA) .... M
Miami, U. of (FL) L
Minnesota, U. of XL
MIT (MA) .... M
▲Mount Holyoke (MA) .... R
Pennsylvania, U. of L
Princeton (NJ) .... M
Rice (TX) .... M
Rutgers (NJ) L
Rochester, U. of (NY) .... M
▲Smith (MA) .... R
Swarthmore (PA) .... R
Tulane (LA) .... M
Union (NY) .... R
Virginia, U. of L
Wake Forest (NC) .... M
Worcester Poly Inst. (MA) .... R
Yale (CT) .... M

GROUP II
Very Selective

Albright (PA) .... R
Arizona State XL
Austin (TX) .... R
Beloit (WI) .... R
Bethel (MN) .... M
California Poly State U. (San Luis Obispo).. L
California, U. of (Davis) XL
California, U. of (Riverside) L
Centre (KY) .... R
Clark (MA) .... R
Colorado, U. of L
Connecticut, U. of XL
Denison (OH) .... R
Florida Inst. of Tech. .... R
Ithaca (NY) .... M
Kansas State L
Knox (IL) .... R
Lewis & Clark (OR) .... R
Louisiana State XL
Maine, U. of L
McDaniel (MD) .... R
Michigan State XL
Mississippi State L
Missouri, U. of XL
Monmouth (IL) .... S

Moravian (PA) .... R
Muhlenberg (PA) .... R
Nebraska, U. of L
Ohio State XL
Oklahoma State L
Pennsylvania State XL
Pittsburgh, U. of (PA) L
Purdue (IN) XL
Ramapo (NJ) .... M
Regis (CO) .... R
Ripon (WI) .... R
Sciences, U. of the (PA) .... S
Siena (NY) .... R
Skidmore (NY) .... R
St. Andrews Presbyterian (NC) .... S
St. John's (MN) .... R
Stony Brook (SUNY) (NY) L
Susquehanna (PA) .... R
Syracuse (NY) L
Virginia Tech. L
Washington State L
Washington, U. of XL
Wisconsin, U. of XL
Wisconsin Lutheran .... S

GROUP III
Selective

California State U. (Fullerton) L
Framingham (MA) .... M
Indiana (PA) L
Misericordia, College (PA) .... S
Nevada, U. of (Reno) L
Northern Illinois U. L

Ohio Northern .... R
Oregon State L
Regis (MA) .... S
Sacred Heart (CT) .... R
Temple (PA) L

BIOLOGY

GROUP I
Most Selective

Albany (SUNY) (NY)	L	Grinnell (IA)	R
Amherst (MA)	R	Hamilton (NY)	R
Austin (TX)	R	Harvard (MA)	M
▲ Barnard (NY)	R	Harvey Mudd (CA)	S
Bates (ME)	R	Haverford (PA)	S
Binghamton (SUNY)(NY)	L	Holy Cross (MA)	R
Boston College (MA)	L	Illinois Wesleyan	R
Boston University (MA)	L	Iowa State	XL
Bowdoin (ME)	R	Johns Hopkins (MD)	M
Brandeis (MA)	R	Kalamazoo (MI)	R
Brown (RI)	M	Kenyon (OH)	R
▲ Bryn Mawr (PA)	S	Lafayette (PA)	R
Bucknell (PA)	R	Lawrence (WI)	R
Buffalo (SUNY)(NY)	L	Lehigh (PA)	M
California Inst. of Tech.	S	Macalester (MN)	R
California, U. of (Berkeley)	XL	Miami, U. of (FL)	L
California, U. of (Los Angeles)	XL	Middlebury (VT)	R
California, U. of (San Diego)	L	Minnesota, U. of (Morris)	R
Carleton (MN)	R	Missouri, U. of (Rolla)	M
Carnegie Mellon (PA)	M	MIT (MA)	M
Case Western Reserve (OH)	M	▲ Mount Holyoke (MA)	R
Centre (KY)	R	New College (FL)	S
Chicago, U. of (IL)	M	North Carolina, U. of	L
Claremont McKenna (CA)	R	Notre Dame (IN)	M
Clarkson (NY)	M	Oberlin (OH)	R
Colby (ME)	R	Occidental (CA)	R
Colgate (NY)	R	Pepperdine (CA)	R
Colorado Col.	R	Pitzer (CA)	S
Columbia (NY)	M	Pomona (CA)	R
Connecticut College	R	Princeton (NJ)	M
Cornell (NY)	L	Providence (RI)	M
Dallas, U. of (TX)	R	Reed (OR)	R
Dartmouth (NH)	M	Rennselaer (NY)	M
Davidson (NC)	R	Rhodes (TN)	R
DePauw (IN)	R	Rice (TX)	R
Dickinson (PA)	R	Richmond, U. of (VA)	M
Duke (NC)	M	Rochester, U. of (NY)	M
Emory (GA)	M	Rutgers (NJ)	L
Franklin & Marshall (PA)	R	Skidmore (NY)	R
Furman (SC)	R	▲ Smith (MA)	R
Geneseo (SUNY) (NY)	M	South, U. of the (TN)	R
Georgetown (DC)	M		
Gettysburg (PA)	R		

GROUP I continues next page

Enrollment Code	
■ *Men Only*	S = Small (less than 1000 students) R = Moderate (1000-3000 students) M = Medium (3000-8000 students)
▲ *Women Only*	L = Large (8000-20,000 students) XL = Extra Large (over 20,000 students)

BIOLOGY, continued

GROUP I, continued

Southern California	L
Southwestern (TX)	R
Stanford (CA)	M
St. Mary's Col. of Maryland	R
St. Olaf (MN)	R
Swarthmore (PA)	R
Trinity (CT)	R
Trinity (TX)	R
Tufts (MA)	M
Tulane (LA)	M
Union (NY)	R
Ursinus (PA)	R
Vanderbilt (TN)	M
Vassar (NY)	R
Vermont, U. of	L
Villanova (PA)	M
Virginia, U. of	L
■ Wabash (IN)	S
Wake Forest (NC)	M
Washington & Lee (VA)	M
Washington U. (MO)	M
▲ Wellesley (MA)	R
Wesleyan (CT)	R
Wheaton (IL)	R
Whitman (WA)	R
Willamette (OR)	R
William & Mary (VA)	M
Williams (MA)	R
Worcester Poly Inst. (MA)	R
Yale (CT)	M
Yeshiva (NY)	R

GROUP II
Very Selective

▲ Agnes Scott (GA)	S
Albright (PA)	R
Allegheny (PA)	R
Alfred (NY)	R
Alma (MI)	R
Arizona State	XL
Arizona, U. of	XL
Auburn (AL)	L
Augustana (IL)	R
Augustana (SD)	R
Belmont (TN)	R
Beloit (WI)	R
Benedictine (IL)	R
Berry (GA)	R
# Bethel (IN)	R
Bethel (MN)	M
Birmingham-Southern (AL)	R
Bryan (TN)	S
Bryn Athyn (PA)	S
Cal. Poly. State U. (San Luis Obispo)	L
California State U. (Chico)	L
California, U. of (Davis)	XL
California, U. of (Irvine)	L
California, U. of (Merced)	R
California, U. of (Riverside)	L
California, U. of (Santa Barbara)	L
California, U. of (Santa Cruz)	M
Canisius (NY)	M
Centenary (LA)	S
Central (IA)	R
Clark (MA)	R
Clarke (IA)	S
Clemson (SC)	L
Coe (IA)	R
Colorado, U. of	L
Columbia College (SC)	R
Concordia (MN)	R
Connecticut, U. of	XL
Cornell Col. (IA)	R
Creighton (NE)	M
Delaware, U. of	L
Denison (OH)	R
Denver, U. of (CO)	M
Drake (IA)	M
Drury (MO)	R
Duquesne (PA)	M
Earlham (IN)	R
Eckerd (FL)	R
Elizabethtown (PA)	R
Elon (NC)	R
Erskine (SC)	S
Evansville (IN)	R

*Also Environmental Biology*

GROUP II continues next page

BIOLOGY, continued

GROUP II, continued

Fairfield (CT)	M
Florida Inst. of Tech	R
Florida International	L
Florida Southern	R
Gannon (PA)	M
Georgetown (KY)	R
Georgia State	L
Georgia, U. of	XL
Gonzaga (WA)	R
Gordon (MA)	R
Grand Valley (MI)	L
Grove City (PA)	R
Guilford (NC)	R
Gustavus Adolphus (MN)	R
Hamline (MN)	R
■ Hampden-Sydney (VA)	S
Hampton (VA)	M
π Harrisburg U. (PA)	S
Hendrix (AR)	R
Hillsdale (MI)	R
Hiram (OH)	R
Hobart & William Smith (NY)	R
Hood (MD)	S
Hope (MI)	R
Houghton (NY)	S
Houston, U. of (TX)	L
Hunter (CUNY)(NY)	L
Idaho, College of	S
Illinois College	S
Illinois, U. of (Chicago)	L
Indiana (PA)	L
Indiana U.	XL
Ithaca (NY)	M
Juniata (PA)	R
Kansas State	L
Kansas, U. of	L
Kentucky, U.of	L
King's (PA)	R
Knox (IL)	R
Lake Forest (IL)	S
LeMoyne (NY)	R
Lewis & Clark (OR)	R

Lipscomb (TN)	R
Linfield (OR)	R
Loras (IA)	R
Loyola (IL)	M
Loyola (LA)	R
Loyola (MD)	R
Luther (IA)	R
Marist (NY)	M
Marquette (WI)	M
Mary Washington (VA)	M
Maryville U. - St. Louis (MO)	R
McDaniel (MD)	R
McKendree (IL)	R
Merrimack (MA)	R
Messiah (PA)	R
Michigan State	XL
Millersville (PA)	M
Millsaps (MS)	S
Minnesota, U. of (Duluth)	M
Minnesota State U. (Moorhead)	M
Missouri, U. of (Kansas City)	M
Mobile, U. of (AL)	R
Monmouth (IL)	S
Montana Tech.	R
Morningside (IA)	S
Mount Mercy (IA)	S
Muhlenberg (PA)	R
Murray State (KY)	M
Nazareth (NY)	R
Nebraska Wesleyan	R
New Hampshire, U. of	L
New Mexico State	L
New Mexico, U. of	L
North Carolina, U. of (Wilmington)	L
North Central (IL)	R
North Dakota, U. of	M
Oglethorpe (GA)	R
Ohio Northern	R
Ohio Wesleyan	R
Oklahoma Christian	R

π *Biotechnology and Biosciences*

GROUP II continues next page

Enrollment Code		
■ *Men Only*	S = Small (less than 1000 students)	R = Moderate (1000-3000 students)	M = Medium (3000-8000 students)
▲ *Women Only*	L = Large (8000-20,000 students)	XL = Extra Large (over 20,000 students)	

BIOLOGY, continued

GROUP II, continued

Oklahoma City U.	R
Oklahoma, U. of	L
Oregon, U. of	L
Oswego (SUNY)(NY)	M
Pacific Lutheran (WA)	R
Pacific University (OR)	R
Presbyterian (SC)	R
Puget Sound (WA)	R
Randolph College (VA)	S
Randolph-Macon (VA)	R
Rhode Island, U. of	L
Ripon (WI)	R
Roanoke (VA)	R
Rochester Inst. of Tech. (NY)	L
Rollins (FL)	R
Rowan (NJ)	M
▲St. Catherine (MN)	R
St. John's (MN)	R
St. Louis (MO)	M
▲St. Mary's College (IN)	R
St. Michael's (VT)	R
St. Norbert (WI)	R
St. Scholastica (MN)	R
Salisbury (MD)	M
Samford (AL)	R
San Diego State U. (CA)	XL
Sciences in Philadelphia (PA)	R
Scranton, U. of (PA)	M
▲Scripps (CA)	S
Seattle Pacific (WA)	R
Siena (NY)	R
South Carolina, U. of	L
South Florida, U. of	L
Spring Hill (AL)	R
Stonehill (MA)	R

Stony Brook (SUNY) (NY)	L
Susquehanna (PA)	R
Texas, U. of (Austin)	XL
Texas Christian	M
Texas Tech U.	L
Transylvania (KY)	S
Truman State (MO)	M
Tulsa, U. of (OK)	R
Utah, U. of	L
Valparaiso U. (IN)	M
Virginia Commonwealth U.	L
Virginia Tech.	L
Washington, U. of	XL
Washington & Jefferson (PA)	R
Washington College (MD)	S
Wells (NY)	S
▲Wesleyan (GA)	S
West Chester (PA)	M
West Florida, U. of	M
Westminster (MO)	S
Westminster (PA)	R
Westminster (UT)	R
Westmont (CA)	R
West Virginia U.	L
Wheaton (MA)	R
William Jewell (MO)	R
Winona State U. (MN)	M
Winthrop (SC)	M
Wisconsin, U. of (Milwaukee)	L
Wisconsin, U. of (Stevens Point)	M
Wittenberg (OH)	R
Wofford (SC)	R
Wooster (OH)	R
Xavier (OH)	R

BIOLOGY continues next page

Enrollment Code		
■ *Men Only*	S = Small (less than 1000 students)	R = Moderate (1000-3000 students)	M = Medium (3000-8000 students)
▲ *Women Only*	L = Large (8000-20,000 students)	XL = Extra Large (over 20,000 students)

BIOLOGY, continued

GROUP III
Selective

Alaska, U. of (Anchorage) .... M	Gwynedd-Mercy (PA) .... S
Alaska, U. of (Fairbanks) .... M	Hardin-Simmons (TX) .... R
▲Alverno (WI) .... R	Heidelberg (OH) .... S
Arcadia (PA) .... R	Holy Names (CA) .... S
Arkansas, U. of L	Houston Baptist (TX) .... R
Aquinas (MI) .... R	# Humboldt State (CA) .... M
Azusa Pacific (CA) .... R	Immaculata (PA) .... S
Baker (KS) .... R	Jacksonville (FL) .... R
Ball State (IN) L	Jacksonville State (AL) .... M
Barry (FL) .... R	Kentucky Wesleyan .... S
▲Bay Path (MA) .... S	Lambuth (TN) .... S
Berea (KY) .... R	Lewis-Clark State (ID) .... R
Bethany (WV) .... S	Lock Haven (PA) .... M
Blackburn (IL) .... S	Long Island U. (C.W. Post)(NY) .... R
Bloomsburg (PA) .... M	Louisiana - Lafayette......................... L
Briar Cliff (IA) .... R	Lycoming (PA) .... R
Bridgewater (VA) .... R	Lynchburg (VA) .... R
Brooklyn (CUNY)(NY)........................ L	Lyndon State (VT) .... R
California Poly State U. (Pomona) L	Maryville (TN) .... S
California State U. (Channel Islands) .... R	Memphis, U. of (TN) L
California State U. (Monterey Bay) .... R	▲Meredith (NC) .... R
Carroll (MT) .... R	Middle Tennessee L
▲Cedar Crest (PA) .... S	Millersville (PA) .... M
Central Michigan L	Milligan (TN) .... S
Colby-Sawyer (NH) .... S	Misericordia, College (PA) .... S
College of Charleston (SC) L	Missouri Southern State .... M
Colorado, U. of (Denver) .... M	Morgan State (MD)............................ M
Daemen (NY) .... R	Mount St. Joseph (OH) .... R
Delaware Valley (PA) .... R	Mount St. Mary's (CA) .... R
DeSales (PA) .... S	Mount Saint Vincent (NY) .... R
Dillard (LA) .... R	Nicholls State (LA) .... M
Doane (NE) .... S	North Carolina (Pembroke) .... R
D'Youville (NY) .... R	North Georgia .... M
East Stroudsburg (PA)........................ M	Northern Illinois U. L
East Tennessee................................. L	Northern Iowa L
Eastern Connecticut .... M	Northern Michigan .... M
Eastern New Mexico .... R	Northland (WI) .... S
Eastern Oregon .... R	Northwestern (IA) .... R
Elmhurst (IL) .... R	Norwich (VT) .... R
Emmanuel (MA) .... S	Penn State (Erie) (PA) .... M
Findlay (OH) .... M	▲Pine Manor (MA) .... S
Fitchburg (MA) .... R	
Fort Lewis (CO) .... M	
Framingham (MA) .... M	**#** *Especially Fisheries Biology*
George Fox (OR) .... R	*GROUP III continues next page*

BIOLOGY, continued

●●● ━━━━━━━━━━━━━━━━━━━ **GROUP III**, continued ━━━━━━━━━━━━━━ ●●●

Pittsburgh, U. of (Bradford)	S
Pittsburg State (KS)	M
Point Park (PA)	R
Puerto Rico (Cayey), U. of	M
Reinhardt (GA)	R
Rhode Island College	M
Rider (NJ)	R
Rockford (IL)	S
Rocky Mountain (MT)	S
Roger Williams (RI)	M
St. Francis (PA)	R
St. Joseph's (IN)	S
St. Joseph's (NY)	R
St. Scholastica (MN)	R
St. Vincent (PA)	R
Salem State (MA)	M
Shippensburg (PA)	M
Shorter (GA)	R
South Alabama	M
South Dakota, U. of	M
South Dakota State U.	M
Southeastern Louisiana	L
Southern Illinois U. (Edwardsville)	L
Southern Mississippi	L
Southern Oregon State U.	M
Southwestern (KS)	S
▲ Spelman (GA)	R

Springfield (MA)	M
Temple (PA)	L
Texas A&M (Corpus Christi)	M
Texas Lutheran	R
Texas, U. of (Arlington)	L
Texas, U. of (San Antonio)	L
Texas, U. of (Tyler)	R
Texas State U. (San Marcos)	L
Thomas More (KY)	R
Tougaloo (MS)	S
Troy State (AL)	M
Utah State	L
Virginia Wesleyan	R
Wartburg (IA)	R
Wayne State (MI)	L
Western Colorado	R
Western Kentucky	L
West Chester (PA)	M
West Virginia Wesleyan	R
Wheeling Jesuit (WV)	R
Wilkes (PA)	R
Wisconsin, U. of (Eau Claire)	L
Wisconsin, U. of (Green Bay)	M
Wisconsin, U. of (Platteville)	M
Wyoming, U. of	L
Xavier University of Louisiana	R

BOTANY / PLANT SCIENCE

GROUP I
Most Selective

California, U. of (Berkeley) XL	Florida, U. of XL
Connecticut College .... R	Miami U. (OH) L
Cornell (NY) L	Michigan, U. of XL
Duke (NC) .... M	North Carolina, U. of L

GROUP II
Very Selective

California, U. of (Davis) XL	Ohio Wesleyan .... R
California, U. of (Riverside) L	Oklahoma, U. of XL
Connecticut, U. of XL	Oklahoma State L
Delaware, U. of L	Pennsylvania State XL
Maine, U. of L	Purdue (IN) XL
Maryland, U. of L	Tennessee, U. of L
Michigan State XL	Texas, U. of (Austin) XL
Montana, U. of .... M	Vermont, U. of L
North Carolina State L	Washington, U. of XL
Ohio U. L	Wisconsin, U. of XL

GROUP III
Selective

Alabama, U. of L	Louisiana State XL
Ball State (IN) L	Northern Arizona XL
Colorado State L	Oregon State L
Eastern Connecticut .... M	San Francisco State (CA) L
Eastern Illinois L	Southeastern Oklahoma State .... M
Hawaii, U. of L	Southern Illinois U. (Carbondale) L
Humboldt State (CA) .... M	Wyoming, U. of L

Enrollment Code		
■ *Men Only*	S = Small (less than 1000 students)	R = Moderate (1000-3000 students)	M = Medium (3000-8000 students)
▲ *Women Only*	L = Large (8000-20,000 students)	XL = Extra Large (over 20,000 students)	

BUSINESS ADMINISTRATION

GROUP I
Most Selective

Albany (SUNY) (NY)	L	Michigan, U. of	XL
American (DC)	M	Missouri, U. of	XL
Babson (MA)	R	MIT (MA)	M
Binghamton (SUNY) (NY)	L	Muhlenberg (PA)	R
Boston College (MA)	L	New Jersey, College of	M
Boston U. (MA)	L	New York U.	L
Bucknell (PA)	R	North Carolina, U. of	L
Buffalo (SUNY) (NY)	L	Notre Dame (IN)	M
California, U. of (Berkeley)	XL	Ohio State	XL
California, U. of (Los Angeles)	XL	Pennsylvania, U. of	L
Carnegie Mellon (PA)	M	Rensselaer (NY)	M
Case Western Reserve U. (OH)	M	Rhodes (TN)	R
Claremont McKenna (CA)	R	Richmond, U. of (VA)	M
Clarkson (NY)	M	Rutgers (NJ)	L
Cornell (NY)	L	Santa Clara U. (CA)	M
Emory (GA)	M	Southern California, U. of	L
Fairfield (CT)	R	Southwestern (TX)	R
Florida, U. of	XL	Syracuse (NY)	L
Florida State	L	Trinity (TX)	R
Franklin & Marshall (PA)	R	Tulane (LA)	M
Furman (SC)	R	U.S. Air Force Academy (CO)	M
Geneseo (SUNY) (NY)	M	Vermont, U. of	L
Georgetown (DC)	M	Villanova (PA)	M
George Washington (DC)	M	Virginia Poly. Institute	L
Georgia Inst. of Tech	L	Virginia, U. of	L
Gettysburg (PA)	R	Wake Forest (NC)	M
Gustavus Adolphus (MN)	R	Washington U. (MO)	M
Illinois, U. of (Urbana-Champaign)	XL	Washington & Lee (VA)	M
Indiana U.	XL	William & Mary (VA)	M
Lafayette (PA)	R	Wisconsin, U. of	XL
Lehigh (PA)	M	Worcester Poly Inst. (MA)	R
Miami, U. of (FL)	L	Yeshiva (NY)	R
Miami U. (OH)	L		

GROUP II
Very Selective

Adelphi (NY)	M	Arizona, U. of	XL
Adrian (MI)	R	Arizona State	XL
▲Agnes Scott (GA)	S	Asbury (KY)	R
Alabama, U. of	L	Auburn (AL)	L
Alabama, U. of (Huntsville)	M	Augsburg (MN)	R
Alaska Pacific	S	Augustana (IL)	R
Albright (PA)	R	Austin (TX)	R
Alfred (NY)	R		
Alma (MI)	R		

GROUP II continues next page

BUSINESS ADMINISTRATION, continued

GROUP II, continued

Baylor (TX) .... M	Evansville (IN) .... R
Belmont (TN) .... R	Flagler (FL) .... R
Bentley (MA) .... M	Florida Atlantic L
---rv (GA) .... R	Florida Gulf Coast U. .... M
---am Southern (AL) .... R	Florida Inst. of Tech. .... R
Bowling Green (OH) L	Florida International .... M
Bradley (IL) .... M	Fordham (NY) L
Brigham Young (UT) XL	Fredonia (SUNY) (NY) .... M
Bryant (RI) .... R	George Mason (VA) L
Buena Vista (IA) .... R	Georgetown College (KY) .... R
Butler (IN) .... R	Gonzaga (WA) .... R
Cal. Poly. State U. (San Luis Obispo) L	Goucher (MD) .... S
California State (Fullerton) L	Grove City (PA) .... R
California, U. of (Riverside) L	Guilford (NC) .... R
California, U. of (Santa Barbara) L	Hampton (VA) .... M
Capital U. (OH) .... R	Hanover (IN) .... R
Centenary (LA) .... S	Harding (AR) .... M
Central Florida, U. of XL	Hendrix (AR) .... R
Charleston, College of (SC) L	Hillsdale (MI) .... R
Christian Brothers (TN) .... R	Hofstra (NY) .... M
Cincinnati, U. of (OH) L	Hood (MD) .... S
Clark (MA) .... R	Houston, U. of (TX) L
Clemson (SC) L	Howard (DC) .... M
Coe (IA) .... R	Idaho, College of .... S
Colorado, U. of L	Idaho, U. of L
Colorado, U. of (Col. Springs) .... M	Illinois College .... S
Columbia College (SC) .... R	Illinois, U. of (Chicago) L
Concordia (MN) .... R	Illinois, U. of (Springfield) .... R
Connecticut, U. of XL	Indiana U. of Pennsylvania L
Creighton (NE) .... M	Indiana Wesleyan .... M
Dayton, U. of (OH) .... M	Iowa State XL
Delaware, U. of L	Iowa, U. of XL
Denver, U. of (CO) .... M	Ithaca (NY) .... M
DePaul (IL) L	James Madison (VA) .... M
Dominican (IL) .... S	John Carroll (OH) .... M
Drake (IA) .... M	▲ Judson (AL) .... S
Dubuque, U. of (IA) .... S	Juniata (PA) .... R
Duquesne (PA) .... M	Kansas, U. of L
Eastern Michigan L	Kansas State L
Eckerd (FL) .... R	Kansas Wesleyan .... S
Elizabethtown (PA) .... R	Kentucky, U. of L
Elon (NC) .... R	
Erskine (SC) .... S	*GROUP II continues next page*

BUSINESS ADMINISTRATION, continued

•• ━━━━━━ GROUP II, continued ━━━━━━ ••

LaSalle (PA)	M
Lebanon Valley (PA)	R
LeMoyne (NY)	R
LeTourneau (TX)	R
Lewis & Clark (OR)	R
Lindenwood (MO)	M
Lipscomb (TN)	R
Longwood (VA)	R
Loras (IA)	R
Loyola (MD)	R
Loyola (LA)	R
Loyola Marymount (CA)	M
Luther (IA)	R
Manhattan (NY)	M
Manhattanville (NY)	R
Marietta (OH)	R
Marist (NY)	M
Marquette (WI)	M
Maryland, U. of	XL
Mary Washington (VA)	M
Massachusetts, U. of	L
Massachusetts, U. of (Lowell)	M
Master's (CA)	R
McDaniel (MD)	R
Messiah (PA)	R
Michigan, U. of (Dearborn)	M
Michigan State	XL
Michigan Tech	M
Millersville (PA)	M
Millsaps (MS)	S
Milwaukee School of Engineering (WI)	R
Minnesota, U. of	XL
Mississippi College	R
Mississippi, U. of	L
Mississippi U. for Women	R
Missouri, U. of (Kansas City)	M
Missouri, U. of (St. Louis)	M
Mobile, U. of (AL)	R
Monmouth (IL)	S
Moravian (PA)	R
Morningside (IA)	S
Nazareth (NY)	R
New Hampshire, U. of	L
Newman University (KS)	S
New Mexico, U. of	L
New Mexico State	L

New Paltz (SUNY)(NY)	M
North Carolina, U. of (Greensboro)	M
North Carolina, U. of (Wilmington)	L
North Dakota, U. of	M
Northeastern (MA)	L
Northwestern (MN)	R
Northern Arizona	XL
Northern Michigan	M
North Florida	L
Oglethorpe (GA)	R
Ohio U.	L
Oklahoma City U. (OK)	R
Oklahoma State	L
Oklahoma, U. of	XL
Old Dominion (VA)	L
Oregon, U. of	L
Oswego (SUNY) (NY)	M
Pacific Lutheran (WA)	R
Pacific, U. of the (CA)	M
Pacific University (OR)	R
Palm Beach Atlantic (FL)	R
Pennsylvania State	XL
Pepperdine (CA)	R
Pittsburgh, U. of (PA)	L
Plattsburgh (SUNY) (NY)	M
Portland State (OR)	L
Portland, U. of (OR)	R
Presbyterian (SC)	R
Principia (IL)	S
Providence (RI)	M
Puerto Rico, U. of	L
Puget Sound (WA)	R
Purdue (IN)	XL
Queens (NC)	R
Ramapo (NJ)	M
Randolph-Macon (VA)	R
Redlands, U. of (CA)	R
Rhode Island, U. of	L
Richard Stockton (NJ)	M
Ripon (WI)	R
Roanoke (VA)	R
Rochester Inst. of Tech (NY)	L
Rockhurst (MO)	R
Rowan (NJ)	M

GROUP II continues next page

BUSINESS ADMINISTRATION, continued

GROUP II, continued

Rutgers-Newark (NJ)	M
Salem College (NC)	S
Salisbury (MD)	M
Samford (AL)	R
San Diego State U. (CA)	XL
San Diego, U. of (CA)	M
San Francisco, U. of (CA)	M
Sciences, U. of the (PA)	S
Scranton, U. of (PA)	M
Seton Hall (NJ)	M
Shaw (NC)	R
Shepherd (WV)	M
Siena (NY)	R
▲ Simmons (MA)	R
Skidmore (NY)	R
Southern Methodist (TX)	M
Spring Hill (AL)	R
St. Bonaventure (NY)	R
▲ St. Catherine (MN)	R
St. John's (MN)	R
▲ St. Joseph's (CT)	S
St. Joseph's U. (PA)	R
St. Louis U. (MO)	M
St. Mary's Col. of CA	R
▲ St. Mary's Col. (IN)	R
St. Mary's Col. (MN)	R
St. Michael's Col. (VT)	R
St. Norbert (WI)	R
# St. Scholastica (MN)	R
Southern Oregon State U.	M
Stetson (FL)	R
Stonehill (MA)	R
Susquehanna U. (PA)	R
Temple (PA)	L

Texas A&M	XL
Texas Christian	M
Texas Tech U.	L
Texas, U. of (Austin)	XL
Texas, U. of (Dallas)	M
Transylvania (KY)	S
▲ Trinity (DC)	S
Truman State (MO)	M
Tulsa, U. of (OK)	R
Ursinus (PA)	R
Utah, U. of	L
Valparaiso (IN)	M
Virginia Military Institute	R
Wartburg (IA)	R
Washington College (MD)	S
Washington State	L
Washington, U. of	XL
Wells (NY)	S
▲ Wesleyan College (GA)	S
Western Michigan	L
Westminster (MO)	S
Westminster (UT)	R
West Virginia U.	L
Whitworth (WA)	R
Wilberforce (OH)	S
William Jewell Col. (MO)	R
Winona State U. (MN)	M
Wisconsin, U. of (Milwaukee)	L
Wisconsin, U. of (Stevens Point)	M
Wittenberg (OH)	R
Wofford (SC)	R
Wyoming, U. of	L
Xavier (OH)	R

Also, Organizational Behavior and Marketing

BUSINESS ADMINISTRATION, continued

GROUP III
Selective

Abilene Christian (TX) .... M	California State U. (Fresno) L
Akron, U. of (OH) L	California State U. (Fullerton) L
Alabama, U. of (Birmingham) .... M	California State U. (Los Angeles) L
Alaska, U. of (Anchorage) .... M	California State U. (Northridge) L
Alaska, U. of (Fairbanks) .... M	California State U. (Sacramento) .... M
Alderson-Broaddus (WV) .... S	California State U. (San Bernardino) ...... M
▲Alverno (WI) .... R	California State U. (San Marcos) .... M
American International (MA) .... R	California State U. (Stanislaus) .... M
Anna Maria (MA) .... S	Campbell (NC) .... R
Appalachian State (NC) L	Canisius (NY) .... M
Aquinas (MI) .... R	Carthage (WI) .... R
Arkansas, U. of L	Castleton (VT) .... R
Ashland (OH) .... R	Catawba (NC) .... S
Assumption (MA) .... R	Cedarville (OH) .... R
Averett (VA) .... S	Central Arkansas .... M
Avila (MO) .... S	Central Connecticut .... M
Azusa Pacific (CA) .... R	Central Oklahoma L
Baker (KS) .... R	Central Washington L
Baldwin-Wallace (OH) .... R	Chaminade (HI) .... R
Barry (FL) .... R	π Champlain (VT) .... R
▲Bay Path (MA) .... R	Chapman (CA) .... R
Baruch (CUNY) (NY) L	▲Chatham (PA) .... S
Belhaven (MS) .... R	Chowan (NC) .... S
Bellarmine (KY) .... R	Christopher Newport (VA) .... M
Belmont Abbey (NC) .... S	Cincinnati, U. of (OH) L
Benedictine (KS) .... R	Citadel, The (SC) .... R
Benedictine (IL) .... R	Clark Atlanta (GA) .... M
▲Bennett (NC) .... S	Coastal Carolina (SC) .... M
Berea (KY) .... R	Coker (SC) .... S
Bethel (MN) .... R	Colorado State L
Blackburn (IL) .... S	Colorado, U. of (Denver) .... M
Bloomsburg (PA) .... M	Columbia College (MO) .... R
Bluffton (OH) .... S	Concordia (CA) .... R
Boise State (ID) L	Concordia (NE) .... R
Brescia (KY) .... S	Concordia-Austin (TX) .... S
Briar Cliff (IA) .... R	Culver-Stockton (MO) .... S
Bridgewater (VA) .... R	Daemen (NY) .... R
Brockport (SUNY) (NY) .... M	Delaware Valley (PA) .... R
Caldwell (NJ) .... S	Dillard (LA) .... R
California Lutheran .... R	Doane (NE) .... S
California Maritime Academy .... S	East Tennessee L
Cal. Poly. State U. (Pomona) L	Eastern (PA) .... R
California State U. (Bakersfield) .... M	Eastern Connecticut .... M
California State U. (Channel Islands) .... R	
California State U. (Dominguez Hills) ..... M	
California State U. (East Bay) .... M	

π Also, Electronic Games &
Interactive Development

GROUP III continues next page

BUSINESS ADMINISTRATION, continued

GROUP III, continued

Eastern Illinois L	Kentucky Wesleyan (KY) .... S
Eastern Nazarene (MA) .... R	King's (PA) .... R
Eastern Oregon .... R	LaSell (MA) .... S
Edgewood (WI) .... S	LaVerne, U. of (CA) .... R
Elmhurst (IL) .... R	Lenoir-Rhyne (NC) .... R
Elmira (NY) .... R	Lesley (MA) .... S
Emory & Henry (VA) .... S	Linfield (OR) .... R
Endicott (MA) .... R	Long Island U. (C.W. Post) (NY) .... R
Eureka (IL) .... S	Louisiana-Lafayette L
Fairleigh Dickinson (NJ) .... M	Louisiana Tech. .... M
Fairmont State (WV) .... M	Louisville (KY) L
Faulkner (AL) .... R	Lyndon State (VT) .... R
Ferris State (MI) L	Maine (Farmington) .... R
Findlay (OH) .... M	Maine, U. of L
Fisk (TN) .... S	Malone (OH) .... R
Florida A&M .... M	Manchester (IN) .... R
Fontbonne (MO) .... R	Marshall (WV) L
Framingham (MA) .... M	▲ Mary Baldwin (VA) .... S
Freed-Hardeman (TN) .... R	Marygrove (MI) .... R
Frostburg (MD) .... M	Mass. Col. of Lib. Arts (N. Adams) .... R
Gannon (PA) .... M	Massachusetts, U. of (Boston) .... M
Gardner-Webb (NC) .... S	Massachusetts, U. of (Dartmouth) .... M
George Fox (OR) .... R	McMurray (TX) .... R
Georgia Southern L	Mercer (GA) .... R
Georgia State L	Mercyhurst (PA) .... R
Graceland (IA) .... R	▲ Meredith (NC) .... R
Grambling (LA) .... M	Merrimack (MA) .... R
Green Mountain (VT) .... S	Middle Tennessee L
Hartford, U. of (CT) .... M	Milligan (TN) .... S
Hartwick (NY) .... R	Mississippi State L
Hastings (NE) .... R	Missouri Southern State .... M
Hawaii Pacific .... M	Monmouth (NJ) .... R
Heidelberg (OH) .... S	Montana, U. of .... M
Henderson State (AR) .... M	Montana State (Billings) .... R
Hillsdale (MI) .... R	Montana State L
Husson (ME) .... S	Montclair State (NJ) .... M
Immaculata (PA) .... S	Montreat (NC) .... S
Indiana Institute of Tech. .... S	■ Morehouse (GA) .... R
Indiana State U. L	Mount Marty (SD) .... R
Iona (NY) .... M	Mount Mercy (IA) .... S
Jacksonville (FL) .... R	Mount St. Joseph (OH) .... R
Jamestown (ND) .... R	
Kennesaw State (GA) .... R	

GROUP III continues next page

Enrollment Code			
■ *Men Only*	S = Small (less than 1000 students)	R = Moderate (1000-3000 students)	M = Medium (3000-8000 students)
▲ *Women Only*	L = Large (8000-20,000 students)	XL = Extra Large (over 20,000 students)	

BUSINESS ADMINISTRATION, continued

••• ——————— GROUP III, continued ——————— •••

Mount St. Mary's (CA) .... R	Quinnipiac (CT) .... R
Mount St. Mary's (MD) .... R	Phillips (OK) .... R
Mount Union (OH) .... R	Radford (VA) .... M
Murray State (KY) .... M	Regis (CO) .... R
Muskingum (OH) .... R	Reinhardt (GA) .... R
Nebraska, U. of L	Rider (NJ) .... M
Nebraska, U. of (Kearney) .... M	Robert Morris (PA) .... M
Nebraska, U. of (Omaha) L	Rockford (IL) .... S
Nevada, U. of (Las Vegas) L	Rocky Mountain (MT) .... S
Nevada, U. of (Reno) L	Roger Williams (RI) .... M
New Orleans, U. of L	Roosevelt (IL) .... R
Niagara (NY) .... R	Sacred Heart (CT) .... R
Nicholls State (LA) .... M	St. Ambrose (IA) .... R
North Carolina, U. of (Charlotte) L	St. Andrews Presbyterian (NC) .... S
North Carolina, U. of (Pembroke) ...... R	St. Cloud (MN) L
North Georgia .... M	St. Edward's (TX) .... M
North Texas L	St. Francis (NY) .... R
Northern Arizona L	St. John Fisher (NY) .... R
Northern Colorado L	St. John's (NY) L
Northern Illinois L	St. Joseph's (IN) .... S
Northern Iowa, U. of L	St. Joseph's (NY) .... R
Northern Kentucky L	St. Martin's (WA) .... S
Northwestern (IA) .... R	St. Mary (KS) .... S
Northwestern U. of Louisiana L	St. Mary's (TX) .... R
Northwood University (MI) .... R	St. Peter's (NJ) .... R
Nova Southeastern (FL) .... R	St. Rose (NY) .... R
Nyack (NY) .... R	St. Thomas (MN) .... M
Oakland U. (MI) .... M	St. Thomas Aquinas (NY) .... R
Oakland City U. (IN) .... R	St. Vincent's (PA) .... R
Ohio Northern .... R	Salem State (MA) .... M
Oral Roberts (OK) .... M	San Francisco State (CA) L
Oregon Inst. of Tech. .... R	San Jose State (CA) L
Ozarks, College of the (MO) .... R	Schreiner (TX) .... S
Pace (NY) .... R	Seattle U. (WA) .... R
Penn State (Erie)(PA) .... M	Shippensburg (PA) .... M
Peru State (NE) .... R	Siena Heights (MI) .... S
Philadelphia U. (PA) .... R	Silver Lake (WI) .... S
▲Pine Manor (MA) .... S	Sioux Falls, U. of (SD) .... R
Pittsburg State (KS) .... M	Simpson (IA) .... R
Pittsburgh, U. of (Greensburg) .... R	Sonoma State (CA) .... M
Pittsburgh, U. of (Johnstown) .... R	South Alabama .... M
Point Loma (CA) .... R	South Carolina, U. of L
Potsdam (SUNY) (NY) .... M	South Dakota, U. of .... M
Presentation (SD) .... S	Southeastern Missouri State L
Puerto Rico (CAYEY), U. of .... M	
Quincy (IL) .... R	*GROUP III continues next page*

GROUP III continues next page

BUSINESS ADMINISTRATION, continued

••• ——— GROUP III, continued ——— •••

Southeastern Oklahoma State	M
Southern Illinois	L
Southern Maine	M
Southern Mississippi	L
Southern Oregon State U.	M
Southern Utah	M
South Florida, U. of	XL
Southwestern Oklahoma	M
▲ Stephens (MO)	S
Suffolk (MA)	R
Tampa, U. of (FL)	R
Taylor (IN)	R
Tennessee, U. of	L
Tennessee, U of (Martin)	M
Texas A&M (Commerce)	M
Texas A&M (Corpus Christi)	M
Texas Lutheran	R
Texas State U. (San Marcos)	L
Texas Wesleyan	R
Texas, U. of (El Paso)	L
Texas, U. of (San Antonio)	L
Texas, U. of (Tyler)	R
Thomas More (KY)	R
Toledo, U. of	L
Towson (MD)	L
Troy State (AL)	M
Utica College (NY)	R
Virginia Commonwealth	L

Virginia Wesleyan	R
Visual Arts, School of (NY)	R
Wagner (NY)	R
Washington & Jefferson (PA)	R
Wayne State (MI)	L
Weber State (UT)	L
West Chester (PA)	M
West Florida, U. of	M
Western Carolina (NC)	M
Western Connecticut State	M
Western New England (MA)	R
Western State (CO)	R
Whittier (CA)	R
Wichita State (KS)	M
Widener (PA)	R
William Paterson (NJ)	M
Winthrop (SC)	M
Wisconsin, U. of (Eau Claire)	L
Wisconsin, U. of (Green Bay)	M
Wisconsin, U. of (LaCrosse)	L
Wisconsin, U. of (Stout)	M
# Wisconsin, U. of (Whitewater)	L
Woodbury (CA)	S
Worcester State (MA)	M
Wright State (OH)	L
Xavier U. of Louisiana	R
York (NE)	S
York (PA)	M
Youngstown State (OH)	L

*Especially Accounting*

CHEMISTRY

GROUP I
Most Selective

Albany (SUNY)(NY)	L	Grinnell (IA)	R
Allegheny (PA)	R	Gustavus Adolphus (MN)	R
Amherst (MA)	R	Hamilton (NY)	R
▲ Barnard (NY)	R	Harvard (MA)	M
Bates (ME)	R	Harvey Mudd (CA)	S
Binghamton (SUNY)(NY)	L	Haverford (PA)	S
Boston College (MA)	L	Holy Cross (MA)	R
Boston U. (MA)	L	Illinois Wesleyan	R
Bowdoin (ME)	R	Illinois, U. of (Urbana-Champaign)	XL
Brandeis (MA)	M	Iowa State	XL
Brown (RI)	M	Johns Hopkins (MD)	M
▲ Bryn Mawr (PA)	S	Kalamazoo (MI)	R
Bucknell (PA)	M	Kenyon (OH)	R
Buffalo (SUNY)(NY)	L	Lafayette (PA)	R
California Inst. of Tech.	S	Lawrence (WI)	R
California, U. of (Berkeley)	XL	Loyola (MD)	M
California, U. of (Los Angeles)	XL	Macalester (MN)	R
California, U. of (San Diego)	L	MIT (MA)	M
Carleton (MN)	R	Miami, U. of (FL)	L
Carnegie Mellon (PA)	M	Michigan, U. of	XL
Case Western Reserve U. (OH)	M	Middlebury (VT)	R
Centre (KY)	R	Missouri, U. of (Rolla)	M
Chicago, U. of (IL)	M	▲ Mount Holyoke (MA)	R
Claremont McKenna (CA)	R	New College (FL)	S
Clarkson (NY)	M	New Jersey, College of	M
Colby (ME)	R	New Jersey Inst. of Tech	M
Colgate (NY)	R	New Mexico Inst. of Tech.	R
Colorado College	R	North Carolina, U. of	L
Columbia (NY)	M	Northeastern (MA)	L
Connecticut College	R	Northwestern (IL)	M
Cornell (NY)	L	Notre Dame (IN)	M
Dartmouth (NH)	M	Oberlin (OH)	R
Davidson (NC)	R	Occidental (CA)	R
DePauw (IN)	R	Pennsylvania State	XL
Drew (NJ)	R	Pomona (CA)	R
Duke (NC)	M	Princeton (NJ)	M
Emory (GA)	M	Puget Sound (WA)	R
Franklin & Marshall (PA)	R	Reed (OR)	R
Furman (SC)	R	Rennselaer (NY)	M
Georgetown (DC)	M	Rhodes (TN)	R
Georgia Inst. of Tech	L		
Gonzaga (WA)	M		

GROUP I continues next page

Enrollment Code	
■ *Men Only*	S = Small (less than 1000 students) R = Moderate (1000-3000 students) M = Medium (3000-8000 students)
▲ *Women Only*	L = Large (8000-20,000 students) XL = Extra Large (over 20,000 students)

CHEMISTRY, continued

GROUP I, continued

Rice (TX)	M	Vanderbilt (TN)	M
Richmond (VA)	M	Vassar (NY)	R
Rochester, U. of (NY)	M	Virginia, U. of	L
Rose-Hulman (IN)	R	■ Wabash (IN)	S
Rutgers (NJ)	L	Wake Forest (NC)	M
▲ Scripps (CA)	S	Washington & Lee (VA)	R
Siena (NY)	R	Washington U. (MO)	M
Skidmore (NY)	R	▲ Wellesley (MA)	R
South, U. of the (TN)	R	Wesleyan (CT)	R
Southwestern (TX)	R	Wheaton (IL)	R
St. Olaf (MN)	R	Wheaton (MA)	R
Stanford (CA)	M	Whitman (WA)	R
Trinity (CT)	R	Willamette (OR)	R
Trinity (TX)	R	Williams (MA)	R
Tufts (MA)	M	Wisconsin, U. of	XL
Union (NY)	R	Worcester Poly Inst.(MA)	R
United States Naval Academy (MD)	M	Yale (CT)	M
United States Air Force Academy (CO)	M	Yeshiva (NY)	R

GROUP II
Very Selective

Adelphi (NY)	M	California, U. of (Santa Cruz)	M
Alabama, U. of (Huntsville)	M	Capital (OH)	R
Albion (MI)	R	Carroll (WI)	R
Alfred (NY)	R	Centenary (LA)	S
Alma (MI)	R	Central (IA)	R
Arcadia (PA)	R	Citadel, The (SC)	R
Arizona, U. of	XL	City College (CUNY)(NY)	L
Arkansas, U. of	L	Clark (MA)	R
Augustana (SD)	R	Clarke (IA)	S
Austin (TX)	R	Clemson (SC)	L
Baylor (TX)	M	Coe (IA)	R
Bemidji State (MN)	M	Colorado, U. of	L
Berea (KY)	R	Concordia (MN)	R
Berry (GA)	R	Converse (SC)	S
Bethany (WV)	S	Creighton (NE)	R
Bethel (MN)	M	Delaware, U. of	L
Birmingham-Southern (AL)	R	Denver, U. of (CO)	M
Bradley (IL)	M	DePaul (IL)	L
Brigham Young (UT)	L	Drake (IA)	M
Brooklyn College (CUNY)(NY)	L	Duquesne (PA)	M
Butler (IN)	R	Earlham (IN)	R
California, U. of (Davis)	XL	Eastern Michigan	L
California, U. of (Irvine)	L		
California, U. of (Santa Barbara)	L		

GROUP II continues next page

CHEMISTRY, continued

•• ━━━━━━━━━━ GROUP II, continued ━━━━━━━━━━ ••

Elizabethtown (PA)	R
Elmhurst (IL)	R
Evansville (IN)	R
Florida Inst. of Tech	R
Florida Southern	R
Florida State	L
Geneva (PA)	R
Georgetown (KY)	R
George Washington (DC)	M
Georgia, U. of	XL
Goucher (MD)	S
Hamline (MN)	R
■ Hampden-Sydney (VA)	S
Hampton (VA)	M
Hanover (IN)	R
π Harrisburg U. (PA)	S
Hendrix (AR)	R
Hiram (OH)	R
Hobart & William Smith (NY)	R
▲ Hollins (VA)	S
Hope (MI)	R
Houghton (NY)	S
Houston, U. of (TX)	L
Howard (DC)	M
Hunter (CUNY)(NY)	L
Huntingdon (AL)	S
Idaho, College of	S
Indiana U.	XL
Iowa, U. of	XL
Ithaca Col.	M
John Carroll (OH)	R
Juniata (PA)	R
Kansas, U. of	L
Kansas Wesleyan	S
Kent State (OH)	L
Knox (IL)	R
Lake Forest (IL)	R
LaSalle (PA)	M
Lebanon Valley (PA)	R
Lehigh (PA)	M
LeMoyne (NY)	R
Lewis & Clark (OR)	R
Linfield (OR)	R
Lipscomb (TN)	R

Loras (IA)	R
Louisiana State	XL
Louisiana-Lafayette	L
Louisville (KY)	L
Loyola (LA)	R
Lycoming (PA)	R
Lyon (AR)	M
Maine, U. of	L
Manhattan (NY)	M
Mansfield (PA)	R
Marist (NY)	M
Marquette (WI)	M
Maryland, U. of (Baltimore County)	M
Mary Washington (VA)	M
Massachusetts, U. of	L
Massachusetts, U. of (Boston)	M
Massachusetts, U. of (Lowell)	M
McKendree (IL)	R
McMurry (TX)	R
Mercer (GA)	M
Merrimack (MA)	R
Michigan State	XL
Michigan, U. of (Dearborn)	M
Millsaps (MS)	S
Minnesota, U. of (Morris)	R
Missouri, U. of (Kansas City)	M
Missouri, U. of (St. Louis)	M
Monmouth (IL)	S
Montana Tech	R
Montana State	L
Morningside (IA)	S
Muhlenberg (PA)	R
Murray State (KY)	M
Nebraska Wesleyan	R
New Hampshire, U. of	L
New Mexico State	L
North Carolina, U. of (Charlotte)	L
North Carolina, U. of (Wilmington)	L
North Carolina State	L
North Central (IL)	R
North Dakota, U. of	M

π *Environmental Chemistry*

GROUP II continues next page

CHEMISTRY, continued

━━ GROUP II, continued ━━

Ohio Northern	R	Stetson (FL)	R
Ohio State	XL	Stonehill (MA)	R
Ohio University	L	Stony Brook (SUNY) (NY)	L
Ohio Wesleyan	R	Susquehanna (PA)	R
Oklahoma, U. of	XL	▲Sweet Briar (VA)	S
Oral Roberts (OK)	M	Syracuse (NY)	L
Oregon, U. of	L	Temple (PA)	L
Otterbein (OH)	R	Tennessee, U. of	XL
Ouachita Baptist (AR)	R	Tennessee, U. of (Chattanooga)	M
Pacific, U. of the (CA)	R	Texas A&M	XL
Pacific Lutheran (WA)	R	Texas A&M (Kingsville)	M
Pittsburgh, U. of (PA)	L	Texas Christian	M
Portland, U. of (OR)	R	Toledo, U. of (OH)	L
Providence (RI)	M	Transylvania (KY)	S
Puerto Rico, U of (Mayaguez)	L	Truman State (MO)	M
Purdue (IN)	XL	Ursinus (PA)	R
Randolph College (VA)	S	Utah State	L
Richard Stockton (NJ)	M	Utah, U. of	L
Ripon (WI)	S	Valparaiso U. (IN)	M
Roanoke (VA)	R	Vermont, U. of	L
Rochester Institute of Tech. (NY)	L	Villanova (PA)	M
Rockhurst (MO)	R	Virginia Military Inst.	R
Rollins (FL)	R	Virginia Tech.	L
St. Edward's (TX)	M	Viterbo (WI)	R
St. John's (MN)	R	Washington & Jefferson (PA)	R
St. Louis (MO)	M	Washington, U. of	XL
▲St. Mary's College (IN)	R	Wayne State (MI)	L
St. Michael's (VT)	R	Wells (NY)	S
St. Thomas (MN)	R	▲Wesleyan (GA)	S
St. Thomas (TX)	R	West Florida, U. of	M
St. Vincent (PA)	R	West Virginia U.	L
San Diego, U. of (CA)	M	Westminster (PA)	R
San Diego State U. (CA)	XL	Westminster (UT)	R
Santa Clara U. (CA)	M	Westmont (CA)	R
Sciences in Philadelphia (PA)	R	Whitworth (WA)	R
Seattle Pacific (WA)	R	Widener (PA)	R
Seattle U. (WA)	R	William Jewell (MO)	R
Shepherd (WV)	M	Winthrop (SC)	M
South Carolina, U. of	L	Wisconsin Lutheran	S
South Dakota, U. of	M	Wisconsin, U. of (Milwaukee)	L
South Dakota School of Mines	R	Wittenberg (OH)	R
South Florida, U. of	L	Wofford (SC)	R
▲Spelman (GA)	R	Wooster (OH)	R
Spring Hill (AL)	R		

CHEMISTRY continues next page

Enrollment Code

■ *Men Only*
▲ *Women Only*

S = Small (less than 1000 students)   R = Moderate (1000-3000 students)   M = Medium (3000-8000 students)
L = Large (8000-20,000 students)   XL = Extra Large (over 20,000 students)

CHEMISTRY, continued

••• ———————————————— **GROUP III** ———————————————— •••
Selective

Abilene Christian (TX)	M	King's (PA)	R
Adrian (MI)	R	Lamar (TX)	M
Akron, U. of (OH)	L	Lambuth (TN)	S
Alabama, U. of (Birmingham)	M	Lewis-Clark State (ID)	R
Andrews (MI)	R	Lock Haven (PA)	M
Aquinas (MI)	R	Long Island U. (Brooklyn)(NY)	M
Ashland (OH)	R	Long Island U. (C.W. Post)(NY)	R
Baldwin-Wallace (OH)	R	Marietta (OH)	R
Benedictine (IL)	R	Marshall (WV)	L
Benedictine (KS)	R	▲ Mary Baldwin (VA)	S
Bethany (KS)	S	Maryville (TN)	R
Bluffton (OH)	S	Massachusetts, U. of (Dartmouth)	M
Brockport (SUNY)(NY)	M	Memphis, U. of (TN)	L
California (PA)	M	Mercyhurst (PA)	R
California State U. (Chico)	L	Middle Tennessee	L
California State U. (Dominguez Hills)	M	Millersville (PA)	M
California State U. (Fresno)	L	Milligan (TN)	S
California State U. (Fullerton)	L	Montana, U. of	M
California State U. (Long Beach)	L	Mount St. Joseph (OH)	R
California State U. (San Jose)	L	Muskingum (OH)	R
California State U. (San Marcos)	M	Nicholls State (LA)	M
Carroll (MT)	R	North Dakota State	L
Carson-Newman (TN)	R	Northern Illinois U.	L
Central Washington	L	Northern Kentucky	L
College of Charleston (SC)	L	Northern Michigan	M
Colorado, U. of (Colorado Springs)	M	Northwestern (IA)	R
Cumberland (KY)	R	Oakland U. (MI)	M
Delaware Valley (PA)	R	Penn State (Erie) (PA)	M
DeSales (PA)	S	Pittsburgh, U. of (Johnstown)	R
East Stroudsburg (PA)	M	Pitzer (CA)	S
Eastern Illinois	L	Puerto Rico, U. of (Cayey)	L
Eastern Washington	L	Queens (CUNY)(NY)	L
Emporia State (KS)	M	Rider (NJ)	R
Framingham (MA)	M	Rockford (IL)	S
Gannon (PA)	M	Rocky Mountain (MT)	S
Georgia State	L	Sacred Heart (CT)	R
Henderson State (AR)	M	St. Ambrose (IA)	R
High Point (NC)	R	St. Francis (PA)	R
Houston Baptist (TX)	R	St. John's (NY)	L
Humboldt State (CA)	M	St. Joseph's (ME)	S
* Husson (ME)	S	St. Mary's (MN)	R
Illinois State	L	St. Mary's U. of San Antonio (TX)	R
Kennesaw State (GA)	R		
Kentucky Wesleyan	R	
King (TN)	S	

* *Chemistry / Pre-Pharmacy*

GROUP III continues next page

CHEMISTRY, continued

━━━ GROUP III, continued ━━━

St. Scholastica (MN) .... R	Union (TN) .... R
Salem State (MA) .... M	Wayne State (NE) .... R
Shippensburg (PA) .... M	West Chester (PA) .... M
Shorter (GA) .... R	Western Carolina (NC) .... M
Sonoma State (CA) .... M	Western Connecticut .... M
South Alabama .... M	Western Illinois L
South Dakota State U. .... M	Western Michigan L
Southern Connecticut .... M	Wheeling Jesuit (WV) .... R
Southern Illinois U. (Carbondale) L	Whittier (CA) .... R
Southern Illinois U. (Edwardsville) ... L	Winona State (MN) .... M
Southern Maine .... M	Wilkes (PA) .... R
Southern Oregon State U. .... M	Wisconsin, U. of (Eau Claire) L
Southwestern Oklahoma .... M	Wisconsin, U. of (LaCrosse).............. L
▲ Sweet Briar (VA) .... S	Wisconsin, U. of (Platteville)............ M
Texas A&M (Corpus Christi) .... M	Wisconsin, U. of (Stevens Point) ...... M
Texas Lutheran .... R	Worcester State (MA) .... M
Thomas More (KY) .... R	Wyoming, U. of L
Tougaloo (AL) .... S	Xavier (OH) .... R
Towson (MD) L	Xavier U. of Louisiana .... R

CLASSICS

GROUP I
Most Selective

Agnes Scott (GA) .... S	Middlebury (VT) .... R
Amherst (MA) .... R	Minnesota, U. of XL
▲ Barnard (NY) .... R	New York U. .... M
Bowdoin (ME) .... R	North Carolina, U. of L
Brown (RI) .... M	Northwestern (IL) .... M
▲ Bryn Mawr (PA) .... S	Notre Dame (IN) .... R
Buffalo (SUNY)(NY) L	Oberlin (OH) .... R
California, U. of (Berkeley) XL	Pennsylvania, U. of L
Carleton (MN) .... R	Pittsburgh, U. of (PA) L
Case Western Reserve (OH) .... M	Princeton (NJ) .... M
Centre (KY) .... R	Reed (OR) .... R
Chicago, U. of (IL) .... M	Rhodes (TN) .... R
Colgate (NY) .... R	St. Olaf (MN) .... R
Columbia (NY) .... M	▲ Scripps (CA) .... S
Connecticut College .... R	Skidmore (NY) .... R
Dallas, U. of (TX) .... R	South, U. of the (TN) .... R
Dartmouth (NH) .... M	Southwestern (TX) .... R
Drew (NJ) .... R	Stanford (CA) .... M
Duke (NC) .... M	Swarthmore (PA) .... R
Emory (GA) .... M	Texas, U. of (Austin) XL
Franklin & Marshall (PA) .... R	Trinity (TX) .... R
Georgetown (DC) .... M	Tufts (MA) .... M
Grinnell (IA) .... R	Vanderbilt (TN) .... M
Gustavus Adolphus (MN) .... R	Virginia, U. of L
Harvard (MA) .... M	■ Wabash (IN) .... S
Haverford (PA) .... S	Wesleyan (CT) .... R
Holy Cross (MA) .... R	Whitman (WA) .... R
Johns Hopkins (MD) .... M	Willamette (OR) .... R
Kalamazoo (MI) .... R	William & Mary (VA) .... R
Kenyon (OH) .... R	Williams (MA) .... R
Macalester (MN) .... R	Wisconsin, U. of XL
Maryland, U. of (Baltimore County) ... M	Yale (CT) .... M
Michigan, U. of XL	

CLASSICS, continued

GROUP II
Very Selective

Baylor (TX)	M	Millsaps (MS) .... S
Beloit (WI)	R	Misericordia, College (PA) .... S
Brooklyn College (CUNY)(NY)	L	Missippi, U. of L
California State U. (Long Beach)	L	Missouri, U. of XL
California, U. of (Santa Barbara)	L	Missouri State L
Catholic U. (DC)	M	Montana, U. of L
Cincinnati, U. of	L	Montclair State (NJ) .... M
Creighton (NE)	M	Nebraska, U. of L
Duquesne (PA)	M	North Carolina (Asheville) .... R
Florida State	L	North Carolina (Greensboro) .... M
Florida, U. of	XL	Ohio State XL
Fordham (NY)	L	Ohio U. L
Georgia, U. of	L	Oklahoma, U. of XL
■ Hampden-Sydney (VA)	S	Puget Sound (WA) .... R
Hanover (IN)	R	Randolph College (VA) .... S
▲ Hollins (VA)	S	Randolph-Macon (VA) .... R
Hope (MI)	R	Rollins (FL) .... R
Howard (DC)	M	St. Anselm (NH) .... R
Hunter (CUNY)(NY)	L	St. John's/St. Benedict (MN) .... R
Illinois, U. of (Chicago)	L	Samford (AL) .... R
Kentucky, U. of	L	Tennessee, U. of XL
Loyola (IL)	M	Vermont, U. of L
Loyola (MD)	M	Virginia Tech. L
Loyola Marymount (CA)	M	Washington, U. of XL
π Mary Washington (VA)	M	Wooster, College of the (OH) .... R
Massachusetts, U. of (Boston)	M	Xavier (OH) .... R

π *Also, Classical Archeology*

Enrollment Code	
■ *Men Only*	S = Small (less than 1000 students) R = Moderate (1000-3000 students) M = Medium (3000-8000 students)
▲ *Women Only*	L = Large (8000-20,000 students) XL = Extra Large (over 20,000 students)

COMPUTER SCIENCE

GROUP I
Most Selective

Albany, (SUNY)(NY) L	Maryland, U. of XL
▲ Barnard (NY) .... R	Michigan, U. of XL
Binghamton (SUNY)(NY) L	MIT (MA) .... M
Boston College (MA) L	Miami U. (OH) L
Brandeis (MA) .... R	Miami, U. of (FL) L
Brown (RI) .... M	Middlebury (VT) .... R
▲ Bryn Mawr (PA) .... S	Missouri, U. of (Rolla) .... M
Bucknell (PA) .... R	▲ Mount Holyoke (MA) .... R
Buffalo (SUNY)(NY) L	New Jersey, College of .... M
California, U. of (Berkeley) XL	New Mexico Inst. of Tech. .... R
California, U. of (Los Angeles) XL	New York U. L
Carleton (MN) .... R	North Carolina, U. of L
* Carnegie Mellon (PA) .... M	North Carolina State L
Case Western Reserve U. (OH) .... M	Pennsylvania State XL
Chicago, U. of (IL) .... M	Pittsburgh, U. of (PA) L
Clarkson (NY) .... M	Princeton (NJ) .... M
Colgate (NY) .... R	Rensselaer (NY) .... M
Colorado School of Mines .... R	Rice (TX) .... M
Cornell (NY) L	Richmond, U. of (VA) .... M
Dallas, U. of (TX) .... R	Rochester, U. of (NY) .... M
Dartmouth (NH) .... M	Rose-Hulman (IN) .... R
Denison (OH) .... R	Rutgers (NJ) L
DePauw (IN) .... R	St. Louis (MO) .... M
Dickinson (PA) .... R	St. Olaf (MN) .... R
Furman (SC) .... R	Stanford (CA) .... M
George Washington (DC) .... M	Stevens Inst. of Tech (NJ) .... R
Georgia Institute of Tech. .... M	Texas A&M XL
Grinnell (IA) .... R	Trinity (TX) .... R
Hamilton (NY) .... R	Union (NY) .... R
Harvard (MA) .... M	United States Air Force Academy (CO) .. M
Harvey Mudd (CA) .... S	United States Military Academy (NY) ..... M
Illinois, U. of XL	Vassar (NY) .... R
Illinois Institute of Technology .... R	Washington, U. of XL
Iowa State XL	Washington U. (MO) .... M
Johns Hopkins (MD) .... M	William & Mary (VA) .... M
Lafayette (PA) .... R	Williams (MA) .... R
Lehigh (PA) .... M	Wisconsin, U. of XL
Loyola (MD) .... M	Worcester Poly. Tech. (MA) .... R
Macalester (MN) .... R	Yeshiva (NY) .... R
Maryland, U. of (Baltimore County) .... M	

* Also, Computer Science & Arts

Enrollment Code

■ *Men Only* **S = Small (less than 1000 students)   R = Moderate (1000-3000 students)   M = Medium (3000-8000 students)**
▲ *Women Only* **L = Large (8000-20,000 students)   XL = Extra Large (over 20,000 students)**

COMPUTER SCIENCE, continued

GROUP II
Very Selective

Adelphi (NY)	M
Alabama, U. of (Huntsville)	M
Allegheny (PA)	R
Alma (MI)	R
Arcadia (PA)	R
Auburn (AL)	L
Augsburg (MN)	R
Bemidji State (MN)	M
Benedictine (IL)	R
▲ Bennett (NC)	S
Bradley (IL)	M
Brooklyn College (CUNY)(NY)	L
Bryant (RI)	R
Buena Vista (IA)	R
Butler (IN)	R
Cal. Poly. State U. (San Luis Obispo)	L
California, U. of (Irvine)	L
California, U. of (Merced)	R
California, U. of (San Diego)	L
California, U. of (Santa Barbara)	L
# California, U. of (Santa Cruz)	M
Capital (OH)	R
Carroll (MT)	R
Carroll (WI)	R
Central (IA)	R
Central Florida, U. of	XL
Clarke (IA)	S
Clemson (SC)	L
Cogswell (CA)	S
Colorado State	L
Denver, U. of (CO)	M
DePaul (IL)	L
Drexel (PA)	M
Duke (NC)	M
Eckerd (FL)	R
Embry-Riddle (FL)	M
Florida Atlantic	L
Florida Inst. of Tech	M
Florida State	L
Gannon (PA)	M
George Mason (VA)	L
Goucher (MD)	R
Harrisburg U. (PA)	S
Hawaii, U. of	L
Hendrix (AR)	R
Hiram (OH)	R
Hofstra (NY)	M
Hunter (CUNY) (NY)	L
Idaho, U. of	L
Illinois College	S
Illinois, U. of (Springfield)	R
Iowa, U. of	XL
James Madison (VA)	M
Juniata (PA)	R
Kansas State	L
Kennesaw State (GA)	R
Kent State (OH)	L
Kentucky, U. of	L
LaSalle (PA)	M
LeTourneau (TX)	R
Linfield (OR)	R
Louisiana State	XL
Maine, U. of	M
Manhattan (NY)	M
Marist (NY)	M
Marquette (WI)	M
Mary Washington (VA)	M
Massachusetts, U. of	L
Massachusetts, U. of (Lowell)	M
McKendree (IL)	R
Mercer (GA)	R
Michigan, U. of (Dearborn)	M
Michigan Tech	M
Millsaps (MS)	S
Minnesota, U. of (Morris)	R
Missouri, U. of (Kansas City)	M
Mobile, U. of (AL)	R
Montana State	L
Montana Tech.	R
Montana, U. of	M
Moravian (PA)	R
Murray State (KY)	M
New Hampshire, U. of	L
New Jersey Inst. of Tech	M
New Mexico State	L
New York Inst. of Tech	M
North Central (IL)	R
North Dakota, U. of	M
North Florida	L

Also, Game Science

GROUP II continues next page

COMPUTER SCIENCE, continued

•• ━━━━━━━━━ GROUP II, continued ━━━━━━━━━ ••

Northeastern (MA)	L	St. John's (MN)	R
Northwestern (IA)	R	St. Norbert (WI)	R
Ohio State	XL	St. Scholastica (MN)	R
Ohio U.	L	St. Thomas (MN)	R
Oklahoma, U. of	XL	San Francisco, U. of (CA)	M
Oklahoma City U.	R	Sciences, U. of the (PA)	S
Oregon, U. of	L	Shippensburg (PA)	M
Oregon State	L	Simpson (IA)	R
Pace (NY)	M	Slippery Rock (PA)	M
Pacific Lutheran (WA)	R	Sonoma State (CA)	M
Pacific University (OR)	R	South Carolina, U. of	L
Pepperdine (CA)	R	South Dakota School of Mines	R
Pittsburgh, U. of (Johnstown)	R	Stetson (FL)	R
Polytechnic Univ. of New York	R	Stonehill (MA)	R
Portland State (OR)	L	Stony Brook (SUNY) (NY)	L
Potsdam (SUNY) (NY)	M	Syracuse (NY)	L
Principia (IL)	S	Taylor (IN)	R
Puerto Rico, U. of (Mayaguez)	L	Texas, U. of	XL
Purdue (IN)	XL	Texas, U. of (Dallas)	M
Queens (CUNY)(NY)	L	Towson (MD)	L
Ramapo (NJ)	M	Transylvania (KY)	S
Regis (CO)	R	Tulsa, U of (OK)	R
Rhode Island, U. of	L	Utah, U. of	L
Richard Stockton (NJ)	M	Virginia Tech.	L
Roanoke (VA)	R	Wayne State (MI)	L
Rochester Inst. of Tech (NY)	L	Webster (MO)	R
Rowan (NJ)	M	Westminster (PA)	R
Rutgers (Camden) (NJ)	M	Westminster (UT)	R
Santa Clara U. (CA)	M	West Virginia U.	L
St. Ambrose (IA)	R	William Jewell (MO)	R
St. Bonaventure (NY)	R	Winthrop (SC)	M
St. Cloud (MN)	L	Winona State U. (MN)	M
St. Edward's (TX)	M	Wofford (SC)	R

COMPUTER SCIENCE continues next page

Enrollment Code	
■ *Men Only*	S = Small (less than 1000 students) R = Moderate (1000-3000 students) M = Medium (3000-8000 students)
▲ *Women Only*	L = Large (8000-20,000 students) XL = Extra Large (over 20,000 students)

COMPUTER SCIENCE, continued

GROUP III
Selective

Alabama, U. of (Birmingham) .... M	Heidelberg (OH) .... S
Arkansas, U. of L	High Point (NC) .... R
Arizona State XL	Husson (ME) .... S
Baker (KS) .... R	Indiana Inst. of Tech. .... S
Baldwin-Wallace (OH) .... R	Iona (NY) .... M
Ball State (IN) L	Jacksonville (FL) .... R
Baruch (CUNY)(NY) L	Jacksonville State (AL) .... M
Belhaven (MS) .... R	Jamestown (ND) .... R
Benedictine (KS) .... R	Johnson C. Smith (NC) .... R
Bloomsburg (PA) .... M	Kansas Wesleyan .... S
Brockport (SUNY) (NY) .... M	Lamar (TX) .... M
Cal. Poly. State U. (Pomona) L	Laverne (CA) .... R
California State U. (Chico) L	Lenoir-Rhyne (NC) .... R
California State U. (East Bay) .... M	Liberty (VA) .... R
California State U. (Monterey Bay) .... R	Long Island U. (Brooklyn)(NY) .... M
California State U. (Northridge) L	Long Island U. (C.W. Post)(NY) .... M
California State U. (Sacramento) .... M	Loras (IA) .... R
California State U. (San Bernardino) ...... M	Louisiana-Lafayette L
California State U. (San Jose) L	Loyola U. (LA) .... M
California State U. (San Marcos) .... M	Lynchburg (VA) .... R
California State U. (Stanislaus) .... M	Marygrove (MI) .... R
Canisius (NY) .... M	Memphis, U. of (TN) L
Catawba (NC) .... S	Midwestern State U. (TX) .... M
π Champlain (VT) .... R	Millersville (PA) .... M
Charleston Southern (SC) .... R	Minnesota State U. (Mankato) L
Christopher Newport (VA) .... M	Minnesota, U. of (Duluth) L
Chowan (NC) .... S	Mississippi College .... R
Clark Atlanta (GA) .... M	Mississippi State L
Coastal Carolina (SC) .... M	Missouri State L
Colorado, U. of (Col. Springs) .... M	Monmouth (NJ) .... M
Colorado, U. of (Denver) .... M	■ Morehouse (GA) .... R
Dakota State (SD) .... R	Mount St. Joseph (OH) .... R
East Stroudsburg (PA) .... M	Mount St. Mary's (NY) .... S
Eastern Connecticut .... M	Mount Union (OH) .... R
Eastern Michigan L	Muskingum (OH) .... R
Eureka (IL) .... S	Nebraska, U. of (Omaha) L
Evansville (IN) .... R	Nevada, U. of (Reno) L
Ferris State (MI) L	New Mexico, U. of L
Fitchburg (MA) .... R	Northeastern Illinois .... M
Florida Gulf Coast U. .... M	Northern Michigan .... M
Frostburg (MD) .... M	Northwestern Louisiana L
Gardner-Webb (NC) .... R	North Carolina (Greensboro) .... M
Georgia State L	Oakland U. (MI) .... M
Great Falls (MT) .... S	
Hawaii Pacific .... M	

π *Electronic Games &*
Interactive Development

GROUP III continues next page

COMPUTER SCIENCE, continued

••• ──────────────── **GROUP III, continued** ──────────── •••

Oklahoma Christian	R		Southern Maine	M
Old Dominion (VA)	L		Southern Polytechnic (GA)	R
Oswego (SUNY)(NY)	M	▲	Spelman (GA)	R
Ozarks, College of the (MO)	R		Temple (PA)	L
Penn State (Harrisburg)(PA)	R		Texas, U. of (Arlington)	L
Pittsburgh, U. of (Bradford)	R		Texas, U. of (San Antonio)	L
Plymouth State (NH)	M		Texas, U. of (Tyler)	R
Quinnipiac (CT)	R		Texas A&M (Corpus Christi)	M
Rider (NJ)	M		Texas State U. (San Marcos)	L
Robert Morris (PA)	R		Walla Walla (WA)	R
Roosevelt (IL)	R		Weber State (UT)	L
St. Joseph's (NY)	R		West Chester (PA)	M
St. Mary (KS)	S		West Florida, U. of	M
▲ St. Mary (NE)	S		West Virginia Wesleyan	R
St. Mary's (MN)	R		Western Carolina (NC)	M
St. Peter's (NJ)	R		Western Kentucky	L
Salem State (MA)	M		Western Michigan	L
San Jose State U. (CA)	L		Western New England (MA)	R
South Alabama	M		Wilkes (PA)	R
South Dakota, U. of	M		William Paterson (NJ)	M
Southeastern Louisiana	L		Wisconsin (LaCrosse)	L
Southern Connecticut	M			

Enrollment Code

■ *Men Only* S = Small (less than 1000 students) R = Moderate (1000-3000 students) M = Medium (3000-8000 students)
▲ *Women Only* L = Large (8000-20,000 students) XL = Extra Large (over 20,000 students)

DANCE/DRAMA/THEATER

GROUP I
Most Selective

Allegheny (PA)... R	Knox (IL).. R
American Acad. of Dramatic Arts (NY) ... S	Lawrence (WI) .... R
American U. (DC) .... M	Macalester (MN) .... R
Amherst (MA) .... R	Maryland, U. of (Baltimore County)...... M
▲ Barnard (NY) .... R	Miami, U. of (FL) L
Binghamton (SUNY)(NY) L	Michigan, U. of XL
Boston College (MA) L	Middlebury (VT) .... R
Boston U. (MA) L	▲ Mount Holyoke (MA) .... R
Brandeis (MA) .... R	New School U. (Eugene Lang) (NY) ...... R
Bucknell (PA) .... M	New York U... L
Buffalo (SUNY)(NY) L	North Carolina, U. of L
California, U. of (Los Angeles) XL	Northwestern (IL) .... M
California, U. of (San Diego) L	Oberlin (OH) .... R
Carleton (MN) .... R	Pennsylvania State XL
* Carnegie Mellon (PA) .... M	Pomona (CA) .... R
Case Western Reserve (OH).............. M	Princeton (NJ) .... M
Colgate (NY) .... R	Rutgers (NJ) L
Colorado College .... R	St. Olaf (MN) .... R
Columbia (NY)...................................... M	Sarah Lawrence (NY) .... R
Connecticut College .... R	Skidmore (NY) .... R
Cornell (NY)... L	South, U. of the (TN) .... R
Dallas, U. of (TX) .... R	Southwestern (TX) .... R
Dartmouth (NH) .... M	Swarthmore (PA) .... R
Davidson (NC) .... R	Tufts (MA) .... M
Denison (OH) .... R	Tulane (LA) .... M
Drew (NJ) .... R	Vassar (NY) .... R
George Washington (DC) .... M	Wake Forest (NC) .... M
Gettysburg (PA) .... R	Wesleyan (CT) .... R
Hamilton (NY) .... R	Whitman (WA)....................................... R
Illinois, U. of XL	William & Mary (VA) .... R
Illinois Wesleyan .... R	Williams (MA) .... R
Juilliard (NY).. S	Yale (CT) .... M
Kenyon (OH) .... R	

* Also Dramatic Writing

DANCE / DRAMA / THEATER continues next page

Enrollment Code		
■ *Men Only*	S = Small (less than 1000 students)	R = Moderate (1000-3000 students)	M = Medium (3000-8000 students)
▲ *Women Only*	L = Large (8000-20,000 students)	XL = Extra Large (over 20,000 students)	

DANCE/DRAMA/THEATER, continued

GROUP II
Very Selective

Adelphi (NY) .... M	Loyola (IL) .... M
▲ Agnes Scott (GA) .... S	Luther (IA) .... R
Alabama, U. of L	Lycoming (PA) .... R
Alma (MI) .... R	Lyon (AR) .... S
Arizona, U. of XL	Maine, U. of L
Arizona State XL	Manhattanville (NY) .... R
Bard (NY) .... R	McDaniel (MD) .... R
Baylor (TX) .... M	Millsaps (MS) .... S
Beloit (WI) .... R	Minnesota State U. (Mankato) L
Bennington (VT) .... S	Minnesota, U. of XL
Birmingham-Southern (AL) .... R	Missouri, U. of (Kansas City) .... M
● Boston Conservatory (MA) .... S	Monmouth (IL) .... S
Brooklyn College (CUNY)(NY) L	Muhlenberg (PA) .... R
Butler (IN) .... R	Nebraska Wesleyan .... R
California Institute of the Arts .... S	Nevada, U. of (Las Vegas) .... M
California, U. of (Irvine).................... L	New Hampshire, U. of .... R
California, U. of (Riverside).............. L	New Mexico, U. of L
Cal. Poly State U. (San Luis Obispo).... L	No. Carolina School of the Arts .... S
Catholic U. (DC) .... M	Occidental (CA) .... R
Central Florida, U. of XL	Ohio U. L
Charleston, College of (SC) L	Oklahoma City U. .... R
Clarke (IA)................................ S	Oklahoma, U. of XL
Clemson (SC) L	Oklahoma State L
Coe (IA) .... R	Pace (NY) .... M
Columbia College Chicago (IL) .... M	Purchase (SUNY) (NY) .... M
Columbia College (SC) .... R	Rollins (FL) .... R
Cornish (WA) .... S	St. Mary's College of Maryland .... R
Creighton (NE) .... M	St. Bonaventure (NY) .... R
DePaul (IL) L	San Diego State (CA) XL
Drake (IA) .... M	Santa Clara (CA) .... M
π Elon (NC) .... R	▲ Scripps (CA) .... S
Emerson (MA) .... M	Seattle Pacific (WA) .... R
Florida, U. of XL	Shepherd (WV) .... R
Florida State L	South Carolina, U. of................ L
Florida Southern .... R	Southern California L
Fordham (NY) L	Southern Methodist (TX) .... M
Fredonia (SUNY)(NY).................... M	Stanford (CA) .... M
George Mason (VA) L	Susquehanna (PA) .... R
Georgia, U. of L	▲ Sweet Briar (VA).................... S
Goucher (MD) .... S	Syracuse (NY) L
Grand Valley (MI) L	Texas Christian .... M
Hanover (IN)............................ R	Texas, U. of XL
Hartwick (NY) .... R	Ursinus (PA) .... R
Hawaii, U. of L	Utah State L
Hofstra (NY) .... M	Utah, U. of L
▲ Hollins (VA).......................... S	Virginia Commonwealth U. L
Hope (WI) .... R	Viterbo (WI) .... R
Houston, U. of (TX)...................... L	Wartburg (IA) .... R
Hunter (CUNY)(NY) L	Washington, U. of XL
Indiana U. XL	Wells (NY) .... S
Iowa, U. of XL	Western Maryland .... R
Ithaca (NY) .... M	West Virginia U. L
James Madison (VA).................... M	Wheaton (MA) .... R
Kansas, U. of L	Wisconsin, U. of XL
Kansas State L	Wisconsin, U. of (Milwaukee) L
LeMoyne (NY) .... R	Wisconsin, U. of (Stevens Point) ...... M
Lindenwood (MO) .... M	Wooster (OH) .... R
Linfield (OR) .... R	
Long Island U.(C.W. Post)(NY) .... R	

● *Dance Only*
π *Music Theatre*

DANCE/DRAMA/THEATER, continued

GROUP III
Selective

+ + Akron, U. of (OH) L	Northern Kentucky L
Alabama, U. of (Birmingham) .... M	Northwestern College (IA) .... R
Alaska, U. of (Fairbanks) .... M	Ohio State XL
Aquinas (MI) .... R	Otterbein (OH) .... R
Arcadia (PA) .... R	Plymouth State (NH) .... M
Arts, U. of the (PA) .... R	# Point Park (PA) .... R
Avila (MO) .... S	Rockford (IL) .... S
Barry (FL) .... R	Rocky Mountain (MT) .... S
Bethany (WV) .... S	Roger Williams (RI) .... M
Belhaven (MS) .... R	Salem State (MA) .... M
** Benedictine (KS) .... R	San Francisco State (CA) L
Boise State (ID) L	Santa Fe, College of (NM) .... S
Brenau (GA) .... R	Seattle U. (WA) .... R
Brockport (SUNY)(NY) .... M	Seton Hill (PA) .... S
California State U. (Long Beach) L	++ Slippery Rock (PA) .... M
California State U. (Northridge) L	Southern Maine .... M
California State U. (Sacramento) .... M	Southern Missippi L
Catawba (NC) .... S	Southern Utah .... M
Central Michigan L	South Florida, U. of L
Coker (SC) .... S	Springfield (MA) .... M
Converse College (SC) .... S	St. Edward's (TX) .... M
Dana (NE) .... S	St. Mary's (MN) .... R
DeSales (PA) .... S	Sterling (KS) .... S
Evansville (IN) .... R	Stephens (MO) .... S
Fontbonne (MO) .... R	Tarleton State (TX) .... M
Franklin (IN) .... S	Temple (PA) L
Greensboro College (NC) .... S	Texas, U. of (El Paso) L
Hartford, U. of (CT) .... M	Texas State U. (San Marcos) L
Illinois State L	Towson (MD) L
Indiana State L	Wagner (NY) .... R
Jacksonville (FL) .... R	Wayne State (MI) L
Johnson State (VT) .... R	Weber State (UT) L
Keene State (NH) .... R	Webster (MO) .... R
Long Island U. (Brooklyn)(NY) .... M	Western Michigan L
Longwood (VA) .... R	* Western St. Coll. of Colorado .... R
Marymount Manhattan (NY) .... R	π West Virginia Wesleyan .... R
▲ Mary Baldwin (VA) .... S	Wichita State (KS) .... M
McPherson (KS) .... S	++ Winthrop(SC) .... M
▲ Meredith (NC) .... R	
Milliken (IL) .... R	π *Music Theater*
Missouri State L	++ *Especially Dance*
Montana, U. of .... M	# *Musical Theater and Dance*
Niagara (NY) .... R	** *Also, Theater Management*
	* *Communication and Theater - One Major*

Enrollment Code

■ *Men Only*	S = Small (less than 1000 students) R = Moderate (1000-3000 students) M = Medium (3000-8000 students)
▲ *Women Only*	L = Large (8000-20,000 students) XL = Extra Large (over 20,000 students)

ECONOMICS

GROUP I
Most Selective

Albany (SUNY)(NY)	L	Miami, U. of (OH)	L
American U. (DC)	M	Michigan, U. of	XL
Amherst (MA)	R	MIT (MA)	M
Babson (MA)	R	Middlebury (VT)	R
▲Barnard (NY)	R	Minnesota, U. of	XL
Bates (ME)	R	▲Mount Holyoke (MA)	R
Binghamton (SUNY)(NY)	L	New York U.	L
Boston College (MA)	L	Northwestern (IL)	M
Boston University (MA)	L	Oberlin (OH)	R
Bowdoin (ME)	R	Occidental (CA)	R
Brandeis (MA)	R	Pennsylvania, U. of	L
Brown (RI)	M	Pomona (CA)	R
▲Bryn Mawr (PA)	S	Princeton (NJ)	M
Bucknell (PA)	M	Reed (OR)	R
California, U. of (Los Angeles)	XL	Rensselaer (NY)	M
California, U. of (San Diego)	L	Rhodes (TN)	R
Carleton (MN)	R	Rice (TX)	M
Carnegie Mellon (PA)	M	Richmond (VA)	R
Carroll (MT)	R	Rochester, U. of (NY)	M
Case Western Reserve (OH)	M	Rose-Hulman (IN)	R
Chicago, U. of (IL)	M	Rutgers (NJ)	L
Claremont McKenna (CA)	R	St. Mary's Col. of Maryland	R
Colby (ME)	R	St. Olaf (MN)	R
Colgate (NY)	R	▲Scripps (CA)	S
Colorado College	R	Skidmore (NY)	R
Colorado School of Mines	R	▲Smith (MA)	R
Columbia (NY)	M	South, U. of the (TN)	R
Connecticut College	R	Southwestern (TX)	R
Cornell (NY)	L	Stanford (CA)	M
Dallas, U. of (TX)	R	Swarthmore (PA)	R
Dartmouth (NH)	M	Texas, U. of	XL
Davidson (NC)	R	Trinity (CT)	R
DePauw (IN)	R	Trinity (TX)	R
Drew (NJ)	R	Tufts (MA)	M
Duke (NC)	M	Tulane (LA)	M
Emory (GA)	M	U.S. Military Academy (NY)	M
Franklin & Marshall (PA)	R	Union (NY)	R
Furman (SC)	R	Vanderbilt (TN)	M
George Washington (DC)	M	Vassar (NY)	R
Georgetown (DC)	M	Villanova (PA)	M
Georgia Inst. of Tech.	M	Virginia, U. of	L
Gettysburg (PA)	R	■Wabash (IN)	S
Grinnell (IA)	R	Wake Forest (NC)	M
Hamilton (NY)	R	Washington & Lee (VA)	R
Harvard (MA)	M	Washington U. (MO)	M
Haverford (PA)	S	▲Wellesley (MA)	R
Holy Cross (MA)	R	Wesleyan (CT)	R
Illinois Wesleyan	R	Whitman (WA)	R
Kalamazoo (MI)	R	Willamette (OR)	R
Kenyon (OH)	R	William & Mary (VA)	R
Lafayette (PA)	R	Williams (MA)	R
Lawrence (WI)	R	Wisconsin, U. of	XL
Lehigh (PA)	M	Worcester Poly. Inst. (MA)	R
Macalester (MN)	R	Yale (CT)	M

ECONOMICS, continued

GROUP II
Very Selective

▲Agnes Scott (GA) .... S	Knox (IL) .... R
Alaska, U. of (Anchorage) .... M	Lake Forest (IL) .... R
# Albion (MI) .... R	Linfield (OR) .... R
Allegheny (PA) .... R	Loras (IA) .... R
Arizona State XL	Loyola (LA) .... R
Assumption (MA) .... R	Loyola Marymount (CA) .... M
Auburn (AL) .... M	Lyon (AR) .... S
Austin (TX) .... R	Maine, U. of L
Baruch (CUNY)(NY) L	Manhattanville (NY) .... R
Beloit (WI) .... R	Maryland, U. of XL
Bentley (MA) .... M	Maryland, U. of (Baltimore County) .... M
Bethany (WV) .... S	Mary Washington (VA) .... M
Bradley (IL) .... M	Massachusetts, U. of L
Brigham Young (UT) L	Mercer (GA) .... R
Bryant (RI) .... R	Michigan State XL
California, U. of (Davis) XL	Michigan, U. of (Dearborn) .... M
California, U. of (Merced) .... R	Missouri, U. of XL
California, U. of (Santa Cruz) .... M	Missouri, U. of (Kansas City) .... M
California State U. (Bakersfield) .... M	Moravian (PA) .... R
California State U. (Long Beach) L	Muhlenberg (PA) .... R
California State U. (Santa Barbara) L	Nebraska, U. of L
Centre (KY) .... R	New Mexico, U. of L
City College (CUNY)(NY) L	North Carolina State L
Clark (MA) .... R	Oglethorpe (GA) .... R
Clemson (SC) L	Ohio State XL
Colorado, U. of L	Ohio Wesleyan (OH) .... R
Connecticut, U. of XL	Oklahoma, U. of XL
Cornell College (IA) .... R	Oneonta (SUNY) (NY) .... M
Delaware, U. of L	Oregon, U. of L
Denison (OH) .... R	Oregon State L
Drake (IA) .... M	Pennsylvania State XL
Florida Atlantic L	Pittsburgh, U. of (PA) L
Florida State L	Providence (RI) .... M
George Mason (VA) L	Puerto Rico, U. of L
Georgia State L	Puget Sound (WA) .... R
Georgia, U. of XL	Randolph-Macon (VA) .... R
Grove City (PA) .... R	Redlands, U. of (CA) .... R
Guilford (NC) .... R	Rhode Island, U. of L
■ Hampden-Sydney (VA) .... S	Richard Stockton (NJ) .... M
Hanover (IN) .... R	Ripon (WI) .... S
Hendrix (AR) .... R	Rochester Inst. of Tech. (NY) L
Hillsdale (MI) .... R	Rollins (FL) .... R
Hobart & William Smith (NY) .... R	St. Catherine (MN) .... R
▲Hollins (VA) .... S	St. John's (MN) .... R
Illinois Col. .... S	St. Lawrence (NY) .... R
Illinois, U. of (Chicago) L	St. Thomas (MN) .... R
Iowa State XL	
John Carroll (OH) .... R	
Kansas, U. of L	

Also, Economics & Business

GROUP II continues next page

Enrollment Code		
■ *Men Only*	S = **Small** (less than 1000 students) R = **Moderate** (1000-3000 students)	M = **Medium** (3000-8000 students)
▲ *Women Only*	L = **Large** (8000-20,000 students) XL = **Extra Large** (over 20,000 students)	

ECONOMICS, continued

GROUP II, continued

St. Michael's (VT)	R
▲Salem Col. (NC)	S
San Diego, U. of (CA)	M
San Diego State (CA)	XL
San Francisco, U. of	M
Santa Clara U. (CA)	M
Seattle U. (WA)	R
Southern Methodist (TX)	L
▲Spelman (GA)	R
Susquehanna (PA)	R
Syracuse (NY)	L
Temple (PA)	L
Texas A&M	XL
Texas, U. of (Dallas)	M
Truman State (MO)	M
Ursinus (PA)	R
Utah State	L
Vermont, U. of	L
Virginia Military Inst.	R
Washington & Jefferson (PA)	R
Washington, U. of	XL
Western Washington U.	R
Westminster Col. (MO)	S
Westmont Col. (CA)	R
Wheaton (MA)	R
Wofford (SC)	R
Wooster (OH)	R
Xavier (OH)	R

GROUP III
Selective

Arkansas, U. of	L
Baldwin-Wallace (OH)	R
Bellarmine (KY)	R
Berea (WV)	R
California State U. (Bakersfield)	M
California State U. (Channel Islands)	R
California State U. (Chico)	L
California State U. (East Bay)	M
California State U. (Northridge)	L
Central Missouri	L
Central Oklahoma	L
East Carolina	L
East Tennessee	L
Eastern Connecticut	M
Eastern Washington	L
Framingham (MA)	M
Hardin-Simmons (TX)	R
Hawaii Pacific	M
Heidelberg (OH)	S
Indiana U.-Purdue U.-Indianapolis (IN)	L
Louisiana-Lafayette	L
Louisiana State	XL
Marshall (WV)	L
Memphis, U. of (TN)	L
Millersville (PA)	M
Mississippi, U. of	L
Monmouth (IL)	S
Montana State	L
Nebraska, U. of (Kearney)	M
Nebraska, U. of (Omaha)	L
Northern Iowa	L
Northern Michigan	M
Northwood University (MI)	R
Oakland U. (MI)	M
Old Dominion (VA)	L
Northern Colorado	L
Queens (CUNY)(NY)	L
Rhode Island College	M
Robert Morris (PA)	M
St. Anselm (NH)	R
St. Cloud (MN)	L
St. Francis (NY)	R
St. John's (NY)	L
St. Vincent (PA)	R
Shepherd (WV)	M
Shippensberg (PA)	M
South Dakota State U.	M
Southern Connecticut	M
Southern Utah	M
Suffolk (MA)	R
Texas, U. of (San Antonio)	L
Toledo, U. of (OH)	L
Washington State	L
Weber State (UT)	L
Whittier (CA)	R
Wilson (PA)	S
Wisconsin, U. of (Milwaukee)	L
Wright State (OH)	L
Wyoming, U. of	L

Enrollment Code		
■ *Men Only*	S = Small (less than 1000 students) R = Moderate (1000-3000 students) M = Medium (3000-8000 students)	
▲ *Women Only*	L = Large (8000-20,000 students) XL = Extra Large (over 20,000 students)	

EDUCATION

GROUP I
Most Selective

Albany (SUNY)(NY)	L	New School U. (Lang) (NY)	R
American U. (DC)	M	North Carolina, U. of	L
Boston College (MA)	L	Pittsburgh, U. of (PA)	L
Boston U. (MA)	L	Occidental (CA)	R
Bucknell (PA)	R	Rutgers (NJ)	L
Buffalo (SUNY) (NY)	L	Skidmore (NY)	R
Connecticut Col.	R	Southern California	L
Dallas, U. of (TX)	R	Southwestern (TX)	R
Dickinson (PA)	R	Stanford (CA)	M
Earlham (IN)	R	Swarthmore (PA)	S
Geneseo (SUNY) (NY)	M	Trinity (TX)	R
Illinois, U. of	XL	➤ Tufts (MA)	M
Iowa, U. of	XL	Vanderbilt (TN)	M
Miami, U. of (FL)	M	▲ Wellesley (MA)	R
Miami U. (OH)	L	Wheaton (IL)	R
Michigan, U. of	XL	William & Mary (VA)	M
New Jersey, College of	M		

➤ *Child Study*

GROUP II
Very Selective

Adelphi (NY)	M	Central (IA)	R
Adrian (MI)	R	Central Florida, U. of	XL
Alaska Pacific	S	Centre (KY)	R
Alfred (NY)	R	Chestnut Hill (PA)	S
Alma (MI)	R	Christian Brothers (TN)	R
Arizona, U. of	XL	Cincinnati, U. of (OH)	L
Asbury (KY)	R	Clarke (IA)	S
Auburn (AL)	L	Clemson (SC)	L
Augustana (IL)	R	Coe (IA)	R
Augustana (SD)	R	Columbia College (SC)	R
Austin (TX)	R	Concordia (MN)	R
Baylor (TX)	L	Connecticut, U. of	XL
Benedictine (IL)	R	Cornell College (IA)	R
Berry (GA)	R	Creighton (NE)	M
π Bethel (IN)	R	Dayton, U. of (OH)	M
Biola (CA)	R	Delaware, U. of	L
Birmingham Southern (AL)	R	DePaul (IL)	L
Bradley (IL)	M	Drake (IA)	M
Bridgewater (MA)	M	Drury (MO)	R
Brigham Young (UT)	XL	Duquesne (PA)	M
Bryan (TN)	S	Eastern Michigan	L
Buena Vista (IA)	R	Elizabethtown (PA)	R
Butler (IN)	R	Elon (NC)	R
California, U. of (Riverside)	L	Erskine (SC)	S
California, U. of (Santa Barbara)	L	Evansville (IN)	R
Calvin (MI)	M	π Flagler (FL)	R
Capital U. (OH)	R	Florida International	L
Carroll (MT)	R		
Carroll (WI)	R	π *Also American Sign Language / Deaf Interpretation*	
Centenary (LA)	S	*GROUP II continues next page*	

EDUCATION, continued

•• ━━━━━━━━━━ **GROUP II, continued** ━━━━━━━━━━ ••

Florida Southern	R	Messiah (PA)	R
Florida State	L	Michigan State	XL
Fredonia (SUNY) (NY)	M	Millersville (PA)	M
Georgetown College (KY)	R	▲ Mills (CA)	S
Georgia, U. of	XL	Millsaps (MS)	S
Gonzaga (WA)	R	Minnesota State U. (Moorhead)	M
Goucher (MD)	R	Minnesota, U. of	XL
Grand Valley (MI)	L	Minnesota, U. of (Duluth)	M
Grove City (PA)	R	Minnesota, U. of (Morris)	R
Guilford (NC)	R	Mississippi, U. of	L
Gustavus Adolphus (MN)	R	Mississippi U. for Women	R
Hamline (MN)	R	Missouri State	L
Hanover (IN)	R	Missouri, U. of (Kansas City)	M
Harding (AR)	M	Missouri, U. of (St. Louis)	M
Hillsdale (MI)	R	Moravian (PA)	R
Hiram (OH)	R	Morningside (IA)	S
Hofstra (NY)	M	Mount St. Mary's (MD)	R
Hood (MD)	S	Nazareth (NY)	R
Houghton (NY)	S	Nebraska, U. of	L
Hunter (CUNY) (NY)	L	New Hampshire, U. of	L
Idaho, College of	S	New Mexico State	L
Illinois College	S	New Orleans (LA)	L
Indiana, U.	XL	New Paltz (SUNY) (NY)	M
Indiana, U. of (PA)	L	North Carolina State	L
Iowa State	XL	North Carolina, U. of (Asheville)	R
James Madison (VA)	M	North Carolina, U. of (Greensboro)	M
Juniata (PA)	R	North Dakota, U. of	M
Kansas, U. of	L	North Florida	L
Kansas State	L	North Texas	L
Kentucky, U. of	L	Ohio Northern	R
Lake Forest (IL)	R	Ohio U.	L
La Salle (PA)	M	Oklahoma, U. of	XL
LeMoyne (NY)	R	Oklahoma State	L
LeTourneau (TX)	R	Oneonta (SUNY)(NY)	M
Lindenwood (MO)	M	Oregon, U. of	L
Lipscomb (TN)	R	Oswego (SUNY)(NY)	M
Loras (IA)	R	Pace (NY)	M
Loyola (MD)	M	Pacific Lutheran (WA)	R
Luther (IA)	R	Pacific, U. of the (CA)	M
Lyon (AR)	S	Pacific U. (OR)	R
Maine, U. of	L	Palm Beach Atlantic (FL)	R
Manhattan (NY)	M	Pennsylvania State	XL
Manhattanville (NY)	R	Plattsburgh (SUNY)(NY)	M
Marquette (WI)	M	Portland, U. of (OR)	R
Maryland, U. of	XL	Potsdam (SUNY) (NY)	M
Maryland, U. of (Baltimore County)	M	Principia (IL)	S
McDaniel (MD)	R	Providence (RI)	M
Mercer (GA)	R		

GROUP II continues next page

EDUCATION, continued

GROUP II, continued

Puerto Rico, U. of	L
Queens (CUNY) (NY)	L
Redlands, U. of (CA)	R
Regis (CO)	R
Ripon (WI)	R
Rockhurst (MO)	R
Rollins (FL)	R
Rowan (NJ)	M
Rutgers (Camden) (NJ)	M
St. Bonaventure (NY)	R
St. Catherine (MN)	R
St. John's/ St. Benedict (MN)	R
St. Joseph's U. (PA)	R
St. Lawrence (NY)	R
St. Louis (MO)	M
St. Martin's (WA)	S
St. Mary's Col. (CA)	R
▲St. Mary's Col. (IN)	R
St. Mary's Col. (MN)	R
St. Michael's (VT)	R
St. Norbert (WI)	R
St. Thomas (MN)	R
Salisbury (MD)	M
San Diego State U. (CA)	XL
Schreiner (TX)	S
Scranton, U. of (PA)	M
Seattle Pacific (WA)	R
Shepherd (WV)	M
Shippensburg (PA)	M
Sonoma State (CA)	M
South Alabama	M
South Florida, U. of	L
Stetson (FL)	R
Susquehanna (PA)	R
Temple (PA)	L
Tennessee, U. of	XL
Tennessee Tech	M
Texas A&M	XL
Texas Christian	M
Texas, U. of (Austin)	XL
Towson (MD)	L
Transylvania (KY)	R
▲Trinity (DC)	S
Truman State (MO)	M
Ursinus (PA)	R
Valparaiso (IN)	R
Washington & Jefferson (PA)	R
Washington State	L
Washington, U. of	XL
Wayne State (MI)	L
Wells (NY)	S
West Chester (PA)	M
West Florida, U. of	M
Western Michigan	L
Western Washington U.	L
Westminster (MO)	R
Westminster (UT)	R
Whitworth (WA)	R
William Jewell Col. (MO)	R
Winona State U. (MN)	M
Wisconsin Lutheran	S
Wisconsin, U. of	XL
Wisconsin, U. of (La Crosse)	L
Wisconsin, U. of (Milwaukee)	L
Wisconsin, U. of (Stevens Point)	M
Wittenberg (OH)	R
Wofford (SC)	R
York (PA)	M

EDUCATION continues next page

Enrollment Code			
■ *Men Only*	S = Small (less than 1000 students)	R = Moderate (1000-3000 students)	M = Medium (3000-8000 students)
▲ *Women Only*	L = Large (8000-20,000 students)	XL = Extra Large (over 20,000 students)	

EDUCATION, continued

••• ━━━━━━━━━━━━━━ **GROUP III** ━━━━━━━━━━━━━ •••
Selective

Akron, U. of (OH)	L
Alaska, U. of (Anchorage)	M
Alderson-Broaddus (WV)	S
▲ Alverno (WI)	R
Anderson (IN)	R
Appalachian State (NC)	L
Aquinas (MI)	R
Arcadia (PA)	R
Arkansas, U. of	L
Arizona State	XL
Ashland (OH)	R
Assumption (MA)	R
Augsburg (MN)	R
Augusta (GA)	M
Averett (VA)	S
Avila (MO)	S
Baker (KS)	R
Baldwin-Wallace (OH)	R
Ball State (IN)	L
Barry (FL)	R
Belhaven (MS)	R
Bellarmine (KY)	R
Belmont (TN)	R
Bemidji State (MN)	M
Benedictine (KS)	R
▲ Bennett (NC)	S
Berea (KY)	R
Bethany (KS)	S
Bethany (WV)	S
Bethel (KS)	S
Bethel (MN)	R
Blackburn (IL)	S
Black Hills State U. (SD)	R
Bloomsburg (PA)	M
Bluffton (OH)	S
Boise State (ID)	L
Bowling Green (OH)	L
Brescia (KY)	S
Brockport (SUNY) (NY)	M
Brooklyn College (CUNY)(NY)	L
Caldwell (NJ)	S
California Baptist	M
California Lutheran	R
California State U. (Bakersfield)	M
California State U. (Channel Islands)	R
California State U. (Fresno)	L
California State U. (Monterey Bay)	R
California State U. (Los Angeles)	L
California State U. (Sacramento)	M

California State U. (San Bernardino)	M
California State U. (San Marcos)	M
California State U. (Stanislaus)	M
California (PA)	M
Canisius (NY)	M
Carson-Newman (TN)	R
Castleton State (VT)	R
Catawba (NC)	S
Cedarville (OH)	R
Central Connecticut	M
Central Michigan U.	L
Central Oklahoma	L
Chaminade (HI)	R
Charleston Southern (SC)	R
Citadel, The (SC)	R
City College (CUNY) (NY)	L
Claflin (SC)	R
Clark Atlanta (GA)	M
Coastal Carolina (SC)	M
Coker (SC)	S
Colby-Sawyer (NH)	S
College of Charleston (SC)	M
Colorado, U. of (Colorado Springs)	M
Concordia (OR)	S
Concordia (NE)	R
▲ Converse (SC)	S
Corban (OR)	S
Cumberland (KY)	R
Daemen (NY)	R
Dakota State (SD)	R
Dana (NB)	S
Dillard (LA)	R
Doane (NE)	S
Dominican (CA)	S
Dordt (IA)	R
Dubuque, U. of (IA)	S
D'Youville (NY)	R
East Carolina (NC)	L
East Central (OK)	M
East Stroudsburg (PA)	M
Eastern Connecticut	M
Eastern Illinois	L
Eastern Kentucky	L
Eastern Mennonite (VA)	R
Eastern Oregon	R
Edgewood (WI)	S
Edinboro (PA)	M
Elmhurst (IL)	R

GROUP III continues next page

EDUCATION, continued

GROUP III, continued

Elmira (NY)	R
Elms (MA)	S
Emporia State (KS)	M
Eureka (IL)	S
Fairmont (WV)	M
Findlay (OH)	M
Fitchburg State (MA)	R
Florida A&M	M
Florida Atlantic	L
Florida Gulf Coast U.	M
Fontbonne (MO)	R
Fort Hays (KS)	M
Framingham State (MA)	M
Franklin (IN)	S
Freed-Hardeman (TN)	R
Friends (KS)	R
Frostburg (MD)	M
Gannon (PA)	M
Geneva (PA)	R
George Fox (OR)	R
Georgia Southern	L
Georgia Southwestern	R
Georgia State	L
Gordon (MA)	R
Graceland (IA)	R
Grambling (LA)	M
Great Falls (MT)	S
Greensboro College (NC)	S
Hannibal-La Grange (MO)	R
Hardin-Simmons (TX)	R
Hartford, U. of (CT)	M
Hastings (NE)	R
Heidelberg (OH)	S
Henderson State (AR)	M
Herbert Lehman (CUNY) (NY)	L
High Point (NC)	R
Holy Names (CA)	S
Houston, U. of (TX)	L
Huntingdon (AL)	S
Huntington (IN)	S
Husson (ME)	S
Illinois State	L
Immaculata (PA)	S
Indiana State U.	L
Indiana U.-Purdue U.-Indianapolis (IN)	L
Iona (NY)	M
Jacksonville (FL)	R
Jacksonville State (AL)	M
Jamestown (ND)	R

Johnson State (VT)	R
▲ Judson (AL)	S
Kansas Wesleyan	S
Kean (NJ)	M
Keene State (NH)	R
Kennesaw State (GA)	R
Kent State (OH)	L
Kentucky Wesleyan	S
King (TN)	S
King's (PA)	R
Kutztown (PA)	M
Lamar (TX)	M
Lambuth (TN)	S
Lasell (MA)	S
Laverne, U. of (CA)	R
Lesley (MA)	S
Lewis-Clark State (ID)	R
Liberty (VA)	R
Linfield (OR)	R
Lock Haven (PA)	M
Long Island U. (Brooklyn)(NY)	M
Long Island U. (C.W.Post)(NY)	M
Longwood (VA)	R
Louisiana College	R
Louisiana-Lafayette	L
Louisiana-Monroe	M
Louisiana Tech.	M
Lynchburg (VA)	R
MacMurray (IL)	S
Maine (Farmington)	R
Manchester (IN)	R
Mansfield (PA)	R
Marietta (OH)	R
Marshall (WV)	L
Marygrove (MI)	R
Maryville (St. Louis) (MO)	R
Marywood (PA)	R
Mass. Coll. of Lib. Arts (N. Adams)	R
Mass. St. Col. System	M
McKendree (IL)	R
McPherson (KS)	S
Memphis, U. of (TN)	L
Mercy (NY)	M
Mercyhurst (PA)	R
Middle Tennessee	L
Millikin (IL)	R
Misericordia, College (PA)	S
Mississippi College	R

GROUP III continues next page

EDUCATION, continued

••• ——————— GROUP III, continued ——————— •••

Mississippi State	L
Missouri Baptist	M
Missouri Southern State	M
Mobile, U. of (AL)	R
Monmouth (IL)	S
Montana, U. of	M
Montana State (Billings)	R
Montclair State (NJ)	M
Montevallo (AL)	R
Mount St. Joseph (OH)	R
Mount Mercy (IA)	S
Mount St. Mary's (NY)	S
Mount Union (OH)	R
Murray State (KY)	M
Muskingum (OH)	R
Nebraska, U. of (Kearney)	M
Nebraska, U. of (Omaha)	L
Nevada, U. of (Las Vegas)	L
Nevada, U. of (Reno)	L
New Mexico, U. of	L
Niagara (NY)	R
Nicholls State (LA)	M
North Dakota State	L
North Georgia	M
Northeastern Illinois	M
Northeastern State (OK)	L
Northern Arizona	L
Northern Colorado	L
Northern Illinois U.	L
Northern Iowa	L
Northern Kentucky	L
Northern Michigan	M
Northern State U. (SD)	R
Northwestern (IA)	R
Northwestern (MN)	R
Northwestern Louisiana	L
Nova Southeastern (FL)	R
Nyack (NY)	R
Oakland (MI)	M
Oakland City U. (IN)	R
Ohio State	L
Ohio Wesleyan	R
Oklahoma Baptist	R
Oklahoma Christian	R

Old Dominion (VA)	L
Olivet Nazarene (IL)	R
Oral Roberts (OK)	M
Otterbein (OH)	R
Ouachita Baptist (AR)	R
Ozarks, College of the (MO)	R
Peru State (NE)	R
Philadelphia Biblical (PA)	S
Piedmont (GA)	S
Pittsburg State (KS)	M
Pittsburgh, U. of (Johnstown)	R
Plymouth State (NH)	M
Point Loma (CA)	R
Point Park (PA)	R
Puerto Rico (Cayey), U. of	L
Radford (VA)	M
Reinhardt (GA)	R
Robert Morris (PA)	R
Rhode Island College	M
Rider (NJ)	R
Rockford (IL)	S
Rocky Mountain (MT)	S
Roger Williams (RI)	R
Roosevelt (IL)	R
Russell Sage (The Sage Colleges)(NY)	R
Sacred Heart (CT)	R
Saginaw Valley (MI)	M
St. Ambrose (IA)	R
St. Andrews Presbyterian (NC)	S
St. Cloud (MN)	L
St. Edward's (TX)	M
St. Francis (IN)	R
St. John Fisher (NY)	R
St. John's (NY)	R
St. Joseph's (IN)	S
St. Joseph's (ME)	S
St. Joseph's (NY)	R
▲St. Joseph Col. (CT)	S
St. Mary (KS)	S
St. Mary (NE)	S
St. Peter's (NJ)	R
St. Rose (NY)	R

GROUP III continues next page

Enrollment Code

■ *Men Only* S = Small (less than 1000 students) R = Moderate (1000-3000 students) M = Medium (3000-8000 students)
▲ *Women Only* L = Large (8000-20,000 students) XL = Extra Large (over 20,000 students)

EDICATION, continued

••• ━━━━━━━━━━━━━━━ **GROUP III, continued** ━━━━━━━━━━━━━━━ •••

St. Scholastica (MN) .... R	Texas State U. (San Marcos) L
St. Thomas Aquinas (NY) .... R	Texas Tech. U. L
▲ Salem College (NC) .... S	Texas, U. of (El Paso) L
Salem State (MA) .... M	Texas Wesleyan .... R
Santa Fe, College of (NM) .... S	Thomas More (KY) .... R
Seton Hall (NJ) .... M	Tougaloo (MS) .... S
Seton Hill (PA) .... S	Troy State (AL) .... M
Shaw (NC) .... R	Union (TN) .... R
Shawnee State (OH) .... R	Utah State L
Shorter (GA) .... R	Wagner (NY) .... R
Siena Heights (MI) .... S	Walsh (OH) .... R
Silver Lake (WI) .... S	Wartburg (IA) .... R
Simpson (IA) .... S	Washburn (KS) .... M
Slippery Rock (PA) .... M	Waynesburg (PA) .... R
South Dakota, U. of .... M	Weber State (UT) L
Southeast Missouri State L	Western Carolina (NC) .... M
Southeastern Louisiana L	Western Connecticut .... M
Southeastern Oklahoma State .... M	Western Illinois L
Southern Connecticut .... M	Western Kentucky L
Southern Illinois U. (Carbondale) ... L	Western New England (MA) .... R
Southern Illinois U. (Edwardsville) . L	Westfield State (MA) .... M
Southern Mississippi L	West Florida, U. of .... M
Southern Nazarene (OK) .... R	West Virginia Wesleyan .... R
Southern Oregon State U. .... M	▲ Wheelock (MA) .... S
Southern Utah .... M	Whittier (CA) .... R
Southwest Baptist (MO) .... R	Widener (PA) .... R
Southwestern Oklahoma .... M	Wilmington (OH) .... S
Springfield (MA) .... M	Wingate (NC) .... R
Stephen F. Austin (TX) L	Winthrop (SC) .... M
▲ Stephens (MO) .... S	Wisconsin, U. of (Oshkosh) L
Sterling (KS) .... S	Wisconsin, U. of (Platteville) ...... M
Tabor (KS) .... S	Wisconsin, U. of (River Falls) ...... M
Tarleton State (TX) .... M	Wisconsin, U. of (Superior) .... M
Taylor (IN) .... R	Worcester State (MA) .... M
Tennessee, U. of (Martin) .... M	Wyoming, U. of L
Texas A&M (Corpus Christi) .... M	Xavier U. of Louisiana .... R
Texas Lutheran .... R	York (NE) .... S

ENGINEERING

GROUP I
Most Selective

Binghamton (SUNY)(NY)	L	Minnesota, U. of	XL
Boston U. (MA)	L	Missouri, U. of (Rolla)	M
Brown (RI)	M	New Mexico Inst. of Mining & Tech.	R
Bucknell (PA)	M	New Jersey, College of	M
Buffalo (SUNY) (NY)	L	Northwestern (IL)	M
California Inst. of Tech.	S	Notre Dame (IN)	M
California, U. of (Berkeley)	XL	Olin (MA)	S
California, U. of (Davis)	XL	Pennsylvania State	XL
California, U. of (Los Angeles)	XL	Pennsylvania, U. of	L
California, U. of (San Diego)	L	Princeton (NJ)	M
California, U. of (Santa Barbara)	L	Rensselaer (NY)	M
Carnegie Mellon (PA)	M	Rice (TX)	M
Case Western Reserve U. (OH)	M	Rochester, U. of	M
Clarkson (NY)	M	Rose-Hulman (IN)	R
Colorado School of Mines	R	Rutgers (NJ)	L
Columbia (NY)	M	▲ Smith (MA)	R
Cooper Union (NY)	S	Southern California, U. of	L
Cornell (NY)	L	Stanford (CA)	M
Dartmouth (NH)	M	Stevens Inst. of Tech. (NJ)	R
Duke (NC)	M	Swarthmore (PA)	R
Florida, U. of	XL	Texas, U. of (Austin)	XL
George Washington (DC)	M	Trinity (CT)	R
Georgia Inst. of Tech.	M	Tufts (MA)	M
Harvey Mudd (CA)	S	Tulane (LA)	M
Illinois Inst. of Tech.	R	Union (NY)	R
Illinois, U. of (Urbana-Champaign)	XL	U.S. Air Force Academy (CO)	M
Iowa State	XL	U.S. Coast Guard Academy (CT)	R
Iowa, U. of	XL	U.S. Military Academy (NY)	M
Johns Hopkins (MD)	M	U.S. Naval Academy (MD)	M
Kettering (MI)	R	Vanderbilt (TN)	M
Lafayette (PA)	R	Villanova (PA)	M
Lehigh (PA)	M	Virginia, U. of	L
Maryland, U. of	XL	Washington U. (MO)	M
MIT (MA)	M	Washington, U. of	L
Miami U. (OH)	L	Worcester Poly. Tech. (MA)	R
Michigan, U. of	XL		

ENGINEERING continues next page

Enrollment Code	
■ *Men Only*	S = Small (less than 1000 students) R = Moderate (1000-3000 students) M = Medium (3000-8000 students)
▲ *Women Only*	L = Large (8000-20,000 students) XL = Extra Large (over 20,000 students)

ENGINEERING, continued

GROUP II
Very Selective

Akron, U. of (OH) L	Gannon (PA) .... R
Alabama, U. of L	Geneva (PA) .... R
Alabama, U. of (Birmingham) .... M	Gonzaga (WA) .... R
Alabama, U. of (Huntsville) .... M	Grand Valley (MI) L
Alaska, U. of (Fairbanks) .... M	Grove City (PA) .... R
Alfred (NY) .... R	Hartford, U. of (CT) .... M
Arizona, U. of XL	Houston, U. of (TX) L
Arizona State XL	Howard (DC) .... M
Arkansas, U. of L	Idaho, U. of L
Auburn (AL) L	Illinois, U. of (Chicago) L
Baylor (TX) .... M	Indiana U./Purdue U./Indianapolis L
Boise State (ID) L	James Madison (VA) L
Bradley (IL) .... M	Kansas, U. of L
Brigham Young (UT) L	Kansas State L
★Butler (IN) .... R	Kentucky, U. of L
California State U. (Fresno) L	Lamar (TX) .... M
California State U. (Fullerton) L	LeTourneau College (TX) .... R
California State U. (Los Angeles) L	Lipscomb (TN) .... R
California State U. (Northridge) L	Louisiana-Lafayette L
California State U. (Sacramento) .... M	Louisiana State XL
California, U. of (Irvine) L	Louisville (KY) L
California, U. of (Merced) .... R	Lowell, U. of (MA) L
California, U. of (Riverside) L	Loyola (MD) .... R
California, U. of (Santa Cruz) .... M	Loyola Marymount (CA) .... M
California Maritime Academy .... S	Maine, U. of L
Cal. Poly State U. (Pomona) L	Manhattan (NY) .... M
Cal. Poly. State U. (San Luis Obispo) L	π Marietta (OH) .... R
Calvin (MI) .... M	Maritime College (SUNY)(NY) .... S
Carroll (MT) .... R	Marquette (WI) .... M
Catholic U. (DC) .... M	Massachusetts, U. of L
Central Connecticut .... M	# Massachusetts, U. of (Dartmouth) .... M
Central Florida, U. of XL	Massachusetts, U. of (Lowell) .... M
Christian Brothers (TN) .... R	Mass. Maritime Academy .... S
Cincinnati, U. of (OH) L	Memphis, U. of (TN) L
Citadel, The (SC) .... R	Mercer (GA) .... R
City College (CUNY)(NY) L	Messiah (PA) .... R
Clemson (SC) L	Michigan State XL
Cogswell (CA) .... S	Michigan Tech. .... M
Colorado State L	Michigan, U. of XL
Colorado, U. of L	Michigan, U. of (Dearborn) .... M
Colorado, U. of (Col. Springs) .... R	Milwaukee Sch. of Engine (WI) .... R
Connecticut, U. of XL	Minnesota State U. (Mankato) L
Dayton, U. of (OH) .... M	Minnesota, U. of (Duluth) .... M
Delaware, U. of L	Mississippi State L
Denver, U. of (CA) .... M	Mississippi, U. of L
Detroit Mercy (MI) .... M	Missouri, U. of XL
Dordt (IA) .... R	Montana Tech. .... R
Drexel (PA) .... M	
★★Embry-Riddle (FL) .... M	
Florida A&M .... M	π *Petroleum Engineering*
Florida Atlantic L	★ *Also, Motorsports Engineering*
Florida Inst. of Tech. .... R	# *Also, Textile Science / Industry*
Florida International L	★★ *Also, Aviation Environmental Science*

GROUP II continues next page

ENGINEERING, continued

•• ━━━━━━━━━ **GROUP II,** continued ━━━━━━━━━ ••

Montana State	L	
Morgan State (MD)	M	
Nebraska, U. of	L	
Nevada, U. of (Las Vegas)	L	
Nevada, U. of (Reno)	L	
New Hampshire, U. of	L	
New Jersey Inst. of Tech.	M	
New Mexico, U. of	L	
New Mexico State U.	L	
New Orleans, U. of	L	
New Paltz (SUNY)(NY)	M	
New York Institute of Tech	M	
North Carolina, U. of (Charlotte)	L	
North Carolina State	L	
North Dakota State	L	
North Dakota, U. of	M	
North Florida, U. of	L	
Northeastern (MA)	L	
Northern Illinois U.	L	
Norwich (VT)	R	
Oakland U. (MI)	M	
Ohio Northern	R	
Ohio State	XL	
Ohio U.	L	
Oklahoma, U. of	XL	
Old Dominion (VA)	L	
Oregon Inst. of Tech.	R	
Oregon State	L	
Pacific, U. of the (CA)	R	
Penn State (Harrisburg)(PA)	R	
Pittsburgh, U. of	L	
Pittsburgh, U. of (Johnstown)	R	
Polytechnic Univ. of NY	R	
Portland, U. of (OR)	R	
Portland State (OR)	M	
Puerto Rico, U. of (Mayaguez)	L	
Purdue (IN)	XL	
+ Rhode Island, U. of	L	
Rochester Inst. of Tech. (NY)	L	
Roger Williams (RI)	M	
Rowan (NJ)	M	
St. Louis U. (MO)	M	
St. Martin's (WA)	S	
San Diego State (CA)	XL	
San Jose State (CA)	L	
Santa Clara U. (CA)	M	
Seattle Pacific (WA)	R	
Seattle U. (WA)	R	
South Alabama	M	

South Carolina, U. of	L	
So. Dakota School of Mines	R	
South Dakota State U.	M	
Southern Illinois U. (Carbondale)	L	
Southern Illinois U. (Edwardsville)	L	
Southern Maine, U. of	M	
Southern Methodist (TX)	L	
Southern Polytechnic (GA)	R	
South Florida, U. of	L	
Stony Brook (SUNY) (NY)	L	
▲ Sweet Briar (VA)	S	
Syracuse (NY)	L	
Tennessee Tech	M	
Tennessee, U. of	XL	
Tennessee, U. of (Chattanooga)	M	
Texas A&M	XL	
Texas A&M (Kingsville)	M	
Texas Tech U.	L	
Texas, U. of (Arlington)	L	
Texas, U. of (Dallas)	M	
Texas, U. of (San Antonio)	L	
Texas, U. of (El Paso)	L	
Texas, U. of (Tyler)	R	
Toledo, U. of (OH)	L	
Tri-State (IN)	R	
Tulsa, U. of (OK)	R	
Tuskegee University (AL)	M	
Utah, U. of	L	
Utah State	L	
Valparaiso (IN)	M	
Virginia Commonwealth	L	
Virginia Military Inst.	R	
Virginia Tech.	L	
Walla Walla (WA)	R	
Washington State	L	
Wayne State (MI)	L	
West Virginia U.	L	
* Western Michigan	L	
Western New England (MA)	R	
Westminster (UT)	R	
Widener (PA)	R	
Wilkes (PA)	R	
Wisconsin, U. of	XL	
Wisconsin, U. of (Milwaukee)	L	
Wisconsin, U. of (Platteville)	M	
Wright State (OH)	L	
Wyoming, U. of	L	

+ *And International Engineering*

* *Also, Engineering Management Technology*

Enrollment Code

■ *Men Only*	S = Small (less than 1000 students) R = Moderate (1000-3000 students) M = Medium (3000-8000 students)
▲ *Women Only*	L = Large (8000-20,000 students) XL = Extra Large (over 20,000 students)

ENGLISH

•━━━━━━━━━━ **GROUP I** ━━━━━━━━━━•
Most Selective

Albany (SUNY)(NY)	L	Kenyon (OH)	R
Allegheny (PA)	R	Knox (IL)	R
American U. (DC)	M	Lafayette (PA)	R
Amherst (MA)	R	Lawrence (WI)	R
Bard (NY)	R	Lehigh (PA)	M
▲Barnard (NY)	R	Macalester (MN)	R
Bates (ME)	R	Maryland, U. of	XL
Binghamton (SUNY)(NY)	L	Miami, U. of (FL)	L
Boston Col. (MA)	L	Miami U. (OH)	L
Bowdoin (ME)	R	Michigan, U. of	XL
Brandeis (MA)	R	Middlebury (VT)	R
Brown (RI)	M	Minnesota, U. of	XL
▲Bryn Mawr (PA)	S	▲Mount Holyoke (MA)	R
Bucknell (PA)	M	New (FL)	S
Buffalo (SUNY) (NY)	L	North Carolina, U. of	L
California, U. of (Berkeley)	XL	New Jersey, College of	M
California, U. of (Los Angeles)	XL	New School U. (Lang)(NY)	R
Carleton (MN)	R	Northwestern (IL)	M
Carnegie Mellon (PA)	M	Notre Dame (IN)	M
Centre (KY)	R	Oberlin (OH)	R
Chicago, U. of (IL)	M	Occidental (CA)	R
Claremont McKenna (CA)	R	Pennsylvania, U. of	L
Colby (ME)	R	Pepperdine (CA)	R
Colgate (NY)	R	Pitzer (CA)	S
Colorado College	R	Pomona (CA)	R
Columbia (NY)	M	Princeton (NJ)	M
Connecticut Col.	R	Puget Sound, U. of (WA)	R
Cornell (NY)	L	Reed (OR)	R
Dallas, U. of (TX)	R	Rhodes (TN)	R
Dartmouth (NH)	M	Rice (TX)	M
Davidson (NC)	R	Richmond, U. of (VA)	M
DePauw (IN)	R	Rochester, U. of (NY)	M
Dickinson (PA)	R	Rutgers (NJ)	L
Drew (NJ)	R	Sarah Lawrence (NY)	R
Duke (NC)	M	Skidmore (NY)	R
Emory (GA)	M	▲Smith (MA)	R
Florida, U. of	XL	South, U. of the (TN)	R
Franklin & Marshall (PA)	R	Southern California	L
Geneseo (SUNY)(NY)	M	Southern Methodist (TX)	M
Georgetown (DC)	M	Southwestern (TX)	R
Gettysburg (PA)	R	Stanford (CA)	M
Grinnell (IA)	R	St. Olaf (MN)	R
Gustavus Adolphus (MN)	R	Swarthmore (PA)	R
Hamilton (NY)	R	Texas, U. of	XL
Harvard (MA)	M	Trinity (CT)	R
Haverford (PA)	S	Trinity (TX)	R
Holy Cross (MA)	R	Tufts (MA)	M
Illinois, U. of	XL	Union (NY)	R
Illinois Wesleyan	R		
➤Iowa, U. of	XL		
Johns Hopkins (MD)	M		
Kalamazoo (MI)	R		

➤ *Also, Creative Writing Track in English*

ENGLISH continues next page

ENGLISH, continued

━━ GROUP I, continued ━━

Vanderbilt (TN) .... M	Wesleyan (CT) .... R
Vassar (NY) .... R	Wheaton (IL) .... R
Virginia, U. of L	Whitman (WA) .... R
■ Wabash (IN) .... S	Willamette (OR) .... R
Wake Forest (NC) .... M	William & Mary (VA) .... R
Washington & Lee (VA) .... R	Williams (MA) .... R
Washington U. (MO) .... M	Wisconsin, U. of XL
▲ Wellesley (MA) .... R	Yale (CT) .... M

GROUP II
Very Selective

Abilene Christian (TX) .... M	Central Florida XL
▲ Agnes Scott (GA) .... S	Central Michigan L
Alabama, U. of L	Chapman (CA) .... R
Albion (MI) .... R	Cincinnati, U. of (OH) L
Albright (PA) .... R	Clark (MA) .... R
Alfred (NY) .... R	Clemson (SC) L
Alma (MI) .... R	Coe (IA) .... R
Arizona, U. of XL	Colorado, U. of L
Arizona State XL	Concordia (MN) .... R
Ashland (OH) .... R	Cornell Col. (IA) .... R
Auburn (AL) L	Creighton (NE) .... M
Augustana (IL) .... R	Delaware, U. of L
Augustana (SD) .... R	Denison (OH) .... R
Baylor (TX) .... M	DePaul (IL) L
Belmont (TN) .... R	Denver, U. of (CO) .... M
Beloit (WI) .... R	Drake (IA) .... M
Bemidji State (MN) .... M	Drury (MO) .... R
Bennington (VT) .... S	Earlham (IN) .... R
Bentley (MA) .... M	Eckerd (FL) .... R
Berea (KY) .... R	Elizabethtown (PA) .... R
Berry (GA) .... R	Emerson (MA) .... M
Bethany (WV) .... S	Evansville (IN) .... R
Birmingham-Southern (AL) .... R	Flagler (FL) .... R
Bradley (IL) .... M	Florida State L
Brigham Young (UT) XL	Fordham (NY) L
Bryn Athyn (PA) .... S	Franciscan U. of Steubenville (OH) .... R
Butler (IN) .... R	Fredonia (SUNY)(NY) .... M
California, U. of (Davis) XL	George Mason (VA) L
California, U. of (Irvine) L	Georgetown College (KY) .... R
Cal Poly State U. (San Luis Obispo) L	Georgia, U. of XL
Calvin (MI) .... M	Gonzaga (WA) .... R
Canisius (NY) .... M	Gordon (MA) .... R
Catholic (DC) .... M	Goucher (MD) .... R
Centenary (LA) .... S	
Central (IA) .... R	*GROUP II continues next page*

Enrollment Code		
■ *Men Only*	S = Small (less than 1000 students) R = Moderate (1000-3000 students) M = Medium (3000-8000 students)	
▲ *Women Only*	L = Large (8000-20,000 students) XL = Extra Large (over 20,000 students)	

ENGLISH, continued

GROUP II, continued

Grand Valley (MI)	L
Grove City (PA)	R
Guilford (NC)	R
Hamline (MN)	R
■ Hampton-Sydney (VA)	S
Hampton (VA)	M
Hanover (IN)	R
Hawaii, U. of	L
Hawaii Pacific	R
Hendrix (AR)	R
Herbert Lehman (CUNY)(NY)	M
Hillsdale (MI)	R
Hiram (OH)	R
Hobart & Wm. Smith (NY)	R
Hofstra (NY)	M
▲ Hollins (VA)	S
Hood (MD)	S
Hope (MI)	R
Houghton (NY)	R
Houston, U. of (TX)	L
Howard (DC)	M
Hunter (CUNY) (NY)	L
Idaho, College of	S
Illinois, U. of (Chicago)	L
Iowa State	XL
John Carroll (OH)	M
▲ Judson (AL)	S
Juniata (PA)	R
Kansas State	L
Kent State (OH)	L
Kentucky, U. of	L
Kentucky Wesleyan	S
Lake Forest (IL)	R
LaSalle (PA)	M
LeMoyne (NY)	R
Lewis & Clark (OR)	R
Lipscomb (TN)	R
Loras (IA)	R
Loyola (LA)	R
Loyola Marymount (CA)	M
Luther (IA)	R
Lycoming (PA)	R
Lyon (AR)	S
Manhattanville (NY)	R
Marietta (OH)	R
Marquette (WI)	M

Mary Washington (VA)	M
Massachusetts, U. of	L
Master's (CA)	R
McDaniel (MD)	R
McKendree (IL)	R
Messiah (PA)	R
Michigan State	XL
▲ Mills (CA)	S
Millsaps (MS)	S
Minnesota, U. of (Morris)	R
Mississippi, U. of	L
Mississippi U. for Women	R
Missouri, U. of	XL
Missouri, U. of (Kansas City)	M
Montana, U. of	M
■ Morehouse (GA)	R
Morgan State (MD)	M
Mount Mercy (IA)	S
Muhlenberg (PA)	R
Murray State (KY)	M
Nazareth (NY)	R
Nevada, U. of (Las Vegas)	L
Nevada, U. of (Reno)	L
New Hampshire, U. of	L
New Mexico State U.	L
New Orleans (LA)	L
New Paltz (SUNY)(NY)	M
North Carolina, U. of (Wilmington)	L
North Carolina State	L
North Central (IL)	R
North Dakota, U. of	M
North Texas	L
Northeastern (MA)	L
Oglethorpe (GA)	R
Ohio State	XL
Ohio U.	L
Ohio Wesleyan	R
Oklahoma Baptist	R
Oklahoma City U.	R
Oklahoma, U. of	XL
Oklahoma State	L
Olivet Nazarene (IL)	S
Oneonta (SUNY)(NY)	M
Oregon, U. of	L

GROUP II continues next page

Enrollment Code	
■ *Men Only*	S = Small (less than 1000 students) R = Moderate (1000-3000 students) M = Medium (3000-8000 students)
▲ *Women Only*	L = Large (8000-20,000 students) XL = Extra Large (over 20,000 students)

ENGLISH, continued

•• ─────────────── **GROUP II, continued** ─────────────── ••

Oswego (SUNY)(NY)	M
Otterbein (OH)	R
Pace (NY)	R
Pacific Lutheran (WA)	R
Pacific University (OR)	R
Pittsburgh, U. of (PA)	L
Portland State (OR)	L
Presbyterian (SC)	R
Principia (IL)	S
Providence (RI)	M
Purchase (SUNY) (NY)	M
Queens (NC)	R
Queens (CUNY)(NY)	L
Ramapo (NJ)	M
Randolph College (VA)	S
Randolph-Macon (VA)	R
Redlands, U. of (CA)	R
Ripon (WI)	S
Roanoke (VA)	R
Rollins (FL)	R
Rutgers (Camden) NJ	M
St. Anselm (NH)	R
St. Bonaventure (NY)	R
▲ St. Catherine (MN)	R
St. Cloud (MN)	L
St. Joseph's U. (PA)	R
St. Lawrence (NY)	R
St. Louis U. (MO)	M
St. Mary's College (CA)	R
▲ St. Mary's Col. (IN)	R
St. Mary's College of Maryland	R
St. Mary's (MN)	R
St. Norbert (WI)	R
St. Rose (NY)	R
St. Scholastica (MN)	R
St. Thomas (MN)	R
Salisbury (MD)	M
Samford (AL)	R
San Diego State (CA)	XL
Santa Clara U. (CA)	M

▲ Scripps (CA)	S
Seattle Pacific (WA)	R
Seton Hall (NJ)	M
Shepherd (WV)	M
Siena (NY)	R
▲ Simmons (MA)	R
Sonoma State (CA)	M
South Carolina, U. of	L
Spring Hill (AL)	R
Stetson (FL)	R
Stony Brook (SUNY) (NY)	L
Susquehanna (PA)	R
▲ Sweet Briar (VA)	S
Texas A&M	XL
Truman State (MO)	M
Tulsa, U. of (OK)	R
Utah State	L
Virginia Poly. Institute	L
Virginia Tech	L
Warren Wilson (NC)	S
Wartburg (IA)	R
Washington & Jefferson (PA)	R
Washington, U. of	XL
Washington State	L
Wells (NY)	S
West Chester (PA)	M
West Virginia U.	L
Western Michigan	L
Western Washington U.	L
Westminster (MO)	S
Westminster (UT)	R
Wheaton (MA)	R
Whitworth (WA)	R
William Jewell (MO)	R
Winona State U. (MN)	M
Winthrop (SC)	M
Wittenberg (OH)	R
Wofford (SC)	S
Wooster (OH)	R
Wyoming, U. of	L

Enrollment Code	
■ *Men Only*	S = Small (less than 1000 students) R = Moderate (1000-3000 students) M = Medium (3000-8000 students)
▲ *Women Only*	L = Large (8000-20,000 students) XL = Extra Large (over 20,000 students)

ENGLISH, continued

GROUP III
Selective

Adrian (MI)	R	Delaware Valley (PA)	R
Akron, U. of (OH)	L	DeSales (PA)	S
Alabama, U. of (Birmingham)	M	Doane (NE)	S
Alabama, U. of (Huntsville)	M	Dordt (IA)	R
Alaska, U. of (Anchorage)	M	D'Youville (NY)	R
▲Alverno (WI)	R	East Carolina	L
Andrews (MI)	R	East Central (OK)	R
Appalachian State (NC)	L	East Tennessee	L
Aquinas (MI)	R	Eastern Illinois	L
Arkansas, U. of	L	Eastern Michigan	L
Arcadia (PA)	R	Eastern Nazarene (MA)	R
Assumption (MA)	R	Eastern Oregon	R
Augsburg (MN)	R	Eastern Washington	L
Augusta (GA)	M	Edinboro (PA)	M
Azusa Pacific (CA)	R	Eureka (IL)	S
Baker (KS)	R	Fairleigh Dickinson (NJ)	M
Baldwin-Wallace (OH)	R	Florida A&M	M
Baruch (CUNY)(NY)	L	Florida Gulf Coast U.	M
Bellarmine (KY)	R	Fort Hays (KS)	M
Belmont Abbey (NC)	S	Fort Lewis (CO)	M
Benedictine (KS)	R	Friends (KS)	R
Bethel (IN)	R	Georgia Southwestern	R
Bethel (KS)	S	Goshen (IN)	R
Brescia (KY)	S	Gwynedd-Mercy (PA)	S
Briar Cliff (IA)	R	Illinois College	S
Bridgewater State (MA)	M	Illinois State	L
Brockport (SUNY)(NY)	M	I.U. P.U.I. (IN)	L
California (PA)	M	Jamestown (ND)	R
California State U. (Bakersfield)	M	Johnson State (VT)	R
California State U. (Channel Islands)	R	Kean (NJ)	M
California State U. (East Bay)	M	Keene State (NH)	R
California State U. (Fresno)	L	Kennesaw State (GA)	R
California State U. (Fullerton)	L	King (TN)	S
California State U. (Monterey Bay)	R	King's (PA)	R
California State U. (Northridge)	L	Kutztown (PA)	M
California State U. (Sacramento)	M	Lewis-Clark State (ID)	R
Campbell (NC)	R	Lindenwood (MO)	M
Carson-Newman (TN)	R	Long Island U. (Brooklyn)(NY)	R
Central Washington	L	Long Island U. (C.W. Post)(NY)	R
Charleston Southern (SC)	R	Longwood (VA)	R
Chestnut Hill (PA)	S	Louisiana College	R
Chowan (NC)	S	Louisiana-Lafayette	L
Christopher Newport (VA)	M	Louisiana State	XL
Citadel, The (SC)	R	Lynchburg (VA)	R
City College (CUNY)(NY)	L	Lyndon State (VT)	R
Colby-Sawyer (NH)	S	Maine (Farmington)	R
Daemen (NY)	R		
Dana (NB)	S		

GROUP III continues next page

ENGLISH, continued

••• ━━━━━━━━━━━━━━━━━━ **GROUP III,** continued ━━━━━━━━━━━━━ •••

Mansfield (PA)	R
▲ Mary Baldwin (VA)	S
Marygrove (MI)	R
Mass. Coll. of Lib. Arts (N. Adams)	R
Massachusetts, U. of (Boston)	M
Memphis, U. of (TN)	L
Mercyhurst (PA)	R
▲ Meredith (NC)	R
Merrimack (MA)	R
Middle Tennessee	L
Millersville (PA)	M
Millikin (IL)	R
Misericordia (PA)	S
Missouri Southern State	M
Montclair State (NJ)	M
Montevallo (AL)	R
Mount St. Joseph (OH)	R
Mount Union (OH)	R
Muskingum (OH)	R
Niagara (NY)	R
Nicholls State (LA)	M
Northeastern Illinois	M
Northeastern State (OK)	L
Northern Colorado	L
Northern Iowa	L
Northern Kentucky	L
Northern Michigan	M
Northwestern (IA)	R
Northwestern (MN)	R
Nyack (NY)	R
Oklahoma Christian	R
Penn State (Erie)(PA)	M
Pittsburgh, U. of (Greensburg)	R
Pittsburg State (KS)	M
Point Park (PA)	R
Plymouth State (NH)	M
Radford (VA)	M
Regis (MA)	S
Rhode Island, U. of	L
Robert Morris (PA)	R
Rockford (IL)	S
Rocky Mountain (MT)	S
▲ Rosemont (PA)	S
Saginaw Valley (MI)	M

St. Ambrose (IA)	R
St. Edward's (TX)	M
St. Francis (NY)	R
St. John Fisher (NY)	R
St. Mary (KS)	S
St. Mary's U. of San Antonio (TX)	R
St. Peter's (NJ)	R
St. Vincent (PA)	R
▲ Salem Col. (NC)	S
Salem State (MA)	M
San Francisco State (CA)	L
Schreiner (TX)	S
Seattle U. (WA)	R
Shippensburg (PA)	M
Siena Heights (MI)	S
Slippery Rock (PA)	M
South Alabama	M
South Dakota, U. of	M
Southeast Missouri State	L
Southeastern Louisiana	L
Southern Connecticut	M
Southern Illinois U. (Carbondale)	L
Southern Maine	M
Southern Nazarene (OK)	R
Southern Utah	M
Southwestern (KS)	S
▲ Spelman (GA)	R
Springfield (MA)	M
Suffolk (MA)	R
Tampa, U. of (FL)	R
Tarleton State (TX)	M
Taylor (IN)	R
Temple (PA)	L
Tennessee, U. of	XL
Tennessee, U. of (Chattanooga)	M
Tennessee, U. of (Martin)	M
Texas, U. of (El Paso)	L
Texas, U. of (San Antonio)	L
Texas, U. of (Tyler)	R
Texas A&M (Corpus Christi)	M
Texas Tech. U.	L
Tougaloo (MS)	S

ENGLISH continues next page

Enrollment Code

■ *Men Only*	S = Small (less than 1000 students)	R = Moderate (1000-3000 students)	M = Medium (3000-8000 students)
▲ *Women Only*	L = Large (8000-20,000 students)	XL = Extra Large (over 20,000 students)	

ENGLISH, continued

GROUP III, continued

▲ Trinity (DC) .... S
Troy State (AL) .... M
Utah, U. of L
Walla Walla (WA) .... R
Walsh (OH) .... R
Weber State (UT) L
Western Carolina (NC) .... M
Western Connecticut .... M
Western Illinois L
Western St. Coll. of Colorado .... R
Westfield (MA) .... M

West Virginia Wesleyan .... R
Wheeling Jesuit (WV) .... R
Wichita State (KS) .... M
Whittier (CA) .... R
Wilkes (PA) .... R
William Paterson (NJ) .... M
Wilmington (OH) .... S
Wisconsin, U. of (Eau Claire) L
Wisconsin, U. of (Milwaukee) .... R
Wisconsin, U. of (Platteville) .... M
Youngstown State (OH) L

FOREIGN LANGUAGES

GROUP I
Most Selective

Albany (SUNY)(NY)	L	Loyola (MD)	M
Allegheny (PA)	R	Macalester (MN)	R
American U. (DC)	M	Maryland, U. of	XL
Bard (NY)	R	Michigan, U. of	XL
▲ Barnard (NY)	R	Middlebury (VT)	R
Bates (ME)	R	Minnesota, U. of	XL
Binghamton (SUNY)(NY)	L	▲ Mt. Holyoke (MA)	R
Boston College (MA)	L	New York U.	M
Boston U. (MA)	L	North Carolina, U. of	L
Bowdoin (ME)	R	Northwestern (IL)	M
Brown (RI)	M	Notre Dame (IN)	M
▲ Bryn Mawr (PA)	S	Pennsylvania, U. of	L
California, U. of (Berkeley)	XL	Pomona (CA)	R
California, U. of (Los Angeles)	XL	Princeton (NJ)	M
Carleton (MN)	R	Reed (OR)	R
Chicago, U. of (IL)	M	Rhodes (TN)	R
Colby (ME)	R	Rochester, U. of (NY)	M
Colgate (NY)	R	Rutgers (NJ)	L
Columbia (NY)	M	▲ Scripps (CA)	S
Connecticut College	R	Skidmore (NY)	R
Dallas, U. of (TX)	R	▲ Smith (MA)	R
Dartmouth (NH)	M	South, U. of the (TN)	R
DePauw (IN)	R	Southwestern (TX)	R
Dickinson (PA)	R	Stanford (CA)	M
Drew (NJ)	R	Swarthmore (PA)	R
Emory (GA)	M	Trinity (TX)	R
Florida, U. of	XL	Tulane (LA)	M
Franklin & Marshall (PA)	R	Vassar (NY)	R
Georgetown (DC)	M	Virginia, U. of	L
Grinnell (IA)	R	Wake Forest (NC)	M
Gustavus Adolphus (MN)	R	Washington & Lee (VA)	R
Harvard (MA)	M	Washington U. (MO)	M
Haverford (PA)	S	▲ Wellesley (MA)	R
Holy Cross (MA)	R	Whitman (WA)	R
Illinois, U. of (Urbana-Champaign)	XL	William & Mary (VA)	M
Kalamazoo (MI)	R	Yale (CT)	M
Lawrence (WI)	R		

FOREIGN LANGUAGES continues next page

Enrollment Code

■ *Men Only*
▲ *Women Only*

S = Small (less than 1000 students)   R = Moderate (1000-3000 students)   M = Medium (3000-8000 students)
L = Large (8000-20,000 students)   XL = Extra Large (over 20,000 students)

FOREIGN LANGUAGES, continued

GROUP II
Very Selective

▲Agnes Scott (GA) .... S
Alabama, U. of L
Arizona, U. of.................................. XL
Arizona State XL
Beloit (WI) .... R
Brigham Young (UT) XL
California, U. of (Santa Barbara) L
Calvin (MI) .... M
Catholic (DC).................................... M
Central (IA) .... R
Centre (KY) .... R
Charleston, College of (SC)............... L
Clark (MA) .... R
Clemson (SC) L
Concordia (MN) .... R
Drake (IA) .... M
Earlham (IN)..................................... R
Eckerd (FL) .... R
Georgia, U. of XL
Grand Valley (MI) L
Gustavus Adolphus (MN) .... R
Hawaii, U. of L
Herbert Lehman (CUNY)(NY) .... M
Hillsdale (MI) .... R
▲Hollins (VA) .... S
Hope (MI) .... R
Hunter (CUNY)(NY) L
Ilinois College .... S
Illinois, U. of (Chicago).................... L
Indiana U. XL
Iowa, U. of....................................... XL
James Madison (VA)......................... L
Kansas, U. of L
Kansas State L
Lake Forest (IL) .... R
Lewis & Clark (OR) .... R
Linfield (OR)..................................... R

Lyon (AR) .... S
▲Mills (CA) .... S
Minnesota, U. of (Morris) .... R
Moravian (PA) .... R
Nazareth (NY)................................... R
Nebraska, U. of L
New Hampshire, U. of L
New Paltz (SUNY)(NY) .... M
North Carolina (Charlotte) L
Ohio State XL
Oregon, U. of L
Pacific University (OR)...................... R
Pepperdine (CA) .... R
Pittsburgh, U. of (PA) L
Portland State (OR) L
Puerto Rico, U. of (Mayaguez) L
Randolph-Macon (VA) .... R
▲Rosemont (PA) .... S
St. Anselm (NH) .... R
South Carolina, U. of........................ L
Stony Brook (SUNY)(NY) L
▲Sweet Briar (VA) .... S
Temple (PA) L
Texas, U. of (Austin) XL
▲Trinity (DC) .... S
Truman State (MO) .... M
Utah, U. of....................................... L
Valparaiso U. (IN) .... M
Vermont, U. of L
Virginia Commonwealth L
Wells (NY) .... S
West Chester (PA) .... M
Wheaton (MA) .... R
Wisconsin, U. of XL
Wittenberg (OH) .... R
Wofford (SC) .... R
Wooster (OH) .... R

GROUP III
Selective

Bethany (WV) .... S
California State U. (Sacramento) ...... M
Carthage (WI) .... R
Eastern Washington .... M
Emory & Henry (VA) .... S
Mansfield (PA) .... R
Montana State.................................. L
New Mexico, U. of L
Northwestern (IA)............................. R

Slippery Rock (PA) .... M
South Alabama .... M
South Florida, U. of L
Southern Oregon State U. .... M
Wayne State (MI).............................. L
Western Michigan L
Wisconsin, U. of (Eau Claire) L
Wisconsin, U. of (Milwaukee) L

FOREIGN LANGUAGES continues next page

FOREIGN LANGUAGES, continued

Some Recommendations by Specific Departments
Compiled initially with the help of Minnesota's Jeff Sheehan, Secondary School Counselor

FRENCH

Arizona, U. of XL	▲Mount Holyoke (MA) .... R
California, U. of (Berkeley) XL	North Carolina, U. of L
Central (IA) .... R	Northwestern (IL) .... M
Colby (ME) .... R	Princeton (NJ) .... M
Columbia (NY) .... M	Rhodes (TN) .... R
Dartmouth (NH) .... M	San Diego State U. (CA) L
Emory (GA) .... R	▲Scripps (CA) .... S
Georgetown (DC) .... M	Tufts (MA) .... M
Harvard (MA) .... M	Tulane (LA) .... M
Holy Cross (MA) .... M	Vassar (NY) .... R
Indiana U. XL	Washington U. (MO) .... M
Indiana (PA) L	▲Wellesley (MA) .... R
▲Mills (CA) .... S	Wittenberg (OH) .... R

GERMAN

Boston College (MA) L	Penn State XL
Brown (RI) .... M	Pennsylvania, U. of............................ L
California, U. of (Berkeley) XL	Princeton (NJ) .... M
California, U. of (Santa Barbara) L	Rhode Island., U. of.......................... L
Colorado, U. of L	Stanford (CA) .... M
Hunter (CUNY)(NY) L	Texas, U. of (Austin) XL
Illinois, U. of (Urbana-Champaign) XL	Williams (MA) .... R
Indiana U. XL	Wisconsin, U. of XL
Indiana (PA) L	Wofford (SC) .... R
Michigan State.................................... XL	

JAPANESE

Brigham Young (UT) XL	Pacific University (OR) .... R
Connecticut College .... R	Pennsylvania, U. of............................ L
Harvard (MA) .... M	Pittsburgh, U. of (PA) L
Hawaii, U. of (Manoa) L	Washington, U. of.............................. XL
Ohio State L	Wisconsin, U. of XL
Oregon, U. of L	

SPANISH

Bradley (IL) .... M	Maryland, U. of.................................... XL
Brigham Young (UT) XL	Massachusetts, U. of (Dartmouth) .... M
Buffalo (SUNY) (NY) L	Messiah (PA) .... R
California State U. (San Marcos) ...... M	Northwestern (IA) .... R
California, U. of (Irvine)...................... M	Pittsburgh, U. of L
California, U. of (San Diego) L	Puerto Rico, U. of (Mayaguez) L
California, U. of (Santa Barbara) L	Rutgers (NJ).. L
Central (IA) .... R	San Diego State U. (CA) L
Colby (ME) .... R	▲Scripps (CA) .... S
George Washington (DC) .... M	Southern Connecticut .... M
Greensboro College (NC) .... S	Texas, U. of XL
Indiana U. XL	Utah, U. of.. L
Kansas, U. of L	Vanderbilt (TN) .... M
Lawrence (WI) .... R	Wisconsin, U. of XL
Lyon (AR) .... S	Worcester State (MA)........................ M

FORESTRY

GROUP I
Most Selective

Florida, U. of XL	South, U. of the (TN) .... R
Illinois, U. of XL	SUNY Coll. of Env. Sci. & Forestry .... R
North Carolina State L	

GROUP II
Very Selective

Arizona, U. of.................................... XL	Missouri, U. of XL
Auburn (AL) L	New Hampshire, U. of L
Clemson (SC) L	Oklahoma State.................................. L
Colorado State L	Pennsylvania State XL
Connecticut, U. of XL	Purdue (IN) XL
Georgia, U. of L	Syracuse (NY) L
Iowa State XL	Tennessee, U. of XL
Kentucky, U. of L	Texas A&M XL
Maine, U. of L	Virginia Tech..................................... L
Massachusetts, U. of L	Washington, U. of............................. XL
Michigan State.................................. XL	West Virginia U. L
Michigan Tech................................... M	Wisconsin, U. of XL
Minnesota, U. of XL	Wisconsin, U. of (Stevens Point) L
Mississippi State L	

GROUP III
Selective

Humboldt State (CA)......................... M	Paul Smith's (NY) .... S
Idaho, U. of L	Southern Illinois (Carbondale)........... L
Montana, U. of .... M	Stephen F. Austin (TX) L
Northern Arizona XL	Utah State L
Oregon State..................................... L	

Enrollment Code		
■ *Men Only*	S = Small (less than 1000 students)	R = Moderate (1000-3000 students)	M = Medium (3000-8000 students)
▲ *Women Only*	L = Large (8000-20,000 students)	XL = Extra Large (over 20,000 students)

GEOGRAPHY

GROUP I
Most Selective

Boston U. (MA)	L	Johns Hopkins (MD)	M
Buffalo (SUNY)(NY)	L	Macalester (MN)	R
California, U. of (Berkeley)	XL	Maryland, U. of	XL
Chicago, U. of (IL)	M	Miami U. (OH)	L
Clark (MA)	R	Michigan, U. of	XL
Colgate (NY)	R	Middlebury (VT)	R
Dartmouth (NH)	M	Minnesota, U. of	XL
Florida, U. of	XL	Sarah Lawrence (NY)	R
George Washington (DC)	M		

GROUP II
Very Selective

Arizona State	XL	Oklahoma, U. of	XL
Bemidji State (MN)	M	Oklahoma State	L
California, U. of (Santa Barbara)	L	Oregon, U. of	L
Colorado, U. of	L	Oneonta (SUNY)(NY)	M
Colorado, U. of (Colorado Springs)	M	Pennsylvania State	XL
Denver, U. of (CO)	M	Radford (VA)	M
DePaul (IL)	L	Salisbury (MD)	M
Florida International	L	San Diego State U. (CA)	L
Georgia, U. of	L	South Carolina, U. of	L
# Harrisburg U. (PA)	S	Syracuse (NY)	L
Hunter (CUNY)(NY)	L	Texas, U. of (Austin)	XL
Indiana U.	XL	Texas, U. of (Dallas)	M
Kansas State	L	Vermont, U. of	L
Kansas, U. of	L	Virginia Poly. Institute	L
Louisiana State	XL	Washington, U. of	XL
Mary Washington (VA)	M	Western Washington U.	L
Michigan State	XL	Wisconsin, U. of (Madison)	XL
New Paltz (SUNY)(NY)	M	Wittenberg (OH)	R
Ohio State	XL		

GROUP III
Selective

Aquinas (MI)	R	Mansfield (PA)	R
Ball State (IN)	M	Massachusetts, U. of (Boston)	M
Bloomsburg (PA)	M	New Orleans (LA)	L
Bridgewater (MA)	M	North Carolina (Charlotte)	L
California State U. (Chico)	L	Salem State (MA)	M
California State U. (Long Beach)	L	Shippensburg (PA)	M
California State U. (Northridge)	L	Slippery Rock (PA)	M
California State U. (Stanislaus)	M	Sonoma State (CA)	M
Carthage (WI)	R	South Dakota State U.	M
Central Connecticut	M	Southern Connecticut	M
Central Michigan	L	Southern Illinois U. (Carbondale)	L
Central Washington	L	Texas A&M (Corpus Christi)	M
Edinboro (PA)	M	Texas State U. (San Marcos)	L
π Elmhurst (IL)	R	Western Illinois	L
Frostburg (MD)	M	Wisconsin, U. of (Eau Claire)	L
++Indiana (PA)	L	Wisconsin, U. of (LaCrosse)	L
Indiana State	L	Wyoming, U. of	L
Keene State (NH)	R		
Louisiana Tech.	M	
Maine (Farmington)	R	

++ *Especially Regional Planning*
# *Geography and Geospatial Imaging*
π *Geography and Environmental Planning*

GEOLOGY

GROUP I
Most Selective

Amherst (MA)	R	Massachusetts, U. of	L
Bates (ME)	R	MIT (MA)	M
Binghamton (SUNY)(NY)	L	Michigan, U. of	XL
Bowdoin (ME)	R	Minnesota, U. of	XL
Brown (RI)	M	▲Mount Holyoke (MA)	R
▲Bryn Mawr (PA)	R	Oberlin (OH)	R
Bucknell (PA)	R	Pennsylvania, U. of	L
California Inst. of Tech.	S	Pennsylvania State	XL
California, U. of (Berkeley)	XL	Pomona (CA)	R
Carleton (MN)	R	Princeton (NJ)	M
Chicago, U. of (IL)	M	Rennselaer (NY)	M
Colgate (NY)	R	Rochester, U. of (NY)	M
Colorado Col.	R	Skidmore (NY)	R
Colorado School of Mines	R	▲Smith (MA)	R
Columbia (NY)	M	South, U. of the (TN)	R
Dartmouth (NH)	M	Union (NY)	R
Franklin & Marshall (PA)	R	Vanderbilt (TN)	M
Furman (SC)	R	Washington & Lee (VA)	R
Geneseo (SUNY) (NY)	M	Washington U. (MO)	M
Gustavus Adolphus (MN)	R	Whitman (WA)	R
Hamilton (NY)	R	William & Mary (VA)	M
Harvard (MA)	M	Williams (MA)	R
Lafayette (PA)	R	Yale (CT)	M
Lehigh (PA)	M		

GROUP II
Very Selective

Alaska, U. of (Fairbanks)	M	College of Charleston (SC)	L
Albany (SUNY) (NY)	L	Colorado State	L
Alabama, U. of	L	Colorado, U. of	L
Albion (MI)	R	Cornell Col. (IA)	R
Allegheny (PA)	R	Dayton, U. of (OH)	M
Arizona State	XL	Denison (OH)	R
Arizona, U. of	XL	Denver, U. of (CO)	M
Beloit (WI)	R	Earlham (IN)	R
Boise State (ID)	L	Eastern Washington	L
Bowling Green (OH)	L	Guilford (NC)	R
Brigham Young (UT)	XL	Hanover (IN)	R
California, U. of (Davis)	XL	Hope (MI)	R
California, U. of (Santa Barbara)	L		
Centenary College (LA)	S		

GROUP II continues next page

	Enrollment Code		
■ *Men Only*	S = Small (less than 1000 students)	R = Moderate (1000-3000 students)	M = Medium (3000-8000 students)
▲ *Women Only*	L = Large (8000-20,000 students)	XL = Extra Large (over 20,000 students)	

GEOLOGY, continued

·· ——————————— GROUP II, continued ——————————— ··

Houston, U. of XL	Purdue (IN) XL
Idaho, U. of L	Rhode Island, U. of.......................... L
Indiana U. XL	St. Lawrence (NY) .... R
Juniata (PA) .... R	St. Thomas (MN) .... M
Mary Washington (VA) .... M	San Diego State (CA) L
Michigan State XL	π South Carolina, U. of L
Michigan Tech .... M	South Dakota School of Mines .... R
Millsaps (MS) .... S	Stony Brook (SUNY) (NY) L
Minnesota, U. of (Duluth) .... M	Texas A&M XL
Minnesota, U. of (Morris) .... R	Texas Christian .... M
New Hampshire, U. of L	Texas, U. of (Austin) XL
New Mexico Inst. of Mining & Tech. ...... R	Tulsa, U. of (OK) .... M
New Mexico, U. of L	Utah, U. of L
North Carolina, U. of (Wilmington).. L	Vermont, U. of .... M
Ohio State XL	Washington, U. of............................ XL
Oklahoma, U. of XL	West Virginia U. L
Oklahoma State L	Wisconsin, U. of XL
Olivet Nazarene (IL) .... S	Wooster, College of (OH) .... R
Oregon State L	

π *Also Geophysics*

··· ——————————— GROUP III ——————————— ···
Selective

Bloomsburg (PA) .... M	Nevada, U. of (Reno) L
Brockport (SUNY)(NY) .... M	Nevada, U. of (Las Vegas) L
Brooklyn College (CUNY) (NY) L	New Mexico State U........................... L
California State U. (Bakersfield) .... M	North Carolina (Wilmington)............ M
California State U. (Chico) L	Northland (WI) .... S
California State U. (East Bay) .... M	Northern Arizona XL
California State U. (Sacramento) ...... M	Northern Illinois U. L
Edinboro (PA) .... M	Oneonta (SUNY)(NY) .... M
Emporia State (KS) .... M	Plattsburgh (SUNY)(NY) .... M
Fort Lewis (CO) .... M	Salem State (MA) .... M
Hartwick (NY).................................. R	Southern Oregon .... M
Hawaii, U. of (Hilo)......................... R	Texas A&M (Corpus Christi) .... M
Lamar (TX) .... M	West Chester (PA) .... M
Louisiana-Lafayette L	Western State Coll. of Colorado........ R
Louisiana State XL	Wisconsin, U. of (River Falls)........... M
Montana, U. of .... M	Wright State (OH) L
Muskingum (OH)............................. R	Wyoming, U. of................................ L

Enrollment Code

■ *Men Only*　　S = Small (less than 1000 students)　　R = Moderate (1000-3000 students)　　M = Medium (3000-8000 students)
▲ *Women Only*　　　L = Large (8000-20,000 students)　　XL = Extra Large (over 20,000 students)

HISTORY

● ━━━━━━━━━━ **GROUP I** ━━━━━━━━━━ ●
Most Selective

Albany (SUNY)(NY) L	Kenyon (OH) .... R
Albion (MI) .... R	Lafayette (PA) .... R
American (DC).......................... M	Lawrence (WI) .... R
Amherst (MA).......................... R	Lehigh (PA) .... M
▲Barnard (NY) .... R	Macalester (MN) .... R
Bates (ME) .... R	Maryland, U. of (Baltimore County) ... M
Binghamton (SUNY)(NY) L	MIT (MA) .... M
Boston Col. (MA).......................... L	Miami U. (OH) L
Boston U. (MA).......................... L	Michigan, U. of XL
Bowdoin (ME) .... R	Middlebury (VT) .... R
Brandeis (MA).......................... R	Minnesota, U. of XL
Brown (RI) .... M	Missouri, U. of (Rolla) .... M
▲Bryn Mawr (PA) .... S	▲Mount Holyoke (MA) .... R
Bucknell (PA) .... M	New College (FL) .... S
Buffalo (SUNY)(NY) L	New Jersey, College of .... M
California, U. of (Berkeley).......................... XL	New York U. L
California, U. of (Los Angeles) XL	North Carolina, U. of L
Carleton (MN).......................... R	Northwestern (IL) .... M
Carnegie Mellon (PA) .... M	Notre Dame (IN) .... M
Case Western Reserve (OH).......................... M	Oberlin (OH) .... R
Centre (KY) .... R	Pennsylvania, U. of L
Chicago, U. of (IL) .... M	Pennsylvania State XL
Claremont McKenna (CA) .... R	Pitzer (CA) .... S
Colgate (NY) .... R	Pomona (CA) .... R
Colorado Col. .... R	Princeton (NJ) .... M
Columbia (NY) .... M	Reed (OR) .... R
Connecticut Col. .... R	Rhodes (TN) .... R
Cornell (NY).......................... L	Rice (TX) .... M
Dallas, U. of (TX) .... R	Richmond, U. of (VA) .... M
Dartmouth (NH) .... M	Rochester, U. of (NY) .... M
Davidson (NC).......................... R	Rutgers (NJ).......................... L
DePauw (IN) .... R	St. Olaf (MN) .... R
Dickinson (PA) .... R	Sarah Lawrence (NY) .... R
Drew (NJ) .... R	▲Smith (MA) .... R
Duke (NC) .... M	South, U. of the (TN) .... R
Emory (GA) .... M	Southwestern (TX) .... R
Florida, U. of XL	Swarthmore (PA) .... R
Furman (SC) .... R	Texas Christian U. (TX) .... M
Geneseo (SUNY)(NY) .... M	Trinity (TX).......................... R
George Washington (DC) .... M	Tufts (MA) .... M
Georgetown (DC) .... M	Tulane (LA) .... M
Georgia Institute of Tech. L	Union (NY) .... R
Gettysburg (PA) .... R	U.S. Air Force Academy (CO).......................... M
Grinnell (IA).......................... R	U.S. Military Academy (NY) .... M
Hamilton (NY) .... R	Vanderbilt (TN) .... R
Harvard (MA).......................... M	Vassar (NY) .... R
Haverford (PA).......................... S	Virginia, U. of L
Holy Cross (MA) .... R	■Wabash (IN) .... S
Illinois, U. of (Urbana-Champaign) XL	Wake Forest (NC) .... M
James Madison (VA) L	Washington & Lee (VA) .... R
Johns Hopkins (MD) .... M	
Kalamazoo (MI) .... R	

GROUP I continues next page

HISTORY, continued

GROUP I, continued

▲Wellesley (MA) .... R
  Wesleyan U. (CT) .... R
  Wheaton (IL) .... R
  Whitman (WA) .... R

  William & Mary (VA) .... M
  Williams (MA) .... R
  Yale (CT) .... M
  Yeshiva (NY) .... R

GROUP II
Very Selective

▲Agnes Scott (GA) .... S
  Albion (MI) .... R
  Alfred (NY) .... R
  Allegheny (PA) .... R
  Alma (MI) .... R
  Arizona State XL
  Arizona, U. of XL
  Auburn (AL) L
  Augustana (IL) .... R
  Austin (TX) .... R
  Bard (NY) .... R
  Baylor (TX) .... M
  Beloit (WI) .... R
  Birmingham-Southern (AL) .... R
  Bryan (TN) .... S
  Bryn Athyn (PA) .... S
  California, U. of (Davis) XL
  California, U. of (Merced) .... R
  California, U. of (Riverside) L
  California, U. of (Santa Cruz) .... M
  Cal. Poly State U. (San Luis Obispo) L
  Calvin (MI) .... M
  Canisius (NY) .... M
  Christendom (VA) .... S
  Cincinnati, U. of (OH) L
  City College (CUNY)(NY) L
  Clark (MA) .... R
  Coe (IA) .... R
  Colorado U. of L
  Connecticut U. of XL
  Cornell College (IA) .... R
  Covenant (GA) .... S
  Delaware, U. of L
  Denison (OH) .... R
  DePaul (IL) L
  Denver, U. of (CO) .... M
  Drake (IA) .... M
  East Carolina L
  Eastern Michigan L
  Elmira (NY) .... R
  Erskine (SC) .... S

  Florida Atlantic L
  Florida State L
  Georgetown College (KY) .... R
  Georgia, U. of L
  Gonzaga (WA) .... R
  Goucher (MD) .... S
  Guilford (NC) .... R
  Gustavus Adolphus (MN) .... R
■Hampden-Sydney (VA) .... S
  Hamline (MN) .... R
  Hanover (IN) .... R
  Hawaii, U. of L
  Hillsdale (MI) .... R
  Hiram (OH) .... R
  Hobart & William Smith (NY) .... R
▲Hollins (VA) .... S
  Hood (MD) .... S
  Houghton (NY) .... S
  Howard (DC) .... M
  Idaho, College of .... S
  Illinois College .... S
  Illinois, U. of (Chicago) L
  Indiana U. XL
  Iowa, U. of XL
  John Carroll (OH) .... R
  Juniata (PA) .... R
  Kansas, U. of L
  Kansas State L
  Kentucky, U. of L
  Kentucky Wesleyan .... S
  Knox (IL) .... R
  Lake Forest (IL) .... R
  LeMoyne (NY) .... R
  Lewis & Clark (OR) .... R
  Linfield (OR) .... R
  Loras (IA) .... R
  Loyola (LA) .... R
  Loyola Marymount (CA) .... M
  Luther (IA) .... R
  Manhattanville (NY) .... R

GROUP II continues next page

Enrollment Code		
■ *Men Only* S = Small (less than 1000 students)	R = Moderate (1000-3000 students)	M = Medium (3000-8000 students)
▲ *Women Only* L = Large (8000-20,000 students)		XL = Extra Large (over 20,000 students)

HISTORY, continued

··━━━━━━━━━━━━ **GROUP II, continued** ━━━━━━━━━━━━··

Mansfield (PA) .... R
Marquette (WI) .... M
Maryland, U. of XL
+ Mary Washington (VA) .... M
Massachusetts, U. of L
Mass. College of Liberal Arts (N. Adams). R
McMurry (TX) .... R
Miami, U. of (FL) .... M
Michigan State XL
Millersville (PA) .... M
Millsaps (MS) .... S
Minnesota, U. of (Morris) .... R
Missouri, U. of XL
Missouri, U. of (Kansas City) .... M
Monmouth (IL) .... S
■ Morehouse (GA) .... R
Muhlenberg (PA) .... R
Nebraska, U. of L
New Mexico State U. L
New Orleans, U. of (LA) L
North Carolina (Asheville) .... R
Northeastern (MA) L
Oglethorpe (GA) .... S
Ohio State XL
Ohio U. L
Oklahoma, U. of XL
Oklahoma City U. .... R
Oklahoma State L
Oregon State L
Ozarks, College of the (MO) .... R
Pittsburgh, U. of (PA) L
Plattsburgh (SUNY)(NY) .... M
Portland, U. of (OR) .... R
Presbyterian (SC) .... R
Providence (RI) .... M
Purchase (SUNY)(NY) .... M
Queens (NC) .... R
Ramapo (NJ) .... M
Randolph-Macon (VA) .... R
Richard Stockton (NJ) .... M
Ripon (WI) .... S
Roanoke (VA) .... R
▲ Rosemont (PA) .... S
Rowan (NJ) .... M
Rutgers (Camden) (NJ) .... M
St. Joseph's (PA) .... R
St. John's/ St. Benedict (MN) .... R
St. Lawrence (NY) .... R
St. Mary's College of Maryland .... R
St. Michael's (VT) .... R
St. Norbert (WI) .... R

St. Scholastica (MN) .... R
St. Thomas (MN) .... R
San Diego State U. (CA) XL
Santa Clara U. (CA) .... M
Seattle U. (WA) .... R
Shepherd (WV) .... M
South Carolina, U. of L
South Florida, U. of L
Southern Methodist (TX) L
Spring Hill (AL) .... R
Stetson (FL) .... R
Stony Brook (SUNY)(NY) L
Susquehanna (PA) .... R
Temple (PA) L
Tennessee, U. of XL
Texas A&M XL
Texas Tech U. L
Texas, U. of (Austin) XL
Texas, U. of (Dallas) .... M
Trinity (CT) .... R
Tulsa, U. of (OK) .... M
Utah, U. of L
Vermont, U. of L
Virginia Tech. L
Virginia Military Institute .... R
Warren Wilson (NC) .... S
Wartburg (IA) .... R
Washington College (MD) .... S
Washington State L
Washington, U. of XL
Washington & Jefferson (PA) .... R
Webster (MO) .... R
Wells (NY) .... S
Western Carolina (NC) .... M
Western Michigan L
Westminster (MO) .... S
Westminster (UT) .... S
Wheaton (MA) .... R
Whittier (CA) .... R
Whitworth (WA) .... R
Willamette (OR) .... R
William Paterson (NJ) .... M
Winona State U. (MN) .... M
Winthrop (SC) .... M
Wisconsin, U. of XL
Wittenberg (OH) .... R
Wofford (SC) .... R
Wooster (OH) .... R
Xavier (OH) .... R

+ And Historic Preservation Major

HISTORY, continued

GROUP III
Selective

Akron, U. of (OH)	L
Alabama, U. of	L
Appalachian State (NC)	L
Arkansas, U. of	L
Assumption (MA)	R
Baldwin-Wallace (OH)	R
Baruch (CUNY)(NY)	L
Bellarmine (KY)	R
Boise State (ID)	L
Briar Cliff (IA)	R
Bridgewater (MA)	M
Bridgewater (VA)	R
Brockport (SUNY)(NY)	M
California State U. (Channel Islands)	R
California State U. (East Bay)	M
California State U. (Fullerton)	L
California State U. (Long Beach)	L
California State U. (San Marcos)	M
Campbell (NC)	R
Capital U. (OH)	R
Carroll (MT)	R
Carson-Newman (TN)	R
Central Connecticut	M
Charleston, U. of (WV)	S
Cumberland (KY)	R
Delaware State	R
East Tennessee	L
Eastern Connecticut	M
Fairmont State (WV)	M
Fitchburg (MA)	R
Fredonia (SUNY)(NY)	M
Georgia Southern	L
Graceland (IA)	R
Hastings (NE)	R
Heidelberg (OH)	S
Holy Names (CA)	S
Houston, U. of (TX)	L
Indiana (PA)	L
I.U. P.U.I. (IN)	L
Kennesaw State (GA)	R
Kutztown (PA)	M
Lambuth (TN)	S
Liberty (VA)	R
Lock Haven (PA)	M
Louisiana College	R
Louisiana State	XL

Manchester (IN)	R
▲ Mary Baldwin (VA)	S
Maryville (TN)	S
Massachusetts U. of (Boston)	M
McPherson (KS)	S
Middle Tennessee	L
Michigan, U. of	XL
Milligan (TN)	S
Misericordia (PA)	S
Mississippi, U. of	L
Montevallo (AL)	R
Morgan State (MD)	M
Mount St. Mary's (MD)	R
Murray State (KY)	M
Muskingum (OH)	R
Nevada, U. of (Las Vegas)	L
New Mexico, U. of	L
North Carolina (Greensboro)	M
Northern Colorado	L
Northern Illinois	L
Northern Iowa	L
Northwestern (IA)	S
Northwestern (MN)	R
Northwestern Louisiana	L
Oklahoma Baptist	R
Old Dominion (VA)	L
Oneonta (SUNY)(NY)	M
Oswego (SUNY)(NY)	M
Pittsburgh, U. of (Greenburg)	R
Quincy (IL)	R
Regis (CO)	R
Reinhardt (GA)	R
Rider (NJ)	R
Rhode Island College	M
St. Ambrose (IA)	R
St. Joseph's (ME)	S
St. Joseph's (NY)	R
St. Mary's (MN)	R
Salem State (MA)	M
Shenandoah (VA)	R
Shippensburg (PA)	M
Simpson (IA)	R
South Dakota, U. of	M
Southern Connecticut	M

GROUP III continues next page

HISTORY, continued

GROUP III, continued

Southern Illinois U. (Carbondale) L
Southern Mississippi L
Stephen F. Austin (TX) L
Tarleton State (TX) .... M
Texas A&M (Corpus Christi) .... M
Texas Lutheran .... R
Texas State U. (San Marcos) L
Texas, U. of (Arlington) L
Texas, U. of (San Antonio) L
Toledo, U. of L
Virginia Wesleyan .... R

Western St. Col. of Colorado .... R
West Kentucky L
West Virginia Wesleyan .... R
Western New England (MA) .... R
Wheeling Jesuit (WV) .... R
Wilkes (PA) .... R
Wilmington (OH) .... S
Wingate (NC) .... R
Wisconsin, U. of (Green Bay) .... M
Wisconsin, U. of (Milwaukee) L

HOME ECONOMICS/FAMILY STUDIES

GROUP I
Most Selective

Florida State	L	Penn State	XL
Iowa State	XL	Wisconsin, U. of	XL

GROUP II
Very Selective

Alabama, U. of	L	Northern Illinois U.	L
Auburn (AL)	L	Oklahoma State	L
# Bradley (IL)	M	Oneonta (SUNY) (NY)	M
Brigham Young (UT)	XL	Purdue (IN)	XL
Connecticut, U. of	XL	Rhode Island, U.of	L
Georgia, U. of	XL	▲ # St. Joseph's (CT)	S
➤ Kansas State	L	π Seattle Pacific (WA)	M
Masters (CA)	R	Utah, U. of	L
Michigan State	XL	Utah State	L
Nebraska, U. of	L	Western Michigan	L
New Hampshire, U. of	L	Wisconsin, U. of (Stout)	M

*Family & Consumer Science*
π *Apparel Design, also Clothing*
➤ *Nutritional & Exercise Sciences*

GROUP III
Selective

Akron, U. of (OH)	L	Nevada, U. of (Reno)	L
Berea (KY)	R	New Mexico State U.	L
California State U. (Fresno)	L	Nicholls State (LA)	M
California State U. (Sacramento)	M	Northwestern Louisiana	L
Central Michigan	L	North Carolina (Greensboro)	M
Eastern Illinois	L	North Dakota State	L
Framingham State (MA)	M	Oregon State	L
Georgia Southern	L	Point Loma (CA)	R
Marywood (PA)	R	Texas Tech. U.	L
Montclair State (NJ)	M	Washington State	L
Montevallo (AL)	R		

JOURNALISM/COMMUNICATIONS

GROUP I
Most Selective

American U. (DC) .... M	North Carolina, U. of L
Boston College (MA) L	Northeastern (MA) L
Boston U. (MA) L	Northwestern (IL) .... M
California, U. of (Los Angeles) XL	Ohio U. L
California, U. of (San Diego) L	# Pomona (CA) .... R
Creighton (NE) .... M	Renssalaer (NY) .... M
DePauw (IN) .... R	▲ # Scripps (CA) .... S
Florida, U. of XL	Southern California L
Illinois, U. of (Urbana-Champaign) XL	Southwestern (TX) .... R
# Kalamazoo (MI) .... R	Stanford (CA) .... M
Macalester (MN) .... R	Syracuse (NY) L
Miami, U. of (FL) L	Trinity (TX) .... R
Michigan, U. of XL	Villanova (PA) .... M
Minnesota, U. of XL	Washington & Lee (VA) .... R
Missouri, U. of XL	Wheaton (IL) .... R
New York U L	Wisconsin, U. of XL

GROUP II
Very Selective

Adelphi (NY) .... M	Emerson (MA) .... M
Alabama, U. of L	Fairfield (CT) .... M
Alabama, U. of (Huntsville) .... M	Flagler (FL) .... R
Alfred (NY) .... R	Florida Inst. of Tech. .... R
Alma (MI) .... R	Fordham (NY) .... M
Arizona State XL	Fredonia (SUNY) (NY) .... M
Arizona, U. of XL	Geneva (PA) .... R
Asbury (KY) .... R	George Mason (VA) L
Auburn (AL) L	Georgetown College (KY) .... R
Boise State (ID) L	Georgia State L
Bryan (TN) .... S	Georgia, U. of XL
California Poly. State U. (SLO) L	Gonzaga (WA) .... R
Canisius (NY) .... M	Hampton (VA) .... M
Capital (OH) .... R	Hanover (IN) .... R
Central Florida, U. of XL	Hastings (NE) .... R
Chapman (CA) .... R	Houston, U. of (TX) L
Charleston, College of (SC) L	Illinois College .... S
Clark (MA) .... R	Indiana State L
Clarke (IA) .... S	Indiana U. XL
Colorado, U. of L	Indiana U. of Pennsylvania L
Colorado, U. of (Colorado Springs) . M	Iowa, U. of XL
Columbia College Chicago (IL) .... M	Ithaca (NY) .... M
Connecticut, U. of XL	James Madison (VA) .... M
Dayton, U. of (OH) .... M	John Carroll (OH) .... M
Delaware, U. of L	Juniata (PA) .... R
Denver, U. of (CO) .... M	Kansas, U. of L
DePaul (IL) L	Kansas State L
Drake (IA) .... M	Kentucky, U. of L
Dubuque, U. of (IA) .... S	
Duquesne (PA) .... M	

*Media Studies*

GROUP II continues next page

JOURNALISM/COMMUNICATIONS, continued

•• ━━━━━━━━━━ GROUP II, continued ━━━━━━━━━━ ••

La Salle (PA)	M
LeMoyne (NY)	R
Linfield (OR)	R
Loras (IA)	R
Louisiana State	XL
Loyola (MD)	R
Loyola Marymount (CA)	M
Maine, U. of	L
Mansfield (PA)	M
Marist (NY)	M
π Marquette (WI)	M
Marshall (WV)	L
Mary Baldwin (VA)	S
Maryland, U. of	XL
Massachusetts, U. of	L
Master's (CA)	R
Memphis, U. of (TN)	L
Michigan State	L
Milligan (TN)	S
▲ Mills College (CA)	S
Minnesota, U. of (Duluth)	M
Mississippi, U. of	L
Mississippi U. for Women	R
Missouri, U. of (Kansas City)	M
Missouri State	L
Montana, U. of	M
Moravian (PA)	R
Muhlenberg (PA)	R
Nevada, U. of (Reno)	L
New Hampshire, U. of	L
North Central (IL)	R
North Florida	L
North Texas	L
Ohio State	XL
Ohio Wesleyan	R
Oklahoma, U. of	XL
Oregon, U. of	L
Oswego (SUNY)(NY)	M
Pennsylvania State	XL
Pepperdine (CA)	R
Pittsburgh, U. of (PA)	L
Plattsburgh (SUNY)(NY)	M
Purchase (SUNY)(NY)	M
Quinnipiac (CT)	R
Ramapo (NJ)	M
Randolph College (VA)	S

Rhode Island, U. of	L
Rowan (NJ)	M
St. Ambrose (IA)	R
St. Bonaventure (NY)	R
St. Cloud (MN)	L
St. Louis (MO)	M
St. Mary's (IN)	R
St. Michael's (VT)	R
St. Norbert (WI)	R
St. Thomas (MN)	M
San Diego State U. (CA)	XL
Santa Clara U. (CA)	M
Scranton, U. of (PA)	M
▲ Simmons (MA)	R
Slippery Rock (PA)	M
South Alabama	M
South Carolina, U. of	L
Southern Illinois U. (Carbondale)	L
Southern Methodist (TX)	M
Spring Hill (AL)	R
▲ Stephens (MO)	S
Suffolk (MA)	R
Susquehanna U. (PA)	R
Temple (PA)	L
Tennessee, U. of	XL
Texas A&M	S
Texas Christian U.	M
Texas, U. of (Arlington)	L
Texas, U. of (Austin)	XL
Tulsa, U. of (OK)	R
Virginia Tech.	L
Wartburg (IA)	R
Washington State	L
Webster (MO)	R
West Florida, U. of	M
West Virginia U.	L
Western Michigan	L
Western Washington U.	L
Westminster (UT)	R
Whitworth (WA)	R
Winona State U. (MN)	L
Wisconsin Lutheran	S
Wisconsin, U. of (Stevens Point)	M
Xavier (OH)	R
York (PA)	R

π *Especially Broadcasting*

JOURNALISM/COMMUNICATIONS continues next page

JOURNALISM/COMMUNICATIONS, continued

GROUP III
Selective

Akron, U. of (OH)	L		I.U. P.U.I. (IN)	L
▲ Alverno (WI)	R		Iona (NY)	M
Appalachian State (NC)	L		Jacksonville (FL)	R
Arkansas, U. of	L		Johnson C. Smith (NC)	R
Augsburg (MN)	R		▲ Judson (AL)	S
+ Azusa Pacific (CA)	R		Keene State (NH)	R
Ball State (IN)	L		Kent State (OH)	L
Bemidji State (MN)	M		Kentucky Wesleyan	S
Bethany (WV)	S		Lewis-Clark State (ID)	R
Bowling Green (OH)	L		Liberty (VA)	R
Bridgewater State (MA)	M		Lindenwood (MO)	M
Brockport (SUNY) (NY)	M		Louisiana-Monroe	M
Buena Vista (IA)	R		Loyola (IL)	M
Butler (IN)	R		Loyola U. (LA)	M
California Lutheran	R		Lynchburg (VA)	R
California State U. (Fullerton)	L		• Lyndon State (VT)	R
California State U. (Long Beach)	L		Marietta (OH)	R
California State U. (Northridge)	L		Marymount Manhattan (NY)	R
California State U. (Sacramento)	M		Mass. College of Lib. Arts (N. Adams)	R
California State U. (San Bernardino)	M		Minnesota, U. of (Duluth)	M
Castleton State (VT)	R		Misericordia, College (PA)	S
Central Missouri	L		Missouri Southern State	M
▲ Chatham (PA)	S		Missouri, U. of (St. Louis)	M
Dana (NE)	S		Monmouth (NJ)	R
East Tennessee	L		Montana, U. of	M
Eastern Connecticut	M		Morningside (IA)	S
Eastern Illinois	L		Montevallo (AL)	R
Eastern Kentucky	L		Mount Saint Vincent (NY)	R
Eastern New Mexico	R		Muskingum (OH)	R
Elon (NC)	R		Murray State (KY)	M
Endicott (MA)	R		Nebraska, U. of	L
Fitchburg (MA)	R		North Carolina, U. of (Greensboro)	M
Florida A&M	M		North Carolina, U. of (Pembroke)	R
Florida Southern	R		North Dakota, U. of	M
Fontbonne (MO)	R		Northern Illinois U.	L
Franklin (IN)	S		Northern Iowa	L
Gwynedd-Mercy (PA)	S		Northern Kentucky	L
Hardin-Simmons (TX)	R		Northwest Missouri State	M
Hartford, U. of (CT)	M		Oakland U. (MI)	M
Hawaii Pacific	M		Oklahoma City U.	R
Hofstra (NY)	M			
Howard (DC)	M			
Hunter (CUNY) (NY)	L			
Idaho, U. of	L			

+ *Media Studies*

• *Also Broadcasting, also Television Studies*

GROUP III continues next page

Enrollment Code			
■ *Men Only*	S = Small (less than 1000 students)	R = Moderate (1000-3000 students)	M = Medium (3000-8000 students)
▲ *Women Only*	L = Large (8000-20,000 students)	XL = Extra Large (over 20,000 students)	

JOURNALISM/COMMUNICATIONS, continued

• • • ━━━━━━━━━━━━━━━━ **GROUP III**, continued ━━━━━━━━━━━━━━━━ • • •

Otterbein (OH)	R
Palm Beach Atlantic (FL)	R
▲ Pine Manor (MA)	S
Point Park (PA)	R
Regis (CO)	R
Regis (MA)	S
Reinhardt (GA)	R
Rider (NJ)	R
Robert Morris (PA)	R
Roger Williams (RI)	M
Roosevelt (IL)	R
St. Edward's (TX)	M
St. John Fisher (NY)	R
St. John's (NY)	L
St. Mary's College (MN)	R
Samford (AL)	R
San Jose State (CA)	L
Seton Hall (NJ)	M
Southeast Missouri State	L
Southeastern Louisiana	L
Southern Connecticut	M

Southern Maine	M
Southern Utah	M
Tampa, U. of (FL)	R
Texas Wesleyan	R
Texas, U. of (El Paso)	L
Towson (MD)	L
Troy State (AL)	M
Virginia Wesleyan	R
Walla Walla (WA)	R
Waynesburg (PA)	R
Weber State (UT)	L
West Chester (PA)	M
Western Illinois	L
Western New England (MA)	R
Westfield (MA)	M
Wichita State (KS)	M
# Wilson (PA)	S
Wingate (NC)	R
Wisconsin, U. of (LaCrosse)	L
Wisconsin, U. of (Whitewater)	L
Worcester State (MA)	M

 # Equine Journalism

MATHEMATICS

GROUP I
Most Selective

▲Agnes Scott (GA)	M
Albany (SUNY)(NY)	L
Allegheny (PA)	R
American U. (DC)	M
▲Barnard (NY)	R
Bates (ME)	R
Binghamton (SUNY) (NY)	L
Boston U. (MA)	L
Bowdoin (ME)	R
Brandeis (MA)	R
▲Bryn Mawr (PA)	R
Bucknell (PA)	M
Buffalo (SUNY)(NY)	L
California Inst. of Tech.	S
California, U. of (Berkeley)	XL
California, U. of (Los Angeles)	XL
California, U. of (San Diego)	L
Carnegie Mellon (PA)	M
Carleton (MN)	R
Case Western Reserve U. (OH)	M
Chicago, U. of (IL)	M
Clarkson (NY)	M
Colby (ME)	R
Colgate (NY)	R
Colorado College	R
Colorado School of Mines	R
Columbia (NY)	M
Connecticut College	R
Cornell (NY)	L
Dartmouth (NH)	M
Davidson (NC)	R
Dickinson (PA)	R
Duke (NC)	M
Florida, U. of	XL
Geneseo (SUNY)(NY)	M
Georgia Inst. of Tech.	L
Grinnell (IA)	R
Harvard (MA)	M
Harvey Mudd (CA)	S
Haverford (PA)	S
Holy Cross (MA)	R
Illinois Inst. of Tech.	R
Illinois, U. of (Urbana-Champaign)	XL
Kenyon (OH)	R
Lehigh (PA)	M

Macalester (MN)	R
Maryland, U. of (Baltimore County)	M
Miami U. (OH)	L
Michigan, U. of	XL
MIT (MA)	M
Middlebury (VT)	R
▲Mount Holyoke (MA)	R
New College (FL)	S
New Jersey, College of	M
New Jersey Inst. of Tech.	M
New Mexico Inst. of Mining & Tech.	R
New York U.	L
Northeastern (MA)	L
Northwestern (IL)	M
Notre Dame (IN)	M
Oberlin (OH)	R
Occidental (CA)	R
Pennsylvania, U. of	L
Pepperdine (CA)	R
Pittsburgh, U. of (PA)	L
Pomona (CA)	R
Princeton (NJ)	M
Providence (RI)	M
Reed (OR)	R
Rensselaer (NY)	M
Rice (TX)	M
Richmond, U. of (VA)	M
Rhodes (TN)	R
Rochester, U. of (NY)	M
Rose-Hulman (IN)	R
Rutgers (NJ)	L
Skidmore (NY)	R
▲Smith (MA)	R
South, U. of the (TN)	R
Stanford (CA)	M
St. Lawrence U. (NY)	R
St. Louis (MO)	M
St. Mary's Col. of Maryland	R
St. Olaf (MN)	R
Stevens Inst. of Technology (NJ)	R
Swarthmore (PA)	R
Syracuse (NY)	L
Trinity (CT)	R

GROUP I continues next page

MATHEMATICS, continued

GROUP I, continued

Tufts (MA) .... M
Tulane (LA) .... M
Union (NY) .... R
United States Air Force Academy (CO) .. M
United States Military Academy (NY) .... M
United States Naval Academy (MD) ...... M
Ursinus (PA) .... R
Vassar (NY) .... R
Villanova (PA) .... M
Virginia, U. of L
Virginia Tech. L
■ Wabash (IN) .... S

Wake Forest (NC) .... M
Washington & Lee (VA) .... R
Washington U. (MO) .... M
▲ Wellesley (MA) .... R
Wesleyan (CT) .... R
Wheaton (IL) .... R
Whitman (WA) .... R
Willamette (OR) .... R
Wisconsin, U. of XL
Worcester Poly Inst. (MA) .... R
Yale (CT) .... M

GROUP II
Very Selective

Abilene Christian (TX) .... M
Adrian (MI) .... R
Alabama, U. of (Birmingham) .... M
Alabama, U. of (Huntsville) .... M
Albion (MI) .... R
Alfred (NY) .... R
Alma (MI) .... R
Arcadia (PA) .... R
Arkansas, U. of L
Arizona, U. of XL
Arizona State XL
Asbury (KY) .... R
Auburn (AL) L
Baylor (TX) .... M
Bellarmine (KY) .... R
Belmont (TN) .... R
Benedictine (IL) .... R
Bentley (MA) .... M
Birmingham-Southern (AL) .... R
Boise State (ID) L
Bowling Green (OH) L
Bryant (RI) .... R
California Poly. State U. (SLO) L
California, U. of (Davis) XL
California, U. of (Irvine) L
California, U. of (Riverside) L
California, U. of (Santa Cruz) .... M
Carroll (MT) .... R
Cincinnati, U. of (OH) L
College of Charleston (SC) L
Colorado, U. of L
Concordia (MN) .... R

Dayton, U. of (OH) .... M
DePaul (IL) L
Earlham (IN) .... R
Evansville (IN) .... R
Fairfield (CT) .... M
Florida Atlantic L
George Mason (VA) L
Grand Valley (MI) L
Hendrix (AR) .... R
Herbert Lehman (CUNY)(NY) .... M
Hiram (OH) .... R
Idaho, College of .... S
Illinois College .... S
Illinois, U. of (Chicago) L
James Madison (VA) L
John Carroll (OH) .... R
Juniata (PA) .... R
Kansas State L
Kennesaw State (GA) .... R
Knox (IL) .... R
Lafayette (PA) .... R
LaSalle (PA) .... M
Lebanon Valley (PA) .... R
Linfield (OR) .... R
Loyola (IL) .... M
Loyola Marymount (CA) .... M
Luther (IA) .... R
Lyon (AR) .... S
Manhattan (NY) .... M
Marist (NY) .... M

GROUP II continues next page

MATHEMATICS, continued

GROUP II, continued

Marquette (WI)	M
Mary Washington (VA)	M
Massachusetts, U. of (Lowell)	M
Michigan State	XL
Michigan Tech	M
Michigan, U. of (Dearborn)	M
Millsaps (MS)	S
Mississippi State	L
Missouri State	L
Montana State	L
Montana Tech.	R
Moravian (PA)	R
■ Morehouse (GA)	R
Muhlenberg (PA)	R
Nazareth (NY)	R
New Mexico State	L
Newman U. (KS)	S
North Carolina State	L
North Dakota, U. of	M
North Florida	L
Ohio Northern	R
Ohio State	XL
Ohio U.	L
Oklahoma, U. of	Xl
Oklahoma State	L
Oregon, U. of	L
Oregon State	L
Otterbein (OH)	R
Pacific, U. of the (CA)	M
Portland, U. of (OR)	R
Potsdam (SUNY) (NY)	M
Principia (IL)	S
Puerto Rico, U. of (Mayaguez)	L
Purdue (IN)	XL
Ramapo (NJ)	M
Rhode Island, U. of	L
Richard Stockton (NJ)	M
Ripon (WI)	R
Roanoke (VA)	R
Rochester Inst. of Tech.	L
Rockhurst (MO)	R
Rowan (NJ)	M
Rutgers (Camden) (NJ)	M
St. Bonaventure (NY)	R

St. Cloud (MN)	L
St. Edward's (TX)	M
St. Joseph's (PA)	R
St. Norbert (WI)	R
Salisbury (MD)	M
Samford (AL)	R
San Diego, U. of (CA)	M
Schreiner (TX)	S
Scranton (PA)	M
Seattle U. (WA)	R
Shippensburg (PA)	M
▲ Simmons (MA)	R
South Carolina, U. of	L
South Dakota School of Mines	R
Southern California, U. of	L
▲ Spelman (GA)	R
Stetson (FL)	R
Stony Brook (SUNY)(NY)	L
▲ Sweet Briar (VA)	S
Temple (PA)	L
Tennessee Tech	M
Texas A&M (Kingsville)	M
Texas, U. of (Austin)	XL
Towson (MD)	L
Transylvania (KY)	R
▲ Trinity (DC)	S
Truman State (MO)	M
Utah, U. of	L
Utah State	L
Valparaiso (IN)	M
Vermont, U. of	M
Virginia Military Institute	R
Virginia Tech.	L
Washburn (KS)	M
Wells (NY)	S
Western New England (MA)	R
Washington, U. of	XL
Wheaton (MA)	R
Winthrop (SC)	M
Wisconsin Lutheran	S
Wofford (SC)	R
Wooster (OH)	R

MATHEMATICS continues next page

Enrollment Code		
■ *Men Only*	S = Small (less than 1000 students)	R = Moderate (1000-3000 students)	M = Medium (3000-8000 students)
▲ *Women Only*	L = Large (8000-20,000 students)	XL = Extra Large (over 20,000 students)

MATHEMATICS, continued

GROUP III
Selective

Aquinas (MI)	R	Millersville (PA)	M
Averett (VA)	S	Minnesota State U. (Moorhead)	M
Baldwin-Wallace (OH)	R	Monmouth (NJ)	R
Ball State (IN)	L	Montana, U. of	M
▲ Bennett (NC)	S	Montana State (Billings)	R
Bloomsburg (PA)	M	Montclair State (NJ)	M
Bluffton (OH)	S	Montevallo (AL)	R
Briar Cliff (IA)	R	Mount St. Joseph (OH)	R
California State U. (Channel Islands)	R	Murray State (KY)	M
California State U. (Dominguez Hills)	M	North Dakota State	L
California State U. (Monterey Bay)	R	Northeastern State (OK)	L
California State U. (San Jose)	L	Northern Illinois U.	L
Christopher Newport (VA)	M	Northern State (OK)	L
City College (CUNY)(NY)	L	Northern Colorado	L
Clark Atlanta (GA)	M	Northern Iowa	L
Colorado, U. of (Denver)	M	Northern Kentucky	L
East Carolina	L	Northern Michigan	M
East Tennessee	L	Northwestern Louisiana	L
Eastern Connecticut	M	Norwich (VT)	R
Eastern Illinois	L	Oakland (MI)	M
Eastern Washington	L	Ozarks, College of the (MO)	R
Findlay (OH)	M	Penn State (Erie)(PA)	M
Fisk (TN)	S	Pittsburgh, U. of (Bradford)	R
Fitchburg (MA)	R	Pittsburgh, U. of (Johnstown)	R
Fontbonne (MO)	R	Plymouth State (NH)	M
Georgia State	L	Radford (VA)	M
High Point (NC)	R	Rhode Island College	M
Humboldt State (CA)	M	Rider (NJ)	R
Indiana (PA)	L	Saginaw Valley (MI)	M
Indiana State	L	St. John's (NY)	L
I.U. P.U.I. (IN)	L	St. Joseph's (NY)	R
Lewis-Clark State (ID)	R	St. Mary's U. of San Antonio (TX)	R
Long Island U. (C.W. Post)(NY)	M	St. Peter's (NJ)	R
Louisiana-Lafayette	L	Shawnee State (OH)	R
Louisiana State	XL	Simpson (IA)	R
Lynchburg (VA)	R	South Dakota, U. of	M
Malone (OH)	R	South Dakota State U.	M
Marshall (WV)	L	Southern Connecticut	M
▲ Meredith (NC)	R	Southern Mississippi	L
Messiah (PA)	R	Southern Oregon State U.	M
Middle Tennessee	L		
Midwestern State U. (TX)	M		

GROUP III continues next page

MATHEMATICS, continued

GROUP III, continued

Southern Polytechnic (GA)	R	Texas, U. of (El Paso)	L
Southern Utah	M	Texas, U. of (San Antonio)	L
Tarleton State (TX)	M	Texas, U. of (Tyler)	R
Taylor (IN)	R	Tuskegee (AL)	M
Tennessee, U. of (Chattanooga)	M	Weber State (UT)	L
Tennessee, U. of (Martin)	M	Western Carolina (NC)	M
Texas A&M (Corpus Christi)	M	Wheeling Jesuit (WV)	R
Texas State U. (San Marcos)	L	Wilkes (PA)	R
Texas Tech. U.	L	Wisconsin, U. of (Eau Claire)	L
Texas, U, of (Arlington)	L	Wisconsin, U. of (Stevens Point)	M

MUSIC

• ━━━━━━━━━━━━━ **GROUP I** ━━━━━━━━━━━━━ •
Most Selective

▲Barnard (NY) .... R
 Beloit (WI) .... R
 Binghamton (SUNY)(NY) L
 Boston College (MA) L
 Boston U. (MA) L
 Bowdoin (ME) .... R
 Brandeis (MA) .... R
 Bucknell (PA) .... R
 Buffalo (SUNY)(NY) L
 California, U. of (Berkeley) XL
 California, U. of (Los Angeles) XL
 California, U. of (San Diego) L
 Carleton (MN).............................. R
 Carnegie-Mellon (PA) .... M
 Case Western Reserve U. (OH) .... M
 Chicago, U. of (IL) .... M
 Cleveland Inst. of Music (OH) .... S
 Colby (ME) .... R
 Columbia (NY) .... M
 Connecticut College .... R
π DePauw (IN) .... R
 Florida, U. of XL
 Furman (SC) .... R
 Geneseo (SUNY) (NY)..................... M
 Gustavus Adolphus (MN) .... R
 Harvard (MA) .... M
 Illinois, U. of (Urbana-Champaign) XL
 Illinois Wesleyan .... R
 Indiana U. XL
 Iowa, U. of XL
 Johns Hopkins (MD) .... M
 Juilliard (NY)............................... S
 Kalamazoo (MI) .... R
 Kenyon (OH) .... R
 Knox (IL).................................... R
 Lawrence (WI) .... R
 Manhattan School of Music (NY) ...... S

 Mannes School of Music (NY) .... S
 Miami, U. of (FL) L
 Miami U. (OH) L
 Michigan, U. of XL
 Minnesota, U. of XL
▲Mount Holyoke (MA) .... R
 New York U. L
 Northwestern (IL) .... M
 Oberlin (OH) .... R
 Pennsylvania State XL
 Pomona (CA) .... R
 Princeton (NJ) .... M
 Rhodes (TN) .... R
 Rice (TX) .... M
 Rochester, U. of (NY) .... M
 Rutgers (NJ) L
 Sarah Lawrence (NY) .... R
▲Scripps (CA) .... S
 Skidmore (NY) .... R
▲Smith (MA) .... R
 Southern California, U. of L
 Southwestern (TX) .... R
 Stanford (CA) .... M
 St. John's (MN) .... R
 St. Mary's College of Maryland .... R
 St. Olaf (MN) .... R
 Swarthmore (PA) .... R
 Texas, U. of (Austin) XL
 Vanderbilt (TN) .... M
 Vassar (NY) .... R
 Virginia, U. of L
 Wheaton (IL) .... R
 Whitman (WA) .... R
 Willamette (OR) .... R
 Wisconsin, U. of XL
 Yale (CT) .... M

π *Music and Music Business*

MUSIC continues next page

	Enrollment Code	
■ *Men Only*	S = Small (less than 1000 students) R = Moderate (1000-3000 students) M = Medium (3000-8000 students)	
▲ *Women Only*	L = Large (8000-20,000 students) XL = Extra Large (over 20,000 students)	

| **MUSIC, continued** |

Alabama, U. of	L	Drake (IA)	M
Alaska Pacific	S	Drury (MO)	R
Arizona State	XL	Elizabethtown (PA)	R
π Asbury (KY)	R	Evansville (IN)	R
Augustana (IL)	R	Florida State	L
Augustana (SD)	M	π Florida Southern	R
Bard (NY)	R	π Fredonia (SUNY) (NY)	M
Baylor (TX)	M	Georgia State	L
Bemidji State (MN)	M	Georgia, U. of	L
Bennington (VT)	S	Gordon (MA)	R
π Berklee College of Music (MA)	R	Harding (AR)	M
Birmingham-Southern (AL)	R	Hiram (OH)	R
Boise State (ID)	L	Hofstra (NY)	M
Boston Conservatory	S	Hope (MI)	R
Brigham Young (UT)	L	Houghton (NY)	S
Bryan (TN)	S	Houston Baptist (TX)	R
Butler (IN)	R	Houston, U. of (TX)	L
Cal. Inst. of the Arts	S	Idaho, College of	S
California, U. of (Riverside)	L	Idaho, U. of	L
California, U. of (Santa Barbara)	L	Illinois, U. of (Chicago)	L
California, U. of (Santa Cruz)	M	Iowa State	XL
Cal. Poly. State U. (San Luis Obispo)	L	Ithaca (NY)	M
Capital (OH)	R	James Madison (VA)	L
Catholic U. (DC)	M	▲ Judson (AL)	S
Centenary (LA)	S	Kansas State	L
Central (IA)	R	Kansas, U. of	L
Central Florida	XL	Kentucky, U. of	L
Chapman (CA)	R	Lake Forest (IL)	R
Cincinnati, U. of	L	π Lebanon Valley (PA)	R
Clark (MA)	R	Lewis & Clark (OR)	R
Clarke (IA)	S	Linfield (OR)	R
Coe (IA)	R	Louisiana State	XL
Colorado, U. of	L	Loyola (IL)	M
Concordia (CA)	R	Luther (IA)	R
Concordia (MN)	R	Maine, U. of	M
▲ Converse (SC)	S	Manhattanville (NY)	R
Cornish (WA)	S	Maryland, U. of	XL
Covenant (GA)	S	Maryville (TN)	S
Creighton (NE)	M	Massachusetts, U. of	L
Curtis Institute of Music (PA)	S	Masters (CA)	R
Dayton, U. of (OH)	M	McDaniel (MD)	R
Denison (OH)	R	Mercer (GA)	R
π Denver, U. of	R		
DePaul (IL)	L		

π *Music and Music Business*

GROUP II continues next page

MUSIC, continued

•• ─────────────── GROUP II, continued ─────────────── ••

Michigan State	XL
Milliken (IL)	R
▲ Mills (CA)	S
Millsaps (MS)	S
Missouri, U. of	XL
Missouri, U. of (Kansas City)	M
Mobile, U. of (AL)	R
Moravian (PA)	R
Morningside (IA)	S
Murray State (KY)	M
π Nazareth (NY)	R
Nebraska, U. of	L
New England Conservatory (MA)	S
New Hampshire, U. of	L
North Carolina School of the Arts	S
North Florida	L
North Texas	L
Northwestern (MN)	R
Ohio State	XL
Ohio U.	L
π Oklahoma City U.	R
Oklahoma State	L
Olivet Nazarene (IL)	R
π Oneonta (SUNY)(NY)	M
Oregon, U. of	L
Pacific Lutheran (WA)	R
Pacific, U. of the (CA)	R
Point Loma (CA)	R
Portland State (OR)	L
π Potsdam (SUNY) (NY)	M
Purchase (SUNY) (NY)	M
π Puget Sound (WA)	R
Queens (NC)	R
Queens (CUNY)(NY)	L
Redlands, U. of (CA)	R
Rhode Island, U. of	L

Roanoke (VA)	R
Rowan (NJ)	M
▲ Salem College (NC)	S
San Francisco Conservatory (CA)	S
Santa Clara U. (CA)	M
Shepherd (WV)	M
Silver Lake (WI)	S
South Carolina, U. of	L
Southern Methodist (TX)	L
St. Ambrose (IA)	R
▲ St. Catherine (MN)	R
Stetson (FL)	R
Stony Brook (SUNY)(NY)	L
Susquehanna (PA)	R
Syracuse (NY)	L
Temple (PA)	M
Texas Christian	M
Texas Tech U.	L
Transylvania (KY)	R
Tulsa, U. of (OK)	M
Utah, U. of	L
Utah State	L
Valparaiso (IN)	R
Wartburg (IA)	R
Washington, U. of	XL
Webster (MO)	R
Wells (NY)	S
West Chester (PA)	M
West Virginia, U. of	L
Western Michigan	L
π Whitworth (WA)	R
William Jewell Col. (MO)	R
Wisconsin Lutheran	S
Wittenberg (OH)	R
Wooster, College of (OH)	R

π *Music and Music Business*

MUSIC continues next page

Enrollment Code		
■ *Men Only*	S = Small (less than 1000 students) R = Moderate (1000-3000 students) M = Medium (3000-8000 students)	
▲ *Women Only*	L = Large (8000-20,000 students) XL = Extra Large (over 20,000 students)	

MUSIC, continued

GROUP III
Selective

Alderson-Broaddus (WV) .... S
▲ Alverno (WI) .... R
Anderson (IN) .... R
Andrews (MI) .... R
Anna Maria (MA) .... S
Aquinas (MI) .... R
Arkansas, U. of L
Arts, U. of the (PA) .... R
➤ Azusa Pacific (CA) .... R
Baker (KS) .... R
π Baldwin-Wallace (OH) .... R
Belhaven (MS) .... S
➤ Belmont (TN) .... R
Benedictine (KS) .... R
Berea (WV) .... R
Bethany (KS) .... S
Bethany (WV) .... R
Bethel (IN) .... R
Bethel (KS) .... S
Bowling Green (OH) L
Bluffton (OH) .... S
Brenau (GA) .... R
Briar Cliff (IA) .... R
Bridgewater (VA) .... R
Brooklyn (CUNY)(NY) L
California State U. (East Bay) .... M
California State U. (Fresno) L
California State U. (Fullerton) L
California State U. (Long Beach) L
California State U. (Northridge) L
California State U. (Sacramento) ...... M
California State U. (San Jose) L
Carson-Newman (TN) .... R
Carthage (WI) .... R
Cedarville (OH) .... R
Central Connecticut .... M
Central Michigan L
Central Oklahoma L
Central Washington L
Charleston Southern (SC) .... R
Christopher Newport (VA) .... M
Coker (SC) .... S
Columbia College (SC) .... R
Cumberland (KY) .... R
Dana (NE) .... S
Doane (NE) .... S
Duquesne (PA) .... M
East Carolina L
Eastern Michigan L

Edgewood (WI) .... S
π Elmhurst (IL) .... R
➤ Five Towns College (NY) .... S
Fort Hays (KS) .... M
Friends (KS) .... R
π Full Sail U. (FL) .... M
Goshen (IN) .... R
Hannibal-La Grange (MO) .... R
Hardin-Simmons (TX) .... R
Hartford, U. of (CT) .... M
Hartwick (NY) .... R
Hastings (NE) .... S
Heidelberg (OH) .... R
Holy Names (CA) .... S
Huntingdon (AL) .... S
Huntington (IN) .... S
Illinois State L
Immaculata (PA) .... S
Indiana (PA) L
Indiana State L
Jacksonville (FL) .... R
Jacksonville State (AL) .... M
John Brown (AR) .... R
Johnson State (VT) .... R
Keene State (NH) .... R
Kent State (OH) L
Kentucky Wesleyan .... R
Kutztown (PA) .... M
Lenoir-Rhyne (NC) .... R
Lock Haven (PA) .... M
Long Island U. (C.W. Post)(NY) .... M
Longwood (VA) .... R
Louisiana College .... R
Louisiana-Lafayette L
Louisiana- Monroe .... M
Louisville (KY) L
π Loyola (LA) .... M
Lynchburg (VA) .... R
Malone (OH) .... R
Mansfield (PA) .... R
Marywood (PA) .... R
Massachusetts, U. of (Boston) .... M
Massachusetts, U. of (Lowell) .... M
McPherson (KS) .... S
Memphis, U. of (TN) L

➤ *Music Business*

π *Music and Music Business*

GROUP III continues next page

MUSIC, continued

•••━━━━━━━━━━ GROUP III, continued ━━━━━━━━ •••

▲ Meredith (NC) .... R
π Middle Tennessee L
  Milligan (TN) .... S
π Minnesota State U. (Moorhead) .... M
  Minnesota, U. of (Duluth) .... M
  Mississippi College .... R
  Missouri Baptist .... M
π Monmouth (NJ) .... R
  Montana, U. of .... M
  Montclair State (NJ) .... M
  Montevallo (AL) .... R
π Montreat (NC) .... S
  Mount St. Joseph (OH) .... R
  Mount St. Mary's (CA) .... R
  Mount Union (OH) .... R
  Muskingum (OH) .... R
  Nevada, U. of (Las Vegas) L
  Nevada, U. of (Reno) L
  New Mexico State U. L
  Northern Colorado L
  Northern Illinois L
  Northern Kentucky L
  Northwestern College (IA) .... R
  Northwestern Louisiana L
  Nyack (NY) .... R
  Oakland City U. (IN) .... R
  Oklahoma Baptist .... R
  Oral Roberts (OK) .... M
π Otterbein (OH) .... R
  Ouachita (AR) .... R
  Peru State (NE) .... R
  Philadelphia Biblical (PA) .... S
  Pittsburg State (KS) .... M
  Reinhardt (GA) .... R
  Rhode Island College .... M
  Rider (NJ) .... M
  Rocky Mountain (MT) .... S
  Roosevelt (IL) .... R
  Samford (AL) .... R
  San Francisco State (CA) L
  Seton Hill (PA) .... S
  Shenandoah (VA) .... R
  Shorter (GA) .... R
  Simpson (IA) .... R

  Slippery Rock (PA) .... M
  Sonoma State (CA) .... M
  South Dakota, U. of .... M
  South Florida, U. of L
  Southeast Missouri State L
  Southeastern Louisiana L
π Southern Illinois U. (Carbondale) L
  Southern Maine .... M
  Southern Mississippi L
π Southern Nazarene (OK) .... R
π Southern Oregon .... M
  Southern Utah .... M
  Southwest Baptist (MO) .... R
  Southwestern (KS) .... S
  Southwestern Oklahoma .... M
  Stephen F. Austin (TX) L
  Sterling (KS) .... S
  Tampa, U. of (FL) .... R
  Tarleton State (TX) .... M
  Taylor (IN) .... R
  Tennessee, U. of (Chattanooga) .... M
  Tennessee Tech .... M
  Texas Lutheran .... R
  Texas State U. (San Marcos) L
  Texas, U. of (El Paso) L
  Texas, U. of (San Antonio) L
  Towson (MD) L
  Truman State (MO) .... M
  Union University (TN) .... R
  Virginia Commonwealth L
  Viterbo (WI) .... R
  Wayne State (MI) L
  Weber State (UT) L
  Western Carolina (NC) .... M
  Western Connecticut .... M
π Western Illlinois L
  Western St. Coll. of Colorado .... R
  Westfield (MA) .... M
π William Paterson (NJ) .... M
  Wingate (NC) .... R
π Wisconsin, U. of (Stevens Point) ...... M
  Wisconsin, U. of (Superior) .... M
  Xavier U. of Louisiana .... R

π *Music and Music Business*

NURSING

GROUP I
Most Selective

Binghamton (SUNY) (NY) L	Miami, U. of (FL) L
Boston Col. (MA) L	Missouri, U. of XL
Buffalo (SUNY)(NY) L	New York U. L
Case Western Reserve U. (OH) .... M	North Carolina, U. of L
Colorado, U. of L	Northern Michigan .... M
Columbia (NY) .... M	Pennsylvania, U. of L
Emory (GA) .... M	Rutgers (NJ) L
Florida, U. of XL	St. Olaf (MN) .... R
Georgetown (DC) .... M	Vanderbilt (TN) .... M
Gustavus Adolphus (MN) .... R	Villanova (PA) .... M
Illinois, U. of XL	Virginia, U. of L
Illinois Wesleyan .... R	Washington, U. of XL
Johns Hopkins (MD) .... M	Wisconsin, U. of L

GROUP II
Very Selective

Adelphi (NY) .... M	Florida Atlantic L
Alabama, U. of L	Florida Gulf Coast U. .... M
Alabama, U. of (Huntsville) .... M	Florida International L
Arizona, U. of XL	Franciscan U. of Steubenville (OH) .... R
Augustana (SD) .... R	George Mason (VA) .... M
Barry (FL) .... R	Gwynedd-Mercy (PA) .... S
Baylor (TX) .... M	Harding (AR) .... M
Belmont (TN) .... R	Hope (MI) .... R
Bethel (MN) .... R	Houston Baptist (TX) .... R
Brigham Young (UT) XL	Hunter (CUNY) (NY) L
Bradley (IL) .... M	Illinois, U. of (Chicago) L
Calvin (MI) .... R	Indiana U. XL
Capital (OH) .... R	Indiana U. of Pennsylvania L
Carroll (WI) .... R	Iowa, U. of XL
Catholic U. (DC) .... M	Kansas, U. of L
Cincinnati, U. of (OH) L	Kentucky, U. of L
Clarke (IA) .... S	LaSalle (PA) .... M
Coe (IA) .... R	Lebanon Valley (PA) .... R
Connecticut, U. of XL	Lipscomb (TN) .... R
Creighton (NE) .... M	Louisiana-Lafayette L
Daemen (NY) .... R	Louisville (KY) L
Delaware, U. of L	Loyola (IL) .... M
Detroit Mercy (MI) .... M	Luther (IA) .... R
Duquesne (PA) .... M	Maine, U. of L
Elmira (NY) .... R	
Evansville (IN) .... R	➤ *Health Policy, also*
Fairfield (CT) .... M	*GROUP II continues next page*

NURSING, continued

GROUP II, continued

Marquette (WI)	M
➤ Maryland, U. of (Baltimore County)	M
Massachusetts, U. of	L
McKendree (IL)	R
McMurry (TX)	R
Mercer (GA)	R
Michigan State	XL
Michigan, U. of	XL
Milwaukee Sch. of Engine (WI)	R
Minnesota, U. of	XL
Mississippi U. for Women	R
Missouri, U. of (St. Louis)	M
Mobile, U. of (AL)	R
Montana Tech.	R
Moravian (PA)	R
Morningside (IA)	S
Mount Mercy (IA)	S
Nazareth (NY)	R
New Hampshire, U. of	L
New Jersey, College of	M
New Mexico, U. of	L
North Dakota, U. of	M
North Florida	L
Northeastern (MA)	L
Ohio Northern	R
Ohio State	XL
Ohio U.	L
Pace (NY)	M
Pacific Lutheran (WA)	R
Pennsylvania State	XL
Pittsburgh, U. of (PA)	L
Portland, U. of (OR)	R
Purdue (IN)	XL
Quinnipiac (CT)	R
Rockhurst (MO)	R
Rutgers-Newark (NJ)	M
Samford (AL)	R
San Diego, U. of (CA)	M
San Francisco, U. of (CA)	M

Scranton (PA)	M
Seattle Pacific (WA)	R
Seton Hall (NJ)	M
Shepherd (WV)	M
▲ Simmons (MA)	R
South Carolina, U. of	L
South Dakota State U.	M
Spring Hill (AL)	R
St. Anselm (NH)	R
▲ St. Catherine (MN)	R
St John's/St. Benedict (MN)	R
St. Louis (MO)	M
▲ St. Mary's College (IN)	R
Tennessee, U. of	XL
Tennessee, U. of (Chattanooga)	M
Tennessee, U. of (Martin)	M
Texas Christian U.	M
Texas, U. of (Health Sci. Ctr.-S. Antonio)	R
Toledo, U. of (OH)	L
Truman State (MO)	M
Union University (TN)	R
Valparaiso U. (IN)	M
Vermont, U. of	M
Viterbo (WI)	R
Virginia Commonwealth	L
Wagner (NY)	R
Washington State	L
Webster (MD)	R
West Virginia U.	L
Western Michigan	L
Westminster (UT)	R
Widener (PA)	R
William Jewell (MO)	R
Winona State U. (MN)	M
Wisconsin, U. of (Milwaukee)	XL
Wyoming, U. of	M
Xavier (OH)	R
York (PA)	M

NURSING continues next page

Enrollment Code		
■ *Men Only*	S = Small (less than 1000 students)	R = Moderate (1000-3000 students)	M = Medium (3000-8000 students)
▲ *Women Only*	L = Large (8000-20,000 students)	XL = Extra Large (over 20,000 students)

NURSING, continued

GROUP III
Selective

Abilene Christian (TX)	M
Akron, U. of (OH)	L
Alabama, U. of (Birmingham)	M
Alabama, U. of (Huntsville)	M
Alaska, U. of (Anchorage)	M
Alaska, U. of (Fairbanks)	M
Alderson-Broaddus (WV)	S
▲ Alverno (WI)	R
Andrews (MI)	R
Arizona State	XL
Avila (MO)	S
Azusa Pacific (CA)	R
Baker (KS)	R
Ball State (IN)	L
Bellarmine (KY)	R
Berea (KY)	R
Bethel (IN)	R
Bethel (KS)	S
Bloomsburg (PA)	M
Boise State (ID)	L
Brenau (GA)	R
Briar Cliff (IA)	R
Brockport (SUNY)(NY)	M
California (PA)	M
California State U. (Bakersfield)	M
California State U. (Chico)	L
California State U. (Dominguez Hills)	M
California State U. (Fresno)	L
California State U. (Fullerton)	L
California State U. (Los Angeles)	L
California State U. (San Jose)	L
Carroll (MT)	R
Carson-Newman (TN)	R
▲ Cedar Crest (PA)	S
Cedarville (OH)	R
Central Arkansas	M
Central Missouri	L
Charleston, U. of (WV)	S
Colby-Sawyer (NH)	S
Colorado, U. of (Colorado Springs)	M
DeSales (PA)	R
Dillard (LA)	R
Dixie State (UT)	M
Dominican (CA)	S
D'Youville (NY)	R
East Carolina (NC)	L
East Stroudsburg (PA)	M
East Tennessee	L
Eastern (PA)	R
Eastern Kentucky	L
Eastern Mennonite (VA)	R
Eastern Michigan	L

Eastern Oregon	R
Eastern Washington	L
Edgewood (WI)	S
Elmhurst (IL)	R
Elms (MA)	S
Emporia State (KS)	M
Fairmont State (WV)	M
Ferris State (MI)	L
Fitchburg (MA)	R
Fort Hays (KS)	M
Gannon (PA)	M
Georgia Southern	L
Georgia Southwestern	R
Georgia State	L
Goshen (IN)	R
Graceland (IA)	R
Grambling (LA)	M
Hardin-Simmons (TX)	R
Hartwick (NY)	R
Hawaii Pacific	M
Henderson State (AR)	M
Herbert Lehman (CUNY)(NY)	M
Holy Names (CA)	S
Howard (DC)	M
Husson (ME)	S
Idaho State	L
Immaculata (PA)	S
Ind.U.-Purdue U.-Indianapolis (IN)	L
Jacksonville (FL)	R
Jacksonville State (AL)	M
Jamestown (ND)	R
Kansas Wesleyan	S
Kean (NJ)	M
Kennesaw State (GA)	R
Kent State (OH)	L
King (TN)	S
Lamar (TX)	M
Lenoir-Rhyne (NC)	R
Lewis-Clark State (ID)	R
Liberty (VA)	R
Long Island U. (Brooklyn)(NY)	M
Louisiana College	R
MacMurray (IL)	S
Malone (OH)	R
Marshall (WV)	L
Marymount (VA)	R
Maryville (St. Louis) (MO)	R
Massachusetts, U. of (Boston)	M
Massachusetts, U. of (Dartmouth)	M
Massachusetts, U. of (Lowell)	M
Memphis, U. of (TN)	L

GROUP III continues next page

NURSING, continued

••• ─────────── **GROUP III, continued** ─────────── •••

Mercy (NY) .... M	St. Joseph's (ME) .... S
Middle Tennessee L	St. Mary, College of (NE) .... S
Midwestern State U. (TX) .... M	# St. Scholastica (MN) .... R
Milligan (TN) .... R	Salem State (MA) .... M
Millikin (IL) .... R	San Diego State (CA) L
Misericordia, College (PA) .... S	Seattle U. (WA) .... R
Mississippi College .... R	Shawnee State (OH) .... R
Missouri Southern State .... M	Shenandoah (VA) .... R
Molloy (NY) .... R	Sonoma State (CA) .... M
Montana State L	South Alabama .... M
Mount St. Joseph (OH) .... R	South Dakota, U. of .... M
Mount St. Mary's (CA) .... R	South Florida, U. of L
Mount St. Mary's (NY) .... S	Southeastern Louisiana L
Mount Saint Vincent (NY) .... R	Southern Illinois U. (Edwardsville) L
Murray State (KY) .... M	Southern Maine, U. of .... M
Nevada, U. of (Las Vegas) L	Southern Mississippi L
Nevada, U. of (Reno) L	Southern Nazarene (OK) .... R
Newman U. (KS) .... S	Southern Utah .... M
New Mexico State U. L	Southwest Baptist (MO) .... R
Nicholls State (LA) .... M	Southwestern (KS) .... S
North Carolina, U. of (Charlotte) L	Southwestern Oklahoma .... M
North Carolina, U. of (Greensboro) ...... M	Stevenson (MD) .... R
North Carolina, U. of (Wilmington) L	Tampa, U. of (FL) .... R
Northern Arizona XL	Texas A&M (Corpus Christi) .... M
Northern Colorado L	Texas, U. of (Arlington) L
Northern Illinois U. L	Texas, U. of (El Paso) L
Northwestern Louisiana L	Texas, U. of (Tyler) .... R
Oakland (MI) .... M	Thomas More (KY) .... R
Oklahoma Baptist .... R	Towson (MD) L
Oklahoma City U. .... R	Troy State (AL) .... M
Old Dominion (VA) L	Tuskegee University (AL) .... M
Olivet Nazarene (IL) .... R	Union (NE) .... R
Oral Roberts (OK) .... M	Union University (TN) .... R
Pittsburgh, U. of (Bradford) .... R	Walla Walla (WA) .... R
Pittsburg State (KS) .... M	Walsh (OH) .... R
Plattsburgh (SUNY) (NY) .... M	Washburn (KS) .... M
Point Loma (CA) .... R	Wayne State (MI) L
Presentation (SD) .... S	Waynesburg (PA) .... R
Quincy (IL) .... R	Weber State (UT) L
Regis (CO) .... R	Western Carolina (NC) .... M
Regis (MA) .... S	Western Connecticut State .... M
Rhode Island, U. of L	Western Kentucky L
Rhode Island College .... M	Wheeling Jesuit (WV) .... R
Robert Morris (PA) .... R	Widener (PA) .... R
Rockford (IL) .... S	Wilkes (PA) .... R
Russell Sage (The Sage Colleges) (NY) .. R	William Paterson (NJ) .... M
Sacred Heart (CT) .... R	Wisconsin, U. of (Eau Claire) L
Saginaw Valley (MI) .... M	Wisconsin, U. of (Oshkosh) L
St. Ambrose (IA) .... R	Worcester State (MA) .... M
St. Francis (IN) .... R	Wright State (OH) L
St. Francis (PA) .... R	Youngstown State (OH) L
▲ St. Joseph (CT) .... S	

Also, Health Informatics and Information Systems

PHARMACY

GROUP I
Most Selective

Buffalo (SUNY) (NY)	L	Michigan, U. of	XL
Butler (IN)	R	Minnesota, U. of	XL
Creighton (NE)	M	North Carolina, U. of	L
Florida, U. of	XL	Purdue (IN)	XL
Illinois, U. of	XL	Rutgers (NJ)	L
Iowa, U. of	XL	Wisconsin, U. of	L

GROUP II
Very Selective

Albany Col. of Pharmacy & Health Sci. (NY)	S	Northwestern Louisiana	L
Arizona, U. of	XL	North Dakota State	L
Auburn (AL)	L	Nova Southeastern (FL)	R
Campbell (NC)	R	Ohio Northern U.	R
Cincinnati, U. of (OH)	L	Ohio State	XL
Connecticut, U. of	XL	Oklahoma, U. of	XL
Drake (IA)	M	Pacific, U. of the (CA)	R
➤ Duquesne (PA)	M	Palm Beach Atlantic (FL)	R
Ferris State (MI)	L	Pittsburgh, U. of	L
Florida A&M	L	Rhode Island, U. of	L
Georgia, U. of	L	Samford (AL)	R
Hawaii, U. of (Hilo)	R	+ Sciences in Philadelphia, U. of (PA)	R
Houston, U. of (TX)	L	South Carolina, U. of	L
Howard (DC)	M	South Dakota State U.	M
Husson (ME)	S	Southern California, U. of	L
Idaho State	L	Southern Illinois U. (Edwardsville)	L
Illinois, U. of (Chicago)	L	Southwestern Oklahoma	M
Kansas, U. of	L	St. John's (NY)	L
Kentucky, U. of	L	St. Louis Col. of Pharmacy (MO)	S
Long Island U. (Brooklyn)(NY)	M	Temple (PA)	L
Louisiana-Monroe	M	Texas, U. of (Austin)	XL
Maryland, U. of	XL	Toledo, U. of	L
Mass. College of Pharmacy	R	Utah, U. of	L
Mercer (GA)	R	Virginia Commonwealth U.	L
Minnesota, U. of (Duluth)	M	Washington State	L
Mississippi, U. of	L	Wayne State (MI)	L
Missouri, U. of (Kansas City)	M	West Virginia U.	L
Montana, U. of	M	Wilkes (PA)	R
New Mexico, U. of	L	Wyoming, U. of	L
Northeastern (MA)	L	Xavier (LA)	R

+ *Also Pharmaceutical Marketing*

➤ *Also, Pharmacy Supply Chain Management*

Enrollment Code

■ *Men Only*
▲ *Women Only*

S = Small (less than 1000 students)   R = Moderate (1000-3000 students)   M = Medium (3000-8000 students)
L = Large (8000-20,000 students)   XL = Extra Large (over 20,000 students)

PHILOSOPHY

GROUP I
Most Selective

Albany (SUNY)(NY) L	Minnesota, U. of XL
American (DC)................................... M	▲ Mount Holyoke (MA) .... R
Austin (TX) .... R	New College (FL) .... S
▲ Barnard (NY) .... R	New School U. (Eugene Lang) (NY) .. R
Bates (ME) .... R	New York U. L
Binghamton (SUNY) (NY) L	North Carolina, U. of L
Boston Col. (MA) L	Notre Dame (IN) .... M
Boston U. (MA) L	Oberlin (OH) .... R
Bowdoin (ME) .... R	Ohio State XL
Brown (RI) .... M	Pennsylvania, U. of L
Bucknell (PA) .... M	Pittsburgh, U. of (PA) L
California, U. of (Berkeley) XL	Pomona (CA) .... R
California, U. of (Los Angeles) XL	Princeton (NJ) .... M
Carleton (MN) .... R	Reed (OR) .... R
Carnegie Mellon (PA) .... M	Rhodes (TN) .... R
Centre (KY) .... R	Richmond, U. of (VA) .... M
Chicago, U. of (IL) .... M	Rochester, U. of (NY) .... M
Claremont McKenna (CA) .... R	Rutgers (NJ) L
Colby (ME) .... R	St. Mary's (MD) .... R
Colgate (NY) .... R	St. Olaf (MN) .... R
Colorado Col. .... R	▲ Smith (MA) .... R
Columbia (NY).................................... M	Southern California L
Connecticut Col. .... R	Southwestern (TX) .... R
Cornell (NY)....................................... L	Stanford (CA) .... M
Creighton (NE) .... M	Swarthmore (PA) .... R
Dallas, U. of (TX) .... R	Texas, U. of (Austin) XL
Davidson (NC) .... R	Trinity (CT) .... R
DePauw (IN) .... R	Trinity (TX) .... R
Duke (NC) .... M	Tufts (MA) .... M
Florida State...................................... L	Tulane (LA) .... M
Florida, U. of XL	Vanderbilt (TN) .... M
Geneseo (SUNY)(NY)......................... M	Vassar (NY) .... R
George Washington (DC) .... M	Villanova (PA) .... M
Georgetown (DC) .... M	■ Wabash (IN) .... S
Gettysburg (PA) .... R	Washington U. (MO) .... M
Hamilton (NY) .... R	Washington, U. of.............................. XL
Harvard (MA)..................................... M	Washington & Lee (VA) .... R
Haverford (PA)................................... S	▲ Wellesley (MA) .... R
Holy Cross (MA) .... R	Wheaton (IL) .... R
Illinois Wesleyan .... R	Whitman (WA).................................... R
Johns Hopkins (MD) .... M	Willamette (OR) .... R
Kenyon (OH) .... R	Willaim & Mary (VA) .... R
Lawrence (WI) .... R	Wisconsin, U. of XL
Macalester (MN)................................ R	Yale (CT) .... M
Michigan, U. of XL	

PHILOSOPHY continues next page

Enrollment Code

■ *Men Only* S = Small (less than 1000 students) R = Moderate (1000-3000 students) M = Medium (3000-8000 students)
▲ *Women Only* L = Large (8000-20,000 students) XL = Extra Large (over 20,000 students)

PHILOSOPHY, continued

GROUP II
Very Selective

Alabama, U. of	L	Elon (NC)	R
Alabama, U. of (Birmingham)	M	Frostburg (MD)	M
Alabama, U. of (Huntsville)	M	Fordham (NY)	L
Allegheny (PA)	R	Fort Hays (KS)	M
Albion (MI)	R	Franciscan U. of Steubenville (OH)	R
Arizona, U. of	XL	George Mason (VA)	L
Asbury (KY)	R	Georgia State	L
Assumption (MA)	R	Georgia, U. of	L
Bellarmine (KY)	R	Gonzaga (WA)	E
Belmont (TN)	R	Gordon (MA)	R
Benedictine (KS)	R	Hamline (MN)	R
Bethel (IN)	R	Hanover (IN)	R
Bethel (MN)	M	Herbert Lehman (CUNY)(NY)	L
Biola (CA)	R	Hobart & Wm. Smith (NY)	R
Bowling Green (OH)	L	Hood (MD)	S
Brooklyn (CUNY)(NY)	L	Illinois, U. of (Chicago)	L
California, U. of (Santa Barbara)	L	Indiana (PA)	L
California, U. of (Santa Cruz)	M	Indiana U.	XL
California State U. (Dominguez Hills)	M	Iowa State	XL
California State U. (Fresno)	L	John Carroll (OH)	R
California State U. (Hayward)	M	Kansas State	L
California State U. (Long Beach)	L	Kent State (OH)	L
California State U. (Northridge)	L	Kutztown (PA)	M
California State U. (Stanislaus)	M	Lake Forest (IL)	R
Calvin (MI)	R	La Salle (PA)	M
Carroll (MT)	R	Lewis & Clark (OR)	R
Catholic (DC)	R	Loras (IA)	R
Central (IA)	R	Louisiana State	XL
Central Florida	XL	Loyola (IL)	M
Christendom (VA)	S	Loyola (LA)	M
Christopher Newport (VA)	M	Loyola (MD)	M
City College (CUNY)(NY)	L	Lycoming (PA)	R
Clarke (IA)	S	Maine, U. of	L
Coastal Carolina (SC)	M	Mansfield (PA)	R
Cornell Col. (IA)	R	Marquette (WI)	M
Dayton, U. of (OH)	M	Maryland, U. of	XL
Denison (OH)	R	Mass. College of Lib. Arts (N.Adams)	R
DePaul (IL)	L	Massachusetts, U. of (Boston)	M
DeSales (PA)	S	Merrimack (MA)	R
Detroit Mercy (MI)	M	Messiah (PA)	R
Doane (NB)	S	Michigan, U. of (Dearborn)	M
Earlham (IN)	R	Michigan State	XL
East Tennessee	L	Milligan (TN)	S
Edinboro (PA)	M		

GROUP II continues next page

PHILOSOPHY, continued

GROUP II, continued

Minnesota, U. of (Morris)	R	St. John's/St. Benedict (MN)	R
Missouri, U. of	XL	St. Joseph's U. (PA)	R
Missouri, U. of (St. Louis)	M	St. Louis (MO)	M
Molloy (NY)	R	▲St. Mary's College (IN)	R
Mount Mercy (IA)	S	St. Mary's (MN)	R
Mount St. Mary's (MD)	R	St. Mary's U. of San Antonio (TX)	R
Muhlenberg (PA)	R	St. Peter's (NJ)	R
Nazareth (NY)	R	St. Norbert (WI)	R
New Hampshire, U. of	L	St. Thomas (MN)	M
New Paltz (SUNY)(NY)	M	St. Thomas, U. of (TX)	R
North Carolina, U. of (Charlotte)	L	Salisbury (MD)	M
Northeastern (MA)	L	San Diego, U. of (CA)	M
Northeastern Illinois	M	Santa Clara U. (CA)	M
Northern Illinois	L	Scranton (PA)	M
Northwestern (IA)	R	Seattle U. (WA)	R
Oklahoma Baptist	R	Seton Hall (NJ)	M
Oneonta (SUNY)(NY)	M	Siena (NY)	R
Oregon State	L	Skidmore (NY)	R
Ozarks, College of the (MO)	R	South Alabama	M
Portland, U. of (OR)	R	South Florida, U. of	L
Providence (RI)	M	Southern Illinois U. (Edwardsville)	L
Purchase (SUNY)(NY)	M	Southern Maine	M
Queens (CUNY)(NY)	L	Stonehill (MA)	R
Redlands (CA)	R	Stony Brook (SUNY) (NY)	L
Regis (CO)	R	Syracuse (NY)	L
Rhode Island College	M	Texas A&M	XL
Richard Stockton (NJ)	M	Transylvania (KY)	R
Rockhurst (MO)	R	Ursinus (PA)	R
Rollins (FL)	R	Utah, U. of	L
Rowan (NJ)	M	Virginia Wesleyan	R
St. Ambrose (IA)	R	Webster (MO)	R
St. Andrews Presbyterian (NC)	S	West Chester (PA)	M
St. Anselm (NH)	R	Westminster (UT)	R
St. Bonaventure (NY)	R	Wheeling Jesuit (WV)	R
▲St. Catherine (MN)	R	Wichita State (KS)	M
St. Cloud (MN)	L	William Jewell (MO)	R
St. Edward's (TX)	M	Wofford (SC)	R
St. Francis (PA)	R	Worcester State (MA)	M
St. John's (NY)	L	Xavier (OH)	R

Enrollment Code

■ **Men Only**   **S = Small** (less than 1000 students)   **R = Moderate** (1000-3000 students)   **M = Medium** (3000-8000 students)
▲ **Women Only**   **L = Large** (8000-20,000 students)   **XL = Extra Large** (over 20,000 students)

PHYSICS

GROUP I
Most Selective

Albany (SUNY)(NY)	L		Kenyon (OH)	R
Allegheny (PA)	R		Kalamazoo (MI)	R
Amherst (MA)	R	#	Kettering (MI)	R
▲ Barnard (NY)	R		Lawrence (WI)	R
Bates (ME)	R		Lehigh (PA)	M
Binghamton (SUNY) (NY)	L		Macalester (MN)	R
Boston U. (MA)	L		Maryland, U. of	XL
Brandeis (MA)	M		MIT (MA)	M
Brown (RI)	M		Miami U. (OH)	L
▲ Bryn Mawr (PA)	S		Michigan, U. of	XL
Buffalo (SUNY)(NY)	L		Michigan, U. of (Dearborn)	M
California Inst. of Tech.	S		Middlebury (VT)	R
California, U. of (Berkeley)	XL		Missouri, U. of (Rolla)	M
California, U. of (San Diego)	L	▲	Mount Holyoke (MA)	R
Carleton (MN)	R		New College (FL)	S
Carnegie Mellon (PA)	M		New Jersey, College of	M
Case Western Reserve U. (OH)	M		New Mexico Inst. of Mining & Tech.	R
Centre (KY)	R		New York U.	L
Chicago, U. of (IL)	M		North Carolina, U. of	L
Clarkson (NY)	M		Northeastern (MA)	L
Colorado School of Mines	R		Northwestern (IL)	M
Columbia (NY)	M		Notre Dame (IN)	M
Connecticut College	R		Oberlin (OH)	R
Cornell (NY)	L		Occidental (CA)	R
Dartmouth (NH)	M		Pennsylvania, U. of	L
Denison (OH)	R		Pennsylvania State	XL
DePauw (IN)	R		Pomona (CA)	R
Dickinson (PA)	R		Princeton (NJ)	M
Florida, U. of	XL		Reed (OR)	R
Franklin & Marshall (PA)	R		Rensselaer (NY)	M
Furman (SC)	R		Rhodes (TN)	R
Geneseo (SUNY) (NY)	M		Rice (TX)	M
Georgetown (DC)	M		Rochester, U. of (NY)	M
Georgia Inst. of Tech.	L		Rose-Hulman (IN)	R
Gettysburg (PA)	R		Rutgers (NJ)	L
Grinnell (IA)	R		St. Olaf (MN)	R
Gustavus Adolphus (MN)	R	▲	Smith (MA)	R
Hamilton (NY)	R		South, U. of the (TN)	R
Harvard (MA)	M		Stanford (CA)	M
Harvey Mudd (CA)	S		Swarthmore (PA)	R
Haverford (PA)	S		Texas, U. of (Dallas)	M
Holy Cross (MA)	R		Trinity (CT)	R
Illinois, U. of (Urbana-Champaign)	XL		Trinity (TX)	R
Illinois Institute of Tech	R		Union (NY)	R
Illinois Wesleyan	R		United States Air Force Academy (CO)	M
Iowa State	XL			
Iowa, U. of	XL			
Johns Hopkins (MD)	M			

 # Applied Physics
GROUP I continues next page

PHYSICS, continued

GROUP I, continued

United States Naval Academy (MD) .. M
Vanderbilt (TN) .... M
Virginia, U. of L
Virginia Tech. L
Wake Forest (NC) .... M
Washington & Lee (VA) .... R
Washington, U. of XL
Washington U. (MO) .... M

▲Wellesley (MA) .... R
Wheaton (IL) .... R
Whitman (WA) .... R
William & Mary (VA) .... M
Worcester Poly. Inst. (MA) .... R
Yale (CT) .... M
Yeshiva (NY) .... R

GROUP II
Very Selective

Adelphi (NY) .... M
▲Agnes Scott (GA) .... S
Alabama, U. of L
Alabama, U. of (Birmingham) .... M
Alabama, U. of (Huntsville) .... M
Albion (MI) .... R
Arizona State XL
Auburn (AL) L
Augsburg (MN) .... R
Baylor (TX) .... M
Beloit (WI) .... R
Bethany (WV) .... S
Bradley (IL) .... M
Cal. Poly. State U. (San Luis Obispo) L
California, U. of (Davis) XL
California, U. of (Irvine) L
California, U. of (Santa Barbara) L
California, U. of (Santa Cruz) .... M
Calvin (MI) .... R
Catholic (DC) .... R
Central Florida XL
Clark (MA) .... R
Clemson (SC) L
Coe (IA) .... R
Colorado, U. of L
Colorado, U. of (Colorado Springs) .... M
Creighton (NE) .... M
Denver, U. of (CO) .... M
Elmhurst (IL) .... R
Evansville, U. of (IN) .... R
Fairfield (CT) .... M
Florida Inst. of Tech. .... R
Florida State L
George Mason (VA) L
Guilford (NC) .... R
Hamline (MN) .... R
Hanover (IN) .... R
Hendrix (AR) .... R
Hope (MI) .... M
Houston, U. of (TX) L

Humboldt State (CA) .... M
Idaho, U. of L
Kansas State L
Kansas, U. of L
Kent State (OH) L
Knox (IL) .... R
Lewis & Clark (OR) .... R
Linfield (OR) .... R
Loras (IA) .... R
Loyola (IL) .... M
Maine, U. of L
Mansfield (PA) .... R
Marietta (OH) .... R
Maryland, U. of (Baltimore County) ...... M
Massachusetts, U. of (Lowell) .... M
McDaniel (MD) .... R
Michigan State XL
Michigan Tech .... M
Mississippi, U. of L
Mississippi State L
Montana State L
Nebraska, U. of L
New Hampshire, U. of L
New Orleans (LA) L
North Carolina State L
Oakland (MI) .... M
Ohio State XL
Ohio U. L
Oklahoma State L
Oregon State L
Pacific University (OR) .... R
Pittsburgh, U. of (PA) L
Presbyterian (SC) .... R
Puerto Rico, U. of (Mayaguez) L
Ramapo (NJ) .... M
Rhode Island, U. of L
Rochester Inst. of Tech. (NY) L
Rollins (FL) .... R

GROUP II continues next page

PHYSICS, continued

GROUP II, continued

Rowan (NJ)	M	Texas, U. of (Austin)	XL
St. John's (MN)	R	Tulsa, U. of (OK)	M
Santa Clara U. (CA)	M	Ursinus (PA)	R
Seattle Pacific (WA)	R	Utah, U. of	L
Shippensburg (PA)	M	Valparaiso U. (IN)	M
Sonoma State (CA)	M	Vermont, U. of	M
South Carolina, U. of	L	Washington State	L
South Dakota School of Mines	R	Wayne State (MI)	L
South Florida, U. of	L	West Virginia	L
Stetson (FL)	R	Westminster (UT)	R
Stevens Institute of Tech. (NJ)	R	Whitworth (WA)	R
Stockton State (NJ)	M	William Jewell (MO)	R
Stony Brook (SUNY) (NY)	L	Wisconsin, U. of	XL
Syracuse (NY)	L	Xavier (OH)	R
Tennessee, U. of	XL		

GROUP III
Selective

Alaska, U. of (Fairbanks)	M	▲ Mary Baldwin (VA)	S
Andrews (MI)	R	Mass. College of Lib. Arts (N. Adams)	R
Arkansas, U. of	L	Massachusetts, U. of (Boston)	M
Ball State (IN)	L	Millersville (PA)	M
Brooklyn Col. (CUNY) (NY)	L	Minnesota State U. (Moorhead)	M
California Poly. State U. (Pomona)	L	Muskingum (OH)	R
California State U. (Dominguez Hills)	M	Nevada, U. of (Reno)	L
California State U. (Northridge)	L	Northern Illinois U.	L
California State U. (San Jose)	L	Northern Michigan	M
Carthage (WI)	R	Northwestern (IA)	R
Christopher Newport (VA)	M	Old Dominion (VA)	L
City Col. (CUNY) (NY)	L	Oneonta (SUNY)(NY)	M
Clark Atlanta (GA)	M	Ozarks, College of the (MO)	R
Doane (NE)	S	Penn State (Erie)(PA)	M
East Stroudsburg (PA)	M	Southern Connecticut	M
Eastern Michigan	L	Southwestern (KS)	S
Edinboro (PA)	M	Suffolk (MA)	R
Fisk (TN)	S	Thomas More (KY)	R
Florida A&M	M	Tuskegee (AL)	M
Fort Lewis (CO)	M	Union (TN)	R
Georgia State	L	Washburn (KS)	M
Goshen (IN)	R	Weber State (UT)	L
Hastings (NE)	R	π West Virginia Wesleyan	R
Indiana (PA)	L	Western Kentucky	L
Indiana State	L	Western Michigan	L
Jacksonville (FL)	R	Wheeling Jesuit (WV)	R
Louisiana-Lafayette	L	Wisconsin, U. of (Milwaukee)	L
Louisiana State	XL		

π *Engineering Physics*

Enrollment Code

■ *Men Only* **S = Small** (less than 1000 students)   **R = Moderate** (1000-3000 students)   **M = Medium** (3000-8000 students)
▲ *Women Only*   **L = Large** (8000-20,000 students)   **XL = Extra Large** (over 20,000 students)

POLITICAL SCIENCE

•————————— **GROUP I** —————————•
Most Selective

Allegheny (PA)	R		Kalamazoo (MI)	R
American U. (DC)	M		Kenyon (OH)	R
Amherst (MA)	R		Lafayette (PA)	R
Binghamton (SUNY)(NY)	L		Lehigh (PA)	M
▲Barnard (NY)	R		Macalester (MN)	R
Bates (ME)	R		MIT (MA)	M
Beloit (WI)	R		Miami, U. of (OH)	L
Boston College (MA)	L		Michigan, U. of	XL
Boston U. (MA)	L		Middlebury (VT)	R
Bowdoin (ME)	R		Minnesota, U. of	XL
Brandeis (MA)	R		▲Mount Holyoke (MA)	R
Brown (RI)	M		Muhlenberg (PA)	R
Bucknell (PA)	R		North Carolina, U. of	L
California, U. of (Berkeley)	XL		Northwestern (IL)	M
California, U. of (Los Angeles)	XL		Notre Dame (IN)	M
California, U. of (San Diego)	L		Oberlin (OH)	R
Carleton (MN)	R		Occidental (CA)	R
Centre (KY)	R		Pennsylvania, U. of	L
Chicago, U. of (IL)	M		Pennsylvania State	XL
Claremont McKenna (CA)	R		Pomona (CA)	R
Colby (ME)	R		Princeton (NJ)	M
Colgate (NY)	R		Rhodes (TN)	R
Colorado Col.	R		Rice (TX)	M
Columbia (NY)	M		Richmond, U. of (VA)	M
Connecticut Col.	R		Rochester, U. of (NY)	M
Connecticut, U. of	XL		Rutgers (NJ)	L
Dallas, U. of (TX)	R		▲Scripps (CA)	S
Dartmouth (NH)	M		▲Smith (MA)	R
Davidson (NC)	M		South, U. of the (TN)	R
DePauw (IN)	R		Southwestern (TX)	R
Dickinson (PA)	R		Stanford (CA)	M
Drew (NJ)	R		Swarthmore (PA)	R
Duke (NC)	M		Texas A&M	XL
Emory (GA)	M		Texas, U. of (Austin)	XL
Florida, U. of	XL		Trinity (TX)	R
Franklin & Marshall (PA)	R		Tufts (MA)	M
Furman (SC)	R		Tulane (LA)	M
Georgetown (DC)	M		Union (NY)	R
George Washington (DC)	M		U.S. Air Force Academy (CO)	M
Gettysburg (PA)	R		U.S. Coast Guard Academy (CT)	R
Grinnell (IA)	R		U.S. Military Academy (NY)	M
Hamilton (NY)	R		U.S. Naval Academy (MD)	M
Harvard (MA)	M		Ursinus (PA)	R
Haverford (PA)	S		Vanderbilt (TN)	M
Holy Cross (MA)	R		Vassar (NY)	R
Illinois, U. of	XL		Villanova (PA)	M
Illinois Wesleyan	R			
Johns Hopkins (MD)	M			

GROUP I continues next page

POLITICAL SCIENCE, continued

━━━━ GROUP I, continued ━━━━

Virginia, U. of	L
■ Wabash (IN)	S
Wake Forest (NC)	M
Washington & Lee (VA)	R
▲ Wellesley (MA)	R
Wesleyan (CT)	R
Wheaton (IL)	R
Whitman (WA)	R
Willamette (OR)	R
William & Mary (VA)	M
Williams (MA)	R
Yale (CT)	M
Yeshiva (NY)	R

GROUP II
Very Selective

▲ Agnes Scott (GA)	S
Albany (SUNY)(NY)	L
Albion (MI)	R
Alma (MI)	R
Arcadia (PA)	R
Auburn (AL)	L
Austin (TX)	R
Belmont (TN)	R
Bethany (WV)	S
Birmingham-Southern (AL)	R
Bradley (IL)	M
Buena Vista (IA)	R
California, U. of (Davis)	XL
California, U. of (Riverside)	L
California, U. of (Santa Barbara)	L
Catholic U. (DC)	M
Clark (MA)	R
Clemson (SC)	L
Colorado State	L
College of Charleston (SC)	L
Cornell College (IA)	R
Creighton (NE)	M
Dayton, U. of (OH)	M
Delaware, U. of	L
Denison (OH)	R
DePaul (IL)	L
Drake (IA)	M
Elon (NC)	R
Emerson (MA)	M
Florida International	L
George Mason (VA)	L
Georgia, U. of	Xl
Gonzaga (WA)	R
Goucher (MD)	R
Grove City (PA)	R
Guilford (NC)	R
Hampden-Sydney (VA)	S
Hawaii, U. of	L
Hendrix (AR)	R
Hillsdale (MI)	R
Hobart & William Smith (NY)	R
Hofstra (NY)	M
▲ Hollins (VA)	S
Hood (MD)	S
Hope (MI)	R
Howard (DC)	M
Hunter (CUNY)(NY)	L
Idaho, College of	S
Illinois College	S
Illinois, U. of (Chicago)	L
Iowa, U. of	XL
James Madison (VA)	M
John Carroll (OH)	R
Kansas, U. of	L
Kennesaw State (GA)	R
Kent State (OH)	L
Knox (IL)	R
Lake Forest (IL)	R
Lipscomb (TN)	R
Lyon (AR)	S
Manhattan (NY)	M
Manhattanville (NY)	R
Marist (NY)	M
Marquette (WI)	M
Maryland, U. of	XL
Maryland, U. of (Baltimore County)	M
Mary Washington (VA)	M
Massachusetts, U. of	L

GROUP II continues next page

POLITICAL SCIENCE, continued

⸺ GROUP II, continued ⸺

McDaniel (MD)	R
Merrimack (MA)	R
Millersville (PA)	M
Millsaps (MS)	S
Minnesota, U. of (Morris)	R
Missouri, U. of	XL
Missouri, U. of (St. Louis)	M
▲Morehouse (GA)	R
North Carolina (Charlotte)	L
North Central (IL)	R
North Texas	L
Oglethorpe (GA)	S
Ohio State	XL
Ohio U.	L
Ohio Wesleyan	R
Oklahoma City U.	R
Oklahoma, U. of	XL
Oklahoma State	L
Oregon, U. of	L
Oswego (SUNY)(NY)	M
Pace (NY)	M
Pacific, U. of the (CA)	M
Pittsburgh, U. of (PA)	L
Portland, U. of (OR)	R
Presbyterian (SC)	R
Providence (RI)	M
Puget Sound (WA)	R
Purchase (SUNY)(NY)	M
Ramapo (NJ)	M
Randolph College (VA)	S
Randolph Macon (VA)	R
Redlands, U. of (CA)	R
Regis (CO)	R
Richard Stockton (NJ)	M
Ripon (WI)	S
Roanoke (VA)	R
St. Anselm (NH)	R
St. Bonaventure (NY)	R
St. Cloud (MN)	L
St. John's (MN)	R
St. John's (NY)	L
St. Joseph's (PA)	R
St. Lawrence (NY)	R
St. Mary's College of Maryland	R

St. Thomas (TX)	R
St. Vincent (PA)	R
San Diego, U. of (CA)	M
San Diego State (CA)	XL
San Francisco, U. of (CA)	M
Santa Clara U. (CA)	M
Seton Hall (NJ)	M
Shepherd (WV)	M
Siena (NY)	R
Skidmore (NY)	R
South Carolina	L
Spring Hill (AL)	R
Stetson (FL)	R
Stonehill (MA)	R
Stony Brook (SUNY)(NY)	L
Susquehanna (PA)	R
▲Sweet Briar (VA)	S
Syracuse (NY)	L
Tampa, U. of (FL)	R
Temple (PA)	L
Texas, U. of (Dallas)	M
Tennessee, U. of	XL
Towson (MD)	L
▲Trinity (DC)	S
Utah, U. of	L
Vermont, U. of	L
Washington, U. of	XL
Washington & Jefferson (PA)	R
Washington College (MD)	S
Webster (MO)	R
West Chester (PA)	M
Western Washington U.	R
Westminster (MO)	S
Westminster (UT)	R
West Virginia U.	L
Wheaton (MA)	R
Wilberforce (OH)	S
Winthrop (SC)	M
Wisconsin, U. of	XL
Wittenberg (OH)	R
Wofford (SC)	R
Wooster, College of the (OH)	R
Wyoming, U. of	L

Enrollment Code

■ *Men Only*　　S = Small (less than 1000 students)　　R = Moderate (1000-3000 students)　　M = Medium (3000-8000 students)
▲ *Women Only*　　L = Large (8000-20,000 students)　　XL = Extra Large (over 20,000 students)

POLITICAL SCIENCE, continued

GROUP III
Selective

Adrian (MI) .... R	Massachusetts, U. of (Boston) .... M
Albright (PA) .... R	Mercyhurst (PA) .... R
Appalachian State (NC) L	Michigan State XL
Arizona State XL	Missouri State L
Azusa Pacific (CA) .... R	Monmouth (NJ) .... R
Baker (KS) .... R	Montana, U. of .... M
Baldwin-Wallace (OH) .... R	Montana State L
Ball State (IN) L	Montana State (Billings) .... R
Belmont Abbey (NC) .... S	Mount St. Mary's (MD) .... R
▲ Bennett (NC) .... S	Mount Union (OH) .... R
Bridgewater (MA) .... M	Muskingum (OH) .... R
Brockport (SUNY)(NY) .... M	Nebraska, U. of (Omaha) L
California State U. (Chico) L	Nevada, U. of (Las Vegas) L
California State U. (Fullerton) L	Nevada, U. of (Reno) L
California State U. (Long Beach) L	New Mexico State U. L
California State U. (Northridge) L	New Orleans, U. of (LA) L
California State U. (Sacramento) ...... M	Northern Arizona XL
California State U. (San Marcos) ...... M	▲ Pine Manor (MA) .... S
California State U. (Stanislaus) .... M	Pittsburgh, U. of (Greensburg) .... R
Campbell (NC) .... R	Queens (CUNY)(NY) L
Carthage (WI) .... R	Radford (VA) .... M
▲ Chatham (PA) .... S	Regis (MA) .... R
Christopher Newport (VA) .... M	Rhode Island, U. of L
City College (CUNY)(NY) L	Rider (NJ) .... R
▲ Converse (SC) .... S	St. Mary's (TX) .... R
Eastern Connecticut .... M	San Jose State (CA) L
Eastern Illinois L	Schreiner (TX) .... S
Eastern Kentucky L	Sioux Falls, U. of (SD) .... R
Eastern Michigan L	South Dakota, U. of .... M
Fairleigh Dickinson (NJ) .... M	Southern Connecticut .... M
Gardner-Webb (NC) .... S	Southern Illinois U. (Carbondale) L
Grambling (LA) .... M	Southern Illinois U. (Edwardsville) L
Hartwick (NY) .... R	▲ Spelman (GA) .... R
Heidelburg (OH) .... S	Suffolk (MA) .... R
Iona (NY) .... M	Texas, U. of (Arlington) L
Illinois State L	Texas, U. of (San Antonio) L
John Jay (CUNY)(NY) .... M	Texas State U. (San Marcos) L
Kutztown (PA) .... M	Utah State L
Laverne (CA) .... R	Virginia Wesleyan .... R
Lock Haven (PA) .... M	Westfield (MA) .... M
Louisiana State XL	Whittier (CA) .... R
Louisville (KY) L	Wisconsin, U. of (Milwaukee) L
Manchester (IN) .... R	York (PA) .... M
▲ Mary Baldwin (VA) .... S	

PRE-LAW

Author's Note: Law School Associations usually recommend that a student choose a major dependent upon one's own individual intellectual interests and upon "the quality of undergraduate education" provided by various departments and colleges. The following recommended colleges have been taken primarily from our recommended departments in English, Economics, and Political Science.

GROUP I
Most Selective

Albany (SUNY) (NY)	L	Franklin & Marshall (PA)	R
Allegheny (PA)	R	Furman (SC)	R
American U. (DC)	M	Georgetown (DC)	M
Amherst (MA)	R	George Washington (DC)	M
Bard (NY)	R	Gettysburg (PA)	R
▲Barnard (NY)	R	Grinnell (IA)	R
Bates (ME)	R	Hamilton (NY)	R
Binghamton (SUNY) (NY)	L	Harvard (MA)	M
Boston Col. (MA)	L	Haverford (PA)	S
Boston U. (MA)	L	Holy Cross (MA)	R
Bowdoin (ME)	R	Illinois, U. of (Chicago)	L
Brandeis (MA)	R	Illinois, U. of (Urbana-Champaign)	XL
Brown (RI)	M	Illinois Wesleyan	R
▲Bryn Mawr (PA)	S	Iowa, U. of	XL
Bucknell (PA)	M	Johns Hopkins (MD)	M
Buffalo (SUNY) (NY)	L	Kalamazoo (MI)	R
California, U. of (Berkeley)	XL	Kenyon (OH)	R
California, U. of (Los Angeles)	XL	Lafayette (PA)	R
California, U. of (San Diego)	L	Macalester (MN)	R
Carleton (MN)	R	Maryland, U. of (Baltimore County)	M
Carnegie Mellon (PA)	M	MIT (MA)	M
Case Western Reserve (OH)	M	Miami, U. of (FL)	L
Centre (KY)	R	Miami U. (OH)	L
Chicago, U. of (IL)	M	Michigan, U. of	XL
Claremont McKenna (CA)	R	Middlebury (VT)	R
Clark (MA)	R	Minnesota, U. of	XL
Clarkson (NY)	M	▲Mount Holyoke (MA)	R
Colby (ME)	R	Muhlenberg (PA)	R
Colgate (NY)	R	New College (FL)	S
Colorado Col.	R	New Jersey, College of	M
Columbia (NY)	M	North Carolina, U. of	L
Connecticut Col.	R	Northwestern (IL)	M
Cornell (NY)	L	Notre Dame (IN)	M
Dallas, U. of (TX)	R	Oberlin (OH)	R
Dartmouth (NH)	M	Occidental (CA)	R
Davidson (NC)	R	Pennsylvania, U. of	L
DePauw (IN)	R	Pennsylvania State	XL
Dickinson (PA)	R	Pitzer (CA)	S
Drew (NJ)	R	Pomona (CA)	R
Duke (NC)	M	Princeton (NJ)	M
Emory (GA)	M		
Florida, U. of	XL		

GROUP I continues next page

PRE-LAW, continued

GROUP I, Continued

Providence (RI)	M
Reed (OR)	R
Rhodes (TN)	R
Richmond, U. of (VA)	M
Rice (TX)	M
Richmond, U. of (VA)	M
Rochester, U. of (NY)	M
Rutgers (NJ)	L
Sarah Lawrence (NY)	R
Skidmore (NY)	R
▲ Smith (MA)	R
South, U. of the (TN)	R
Southwestern (TX)	R
Stanford (CA)	M
St. Louis (MO)	M
St. Olaf (MN)	R
Swarthmore (PA)	R
Trinity (CT)	R
Trinity (TX)	R
Tufts (MA)	M
Tulane (LA)	M
Union (NY)	R
Vanderbilt (TN)	M
Vassar (NY)	R
Villanova (PA)	M
Virginia, U. of	L
■ Wabash (IN)	S
Wake Forest (NC)	M
Washington & Lee (VA)	R
Washington U. (MO)	M
▲ Wellesley (MA)	R
Wesleyan U. (CT)	R
Wheaton (IL)	R
Whitman (WA)	R
Williams (MA)	R
Wisconsin, U. of	XL
Worcester Poly. Inst. (MA)	R
Yale (CT)	M

GROUP II
Very Selective

▲ Agnes Scott (GA)	S
Alabama, U. of	L
Albion (MI)	R
Alfred (NY)	R
Alma (MI)	R
Arcadia (PA)	R
Arizona, U. of	XL
Augsburg (MN)	R
Augustana (IL)	R
Baylor (TX)	R
Belmont (TN)	R
Bennington (VT)	S
Birmingham-Southern (AL)	R
Bradley (IL)	M
Brigham Young (UT)	XL
Butler (IN)	R
California, U. of (Davis)	XL
California, U. of (Irvine)	L
California, U. of (Riverside)	L
California, U. of (Santa Barbara)	L
Calvin (MI)	M
Catholic (DC)	R
Chapman (CA)	R
City College (CUNY)(NY)	L
Clark (MA)	R
Columbia Col. (SC)	R
Connecticut, U. of	XL
Cornell Col. (IA)	R
Creighton (NE)	M
Dayton, U. of (OH)	M
Delaware, U. of	L
Denison (OH)	R
Denver, U. of (CO)	M
DePaul (IL)	L
Drake (IA)	M
Drury (MO)	R
Evansville (IN)	R
Elizabethtown (PA)	R
Flagler (FL)	R
Florida Institute of Technology	R
Fordham (NY)	L
George Mason (VA)	L
Georgetown College (KY)	R
Georgia, U. of	XL
Gonzaga (WA)	R
Goucher (MD)	R

GROUP II continues next page

Enrollment Code

■ *Men Only*	S = Small (less than 1000 students) R = Moderate (1000-3000 students) M = Medium (3000-8000 students)
▲ *Women Only*	L = Large (8000-20,000 students) XL = Extra Large (over 20,000 students)

PRE-LAW, continued

GROUP II, continued

Grand Valley (MI)	L
Guilford (NC)	R
Hamline (MN)	R
■ Hampden-Sydney (VA)	S
Hampton (VA)	M
Hawaii Pacific	R
Hartwick (NY)	R
Hendrix (AR)	R
Hiram (OH)	R
Hobart & Wm. Smith (NY)	R
Hofstra (NY)	M
Hood (MD)	S
Hope (MI)	R
Howard (DC)	M
Hunter (CUNY) (NY)	L
Idaho, College of	S
Illinois College	S
Illinois, U. of (Chicago)	L
Indiana (PA)	L
Iowa State	XL
James Madison (VA)	L
Juniata (PA)	R
Kansas State	L
Knox (IL)	R
Lake Forest (IL)	R
LaSalle (PA)	M
Lawrence (WI)	R
Lebanon Valley (PA)	R
Loras (IA)	R
Loyola (LA)	R
Loyola (MD)	M
Manhattan (NY)	M
Marietta (OH)	R
Marquette (WI)	M
Maryland, U. of	XL
Massachusetts, U. of	L
Mercyhurst (PA)	R
Michigan State	XL
Michigan, U. of (Dearborn)	M
Millersville (PA)	M
Millsaps (MS)	S
Minnesota, U. of (Morris)	R
Mississippi, U. of	L
Missouri, U. of	XL
Nebraska, U. of	L
New Hampshire, U. of	L
North Carolina, U. of (Charlotte)	L
North Carolina, U. of (Wilmington)	L
North Carolina State	L

North Central (IL)	R
Oglethorpe (GA)	S
Ohio State	XL
Ohio U.	L
Ohio Wesleyan	R
Oklahoma City U.	R
Oklahoma, U. of	XL
Oneonta (SUNY) (NY)	M
Oregon, U. of	L
Oswego (SUNY)(NY)	M
Pittsburgh, U. of (PA)	L
Portland State (OR)	L
Presbyterian (SC)	R
Principia (IL)	S
Puget Sound (WA)	R
Purchase (SUNY) (NY)	M
Queens (NC)	R
Randolph College (VA)	S
Randolph-Macon (VA)	R
Redlands, U. of (CA)	R
Ripon (WI)	S
Rowan (NJ)	M
Rutgers (Camden) (NJ)	M
▲ Salem College (NC)	S
Salisbury (MD)	M
San Diego, U. of	M
San Diego State (CA)	XL
San Francisco, U. of (CA)	M
Santa Clara U. (CA)	R
▲ Scripps (CA)	S
Seton Hall (AL)	M
Siena (NY)	R
South Carolina, U. of	L
South Dakota, U. of	M
Spring Hill (AL)	R
St. Bonaventure (NY)	R
St. Cloud (MN)	L
St. John's (MN)	R
St. Lawrence (NY)	R
▲ St. Mary's Col. (IN)	R
Stetson (FL)	R
Stonehill (MA)	R
Stony Brook (SUNY) (NY)	L
▲ Sweet Briar (VA)	S
Syracuse (NY)	L
▲ Trinity (DC)	S
Tuskegee (AL)	M

GROUP II continues next page

PRE-LAW, continued

GROUP II, continued

Ursinus (PA)	R	West Virginia U.	L
Vermont, U. of	L	Western New England (MA)	R
Virginia Commonwealth U.	L	Western Washington U.	L
Virginia Military Inst.	R	Westminster Col. (MO)	S
Warren Wilson (NC)	S	Westmont (CA)	R
Washington & Jefferson (PA)	R	Wheaton (MA)	R
Washington College (MD)	S	Wilberforce (OH)	S
Washington, U. of	XL	Wittenberg (OH)	R
Wells (NY)	S	Wofford (SC)	R
West Chester (PA)	M	Wooster (OH)	R

GROUP III
Selective

Adrian (MI)	R	Louisiana State	XL
Albright (PA)	R	Lynchburg (VA)	R
Arkansas, U. of	L	Massachusetts, U. of (Boston)	M
Baldwin-Wallace (OH)	R	Missouri State	L
Belmont Abbey (NC)	S	Molloy (NY)	R
▲Bennett (NC)	S	Mount St. Joseph (OH)	R
Bethany (WV)	S	Mount St. Mary's (MD)	R
Brockport (SUNY)(NY)	M	Mount St. Vincent (NY)	R
California State U. (Channel Islands)	R	Niagara (NY)	R
California State U. (Long Beach)	L	Northland (WI)	S
California State U. (Monterey Bay)	R	Radford (VA)	M
California State U. (Northridge)	L	Rhode Island, U. of	L
Campbell (NC)	R	Roanoke (VA)	R
▲Chatham (PA)	S	Rockford (IL)	S
Chestnut Hill (PA)	S	▲Rosemont (PA)	S
Citidel, The (SC)	R	St. Anselm (NH)	R
Emerson (MA)	M	St. Francis (PA)	R
Fairleigh Dickinson (NJ)	M	St. Mary's (TX)	R
Fisk (TN)	S	San Francisco State (CA)	L
Florida A&M	M	Schreiner (TX)	S
Fort Lewis (CO)	M	Seattle U. (WA)	R
Gwynedd-Mercy (PA)	S	▲Spelman (GA)	R
Hawaii, U. of	L	▲Stephens (MO)	S
Heidelberg (OH)	S	Temple (PA)	L
▲Hollins (VA)	S	Tennessee, U. of	XL
Husson (ME)	S	Utah, U. of	L
Illinois State	L	Virginia Wesleyan	R
Laverne (CA)	R	Whittier (CA)	R
Longwood (VA)	R	Wilson (PA)	S
Louisiana College	R	Wisconsin, U. of (Milwaukee)	L
Louisiana-Lafayette	L	Wyoming, U. of	L

Enrollment Code	
■ *Men Only*	S = Small (less than 1000 students) R = Moderate (1000-3000 students) M = Medium (3000-8000 students)
▲ *Women Only*	L = Large (8000-20,000 students) XL = Extra Large (over 20,000 students)

PRE-MED/PRE-DENTAL

Author's Note: In addition to general college requirements and requirements of their major department, premedical and predental students must usually pass with a good grade the following: general chemistry, zoology, organic chemistry, general biology, English composition or literature, and general physics.

Other required or highly recommended courses are: advanced biology, psychology or sociology, physical chemistry, calculus, and quantitative chemistry. Of course, the wise path to follow is to consult the exact course requirements of the school you expect to apply to. The recommended colleges below are taken primarily from our recommended departments in biology and chemistry.

GROUP I
Most Selective

Albany (SUNY) (NY) L	Florida, U. of XL
Allegheny (PA) .... R	Franklin & Marshall (PA) .... R
American U. (DC) .... M	Furman (SC) .... R
Amherst (MA) .... R	Geneseo (SUNY) (NY) .... M
Bates (ME) .... R	Georgetown (DC) .... M
Binghamton (SUNY) (NY) L	Gettysburg (PA) .... R
Boston Col. (MA) L	Grinnell (IA) .... R
Boston U. (MA) L	Hamilton (NY) .... R
Bowdoin (ME) .... R	Harvard (MA) .... M
Brandeis (MA) .... R	Harvey Mudd (CA) .... S
Brown (RI) .... M	Haverford (PA) .... S
▲ Bryn Mawr (PA) .... S	Holy Cross (MA) .... R
Bucknell (PA) .... M	Illinois, U. of (Urbana-Champaign) XL
Buffalo (SUNY) (NY) L	Illinois Wesleyan .... R
California Inst. of Tech. .... S	Iowa State XL
California, U. of (Berkeley) XL	Iowa, U. of XL
California, U. of (Los Angeles) XL	Johns Hopkins (MD) .... M
California, U. of (San Diego) L	Kalamazoo (MI) .... R
Carleton (MN) .... R	Kenyon (OH) .... R
Carnegie-Mellon (PA) .... M	Knox (IL) .... R
Case Western Reserve U. (OH) .... M	Lafayette (PA) .... R
Centre (KY) .... R	Lawrence (WI) .... R
Chicago, U. of (IL) .... M	Lehigh (PA) .... M
Claremont McKenna (CA) .... R	Macalester (MN) .... R
Clark (MA) .... R	Miami, U. of (FL) L
Colby (ME) .... R	Miami, U. of (OH) L
Colgate (NY) .... R	MIT (MA) .... M
Colorado Col. .... R	Michigan, U. of XL
Colorado School of Mines .... R	Middlebury (VT) .... R
Columbia (NY) .... M	▲ Mount Holyoke (MA) .... R
Cornell (NY) L	New College (FL) .... S
Dallas, U. of (TX) .... R	New Jersey, College of .... M
Dartmouth (NH) .... M	North Carolina, U. of L
Davidson (NC) .... R	Northwestern (IL) .... M
DePauw (IN) .... R	Notre Dame (IN) .... M
Dickinson (PA) .... M	Oberlin (OH) .... R
Drew (NJ) .... R	Occidental (CA) .... R
Duke (NC) .... R	Pitzer (CA) .... S
Emory (GA) .... M	Pomona (CA) .... R
Fairfield (CT) .... M	

GROUP I continues next page

PRE-MED/PRE-DENTAL, continued

GROUP I, continued

Princeton (NJ)	M
Providence (RI)	M
Puget Sound (WA)	R
Reed (OR)	R
Rhodes (TN)	R
Rice (TX)	M
Richmond, U. of (VA)	M
Rochester, U. of (NY)	M
Rutgers (NJ)	L
Santa Clara, U. of (CA)	M
Skidmore (NY)	R
▲ Smith (MA)	R
South, U. of the (TN)	R
Southwestern (TX)	R
Stanford (CA)	M
Stetson (FL)	R
St. Mary's College of Maryland	R
St. Olaf (MN)	R
Swarthmore (PA)	S
Texas, U. of (Austin)	XL
Trinity (CT)	R
Trinity (TX)	R
Tufts (MA)	M
Tulane (LA)	M
Union (NY)	R
Ursinus (PA)	R
Vanderbilt (TN)	M
Vassar (NY)	R
Villanova (PA)	M
Virginia, U. of	L
■ Wabash (IN)	S
Wake Forest (NC)	M
Washington & Lee (VA)	M
Washington U. (MO)	M
▲ Wellesley (MA)	R
Wesleyan (CT)	R
Wheaton (IL)	R
Whitman (WA)	R
Willamette (OR)	R
William & Mary (VA)	M
Williams (MA)	R
Yale (CT)	M
Yeshiva (NY)	R

GROUP II
Very Selective

▲ Agnes Scott (GA)	S
Alabama, U. of	l
Albion (MI)	R
Albright (PA)	R
Alfred (NY)	R
Alma (MI)	R
Arizona State	XL
Arizona, U. of	XL
Augustana (SD)	M
Austin (TX)	R
Baylor (TX)	M
Berry (GA)	R
Bethany (WV)	S
Birmingham-Southern (AL)	R
Brigham Young (UT)	XL
Butler (IN)	R
California, U. of (Davis)	XL
California, U. of (Irvine)	L
California, U. of (Riverside)	L
California, U. of (Santa Barbara)	L
California, U. of (Santa Cruz)	M
Canisius (NY)	M
Carroll (WI)	R
Centenary (LA)	S
Chapman (CA)	R
City College (CUNY)(NY)	L
College of Charleston (SC)	L
Columbia Col. (SC)	R
Colorado, U. of	L
Concordia (MN)	R
Connecticut, U. of	XL
Cornell (IA)	R
Creighton (NE)	M
Dayton, U. of (OH)	M

GROUP II continues next page

Enrollment Code	
■ *Men Only*	S = Small (less than 1000 students) R = Moderate (1000-3000 students) M = Medium (3000-8000 students)
▲ *Women Only*	L = Large (8000-20,000 students) XL = Extra Large (over 20,000 students)

PRE-MED/PRE-DENTAL, continued

GROUP II, continued

Delaware, U. of	L
DePaul (IL)	L
Denison (OH)	R
Denver, U. of (CO)	M
DeSales (PA)	R
Duquesne (PA)	M
Earlham (IN)	R
Eckerd (FL)	R
Erskine (SC)	S
Evansville (IN)	R
Florida State	L
Fordham (NY)	M
Franklin (IN)	S
Gannon (PA)	M
Georgia, U. of	XL
Gonzaga (WA)	R
Goucher (MD)	R
Grove City (PA)	R
Guilford (NC)	R
Gustavus Adolphus (MN)	R
Hamline (MN)	R
Hanover (IN)	R
Harrisburg U. (PA)	S
Hawaii Pacific	R
■ Hampden-Sydney (VA)	S
Hendrix (AR)	R
Hiram (OH)	R
Hobart & Wm. Smith (NY)	R
Hofstra (NY)	M
▲ Hollins (VA)	S
Hood (MD)	S
Hope (MI)	R
Houghton (NY)	S
Houston Baptist (TX)	R
Houston, U. of (TX)	L
Howard (DC)	M
Huntingdon (AL)	S
Idaho, College of	S
Illinois, U. of (Chicago)	L
Indiana U.	XL
Indiana Wesleyan	M
Ithaca Col. (NY)	M

James Madison (VA)	L
Juniata (PA)	R
Kansas, U. of	L
Kansas State	L
Kentucky, U. of	L
Knox (IL)	R
Lake Forest (IL)	R
LaSalle (PA)	M
Lebanon Valley (PA)	R
Lewis & Clark (OR)	R
Lipscomb (TN)	R
Loyola (IL)	M
Loyola (LA)	R
Loyola (MD)	M
Lycoming (PA)	R
Manhattan (NY)	M
Marquette (WI)	M
Mary Washington (VA)	M
Maryland, U. of (Baltimore County)	M
Massachusetts, U. of	L
McDaniel (MD)	R
Michigan State	XL
Michigan, U. of (Dearborn)	M
Millsaps (MS)	R
Minnesota, U. of (Morris)	R
Mississippi, U. of	L
Mississippi State	L
Missouri, U. of	XL
Monmouth (IL)	S
Moravian (PA)	R
Morningside (IA)	S
Muhlenberg (PA)	R
Nebraska Wesleyan	R
Nevada, U. of (Reno)	L
New Hampshire, U. of	L
New Mexico, U. of	L
New York U.	L
North Carolina, U. of (Charlotte)	L
North Central (IL)	R

GROUP II continues next page

Enrollment Code		
■ *Men Only* ▲ *Women Only*	S = Small (less than 1000 students)	R = Moderate (1000-3000 students)	M = Medium (3000-8000 students)
	L = Large (8000-20,000 students)	XL = Extra Large (over 20,000 students)	

PRE-MED/PRE-DENTAL, continued

GROUP II, continued

Oglethorpe (GA)	S
Ohio State	XL
Ohio Wesleyan	R
Oregon, U. of	L
Pacific, U. of the (CA)	R
Pacific Lutheran (OR)	R
Pacific University (OR)	R
Pennsylvania State	XL
Pittsburgh, U. of (PA)	L
Point Loma (CA)	R
Presbyterian (SC)	R
Purchase (SUNY)(NY)	M
Randolph College (VA)	S
Randolph-Macon (VA)	R
Redlands, U. of (CA)	R
Regis (CO)	R
Richard Stockton (NJ)	M
Ripon (WI)	S
Rowan (NJ)	M
St. Francis (PA)	R
St. John's (MN)	R
St. Joseph's U. (PA)	R
St. Louis (MO)	M
St. Louis Col. of Pharmacy (MO)	S
St. Scholastica (MN)	R
St. Thomas, U. of (MN)	S
St. Thomas, U. of (TX)	R
San Diego, U. of (CA)	M
San Diego State U. (CA)	XL
San Francisco, U. of (CA)	M
Scranton, U. of (PA)	M
▲ Scripps (CA)	S

Seton Hall (NJ)	M
Siena (NY)	R
Spring Hill (AL)	R
Stetson (FL)	R
Stonehill (MA)	R
Stony Brook (SUNY) (NY)	L
Susquehanna (PA)	R
Tennessee, U. of	XL
Texas A&M	XL
Transylvania (KY)	S
Truman State (MO)	M
Tuskegee (AL)	M
Utah, U. of	L
Valparaiso U. (IN)	M
Vermont, U. of	L
Virginia Tech.	L
Washington College (MD)	S
Washington & Jefferson (PA)	R
Washington, U. of	XL
Wells (NY)	S
West Florida, U. of	M
West Virginia U	L
Westminster (MO)	S
Westminster (PA)	R
Westmont (CA)	R
Wheaton (MA)	R
Winona State U. (MN)	M
Wisconsin, U. of	XL
Wittenberg (OH)	R
Wofford (SC)	R
Wooster (OH)	R
Wyoming, U. of	L

PRE-MED / PRE-DENTAL continues next page

Enrollment Code

■ *Men Only*
▲ *Women Only*

S = Small (less than 1000 students)   R = Moderate (1000-3000 students)   M = Medium (3000-8000 students)
L = Large (8000-20,000 students)   XL = Extra Large (over 20,000 students)

PRE-MED/PRE-DENTAL, continued

GROUP III
Selective

Abilene Christian (TX)	M	Louisiana College	R
American International (MA)	R	Louisiana-Lafayette	L
Benedictine (IL)	R	Louisiana State	XL
▲ Bennett (NC)	S	Lynchburg (VA)	R
Blackburn (IL)	S	Mount St. Joseph (OH)	R
Brooklyn Col. (CUNY) (NY)	L	Mount St. Mary's (MD)	R
California State U. (Channel Islands)	R	Nicholls State (LA)	M
California State U. (Fullerton)	L	Nova Southeastern (FL)	R
California State U. (Monterey Bay)	R	Rider (NJ)	R
California State U. (San Jose)	L	▲ Spelman (GA)	R
Carroll (MT)	R	St. Mary's (TX)	R
Carson-Newman (TN)	R	St. Vincent (PA)	R
Delaware Valley (PA)	R	South Dakota, U. of	M
Dillard (LA)	R	Temple (PA)	L
Dominican (CA)	S	Texas, U. of (San Antonio)	L
East Carolina (NC)	L	Thomas More (KY)	R
Elmhurst (IL)	R	Toledo, U. of (OH)	L
Findlay (OH)	M	Virginia Commonwealth	L
Florida A&M	M	Virginia Wesleyan	R
Florida Southern	R	Walla Walla (WA)	R
Freed-Hardeman (TN)	R	Wartburg (IA)	R
Gardner-Webb (NC)	R	Wayne State (MI)	L
Heidelberg (OH)	S	Wilkes (PA)	R
Ind.U.-Purdue U.-Indianapolis (IN)	L	Wisconsin, U. of (Stevens Point)	M
Jacksonville (FL)	R	Xavier U. of Louisiana	R
Kentucky Wesleyan	S		

Enrollment Code

■ *Men Only*
▲ *Women Only*

S = Small (less than 1000 students)   R = Moderate (1000-3000 students)   M = Medium (3000-8000 students)

L = Large (8000-20,000 students)   XL = Extra Large (over 20,000 students)

PSYCHOLOGY

GROUP I
Most Selective

Allegheny (PA)......................R	Lafayette (PA) ....R
American U. (DC) ....M	Lehigh (PA) ....M
Amherst (MA)........................R	Macalester (MN)......................R
Bard (NY) ....R	Miami, U. of (FL) L
▲Barnard (NY)........................R	Miami U. (OH) L
Bates (ME) ....R	Michigan, U. of XL
Binghamton (SUNY) (NY) L	Minnesota, U. of XL
Boston U. (MA) L	▲Mount Holyoke (MA)............R
Brandeis (MA) ....R	New College (FL) ....S
▲Bryn Mawr (PA) ....S	New Jersey, College of ....M
Bucknell (PA)..........................M	New York U. L
Buffalo (SUNY)(NY) L	North Carolina, U. of L
California, U. of (Berkeley)..............XL	Northwestern (IL) ....M
California, U. of (Los Angeles) XL	Notre Dame, U of (IN)............M
California, U. of (San Diego) L	Occidental (CA) ....R
Carleton (MN)........................R	Pennsylvania, U. of.................L
Carnegie-Mellon (PA) ....M	Pennsylvania State XL
Case Western Reserve U. (OH) ....M	Pitzer (CA) ....S
Centre (KY) ....R	Pomona (CA) ....S
Chicago, U. of (IL) ....M	Princeton (NJ) ....M
Claremont McKenna (CA) ....R	Reed (OR) ....R
Clarkson (NY) ....M	Richmond, U. of (VA) ....R
Colby (ME) ....R	Rhodes (TN) ....R
Colgate (NY) ....R	Rochester, U. of (NY) ....M
Colorado College ....R	Rutgers (NJ) L
Columbia (NY) ....M	▲Scripps (CA) ....S
Connecticut Col. ....R	▲Simmons (MA) ....R
Dallas, U. of (TX) ....R	Skidmore (NY) ....R
Dartmouth (NH) ....M	▲Smith (MA) ....R
Davidson (NC) ....R	Southwestern (TX) ....R
DePauw (IN) ....R	Stanford (CA) ....M
Dickinson (PA) ....R	St. Louis (MO) ....M
Drew (NJ) ....R	St. Mary's College of Maryland ....R
Duke (NC) ....M	St. Olaf (MN) ....R
Emory (GA) ....M	Swarthmore (PA) ....R
Franklin & Marshall (PA) ....R	Tufts (MA) ....M
Furman (SC) ....R	Tulane (LA) ....M
Georgetown (DC) ....M	Union (NY) ....R
George Washington (DC) ....M	Vanderbilt (TN) ....M
Georgia Institute of Tech. L	Vassar (NY) ....R
Gettysburg (PA) ....R	Virginia, U. of L
Grinnell (IA) ....R	■Wabash (IN) ....S
Gustavus Adolphus (MN) ....R	Wake Forest (NC) ....M
Harvard (MA)..........................M	Washington U. (MO) ....M
Haverford (PA) ....S	Wesleyan (CT) ....R
Holy Cross (MA) ....R	Wheaton (IL) ....R
Illinois, U. of (Urbana-Champaign) XL	Whitman (WA)..........................R
Illinois Wesleyan ....R	Willamette (OR) ....R
James Madison (VA)...............L	Williams (MA) ....R
Johns Hopkins (MD) ....M	Yale (CT) ....M
Kalamazoo (MI) ....R	Yeshiva (NY) ....M
Kenyon (OH) ....R	

PSYCHOLOGY continues next page

PSYCHOLOGY, continued

GROUP II
Very Selective

Adelphi (NY)	M	Elmira (NY)	R
▲ Agnes Scott (GA)	S	Elon (NC)	R
Alabama, U. of	L	Fairfield (CT)	M
Alabama, U. of (Huntsville)	M	Fairmont (WV)	M
Albany (SUNY) (NY)	L	Flagler (FL)	R
Albright (PA)	R	Florida Atlantic	L
Alfred (NY)	R	Florida Inst. of Tech.	R
Alma (MI)	R	Florida International	L
Arizona State	XL	Florida State	L
Arizona, U. of	XL	Gannon (PA)	R
Assumption (MA)	R	George Mason (VA)	L
Belmont (TN)	R	Georgia State	`L
Beloit (WI)	R	Grand Valley (MI)	L
▲ Bennett (NC)	S	Guilford (NC)	R
Berry (GA)	R	Hamline (MN)	R
Bethany (WV)	S	Hampton (VA)	M
Bowling Green (OH)	L	Hanover (IN)	R
Birmingham-Southern (AL)	R	Hendrix (AR)	R
Brigham Young (UT)	XL	Herbert Lehman (CUNY) (NY)	L
Cal. Poly State U. (SLO)	L	Hobart & Wm. Smith (NY)	R
California, U. of (Irvine)	L	Hofstra (NY)	M
California, U. of (Merced)	R	Hood (MD)	S
California, U. of (Riverside)	L	Hope (MI)	R
California, U. of (Santa Barbara)	L	Houghton (NY)	S
California, U. of (Santa Cruz)	M	Houston, U. of (TX)	L
Carroll (WI)	R	Hunter (CUNY) (NY)	L
Catholic (DC)	R	Illinois, U. of (Chicago)	L
Central Florida, U. of	XL	Indiana U.	XL
Chapman (CA)	R	Iowa, U. of	XL
Cincinnati, U. of	L	John Carroll (OH)	R
Clark (MA)	R	Kansas State	L
Coe (IA)	R	Kansas, U. of	L
College of Charleston (SC)	L	Kean (NJ)	M
Colorado State	L	Kentucky, U. of	L
Colorado, U. of	L	Lake Forest (IL)	R
Concordia (MN)	R	LaSalle (PA)	M
Connecticut, U. of	XL	Lebanon Valley (PA)	R
Cornell Col. (IA)	R	LeMoyne (NY)	R
Creighton (NE)	M	Loras (IA)	R
Delaware, U. of	L	Louisiana State U.	L
Denison (OH)	R	Loyola (IL)	M
Denver, U. of (CO)	M	Loyola (MD)	M
DePaul (IL)	L	Luther (IA)	R
Dubuque, U. of (IA)	S	Lycoming (PA)	R
Earlham (IN)	R	Maine, U. of	L
Eastern Michigan	L		
Eckerd (FL)	R		

GROUP II continues next page

Enrollment Code

■ *Men Only* S = Small (less than 1000 students)   R = Moderate (1000-3000 students)   M = Medium (3000-8000 students)
▲ *Women Only*   L = Large (8000-20,000 students)   XL = Extra Large (over 20,000 students)

| **PSYCHOLOGY, continued** |

GROUP II, continued

Manhattanville (NY) .... R
Marist (NY) .... M
Marquette (WI) .... R
Maryville (TN) .... S
Mary Washington (VA) .... M
Massachusetts, U. of L
Mercer (GA) .... R
Merrimack (MA) .... R
Michigan State XL
Millersville (PA) .... M
▲ Mills (CA) .... S
Minnesota, U. of (Morris) .... R
Missouri, U. of XL
Missouri, U. of (Kansas City) .... M
Missouri, U. of (St. Louis) .... M
Moravian (PA) .... R
Morningside (IA) .... S
Muhlenberg (PA) .... R
Nebraska Wesleyan .... R
Nevada, U. of (Las Vegas) L
New Paltz (SUNY) (NY) .... M
New Mexico, U. of L
New School U. (Eugene Lang) (NY) ..... R
Newman U. (KS) .... S
North Carolina (Asheville) .... R
North Carolina, U. of (Charlotte) L
North Carolina, U. of (Wilmington) .. L
North Carolina State L
Northern Colorado, U. of L
Northeastern (MA) L
Ohio State XL
Ohio U. L
Ohio Wesleyan .... R
Oklahoma City U. .... R
Oklahoma, U. of XL
Oklahoma State L
Oregon, U. of L
Oswego (SUNY) (NY) .... M
Pace (NY) .... M
Pittsburgh, U. of (PA) L
Portland State (OR) L
Puerto Rico, U. of L
Queens (CUNY) (NY) L
Quinnipiac (CT) .... R
Ramapo (NJ) .... M
Randolph College (VA) .... S
Randolph-Macon (VA) .... R
Rhode Island, U. of L
Richard Stockton (NJ) .... M
Roanoke (VA) .... R
Rockhurst (MO) .... R

Rollins (FL) .... R
Rowan (NJ) .... M
Rutgers-Newark (NJ) .... M
St. Lawrence (NY) .... R
St. Mary's College (CA) .... R
St. Michael's (VT) .... R
St. Thomas, U. of (TX) .... R
Salisbury (MD) .... M
San Diego State U. (CA) XL
San Francisco, U. of (CA) .... M
Santa Clara, U. of (CA) .... M
Seattle Pacific (WA) .... R
Shepherd (WV) .... M
Siena (NY) .... R
Southern California L
Stetson (FL) .... R
Stonehill (MA) .... R
Stony Brook (SUNY) (NY) L
Susquehanna (PA) .... R
▲ Sweet Briar (VA) .... S
Syracuse (NY) L
Temple (PA) L
Texas, U. of (Austin) XL
Towson (MD) L
Transylvania (KY) .... R
Tulsa, U. of (OK) .... R
Valparaiso U. (IN) .... M
Vermont, U of L
Virginia Tech. L
Virginia, U. of L
Washington College (MD) .... S
Washington & Jefferson (PA) .... R
Washington, U. of XL
Webster (MO) .... R
Wells (NY) .... S
West Florida, U. of .... M
West Virginia U. L
Western Michigan L
Western Washington U. .... R
Westminster (MO) .... S
Westminster (UT) .... R
Westmont (CA) .... R
Wheaton (MA) .... R
Whitworth (WA) .... R
Winthrop (SC) .... M
Wisconsin, U. of XL
Wisconsin Lutheran .... S
Wittenberg (OH) .... R
Wofford (SC) .... R
Xavier (OH) .... R

PSYCHOLOGY continues next page

PSYCHOLOGY, continued

GROUP III
Selective

Akron, U. of (OH)	L	Chaminade (HI)	R
Alabama, U. of (Birmingham)	M	Coker (SC)	S
Alaska Pacific	S	Colby-Sawyer (NH)	S
▲Alverno (WI)	R	Colorado, U. of (Colorado Springs)	M
American International (MA)	R	Colorado, U. of (Denver)	M
Aquinas (MI)	R	Concordia (OR)	S
Arcadia (PA)	R	Corban (OR)	S
Arkansas, U. of	L	Delaware State	R
Averett (VA)	S	Dominican (CA)	S
Baker (KS)	R	Dominican (IL)	S
Baldwin-Wallace (OH)	R	D'Youville (NY)	R
Ball State (IN)	L	East Carolina	L
▲Bay Path (MA)	R	Eastern Connecticut	M
Bemidji State (MN)	M	Eastern Illinois	L
Bethel (MN)	R	Edgewood (WI)	S
Biola (CA)	R	Elmhurst (IL)	R
Blackburn (IL)	S	Findlay (OH)	M
Bridgewater (MA)	M	Fitchburg (MA)	R
Bridgewater (VA)	R	Framingham (MA)	M
Brockport (SUNY)(NY)	M	Franciscan U. of Steubenville (OH)	R
Brooklyn (CUNY)(NY)	L	George Fox (OR)	R
Caldwell (NJ)	S	Hawaii, U. of (Hilo)	R
California (PA)	M	▲Hollins (VA)	S
California Baptist	M	Holy Names (CA)	S
California Lutheran	R	John Jay College (CUNY)(NY)	M
California State U. (Bakersfield)	M	Johnson C. Smith (NC)	R
California State U. (Channel Islands)	R	▲Judson (AL)	S
California State U. (Chico)	L	Keene State (NH)	R
California State U. (Dominguez Hills)	M	Kentucky Wesleyan	S
California State U. (Long Beach)	L	Kutztown (PA)	M
California State U. (Los Angeles)	L	Laverne (CA)	R
California State U. (Northridge)	L	Liberty (VA)	R
California State U. (Sacramento)	M	Lindenwood (MO)	M
California State U. (San Bernardino)	M	Lock Haven (PA)	M
California State U. (San Marcos)	M	Long Island U. (C.W.Post)(NY)	M
California State U. (Stanislaus)	M	Longwood (VA)	R
Canisius (NY)	M	Lyndon State(VT)	R
Carson-Newman (TN)	R	Lyon (AR)	S
Carthage (WI)	R	Maine, U. of (Farmington)	R
Castleton State (VT)	R	Manchester (IN)	R
▲Cedar Crest (PA)	S	Marshall (WV)	L
Central Connecticut	M	▲Mary Baldwin (VA)	S
Central Michigan	L	Marymount (VA)	R
Central Washington	L		

GROUP III continues next page

Enrollment Code

■ *Men Only*   S = Small (less than 1000 students)   R = Moderate (1000-3000 students)   M = Medium (3000-8000 students)
▲ *Women Only*   L = Large (8000-20,000 students)   XL = Extra Large (over 20,000 students)

PSYCHOLOGY, continued

GROUP III, continued

Marymount Manhattan (NY)	R
Marywood (PA)	R
Massachusetts, U. of (Dartmouth)	M
Memphis, U. of (TN)	L
Mercy (NY)	M
▲Meredith (NC)	R
Middle Tennessee	L
Millersville (PA)	M
Minnesota State U. (Moorhead)	M
Minnesota, U. of (Duluth)	L
Molloy (NY)	R
Montclair State (NJ)	M
Mount St. Joseph (OH)	R
Muskingum (OH)	R
New Hampshire, U. of	L
North Carolina (Greensboro)	M
Northeastern State (OK)	L
Northern Arizona	L
Northern Iowa, U. of	L
Northwestern (IA)	R
Northwestern (MN)	R
Nyack (NY)	R
Oakland City U. (IN)	R
Oklahoma Baptist	R
Otterbein (OH)	R
Ozarks, College of the (MO)	R
Palm Beach Atlantic (FL)	R
Penn State (Harrisburg)(PA)	R
Peru State (NE)	R
▲Pine Manor (MA)	S
Pittsburgh, U.of (Greensburg)	R
Plattsburgh (SUNY)(NY)	M
Point Park (PA)	R
Potsdam (SUNY)(NY)	M
Purchase (SUNY)(NY)	M
Radford (VA)	M
Regis (CO)	R
Rhode Island College	M
Rockford (IL)	S
Roger Williams (RI)	M
Roosevelt (IL)	R
▲Rosemont (PA)	S
Russell Sage/The Sage Colleges (NY)	R
Sacred Heart (CT)	R
St. Ambrose (IA)	R
St. Anselm (NH)	R
St. Edward's (TX)	M
St. Francis (NY)	R
St, John's (NY)	L
St. Joseph's (IN)	S
St. Joseph's (NY)	R
St. Martin's (WA)	S
St. Mary (KS)	S
St. Mary, College of (NE)	S
St. Scholastica (MN)	R
St. Thomas Aquinas (NY)	R
St. Vincent (PA)	R
Salem State (MA)	M
Seton Hall (NJ)	M
Siena Heights (MI)	S
Shippensburg (PA)	M
Simpson (IA)	R
Sonoma State (CA)	M
South Dakota, U. of	M
Southern Connecticut	M
Southern Illinois U. (Carbondale)	L
Southern Oregon State U.	M
Southwest Baptist (MO)	R
Springfield (MA)	M
Staten Island (CUNY)(NY)	M
▲Stephens (MO)	S
Suffolk (MA)	R
Taylor (IN)	R
Tennessee, U. of (Chattanooga)	M
Texas A&M (Corpus Christi)	M
Texas, U. of (El Paso)	L
Texas, U. of (San Antonio)	L
Texas, U. of (Tyler)	R
Texas Wesleyan	R
Virginia Commonwealth U.	L
Virginia Wesleyan	R
Wayne State (MI)	L
Waynesburg (PA)	R
Western Kentucky	L
Western New England (MA)	R
Westfield (MA)	M
Wheeling Jesuit (WV)	R
Wilkes (PA)	R
Wilson (PA)	S
Wisconsin, U. of (Green Bay)	M
Wisconsin, U. of (Stout)	M
Worcester State (MA)	M
Wyoming, U. of	L
Xavier University of Louisiana	R
York (NE)	S

RELIGIOUS STUDIES

GROUP I
Most Selective

▲ Agnes Scott (GA) .... S	North Carolina, U. of L
▲ Barnard (NY) .... R	Northwestern (IL) .... M
Bates (ME) .... R	Notre Dame (IN) .... M
Boston College (MA) L	Oberlin (OH) .... R
Bowdoin (ME) .... R	Occidental (CA) .... R
Brown (RI) .... M	Pennsylvania, U. of L
California, U. of (Berkeley) XL	Pepperdine (CA) .... R
Carleton (MN) .... R	Pittsburgh, U. of (PA) L
Case Western Reserve (OH) .... M	Pomona (CA) .... R
Centre (KY) .... R	Princeton (NJ) .... M
Chicago, U. of (IL) .... M	Providence (RI) .... M
Claremont McKenna (CA) .... R	Rhodes (TN) .... R
Colby (ME) .... R	Richmond, U. of (VA) .... M
Colgate (NY) .... R	Rutgers (NJ) L
Columbia (NY) .... M	St. Joseph's (PA) .... R
Dartmouth (NH) .... M	St. Mary's College of Maryland .... R
Davidson (NC) .... R	St. Olaf (MN) .... R
DePauw (IN) .... R	South, U. of the (TN) .... R
Dickinson (PA) .... R	Southwestern (TX) .... R
Drew (NJ) .... R	Stanford (CA) .... M
Duke (NC) .... M	Texas, U. of XL
Emory (GA) .... M	Trinity (CT) .... R
Furman (SC) .... R	Villanova (PA) .... M
Georgetown (DC) .... M	Virginia, U. of L
Grinnell (IA) .... R	■ Wabash (IN) .... S
Gustavus Adolphus (MN) .... R	Wake Forest (NC) .... M
Hamilton (NY) .... R	▲ Wellesley (MA) .... R
Haverford (PA) .... S	Wesleyan (CT) .... R
Holy Cross (MA) .... R	Wheaton (IL) .... R
Kenyon (OH) .... R	Whitman (WA) .... R
Lawrence (WI) .... R	Willamette (OR) .... R
Macalester (MN) .... R	William & Mary (VA) .... M
Middlebury (VT) .... R	Wofford (SC) .... R
▲ Mount Holyoke (MA) .... R	Yale (CT) .... M
New College (FL) .... S	

RELIGIOUS STUDIES continues next page

Enrollment Code

■ *Men Only*	S = Small (less than 1000 students) R = Moderate (1000-3000 students) M = Medium (3000-8000 students)
▲ *Women Only*	L = Large (8000-20,000 students) XL = Extra Large (over 20,000 students)

RELIGIOUS STUDIES

GROUP II
Very Selective

Alaska Pacific	S	Hendrix (AR)	R
Arizona State	XL	Hiram (OH)	R
Asbury (KY)	R	Hood (MD)	S
Augsburg (MN)	R	Hope (MI)	R
Augustana (SD)	R	Houghton (NY)	S
Austin (TX)	R	Huntingdon (AL)	S
Baylor (TX)	M	Indiana Wesleyan	M
Belmont (TN)	R	Iowa, U. of	XL
Berea (KY)	R	John Carroll (OH)	R
Bethany (WV)	S	LaSalle (PA)	M
Bethel (IN)	R	LeMoyne (NY)	R
Bethel (MN)	M	Lipscomb (TN)	R
Biola (CA)	R	Loras (IA)	R
Birmingham-Southern (AL)	R	Loyola (IL)	M
Brigham Young (UT)	XL	Loyola (LA)	R
Bryan (TN)	S	Loyola Marymount (CA)	M
Bryn Athyn (PA)	S	Luther (IA)	R
California, U. of (Santa Barbara)	L	Lycoming (PA)	R
Capital (OH)	R	Manhattan (NY)	M
Catholic U. (DC)	M	Manhattanville (NY)	R
Central (IA)	R	Marquette)WI)	M
Christendom (VA)	S	Master's (CA)	R
Christian Brothers (TN)	R	McMurry (TX)	R
Concordia (CA)	R	Mercer (GA)	R
Creighton (NE)	M	Merrimack (MA)	R
Dana (NE)	S	Messiah (PA)	R
Dayton, U. of (OH)	M	Muhlenberg (PA)	R
Denver, U. of (CO)	M	Nazareth (NY)	R
DePaul (IL)	L	Newman U. (KS)	S
Detroit Mercy (MI)	M	North Carolina (Charlotte)	L
Drury (MO)	R	Oklahoma City U.	R
Duquesne (PA)	M	Pacific Lutheran (WA)	R
Earlham (IN)	R	Portland, U. of (OR)	R
Eckerd (FL)	R	Presbyterian (SC)	R
Elizabethtown (PA)	R	Roanoke (VA)	R
Florida State	L	Rockhurst (MO)	R
Fordham (NY)	M	Rollins (FL)	R
Geneva (PA)	R	Rowan (NJ)	M
Gonzaga (WA)	R	St. Anselm (NH)	R
Gordon (MA)	R	St. Bonaventure (NY)	R
Guilford (NC)	R	St. Edward's (TX)	M
Hamline (MN)	R	St. Francis (PA)	R
■ Hampden-Sydney (VA)	S		
Hanover (IN)	R		
Harding (AR)	M		

GROUP II continues next page

RELIGIOUS STUDIES, continued

•• ━━━━━━━━━━━━━━━ **GROUP II**, continued ━━━━━━━━━━━━━━━ ••

St. John's (MN)	R
St. Louis U. (MO)	M
St. Mary's (MN)	R
St. Mary's College (CA)	R
▲ St. Mary's College (IN)	R
St. Mary's U. of San Antonio (TX)	R
St. Michael's (VT)	R
St. Norbert (WI)	R
St. Scholastica (MN)	R
St. Thomas (MN)	R
St. Thomas, U. of (TX)	R
Sanford (AL)	R
San Diego, U. of (CA)	M
Santa Clara U. (CA)	M
Scranton (PA)	M
Seattle Pacific (WA)	R
Siena (NY)	R
Southern Methodist (TX)	L
Stetson (FL)	R

Spring Hill (AL)	R
Stony Brook (SUNY) (NY)	L
Stonehill (MA)	R
Syracuse (NY)	L
Tennessee, U. of	XL
Texas Christian U.	M
Texas Wesleyan	R
Union (NE)	R
Valparaiso U. (IN)	M
Vermont, U. of	L
Wartburg (IA)	R
Westmont (CA)	R
Whitworth (WA)	R
Wisconsin Lutheran	S
Wittenberg (OH)	R
Wofford (SC)	R
Wooster (OH)	R
Xavier (OH)	R

RELIGIOUS STUDIES continues next page

Enrollment Code

■ *Men Only*   S = Small (less than 1000 students)   R = Moderate (1000-3000 students)   M = Medium (3000-8000 students)
▲ *Women Only*   L = Large (8000-20,000 students)   XL = Extra Large (over 20,000 students)

RELIGIOUS STUDIES, continued

GROUP III
Selective

Abilene Christain (TX)	M	
Andrews (MI)	R	
Aquinas (MI)	R	
Azusa Pacific (CA)	R	
Barry (FL)	R	
Belhaven (MS)	R	
Benedictine (KS)	R	
# Bethel (IN)	R	
Bluffton (OH)	S	
Brescia (KY)	S	
Briar Cliff (IA)	R	
California State U. (Chico)	L	
California State U. (Fullerton)	L	
California State U. (Long Beach)	L	
Carthage (WI)	R	
Chaminade (HI)	R	
Columbia College (SC)	R	
Concordia (NE)	R	
Cumberland (KY)	R	
De Sales (PA)	S	
Doane (NE)	S	
Dordt (IA)	R	
Eastern Mennonite (VA)	R	
Fort Lewis (CO)	M	
Franciscan U. of Steubenville (OH)	R	
Freed-Hardeman (TN)	R	
Gannon (PA)	M	
George Fox (OR)	R	
Greensboro College (NC)	S	
Hardin-Simmons (TX)	R	
Hastings (NE)	R	
High Point (NC)	R	
Holy Names (CA)	S	
John Brown (AR)	R	
▲ Judson (AL)	S	
Kentucky Wesleyan	R	
King (TN)	S	
Lambuth (TN)	S	
Liberty (VA)	R	
Louisiana College	R	
Louisiana State	XL	
Maryville (TN)	S	
Marywood (PA)	R	
Mercyhurst (PA)	R	
▲ Meredith (NC)	R	
Milligan (TN)	S	
Mississippi College	R	

Montreat (NC)	S
■ Morehouse (GA)	R
Mount St. Joseph (OH)	R
Mount St. Mary's (CA)	R
Muskingum (OH)	R
Niagara (NY)	R
Northland (WI)	S
Northwestern (IA)	S
Northwestern (MN)	R
Nyack (NY)	R
Oakland City U. (IN)	R
Oklahoma Baptist	R
Oklahoma Christian	R
Olivet Nazarene (IL)	R
Oral Roberts (OK)	M
Ouachita Baptist (AR)	R
Palm Beach Atlantic (FL)	R
Philadelphia Biblical (PA)	S
Quincy (IL)	R
Regis (CO)	R
▲ Rosemont (PA)	R
Sacred Heart (CT)	R
St. Ambrose (IA)	R
▲ St. Catherine (MN)	R
St. Francis (IN)	R
St. John's (NY)	L
St. Joseph's U. (PA)	R
St. Martin's (WA)	S
St. Mary, College of (NE)	S
St. Peter's (NJ)	R
St. Vincent (PA)	R
Seattle U. (WA)	R
Seton Hall (NJ)	M
Silver Lake (WI)	S
Simpson (IA)	R
Southern Nazarene (OK)	R
Southwest Baptist (MO)	R
Tabor (KS)	S
Taylor (IN)	R
Texas Lutheran	R
Union University (TN)	R
Virginia Commonwealth U.	L
Virginia Wesleyan	R
Walsh (OH)	R
Wheeling Jesuit (WV)	R
York (NE)	S

 # Also, Youth Ministry, Ministerial Studies

SOCIOLOGY

GROUP I
Most Selective

Amherst (MA) .... R	Illinois Wesleyan .... R
Bard (NY) .... R	Johns Hopkins (MD) .... M
▲ Barnard (NY) .... R	Kalamazoo (MI) .... R
Binghamton (SUNY)(NY) .... M	Kenyon (OH) .... R
Boston College (MA) L	Lycoming (PA) .... R
Bowdoin (ME) .... R	Maryland, U. of XL
▲ Bryn Mawr (PA) .... S	Michigan, U. of XL
Bucknell (PA) .... M	Minnesota, U. of XL
California, U. of (Berkeley) XL	New Jersey, College of .... M
California, U. of (Los Angeles) XL	North Carolina, U. of L
Chicago, U. of (IL) .... M	Northwestern (IL) .... M
Clarkson (NY) .... M	Notre Dame (IN) .... M
Colorado College .... R	Oberlin (OH) .... R
Columbia (NY) .... M	Pennsylvania, U. of L
Connecticut College .... R	Pennsylvania State XL
Dartmouth (NH) .... M	Pitzer (CA) .... S
DePauw (IN) .... R	Pomona (CA) .... R
Duke (NC) .... M	Princeton (NJ) .... M
Emory (GA) .... M	Rutgers (NJ) L
Florida, U. of XL	Southwestern (TX) .... R
Franklin & Marshall (PA) .... R	Stanford (CA) .... M
Geneseo (SUNY)(NY) .... M	Trinity (TX) .... R
Georgetown (DC) .... M	Union (NY) .... R
George Washington (DC) .... M	Virginia, U. of L
Gettysburg (PA) .... S	Wake Forest (NC) .... M
Grinnell (IA) .... R	Wheaton (IL) .... R
Harvard (MA) .... M	Whitman (WA) .... R
Holy Cross (MA) .... R	Willamette (OR) .... R
Illinois, U. of (Urbana-Champaign) XL	Yale (CT) .... M

SOCIOLOGY continues next page

Enrollment Code	
■ *Men Only*	S = Small (less than 1000 students) R = Moderate (1000-3000 students) M = Medium (3000-8000 students)
▲ *Women Only*	L = Large (8000-20,000 students) XL = Extra Large (over 20,000 students)

SOCIOLOGY, continued

GROUP II
Very Selective

Albany (SUNY) (NY)	L	McDaniel (MD)	R
Appalachian State (NC)	L	Merrimack (MA)	R
Arizona, U. of	XL	Mississippi State	L
Asbury (KY)	R	Moravian (PA)	R
Augsburg (MN)	R	■ Morehouse (GA)	R
Belmont (TN)	R	Mount Mercy (IA)	S
Beloit (WI)	R	New College (FL)	S
Brigham Young (UT)	XL	New Mexico, U. of	L
Brown (RI)	M	North Carolina (Asheville)	R
California, U. of (Santa Barbara)	L	North Carolina, U. of (Wilmington)	L
Catholic (DC)	R	North Texas	L
Cincinnati, U. of (OH)	L	Ohio U.	L
City College (CUNY)(NY)	L	Oklahoma State	L
Clark (MA)	R	Oregon, U. of	L
Clemson(SC)	L	Oregon State	L
College of Charleston (SC)	L	Pace (NY)	M
Colorado, U. of	L	Portland State (OR)	L
Concordia (MN)	R	Principia (IL)	S
Connecticut, U. of	XL	Puget Sound (WA)	R
Cornell Col. (IA)	R	Purdue (IN)	XL
Covenant (GA)	S	Queens (CUNY)(NY)	L
Dayton, U. of (OH)	M	Quinnipiac (CT)	R
Denison (OH)	R	Regis (CO)	R
Denver, U. of (CO)	M	Roanoke (VA)	R
Drake (IA)	M	Rutgers (Camden) (NJ)	M
Earlham (IN)	R	St. Lawrence (NY)	R
Florida International	L	St. Mary's Col. (CA)	R
Georgetown College (KY)	R	▲ Salem Col. (NC)	S
Gordon (MA)	R	San Diego State U. (CA)	XL
Hamline (MN)	R	San Francisco, U. of (CA)	M
Hanover (IN)	R	▲ Simmons (MA)	R
Hawaii, U. of	L	South Dakota School of Mines	R
Hendrix (AR)	R	Stony Brook (SUNY)(NY)	L
Herbert Lehman (CUNY)(NY)	M	Syracuse (NY)	L
Hobart & Wm. Smith (NY)	R	Texas A&M	XL
Hofstra (NY)	M	Towson (MD)	L
▲ Hollins (VA)	S	▲ Trinity (DC)	S
Howard (DC)	M	Vermont, U. of	L
Illinois College	S	Washington State	L
Indiana U.	XL	Washington, U. of	XL
Iowa, U. of	XL	Wells (NY)	S
Iowa State	XL	West Virginia U.	L
James Madison (VA)	M	Westminster (PA)	R
John Carroll (OH)	R	Western Washington U.	L
Kansas State	L	Wheaton (MA)	R
Knox (IL)	R	Winona State U. (MN)	M
Lake Forest (IL)	R	Wisconsin, U. of	XL
Lebanon Valley (PA)	R	Wisconsin, U. of (Stevens Point)	M
Lewis & Clark (OR)	R	Wofford (SC)	R
Louisiana State	XL	Wooster (OH)	R
Loyola Marymount (CA)	M		
Manhattanville (NY)	R		

SOCIOLOGY continues next page

SOCIOLOGY, continued

GROUP III
Selective

Adrian (MI)	R	Kean (NJ)	M
Akron, U. of (OH)	L	Keene State (NH)	R
Alabama, U.of (Huntsville)	M	Illinois State	L
Albright (PA)	R	Indiana (PA)	L
Aquinas (MI)	R	Indiana U.-Purdue U.-Indianapolis (IN)	L
Augusta (GA)	M	Lamar (TX)	M
Averett (VA)	S	Lenoir-Rhyne (NC)	R
Baldwin-Wallace (OH)	R	Longwood (VA)	R
Belmont Abbey (NC)	S	Louisville (KY)	L
Benedictine (KS)	R	Lynchburg (VA)	R
Biola (CA)	R	Manchester (IN)	R
Bridgewater (VA)	R	▲ Mary Baldwin (VA)	S
Bridgewater State (MA)	M	Mass. Col. of Lib. Arts. (N. Adams)	R
California State U. (Fresno)	L	Massachusetts, U. of (Boston)	M
California State U. (East Bay)	M	Massachusetts, U. of (Dartmouth)	M
California State U. (Fullerton)	L	Michigan State	XL
California State U. (Los Angeles)	L	Millersville (PA)	M
California State U. (Northridge)	L	Minnesota, U. of (Duluth)	M
California State U. (Sacramento)	M	Missouri State	L
California State U. (San Bernardino)	M	Montana, U. of	M
California State U. (San Marcos)	M	Montana State (Billings)	R
Castleton State (VT)	R	π Mount St. Joseph (OH)	R
Central Connecticut	M	Nevada, U. of (Las Vegas)	L
Coker (SC)	S	Nevada, U. of (Reno)	L
Colorado, U. of (Colorado Springs)	M	New Orleans (LA)	L
Doane (NE)	S	North Carolina, U. of (Pembroke)	R
D'Youville (NY)	R	Northern Colorado	L
Eastern (PA)	R	Northern Illinois	L
Eastern Connecticut	M	Northern Michigan	M
Eastern Michigan	L	Northland (WI)	S
Fisk (TN)	S	Old Dominion (VA)	L
Fort Hays (KS)	M	Piedmont (GA)	S
Framingham State (MA)	M	Pittsburgh, U. of (Bradford)	R
Gardner-Webb (NC)	S	Randolph-Macon (VA)	R
George Fox (OR)	R	Rhode Island College	M
Georgia State	L	▲ Rosemont (PA)	R
Grambling (LA)	M	St. Anselm (NH)	R
Hartford, U. of (CT)	M	▲ St. Catherine (MN)	R
Hartwick (NY)	R	St. Francis (PA)	R
Hunter (CUNY)(NY)	L		
Johnson C. Smith (NC)	R		

π *Criminology / Sociology*

GROUP III continues next page

Enrollment Code

■ *Men Only*   S = Small (less than 1000 students)   R = Moderate (1000-3000 students)   M = Medium (3000-8000 students)

▲ *Women Only*   L = Large (8000-20,000 students)   XL = Extra Large (over 20,000 students)

SOCIOLOGY, continued

GROUP III, continued

St. John's (NY) L	Temple (PA) L
St. Mary's U. of San Antonio (TX) .... R	Virginia Wesleyan .... R
St. Rose (NY) .... R	Wagner (NY) .... R
Salem State (MA) .... M	West Chester (PA) .... M
Shaw (NC) .... R	Western Connecticut State .... M
Shippensburg (PA) .... M	Western Illinois L
Simpson (IA) .... R	Western Kentucky L
Sonoma State (CA) .... M	Western Michigan L
South Alabama .... M	Whitman (WA) .... R
Southern Connecticut .... M	William Paterson (NJ) .... M
Southern Oregon State U. .... M	Wilson (PA) .... S
▲ Spelman (GA) .... R	Wisconsin, U. of (LaCrosse) L
Springfield (MA) .... M	Wisconsin, U. of (Superior) .... M
Suffolk (MA) .... R	Wisconsin, U. of (Whitewater) L
Tarleton State (TX) .... M	Xavier U. of Louisiana .... R

Enrollment Code		
■ *Men Only*	S = Small (less than 1000 students)	R = Moderate (1000-3000 students)	M = Medium (3000-8000 students)
▲ *Women Only*	L = Large (8000-20,000 students)	XL = Extra Large (over 20,000 students)

ZOOLOGY

GROUP I
Most Selective

California, U. of (Berkeley)	XL	Michigan, U. of	XL
Cornell (NY)	L	North Carolina, U. of	L
Florida, U. of	XL	Pennsylvania State	XL
Miami, U. of (OH)	L	Wisconsin, U. of	XL

GROUP II
Very Selective

Arizona State	XL	Michigan State	XL
Brigham Young (UT)	XL	New Hampshire, U. of	L
California, U. of (Davis)	XL	North Carolina State	L
California, U. of (Santa Barbara)	L	North Central (IL)	R
Clemson (SC)	L	Ohio Wesleyan	R
Connecticut, U. of	XL	Ohio U.	L
Georgia, U. of	L	Oklahoma, U. of	XL
Hawaii, U. of	L	Oklahoma State	L
Indiana U.	XL	Oswego (SUNY)(NY)	M
Iowa State	XL	Texas A&M	XL
Kansas, U. of	L	Texas, U. of (Austin)	XL
Kentucky, U. of	XL	Vermont, U. of	L
Maryland, U. of	XL	Washington State	L
Massachusetts, U. of	L	Washington, U. of	XL

GROUP III
Selective

Cal. Poly. State U. (Pomona)	L	Oregon State	L
California State U. (San Jose)	L	San Francisco State	L
Colorado State	L	San Jose State (CA)	L
Eastern Illinois	L	Southeastern Oklahoma State	M
Howard (DC)	M	Southern Illinois U. (Carbondale)	L
Louisiana-Lafayette	L	Tennessee, U. of	XL
Louisiana State	XL	Weber State (UT)	L
Montana, U. of	M	Wyoming, U. of	L

Enrollment Code		
■ *Men Only*	S = Small (less than 1000 students)	R = Moderate (1000-3000 students)	M = Medium (3000-8000 students)
▲ *Women Only*	L = Large (8000-20,000 students)	XL = Extra Large (over 20,000 students)

SECTION TWO

MISCELLANEOUS MAJORS

ACTUARIAL SCIENCE

Abilene Christian (TX)
Albany (SUNY) (NY)
Ball State (IN)
Bellarmine (KY)
Bentley (MA)
Bradley (IL)
Brigham Young (UT)
Bryant (RI)
Butler (IN)
Carroll (MT)
Carroll (WI)
Central Florida
Central Michigan
Central Missouri
Central Oklahoma
Connecticut, U. of
Drake (IA)
Edinboro (PA)
Elizabethtown (PA)
Eastern Michigan
Florida State
Georgia State
Illinois, U. of
Iowa, U. of
Lebanon Valley (PA)
LeMoyne (NY)
Lycoming (PA)

Maryville (MO)
Minnesota State (Moorhead)
Minnesota, U. of
Nebraska, U. of
New York U.
North Central (IL)
Northern Iowa
Northwestern (IA)
Ohio State
Pennsylvania State
Pennsylvania, U. of
Purdue (IN)
Rider (NJ)
Robert Morris (PA)
Roosevelt (IL)
St. John's (NY)
▲ St. Mary's (IN)
St. Thomas (MN)
San Franciso State
Seton Hill (PA)
Temple (PA)
Thiel (PA)
Texas, U. of (San Antonio)
Valparaiso (IN)
Wisconsin, U. of
Worcester Poly (MA)

AFRICANA STUDIES

Albany (SUNY) (NY)
Bard (NY)
▲ Barnard (NY)
Bates (ME)
Binghamton (SUNY)(NY)
Bowdoin (ME)
Bowling Green (OH)
Brooklyn (CUNY) (NY)
California, U. of (Berkeley)
California, U. of (Santa Barbara)
Chicago, U. of (IL)
City (CUNY)(NY)
Coe (IA)
Columbia (NY)
Connecticut, U. of
Denison (OH)
Duke (NC)
Earlham (IN)
Eastern Illinois
Emory (GA)
Florida, U. of
Franklin & Marshall (PA)
Harvard (MA)
Herbert Lehman (CUNY)(NY)
Howard (DC)
Illinois, U. of (Chicago)
Kansas, U. of
Knox (IL)
Louisiana State
Louisville (KY)
Loyola Marymount (CA)
Luther (IA)

Massachusetts, U. of
Mercer (GA)
Michigan State
Minnesota, U. of
■ Morehouse (GA)
Nebraska, U. of (Omaha)
New York U.
North Carolina (Chapel Hill)
Northwestern (IL)
Notre Dame (IN)
Oberlin (OH)
Ohio State U.
Pennsylvania, U. of
Pittsburgh, U. of (PA)
Princeton (NJ)
Portland State (OR)
Rochester, U. of (NY)
Rutgers (NJ)
San Diego State (CA)
San Francisco State (CA)
Stanford (CA)
Stony Brook (SUNY)(NY)
Texas, U. of
Toledo, U. of (OH)
Vassar (NY)
Washington U. (MO)
▲ Wellesley (MA)
Wesleyan (CT)
Wooster (OH)
Wisconsin, U. of
Wisconsin, U. of (Milwaukee)
Yale (CT)

ALTERNATIVE COLLEGES (see page ix)

Atlantic, College of the (ME)
Berea (WV)
Deep Springs (CA)
Eugene Lang (NY)
Evergreen (WA)
Goddard (VT)
Hampshire (MA)
Marlboro (VT)
New College (FL)

New School U.-Eugene Lang Coll. (NY)
Prescott (AZ)
St. John's (MD) (NM)
Shimer (IL)
Simon's Rock (MA)
Sterling (VT)
Thomas Aquinas (CA)
Unity (ME)
Warren Wilson (NC)

■ *Men Only*
▲ *Women Only*

ANIMAL SCIENCE

Arizona, U. of
Arkansas, U. of
Auburn (AL)
Berry (GA)
Brigham Young (UT)
Cal Poly (Pomona)
Cal Poly (SLO)
Cal State U. (Fresno)
California, U. of (Davis)
Clemson (SC)
Colorado State
Connecticut, U. of
Cornell (NY)
Delaware Valley (PA)
Delaware, U. of
Florida, U. of
Georgia U. of
Hampshire (MA)
Hawaii, U. of
Idaho, U. of
Illinois, U. of
Iowa State
Kansas State
Kentucky, U. of
Louisiana State U.
Maine, U. of
Maryland, U. of
Massachusetts, U. of
Michigan State
Minnesota, U. of
Mississippi State
Missouri, U. of

Montana, U. of (Bozeman)
Nebraska, U. of
Nevada, U of (Reno)
New Hampshire, U. of
New Mexico State
North Carolina State
North Dakota State U.
Ohio State
Oklahoma State
Oregon State
Ozarks, College of the (MO)
Pennsylvania State
Purdue (IN)
Rhode Island, U. of
Rutgers (NJ)
South Dakota State
Southern Illinois (Carbondale)
Southwest Missouri
Tarleton State (TX)
Tennessee
Texas A&M
Texas A&M (Kingsville)
Texas Tech
Utah State
Vermont, U. of
Virginia Poly
Washington State
West Virginia U.
Wisconsin, U.of
Wisconsin, U.of (Platteville)
Wisconsin, U.of (River Falls)
Wyoming, U. of

■ *Men Only*
▲ *Women Only*

APPLIED MATHEMATICS

American (DC)
Auburn (AL)
▲ Barnard (NY)
Boston U. (MA)
Brown (RI)
Bryant (RI)
Cal Tech
California, U. of (Berkeley)
California, U. of (Los Angeles)
California, U. of (Merced)
California, U. of (San Diego)
Carnegie-Mellon (PA)
Case Western (OH)
Chicago, U. of (IL)
Clarkson (NY)
Colgate (NY)
Colorado, U. of
Columbia (NY)
Connecticut, U. of
Florida State
George Washington (DC)
Georgia Tech
Harvard (MA)
Houston, U. of (TX)
Idaho, U. of
Illinois Inst. of Tech
Kettering (MI)
Lehigh (PA)
Michigan, U. of
Missouri, U. of (Rolla)
Montana State

Nevada, U. of (Reno)
New Jersey Inst of Tech.
North Carolina (Asheville)
Northwestern (IL)
Oregon Inst. of Tech.
Pacific, U. of the (CA)
Pittsburgh, U. of (PA)
Pittsburgh (Bradford)
Pitzer (CA)
Purdue (IN)
Queens (CUNY)(NY)
Rice (TX)
Robert Morris (PA)
Rochester, U. of (NY)
Rochester Inst. of Tech (NY)
Rutgers (NJ)
San Jose State (CA)
Sioux Falls, U. of (SD)
Stony Brook (SUNY)(NY)
Tulane (LA)
Tulsa (OK)
Union (NY)
Virginia, U. of
Wake Forest (NC)
Washington U. (MO)
Western Michigan
Western Washington
Wisconsin
Worcester Poly (MA)
Yale (CT)

ARABIC

Binghamton (SUNY)(NY)
Brigham Young (UT)
California, U. of (Los Angeles)
Chicago, U. of (IL)
Georgetown (DC)
Harvard (MA)
Michigan, U. of

Notre Dame (IN)
Ohio State
Stevens Inst. of Tech. (NJ)
Texas, U. of
U.S. Military Academy (NY)
U.S. Naval Academy (MD)

■ *Men Only*
▲ *Women Only*

ARCHAEOLOGY

Baylor (TX)
Boston U. (MA)
Bowdoin (ME)
Brown (RI)
▲ Bryn Mawr (PA)
Cornell (IA)
Cornell (NY)
Dartmouth (NH)
Dickinson (PA)
Evansville (IN)
Florida State
George Washington (DC)
Hamilton (NY)
Harvard (MA)
Haverford (PA)
Hunter (CUNY) (NY)
Johns Hopkins (MD)
Kent State (OH)
Maryland, U. of
π Mary Washington, U. of (VA)

Mercyhurst (PA)
Michigan, U. of
Missouri, U. of
New York U.
North Carolina, U. of (Greensboro)
North Carolina (Charlotte)
Oberlin (OH)
Potsdam (SUNY)(NY)
Rhode Island College
Texas, U. of
Virginia
Washington & Lee (VA)
Washington U. (MO)
▲ Wellesley (MA)
Wesleyan (CT)
West Florida
Wheaton (IL)
Wisconsin (La Crosse)
Wooster (OH)
Yale (CT)

π *Classical Archeology*

ART THERAPY

Alverno (WI)
Anna Maria (MA)
Arcadia (PA)
Avila (MO)
Barat (IL)
Bowling Green (OH)
Brescia (KY)
Capital U. (OH)
Carlow (PA)
▲ Cedar Crest
▲ Converse (SC)
▲ Edgewood (WI)
Emporia State (KS)
Harding (AR)
Indianapolis, U. of
Lesley (MA)
Long Island U. (CW Post)(NY)

Marygrove (MI)
Marian Col. of Fond du Lac (WI)
Mercyhurst (PA)
▲ Meredith (NC)
Millikin (IL)
Pittsburg (KS)
Russell Sage (NY)
St. Andrews (NC)
St. Thomas Aquinas (NY)
Santa Fe, Col. of (NM)
Seton Hill (PA)
Southern Illinois (Edwardsville)
Spring Hill (AL)
Springfield (MA)
St. Thomas Aquinas (NY)
Wisconsin (Superior)

■ *Men Only*
▲ *Women Only*

ATMOSPHERIC SCIENCES / METEOROLOGY

Albany (SUNY) (NY)
Arizona, U. of
Brockport (SUNY) (NY)
California (PA)
California, U. of (Davis)
Cornell (NY)
Creighton (NE)
Embry-Riddle (FL)
Florida Inst. of Tech.
Florida State
Hawaii
Iowa State
Kansas
Louisiana-Lafayette
Louisiana-Monroe
Lyndon State (VT)
Metropolitan State (CO)
Millersville (PA)
Nebraska
North Carolina, U. of (Asheville)
North Carolina State
North Dakota, U. of

Northern Illinois
Northland (WI)
Oklahoma, U. of
Oneonta (SUNY) (NY)
Pennsylvania State
Plymouth State (NH)
Purdue (IN)
St. Louis University (MO)
San Francisco State (CA)
San Jose State (CA)
South Alabama
Stony Brook (SUNY)(NY)
Texas A&M
Utah, U. of
Valparaiso (IN)
Washington, U. of
Western Illinois
Western Connecticut
Wilkes-Barre (PA)
Wisconsin, U. of
Wisconsin, U. of (Milwaukee)

■ *Men Only*
▲ *Women Only*

AUDIOLOGY/SPEECH/LANGUAGE THERAPY

Abilene Christian (TX)
Adelphi (NY)
Akron, U. of (OH)
Andrews (MI)
Arizona
Arizona State
Auburn (AL)
Augustana (IL)
Ball State (IN)
Bloomsburg (PA)
Boston U.
Brescia (KY)
Brooklyn (CUNY)(NY)
Buffalo (SUNY)(NY)
California State U. (East Bay)
California State U. (Fresno)
California State U. (San Marcos)
Clarion (PA)
Colorado
Columbia (SC)
East Tennessee
East Stroudsburg (PA)
Eastern Illinois
Eastern Washington
Elmhurst (IL)
Elmira (NY)
Florida
Florida State
Fontbonne (MO)
Fredonia (SUNY)(NY)
Geneseo (SUNY)(NY)
Geneva (PA)
George Washington (DC)
Hardin-Simmons (TX)
Hampton (VA)
Hawaii
Hofstra (NY)
Illinois, U. of
Iona (NY)
Iowa, U. of
Ithaca (NY)
James Madison (VA)
Kansas
Kean (NJ)
Lamar (TX)
LaSalle (PA)
Long Island U (Brooklyn)(NY)
Longwood (VA)
Louisiana-Lafayette
Loyola (MD)
Maine, U. of
Marquette (WI)

Marshall (WV)
Maryland, U. of
Marymount Manhattan (NY)
Maryville (TN)
Massachusetts, U. of
Mercy (NY)
Miami U. (OH)
Michigan State
Minnesota, U. of
Minnesota State U. (Moorhead)
Misericordia, College (PA)
Mississippi, U. of
Mississippi U. for Women
Montevallo (AL)
Moorhead (MN)
Nazareth (NY)
Nebraska
Nevada, U. of (Reno)
New Hampshire, U. of
New Mexico, U. of
New Paltz (SUNY) (NY)
New York U.
North Colorado
North Dakota, U. of
North Iowa
North Michigan
Northern Illinois
Northwestern (IL)
Ohio U.
Oklahoma
Pace (NY)
Pacific, U. of the (CA)
Pittsburgh, U. of (PA)
Plattsburg (SUNY) (NY)
Portland State (OR)
Purdue (IN)
Redlands (CA)
Richard Stockton (NJ)
Rhode Island
Rockhurst (MO)
St. John's (NY)
St. Louis U. (MO)
St. Rose (NY)
San Diego State (CA)
Science and Arts of Oklahoma
S. Alabama
S. Dakota, U. of
S. Florida
Southeastern Louisiana
Southern Connecticut

AUDIOLOGY/SPEECH/LANGUAGE
THERAPY continues next page

AUDIOLOGY/SPEECH/LANGUAGE THERAPY, continued

Syracuse (NY)
Tennessee
Texas
Texas (Dallas)
Texas Christian
Towson (MD)
Tulsa (OK)
Utah State

Washington, U. of
Wayne State (MI)
West Virginia
Western Michigan
Western Washington
Worcester State (MA)
Wisconsin
Wyoming

AVIATION MANAGEMENT

Aeronautics, College of (NY)
Alaska, U. of (Anchorage)
Auburn (AL)
Central Missouri
Daniel Webster (NH)
Dowling (NY)
Dubuque, U. of (IA)
Eastern Kentucky
Eastern Michigan
Embry-Riddle (FL)
Fairmont (WV)
Farmingdale (SUNY)(NY)
Florida Inst. of Tech.
Hampton (VA)
Henderson (AR)
Jacksonville (FL)
LeTourneau (TX)
Lewis (IL)

Louisiana-Monroe
Lynn (FL)
Metropolitan State (CO)
Middle Tennessee
Minnesota State U. (Mankato)
New Haven (CT)
North Dakota, U. of
Purdue (IN)
Robert Morris (PA)
Rocky Mountain (MT)
St. Francis (NY)
St. Louis (MO)
Southeastern Louisiana
Southern Illinois U.
Tarleton State (TX)
Western Michigan
Westfield State (MA)

AVIATION SCIENCE

Andrews (MI)
Averett (VA)
Baylor (TX)
Bowling Green (OH)
Daniel Webster (NH)
Dowling (NY)
Embry-Riddle (FL)
Fairmont (WV)
Florida Inst. of Tech.
Geneva (PA)
Georgia Institute of Technology
Grace (NE)
Hampton (VA)
Henderson State (AR)
\# Illinois, U. of
Kansas State
Kent State (OH)
Lewis (IL)
● Louisiana Tech.

Metropolitan State (CO)
Minnesota State U. (Mankato)
North Dakota, U. of
Northwestern (LA)
Ohio State
Ohio University
Oklahoma State
Purdue (IN)
Rocky Mountain (MT)
St. Cloud State (MN)
St. Louis U. (MO)
Salem State (MA)
Salem International (WV)
San Jose State (CA)
Southern Illinois
Walla Walla (WA)
Western Michigan
Westminster (UT)

BIOMEDICAL ENGINEERING

Alabama (Birmingham)
Boston U. (MA)
Brown (RI)
California, U. of (Berkeley)
California, U. of (Davis)
California, U. of (Santa Cruz)
City College (CUNY)(NY)
Cornell (NY)
Duke (NC)
Illinois Inst. of Tech.
Johns Hopkins (MD)
LeTourneau (TX)
Marquette (WI)
Michigan, U. of
Michigan Tech.
Milwaukee Sch. of Engine (WI)
North Carolina, U. of
North Carolina State

Northwestern (IL)
Ohio State
Pennsylvania, U. of
Purdue (IN)
Rensselaer (NY)
Rochester, U. of (NY)
Rose-Hulman (IN)
Rutgers (NJ)
Southern California
Stanford (CA)
Texas, U. of
Tulane (LA)
Vanderbilt (TN)
Western New England (MA)
Wisconsin, U. of
Worcester Poly Tech (MA)
Wright State (OH)
Yale (CT)

BIOPHYSICS

Alabama (Birmingham)
Brown (RI)
Buffalo (SUNY)(NY)
California, U. of (Irvine)
California, U. of (San Diego)
Centenary (LA)
Chicago U. of (IL)
Columbia (NY)
Connecticut, U. of
Geneseo (SUNY)(NY)
■ Hampden-Sydney (VA)
Hampshire (MA)
Harvard (MA)
Houston, U. of (TX)
Illinois Institute of Tech.
Illinois, U. of

Iowa State
Johns Hopkins (MD)
Michigan, U. of
Minnesota, U. of
Oklahoma City U.
Oregon State
Pennsylvania, U. of
Pitzer (CA)
Rensselaer (NY)
Rice (TX)
St. Bonaventure (NY)
Scranton, U. of (PA)
Suffolk (MA)
Temple (PA)
Walla Walla (WA)
Washington U. (MO)

CERAMICS

Alfred (NY)
Arcadia (PA)
Bennington (VT)
Bowling Green (OH)
Cleveland Institute of Art (OH)
Colorado State
East Carolina (NC)
Hartford, U. of (CT)
Kansas, U. of
Kansas City Art Institute (MO)
Maryland Inst. College of Art
Massachusetts College of Art
Memphis College of Art (TN)
Miami (FL)

Montevallo (AL)
Moore (PA)
Museum of Fine Arts (MA)
New Paltz (SUNY)(NY)
North Texas
Oklahoma, U. of
Oneonta (SUNY)(NY)
Pratt (NY)
Rhode Island School of Design
San Jose State (CA)
Syracuse (NY)
Temple (PA)
Washington, U. of
Wichita State (KS)

CHINESE

Bard (NY)
Bates (ME)
California St U. (Long Beach)
California, U. of (Berkeley)
California, U. of (Davis)
California, U. of (Irvine)
California, U. of (Los Angeles)
California, U. of (Riverside)
California, U. of (Santa Barbara)
Colorado, U. of
Connecticut, U. of
Dartmouth (NH)
Florida State
George Washington (DC)
Georgetown (DC)
Grinnell (IA)
Hamilton (NY)
■ Hampden-Sydney (VA)
Harvard (MA)
Hawaii, U. of
Hunter (CUNY)(NY)
Lawrence (WI)
Maryland, U. of
Massachusetts, U. of

Michigan, U. of
Middlebury (VT)
Minnesota, U. of
Montana, U. of
Notre Dame (IN)
Ohio State
Oregon, U. of
Pittsburgh, U. of
Pomona (CA)
Reed (OR)
Rutgers (NJ)
San Francisco State (CA)
San Jose (CA)
Scripps (CA)
Tufts (MA)
U.S. Military Academy (NY)
U.S. Naval Academy (MD)
Vassar (NY)
Washington, U. of
▲ Wellesley (MA)
Williams (MA)
Wisconsin, U. of
Yale (CT)

CINEMATOGRAPHY/FILM STUDIES/VIDEO PRODUCTION

Arizona State
* Arts, U. of the (PA)
Bard (NY)
Bennington (VT)
Bowling Green (OH)
Boston U. (MA)
Brooklyn (CUNY) (NY)
Brown (RI)
California College of theArts
California State U. (Long Beach)
California, U. of (Berkeley)
California, U. of (Irvine)
California, U. of (Los Angeles)
California, U. of (Santa Barbara)
California, U. of (Santa Cruz)
California Institute of the Arts
Central Florida
Chapman (CA)
Chicago, U. of (IL)
Claremont-McKenna (CA)
Clark (MA)
Cogswell (CA)
Columbia (IL)
Colgate (NY)
Columbia College Chicago (IL)
Columbia College Hollywood (CA)
Colorado State
Colorado, U. of
Columbia (IL)
Columbia (NY)
Columbus Coll. of Art & Design (OH)
Denison (OH)
DePauw (IN)
DeSales (PA)
Eastern New Mexico University
Eastern Washington
Emerson (MA)
Emory (GA)
Evergreen State (WA)
Florida
Florida State
Full Sail U. (FL)
Georgia State
Hampshire (MA)
Hofstra (NY)

**▲Hollins
Howard (DC)
Hunter (CUNY) (NY)
Iowa
Ithaca (NY)
Kansas
Lawrence (WI)
Louisiana-Monroe
Loyola-Marymount (CA)
Massachusetts College of Art
Memphis (TN)
Michigan
Middlebury (VT)
Muhlenberg (PA)
New Orleans, U. of (LA)
New York U.
North Carolina, U. of (Greensboro)
North Carolina, U. of (Wilmington)
North Carolina School of the Arts
North Carolina State
North Texas
Northern Michigan
Northwestern (IL)
Oberlin (OH)
Oklahoma
Oklahoma City U.
Pennsylvania State
Pittsburgh, U. of (PA)
Pitzer (CA)
Point Park (PA)
Purchase (SUNY) (NY)
Purdue (IN)
Queens (CUNY) (NY)
Rhode Island College
Rhode Island School of Design
Rochester Inst. of Tech. (NY)
Rochester, U. of (NY)
San Francisco Art Institute (CA)
*** San Francisco State (CA)
Santa Fe (NM)
Sarah Lawrence (NY)

CINEMATOGRAPHY continues next page

* and Writing for Media Performance
** Film and Photography
*** Especially Animation
 # Also Animation

■ *Men Only*
▲ *Women Only*

CINEMATOGRAPHY/FILM STUDIES/VIDEO PRODUCTION, continued

Southern California
Southern Methodist (TX)
Syracuse (NY)
Temple (PA)
Texas Christian
Texas, U. of
Toledo (OH)
Towson (MD)

Utah, U. of
Visual Arts, School of (NY)
Wayne State (MI)
Webster (MO)
Wesleyan (CT)
Wisconsin (Milwaukee)
Woodbury (CA)
Yale (CT)

COGNITIVE SCIENCE

California State U. (Fresno)
Carnegie-Mellon (PA)
Case Western Reserve (OH)
Georgia, U. of
George Fox (OR)

Lehigh (PA)
N. Michigan
Occidental (CA)
Richmond, U. of (VA)
Texas, U. of (Dallas)

COMPUTER ENGINEERING

Alabama, U. of (Huntsville)
Arkansas, U. of
Arizona, U. of
Arizona State
Auburn (AL)
Binghamton (SUNY)(NY)
Boston U. (MA)
Brown (RI)
California, U. of (Berkeley)
California, U. of (Davis)
California, U. of (Los Angeles)
California, U. of (San Diego)
California, U. of (Santa Cruz)
California Poly. (SLO)
California State U. (Long Beach)
Carnegie-Mellon (PA)
Case Western Reserve (OH)
Central Florida
Clarkson (NY)
Clemson (SC)
Colorado, U. of
Columbia (NY)
Cornell (NY)
Drexel (PA)
Florida Atlantic
Florida Inst. of Tech.
Florida State
Florida, U. of
George Mason (VA)
George Washington (DC)
Georgia Tech.
Gonzaga (WA)
Harvey Mudd (CA)
Illinois, U. of
Illinois, U. of (Chicago)
Illinois Inst. of Tech.
I.U.P.U.I. (IN)
Iowa
Iowa State
Johns Hopkins (MD)
Kansas, U. of
Kansas State
Kentucky, U. of
Kettering (MI)
Lehigh (PA)
Louisville, U. of (KY)
Marquette (WI)

Maryland, U. of
Maryland, U. of (Baltimore Co.)
Massachusetts, U. of (Dartmouth)
Massachusetts, U. of (Lowell)
MIT (MA)
Mercer (GA)
Michigan, U. of
Michigan State
Michigan Tech.
Milwaukee Sch. of Engin. (WI)
Missouri, U. of (Rolla)
Montana State
Nebraska, U. of
New Jersey Inst. of Tech.
New Mexico, U. of
New Mexico State U.
North Carolina (Charlotte)
North Carolina State
Northeastern (MA)
Northwestern (IL)
Notre Dame (IN)
Ohio State
Oklahoma, U. of
Oklahoma State
Old Dominion (VA)
Olin (MA)
Oregon Institute of Tech.
Pacific, U. of the (CA)
Pennsylvania State
Pennsylvania, U. of
Pittsburgh, U. of (PA)
Princeton (NJ)
Puerto Rico (Mayaguez)
Purdue (IN)
Rensselaer (NY)
Rice (TX)
Rochester, U. of (NY)
Rochester Inst. of Tech. (NY)
Rose-Hulman (IN)
San Diego State (CA)
San Jose State (CA)
Santa Clara (CA)
South Dakota School of Mines
South Florida

■ *Men Only*
▲ *Women Only*

COMPUTER ENGINEERING continues
next page

COMPUTER ENGINEERING, continued

Southern Illinois U. (Carbondale)
Stevens Institute of Tech (NJ)
Stony Brook (SUNY) (NY)
Tennessee, U. of (Chattanooga)
Texas A&M
Texas, U. of
Texas, U. of (Arlington)
Union (NY)

Utah, U. of
Vanderbilt (TN)
Virginia Poly Tech.
Washington, U. of
Washington U. (MO)
Worcester Poly Tech. (MA)
Wright State (OH)
Wyoming, U. of

COMPUTER GRAPHICS

Allegheny (PA)
American (DC)
Andrews (MI)
Arts, U. of the (PA)
Central Oklahoma
Champlain (VT)
Cogswell (CA)
Columbia College Chicago (IL)
Columbus Coll. of Art & Design (OH)
Dominican (IL)
Dubuque (IA)
E. Michigan
Embry-Riddle (FL)
Fashion Institute of Tech. (NY)
Huntingdon (AL)
Jacksonville (FL)
\# John Brown (AR)
LaSalle (PA)
Lewis (IL)
Long Island U. (Brooklyn)(NY)
Loyola Marymount (CA)
Lyndon State (VT)

Memphis College of Art (TN)
Monmouth (NJ)
Montserrat (MA)
New York Institute of Tech.
+ Ohio State University
Parsons (NY)
Pratt Institute (NY)
Purdue (IN)
+ Ringling (FL)
Robert Morris (PA)
Rochester Institute of Tech (NY)
Stetson (FL)
Stevenson (MD)
Springfield (MA)
Syracuse (NY)
Taylor (IN)
Tampa (FL)
+ Texas, U. of (Dallas)
Visual Arts (NY)
Western Michigan
Woodbury (CA)

\# Digital Media Arts
+ And Especially Computer Animation

■ *Men Only*
▲ *Women Only*

CREATIVE WRITING

▲ Agnes Scott (GA)
Alabama, U. of
Alderson-Broaddus (WV)
Allegheny (PA)
Arizona, U. of
Ashland (OH)
Bard (NY)
Belhaven (MS)
Belmont (TN)
Beloit (WI)
Bennington (VT)
Bowling Green (OH)
* Briar Cliff (IA)
California Institute of the Arts
California, U. of (Riverside)
California, U. of (Santa Cruz)
Carlow (PA)
●● Carnegie Mellon (PA)
Chapman (CA)
Columbia (NY)
Columbia College Chicago (IL)
Creighton (NE)
Dana (NE)
Dominican (CA)
East Carolina (NC)
Eastern Kentucky
Eckerd (FL)
Emerson (MA)
Evansville (IN)
Evergreen (WA)
Florida State
Franklin & Marshall (PA)
Grand Valley (MI)
Hamilton (NY)
▲ Hollins (VA)
Houston, U. of (TX)
Iowa
Kenyon (OH)
Knox (IL)

* Lafayette (PA)
Lewis-Clark State (ID)
Linfield (OR)
Long Island U. (Southampton)(NY)
Loras (IA)
Lycoming (PA)
Maine (Farmington)
Memphis, U. of (TN)
Michigan, U. of
New Paltz (SUNY)(NY)
New School U. (Lang) (NY)
North Carolina (Wilmington)
Oberlin (OH)
Oregon, U. of
Pacific U. (OR)
Pittsburgh, U. of (PA)
Pittsburgh (Johnstown) (PA)
Princeton (NJ)
Purchase (SUNY) (NY)
Redlands (CA)
Roger Williams (RI)
Saginaw Valley (MI)
St. Andrews (NC)
St. Cloud (MN)
▲ Salem (NC)
San Francisco State (CA)
Santa Clara (CA)
Santa Fe, College of (NM)
Sarah Lawrence (NY)
Southern California
▲ Stephens (MO)
Susquehanna (PA)
▲ Sweet Briar (VA)
Texas, U. of (El Paso)
Vanderbilt (TN)
Warren Wilson (NC)
Wheaton (MA)
Wichita State (KS)

* *Writing Major*
●● *Also, Dramatic Writing*
English & Creative Writing

■ *Men Only*
▲ *Women Only*

CRIMINAL JUSTICE

Adelphi (NY)
Alaska, U. of (Anchorage)
Albany (SUNY) (NY)
Anna Maria (MA)
Arcadia (PA)
Arizona, U. of
Bloomsburg (PA)
Bowling Green (OH)
Brockport (SUNY) (NY)
Buena Vista (IA)
California State U. (Bakersfield)
California State U. (Fresno)
California State U. (Fullerton)
California State U. (Long Beach)
California State U. (Los Angeles)
California State U. (Sacramento)
California State U. (San Bernardino)
California, U. of (Irvine)
Castleton (VT)
Central Missouri
Chadron State (NE)
Chaminade (HI)
Columbia (MO)
Dayton, U. of (OH)
Delaware, U. of
Dillard (LA)
East Tennessee
Eastern Kentucky
Eastern Washington
Edinboro (PA)
Elmira (NY)
Fairmont State (WV)
Florida Atlantic
Florida Gulf Coast U.
Florida International
Florida Southern
● Florida State
Gannon (PA)
George Washington (DC)
Georgia State
Grambling (LA)
Grand Valley (MI)
Great Falls, U. of (MT)
Guilford (NC)
Hamline (MN)
■ Hampden-Sydney (VA)
Hannibal-La Grange (MO)

Hardin-Simmons (TX)
★ Husson (ME)
Illinois (Chicago)
Indiana
Indiana State
Iona (NY)
Jacksonville State (AL)
John Jay (CUNY) (NY)
Juniata (PA)
Kentucky Wesleyan
Kutztown (PA)
Lindenwood (MO)
Long Island U. (C.W. Post)(NY)
Longwood (VA)
Loras (IA)
Louisiana-Monroe
Louisville (KY)
Lycoming (PA)
Madonna (MI)
Mansfield (PA)
Marist (NY)
Marshall (WV)
Maryland
Massachusetts State College
  (Westfield)
Massachusetts, U. of (Lowell)
Mercy (NY)
Mercyhurst (PA)
Michigan State
Minnesota State U. (Mankato)
Minnesota State U. (Moorhead)
Missouri, U. of (St. Louis)
Mitchell (CT)
Mount Mercy (IA)
Nebraska, U. of (Omaha)
New Haven (CT)
New Mexico State
North Carolina (Charlotte)
North Carolina (Wilmington)
North Carolina Wesleyan
North Florida

★ *Criminal Justice / Psychology*
  - Double Major (5-Year)

Military Leadership and
  National Security Studies
● *Also, Computer Criminology*

■ *Men Only*
▲ *Women Only*

CRIMINAL JUSTICE continues next page

CRIMINAL JUSTICE, continued

North Michigan
Northeastern (MA)
Northeastern State (OK)
Norwich (VT)
Ohio Northern
Ohio State
Old Dominion (VA)
Pace (NY)
Pittsburgh (Bradford)
Portland, U. of (OR)
Potsdam (SUNY) (NY)
Quinnipiac (CT)
Radford (VA)
Regis (CO)
Richard Stockton (NJ)
Richmond (VA)
Roanoke (VA)
Roger Williams (RI)
Rowan (NJ)
Sacred Heart (CT)
Saginaw Valley (MI)
St. Ambrose (IA)
St. Anselm (NH)
St. Cloud (MN)
St. Edward's (TX)
St. Francis (NY)
St. John's (NY)
St. Leo (FL)
St. Peter's (NJ)
Salem State (MA)
Salve Regina-The Newport College (RI)
Sam Houston State (TX)
San Diego State (CA)
San Francisco State
San Jose State (CA)

Seton Hall (NJ)
●● Shippensburg (PA)
Simpson (IA)
South Dakota, U. of
South Florida
Southern Illinois U.
   (Carbondale)
Southern Oregon
Southern Polytechnic (GA)
Southwest Texas
Tampa, U. of (FL)
Tarleton State (TX)
Texas, U. of (El Paso)
Texas, U. of (Tyler)
Texas, U. of (San Antonio)
Toledo (OH)
Towson (MD)
Utica (NY)
Washburn (KS)
Waynesburg (PA)
Weber State (UT)
Western Carolina (NC)
Western Connecticut
Western Illinois
Western New England (MA)
Westfield State (MA)
West Virginia Wesleyan
Wilmington (OH)
Wisconsin (Milwaukee)
Wisconsin (Platteville)
Wisconsin (Whitewater)
Worcester State (MA)
York (PA)
Youngstown State (OH)

●● *Also, Pre-Forensic Science*

DESIGN/COMMERCIAL ART

Alfred (NY)
Art Center College of Design (CA)
Arts, U. of the (PA)
Brenau (GA)
Brigham Young (UT)
California College of Arts
    & Crafts
California Inst. of the Arts
California Poly (SLO)
California, U. of (Davis)
Carnegie Mellon (PA)
Carthage (WI)
Central Oklahoma
Champlain (VT)
Chowan (NC)
Cincinnati, U. of (OH)
Cleveland Institute of Art (OH)
Columbia College Chicago (IL)
Columbus College of Art &
    Design (OH)
Cornish (WA)
Creighton (NE)
Drake (IA)
Dubuque (IA)
Edgewood (WI)
Endicott (MA)
Fashion Inst. of Tech. (NY)
Flagler (FL)
Florida A&M
Fort Hays (KS)
Grand Valley (MI)
Illinois, U. of
Iowa State
John Brown (AR)
Kansas City Art Institute (MO)
Kean (NJ)
Kendall Coll. of Art
    & Design (MI)
Kent State (OH)

Long Island U. (C.W. Post)(NY)
Lyndon State (VT)
Maryland Institute - College
    of Art
Maryland, U. of
Maryville (MO)
Massachusetts College of Art
Massachusetts, U. of
    (Dartmouth)
Memphis College of Art
Milliken (IL)
Montserrat (MA)
Moore (PA)
Moravian (PA)
Morningside (IA)
** New Jersey, College of
New York Inst.of Technology
North Carolina State
Ohio State
Otis College of Art and
    Design (CA)
Parsons School of Design (NY)
Pratt (NY)
Purchase (SUNY) (NY)
Rhode Island School of
    Design
+ Ringling (FL)
Rochester Inst. of Tech. (NY)
* Roger Williams (RI)
St. Mary's (MN)
San Jose State (CA)
Southern Illinois U.
    (Carbondale)
Stevenson (MD)
Texas Christian
Texas State
Visual Arts, School of (NY)
** Woodbury (CA)

Graphic Design Communications
***Especially Graphic Design*
#*Digital Media Arts*
+*And Business Art and Design*

EAST ASIAN STUDIES

Bates (ME)
Berea (KY)
Binghamton (SUNY) (NY)
Bowdoin (ME)
▲ Bryn Mawr (PA)
Bucknell (PA)
California, U. of (Davis)
California, U. of (Los Angeles)
California, U. of (San Diego)
Chicago, U. of (IL)
Coe (IA)
Colgate (NY)
Colorado College
Columbia (NY)
Connecticut College
Cornell (NY)
Denison (OH)
Denver, U. of (CO)
DePauw (IN)
Furman (SC)
George Washington (DC)
Hamilton (NY)
Hamline (MN)
Harvard (MA)
Hawaii, U. of
Hofstra (NY)
Illinois, U. of
Indiana
John Carroll (OH)
Kansas, U. of
Lawrence (WI)
Lehigh (PA)
Lewis & Clark (OR)
Macalester (MN)
Manhattanville (NY)
Maryland, U. of
Middlebury (VT)
▲ Mount Holyoke (MA)
New York U.

North Carolina
North Central (IL)
Oberlin (OH)
Occidental (CA)
Ohio State
Oregon, U. of
Pennsylvania, U. of
Pomona (CA)
Princeton (NJ)
Puget Sound (WA)
Redlands (CA)
Reed (OR)
Rice (TX)
Rutgers (NJ)
St. Olaf (MN)
San Francisco, U. of (CA)
Sarah Lawrence (NY)
▲ Simmons (MA)
Skidmore (NY)
▲ Smith (MA)
South, U. of the (TN)
Stanford (CA)
Swarthmore (PA)
Texas, U. of
Ursinus (PA)
Utah, U. of
Vassar (NY)
Washington & Lee (VA)
Washington U. (MO)
Washington, U. of
▲ Wellesley (MA)
Wesleyan (CT)
Western Washington
Westmont (CA)
Willamette (OR)
Wisconsin, U. of
Wittenberg (OH)
Yale (CT)

■ *Men Only*
▲ *Women Only*

E-COMMERCE

Bellevue (NE)
California State U.
  (Monterey Bay)
Carnegie Mellon (PA)
Castleton State (VT)
Champlain (VT)
Christopher Newport (VA)
Clarkson (NY)
DePaul (IL)
Emory (GA)
Harrisburg U. (PA)
Jacksonville State (AL)
▲ Judson (AL)
Misericordia (PA)

New Jersey Inst. of Tech.
North Dakota State
Nothern State U. (SD)
Northwestern Oklahoma
Old Dominion (VA)
San Jose State (CA)
Scranton (PA)
Seattle U. (WA)
Southern Alabama
Texas Christian
Thomas (ME)
Towson (MD)
Utah State

ENTOMOLOGY

Auburn (AL)
California State U.
  (Stanislaus)
California, U. of (Davis)
California, U. of (Riverside)
Colorado State
Cornell (NY)
Delaware, U. of
Florida A & M
Florida, U. of
Georgia, U. of
Harvard (MA)
Hawaii, U. of
Idaho, U. of
Illinois, U. of
Iowa State
Kentucky, U. of

Maine, U. of
Michigan State
Nebraska, U. of
New Mexico State
North Carolina State
Ohio State
Oklahoma State
Oregon State
Purdue (IN)
Rutgers (NJ)
San Jose State (CA)
Texas A & M
Utah State
Virginia Tech.
Washington State
Wisconsin, U. of

■ *Men Only*
▲ *Women Only*

ENTREPRENEUR STUDIES

American (DC)
American International (MA)
Arizona, U. of
Babson (MA)
Baylor (TX)
Black Hills State U. (SD)
Boise State (ID)
Bradley (IL)
Brown (RI)
Buena Vista (IA)
California State U.
   (San Bernardino)
California, U. of (Riverside)
Canisius (NY)
Case Western Reserve (OH)
Catawba (NC)
Central Connecticut
Chowan (NC)
Colorado State
Columbia College (SC)
Connecticut, U. of
Creighton (NE)
Dayton (OH)
Duquesne (PA)
Eastern Michigan
Fairleigh Dickinson (NJ)
Ferris State U. (MI)
Florida State
Gannon (PA)
Gonzaga (WA)
Hampton (VA)
Hartford, U. of (CT)
Hawaii Pacific
Hofstra (NY)
Houston Baptist (TX)
Houston, U. of (TX)
Illinois
Indiana
Juniata (PA)
Louisiana State U.
Lourdes (OH)
Loyola Marymount (CA)
Lyndon State (VT)
Lynn (FL)
Marquette (WI)
Maryland, U. of
Miami (FL)

Middle Tennessee
Millikin (IL)
Mississippi U. for Women
Montana State
Muhlenberg (PA)
New Mexico
Northeastern (MA)
Northeastern State (OK)
Northern Kentucky
North Carolina (Greensboro)
North Central (IL)
North Dakota
North Texas
Northwood (MI)
Ohio University
Oklahoma, U. of
Oregon, U. of
Oregon Inst. of Tech.
Palm Beach Atlantic (FL)
Pennsylvania, U. of
Pittsburgh (Bradford) (PA)
Plattsburgh (SUNY) (NY)
Portland State (OR)
Quinnipiac (CT)
Reinhardt (GA)
Rensselaer (NY)
Rider (NJ)
Rowan (NJ)
St. Mary's (TX)
St. Thomas (MN)
Seton Hill (PA)
Southern California
▲ Stephens (MO)
Syracuse (NY)
Texas Christian
Virginia Commonwealth
Washington & Jefferson (PA)
Washington State
Waynesburg (PA)
Western Carolina (NC)
Wheeling Jesuit (WV)
Wichita State (KS)
Winthrop (SC)
Wisconsin, U. of
Wyoming
Xavier (LA)
Xavier (OH)

■ *Men Only*
▲ *Women Only*

ENVIRONMENTAL STUDIES

Adelphi (NY)
Alaska Pacific
Albion (MI)
Alfred (NY)
Allegheny (PA)
American (DC)
Atlantic, College of the (ME)
▲ Barnard (NY)
Bates (ME)
Beloit (WI)
Berry (GA)
Bethel (KS)
Birmingham-Southern (AL)
Bowdoin (ME)
Brenau (GA)
Briar Cliff (IA)
Brockport (SUNY)(NY)
Brown (RI)
Bucknell (PA)
California State U. (Channel Islands)
California, U. of (Davis)
California, U. of (Merced)
California, U. of (Riverside)
California, U. of (Santa Barbara)
California, U. of (Santa Cruz)
Carleton (MN)
Carroll (WI)
Case Western Reserve
Centenary (LA)
Central (IA)
Chapman (CA)
Chestnut Hill (PA)
Chicago, U. of (IL)
Claremont McKenna (CA)
Clark (MA)
Clarkson (NY)
Colby (ME)
Colgate (NY)
Colorado, U. of
Connecticut College
Connecticut, U. of
Dartmouth (NH)
Davis & Elkins (WV)
Delaware Valley (PA)
Denison (OH)
Denver, U. of (CO)
DePaul (IL)

\# Depauw (IN)
Dickinson (PA)
Doane (NE)
Dordt (IA)
Drake (IA)
Dubuque (IA)
Duke (NC)
Earlham (IN)
Eastern Connecticut
Eastern Kentucky
Eckerd (FL)
Elizabethtown (PA)
Endicott (MA)
Evergreen State (WA)
Florida Gulf Coast
Florida, U. of
Florida Institute of Tech.
Fordham (NY)
Franklin & Marshall (PA)
George Fox (OR)
Georgetown College (KY)
Georgia
Gettysburg (PA)
Green Mountain (VT)
Harvard (MA)
Hawaii Pacific
Hiram (OH)
Idaho
Jacksonville (FL)
Johnson State (VT)
Juniata (PA)
Knox (IL)
Lake Forest (IL)
Lawrence (WI)
Lesley (MA)
Lewis & Clark (OR)
Linfield (OR)
Long Island U. (C.W. Post)(NY)
Loyola (IL)
Lynchburg (VA)
Lyndon (VT)
Macalester (MN)
Manchester (IN)
Marietta (OH)

\# *Environmental Geoscience*
π *Environmental & Occupational Health*

■ *Men Only*
▲ *Women Only*

ENVIRONMENTAL STUDIES continues next page

ENVIRONMENTAL STUDIES, continued

Marist (NY)
Maritime College (SUNY)(NY)
Maryville (MO)
Miami, U. of (FL)
Michigan, U. of
Michigan State
Michigan Tech.
Middlebury (VT)
Minnesota, U. of
Monmouth (IL)
Montana State (Billings)
Montreat (NC)
Moravian (PA)
Nebraska, U. of
Nevada, U. of (Reno)
New Hampshire, U. of
New Mexico Inst. of Min. & Tech.
π New Mexico State
North Carolina (Asheville)
North Carolina (Greensboro)
North Carolina (Wilmington)
Northern Arizona
Northland (WI)
* Northwestern (IA)
Oberlin (OH)
Ohio Wesleyan
Oneonta (SUNY) (NY)
Oregon Inst. of Tech.
● Oregon State
Pacific U. (OR)
Pennsylvania State
Pennsylvania, U. of
Pittsburgh (Bradford)
Pittsburgh, U. of (PA)
Pitzer (CA)
Plattsburgh (SUNY)(NY)
Portland State (OR)
Prescott (AZ)
Purchase (SUNY) (NY)
Queens (NC)
Ramapo (NJ)
Randolph (VA)
Redlands (CA)
Reed (OR)

Rensselaer (NY)
Rhode Island, U. of
Richard Stockton (NJ)
Ripon (WI)
Rochester Inst. of Tech. (NY)
Rocky Mountain (MT)
Rutgers (NJ)
Sacred Heart (CT)
St. Anselm (NH)
St. John's (NY)
St. Lawrence (NY)
St. Michael's (VT)
St. Norbert (WI)
Salisbury (MD)
Santa Fe, College of (NM)
Sarah Lawrence (NY)
Sciences, U. of the (PA)
Shepherd (WV)
Skidmore (NY)
South, U. of the (TN)
South Florida
Southeast Missouri State
Southwestern (TX)
▲ Spelman (GA)
Stanford (CA)
Stephen. F. Austin (TX)
Stockton State (NJ)
SUNY College of Env.
    Sci. & Forestry
▲ Sweet Briar (VA)
Susquehanna (PA)
Tarleton State (TX)
Texas (El Paso)
Thomas More (KY)
Toledo, U. of (OH)
Unity (ME)
Ursinus (PA)
Utah State
Valparaiso (IN)
Vassar (NY)
Vermont, U. of
Virginia, U. of

● *Also, Environmental Engineering*
* *Environmental Science*
π *Environmental and Occupational Health*

ENVIRONMENTAL STUDIES, continued

Warren Wilson (NC)
Washington & Jefferson (PA)
Washington State
Washington, U. of
Wesleyan (CT)
Western Washington
West Virginia Wesleyan
Westfield State (MA)

Westminster (MO)
Westminster (UT)
Whitman (WA)
Wilson (PA)
Wisconsin
Wisconsin (Green Bay)
Worcester Poly (MA)
Yale (CT)

EQUESTRIAN STUDIES

Averett (VA)
Bethany (WV)
Centenary (NJ)
Colorado State
Delaware Valley (PA)
Findlay (OH)
\# Johnson & Wales (RI)
▲ Judson (AL)
Lake Erie (OH)
\# Louisville
North Dakota State

Otterbein (OH)
Puerto Rico, U. of (Rio Piedras)
Rocky Mountain (MT)
St. Andrews (NC)
Salem International (WV)
▲ Stephens (MO)
Truman State (MO)
Virginia Intermont
William Woods (MO)
* Wilson (PA)

\# *Equine Business*
* *Also, Equine Journalism*

■ *Men Only*
▲ *Women Only*

EXERCISE SCIENCE/WELLNESS/MOVEMENT

Abilene Christian (TX)
Adelphi (NY)
Adrian (MI)
Alma (MI)
Austin (TX)
Ball State (IN)
* Belhaven (MS)
Black Hills State U. (SD)
Bloomsburg (PA)
Bluffton (OH)
Boston U.
Bridgewater (VA)
Brigham Young (UT)
Brockport (SUNY) (NY)
Buena Vista (IA)
Cal Poly (SLO)
California State U. (Fresno)
California State U. (Fullerton)
California State U.
    (Long Beach)
California State U.
    (San Bernardino)
California State U.
    (San Marcos)
Carthage (WI)
Castleton (VT)
Central (IA)
Chapman (CA)
Colby-Sawyer (NH)
Colorado, U. of
Concordia (NE)
Connecticut, U. of
Cumberland (KY)
Dayton (OH)
DePauw (IN)
Drury (MO)
East Stroudsburg (PA)
Eastern Nazarene (MA)
Evansville (IN)
Fitchburg (MA)
Florida Atlantic
Fort Lewis (CO)
Georgetown (KY)
George Washington (DC)
Gordon (MA)
Greensboro (NC)
Hendrix (AR)

High Point (NC)
Houston Baptist (TX)
Houston (TX)
Humboldt State (CA)
Idaho, U. of
Illinois, U. of (Chicago)
▲ Immaculata (PA)
Indiana Wesleyan
Ithaca (NY)
James Madison (VA)
Kennesaw State (GA)
Lipscomb (TN)
Linfield (OR)
Lynchburg (VA)
Lyndon State (VT)
Massachusetts, U. of
Massachusetts, U. of (Lowell)
▲ Meredith (NC)
Miami U. (OH)
Millersville (PA)
Mississippi U. for Women
Nevada, U. of (Las Vegas)
New Hampshire, U. of
New Jersey, College of
North Georgia
North Texas
Northeastern Illinois
Northern State U. (SD)
Otterbein (OH)
Pacific U. (OR)
Penn State
Pittsburgh, U. of (PA)
Puget Sound (WA)
Ripon (WI)
▲ St. Catherine (MN)
St. Scholastica (MN)
San Francisco State (CA)
Schreiner (TX)
Scranton (PA)
Shaw (NC)
Skidmore (NY)
Slippery Rock (PA)
Southwestern (TX)
Southwest Texas State

■ *Men Only*
▲ *Women Only*

* *Exercise Science and*
Sports Medicine

EXERCISE SCIENCE/WELLNESS/MOVEMENT, continued

Springfield (MA)
Sterling (KS)
Stetson (FL)
Tampa, U. of (FL)
Tennessee, U. of
Texas A&M
Texas A&M (Corpus Christi)
Texas A&M (Kingsville)
Toledo (OH)
Transylvania (KY)
Texas A&M (Commerce)
Texas (El Paso)
Texas Lutheran

Texas Women's
Utah
Westfield (MA)
Western State College of
   Colorado
Western Maryland
West Virginia U.
West Virginia Wesleyan
Whitworth (WA)
Willamette (OR)
Wisconsin (La Crosse)
Wyoming

FASHION DESIGN / MERCHANDISING

Akron, U. of (OH)
Albright (PA)
Auburn (AL)
Baylor (TX)
Bowling Green (OH)
Brenau (GA)
California College of
   Arts & Crafts
California State U. (Fresno)
California State U.
   (Sacramento)
Central Washington
Cincinnati (OH)
Colorado State
Columbus College of Art &
   Design (OH)
Columbia College Chicago (IL)
Delaware, U. of
Dominican (IL)
Drexel (PA)
Florida State
Framingham (MA)
Eastern Michigan
Hawaii, U. of
High Point (NC)
Illinois, U. of
Indiana (PA)
Iowa State
Kansas State

Kent State (OH)
Kentucky, U. of
Lasell (MA)
Lynn (FL)
Marist (NY)
Marymount (VA)
▲ Meredith (NC)
Moore College of Art (PA)
Nebraska, U. of
North Carolina (Greensboro)
Oklahoma State
Oregon State
Otis (CA)
Parsons (NY)
Philadelphia U. (PA)
Pratt (NY)
Rhode Island School of Design
Rhode Island, U. of
School of the Art Institute of
   Chicago (IL)
Southern New Hampshire
▲ Stephens (MO)
Tarleton State (TX)
Texas Christian
Virginia Commonwealth U.
Washington State
Western Michigan
Wisconsin, U. of
Wisconsin, U. of (Stout)

■ *Men Only*
▲ *Women Only*

Especially Interior Design

FIREFIGHTING

Anna Maria (MA)
Cogswell (CA)
Holy Family (PA)
John Jay (CUNY) (NY)
Madonna (MI)

Maryland, U. of (Univ.
    College)
New Haven (CT)
Salem State (MA)

FORENSIC SCIENCES / TECHNOLOGY

▲ Bay Path (MA)
Bemidji State (MN)
Central Florida
▲ Cedar Crest (PA)
Chaminade (HI)
Colorado (Colorado Springs)
π Dakota State (SD)
Defiance (OH)
DeSales (PA)
Duquesne (PA)
Eastern Kentucky
Eastern Washington
Edinboro (PA)
Florida Gulf Coast U.
● Florida State
Great Falls, U. of (MT)
* Guilford (NC)
+ Gwynedd-Mercy (PA)
Hamline (MN)
Harrisburg U. (PA)
John Jay (CUNY)(NY)
Kansas State
Keystone (PA)
King (TN)
Long Island U.
    (C.W. Post)(NY)
Loyola (IL)
Marygrove (MI)
Mercyhurst (PA)
Miami, U. of (FL)

Mississippi, U. of
Mount Marty (SD)
New Haven, U. of (CT)
**New Jersey, College of
North Dakota, U. of
Northern Kentucky
Ohio U.
Pace (NY)
Quincy (IL)
St. Andrews (NC)
St. Francis (PA)
St. Scholastica (MN)
San Jose State (CA)
**Scranton (PA)
Seattle U. (WA)
Seton Hill (PA)
Southern Mississippi
Tampa, U. of (FL)
Texas, U. of (San Antonio)
Thomas More (KY)
**Towson (MD)
Tri-State (IN)
Virginia Commonwealth U.
Waynesburg (PA)
West Virginia U.
**Western New England (MA)
**Winthrop (SC)

* *Forensic Biology*
** *Forensic Chemistry*
+ *Forensic Psychology*
# *Forensic Biotechnology*
● *Also, Computer Criminology*
π *Scientific Forensic Technology*

■ *Men Only*
▲ *Women Only*

GENETICS

Ball State (IN)
California, U. of (Berkeley)
California, U. of (Davis)
California, U. of (Irvine)
California, U. of (Los Angeles)
Carnegie Mellon (PA)
▲ Cedar Crest (PA)
Chicago, U. of (IL)
Clemson (SC)
Connecticut, U. of
Cornell (NY)
Florida State
Fredonia (SUNY)(NY)
Georgia, U. of
Harvard (MA)
Illinois, U. of

Illinois, U. of (Chicago)
Iowa State
Kansas
Maryland, U. of
Minnesota
Ohio State
Ohio Wesleyan
Otterbein (OH)
Purdue (IN)
Rochester, U. of (NY)
Rutgers (NJ)
Texas A & M
Vermont, U. of
Washington State
Western Kentucky
Wisconsin, U. of

GERONTOLOGY/GERIATRIC SERVICES

Alfred (NY)
Arkansas, U. of (Pine Bluff)
Bethune-Cookman (FL)
Black Hills State U. (SD)
California (PA)
California State U. (Sacramento)
Case Western (OH)
Central Washington
East Stroudsburg (PA)
Florida Gulf Coast U.
Fort Hays (KS)
Gwynedd-Mercy (PA)
Ithaca (NY)
Kent State (OH)
King's (PA)
Langston (OK)
Lindenwood (VA)
Lourdes (OH)
Madonna (MI)
Massachusetts (Boston)
Miami U. (OH)
Minnesota State U.
   (Moorhead)

Mount St. Mary's (CA)
Mount St. Joseph (OH)
North Carolina (Greensboro)
North Colorado
North Texas
Oneonta (SUNY)(NY)
Quinnipiac (CT)
Roosevelt (IL)
Richard Stockton (NJ)
St. Bonaventure (NY)
St. Mary's (CA)
San Diego State (CA)
Scranton (PA)
Shaw (NC)
South Florida
Southern California
Southwest Missouri
Springfield (MA)
Stephen F. Austin (TX)
Towson (MD)
Wagner (NY)
Washburn (KS)
Weber State (UT)

■ *Men Only*
▲ *Women Only*

Also, Aging Services Administration
/ Social Work

HEALTH SERVICES ADMINISTRATION

Alfred (NY)
Appalachian State (NC)
Arcadia (PA)
Arizona
Carlow (PA)
Creighton (NE)
Detroit Mercy (MI)
Eastern Michigan
Eastern Washington
Florida Atlantic
* Georgetown (DC)
Herbert Lehman (CUNY)(NY)
James Madison (VA)
Kentucky
Madonna (MI)
▲ Mary Baldwin (VA)
Michigan (Dearborn)
Missouri, U. of
Mount Mercy (IA)
North Carolina
Northeastern (MA)
Ohio U.

Oregon State
Pennsylvania State
Providence College (RI)
Quinnipiac (CT)
Regis (CO)
Robert Morris (PA)
St. Joseph's (NY)
Saint Scholastica (MN)
Scranton (PA)
South Dakota, U. of
Springfield (MA)
Stonehill (MA)
Utah, U. of
Washburn (KS)
Washington, U. of
Weber State (UT)
William Paterson (NJ)
Wisconsin, U. of
   (Eau Claire)
* Wisconsin, U. of
   (Milwaukee)

* *Health Systems Administration*
# *Community Health*

HISPANIC STUDIES/LATIN AMERICAN STUDIES

Adelphi (NY)
Albany (SUNY) (NY)
American (DC)
Arizona, U. of
Assumption (MA)
Austin (TX)
▲ Barnard (NY)
Binghamton (SUNY) (NY)
Brandeis (MA)
California, U. of (Berkeley)
California, U. of
    (Santa Barbara)
California, U. of
    (Santa Cruz)
California State
    (Long Beach)
Carnegie-Mellon (PA)
Chicago, U. of (IL)
City (CUNY) (NY)
Colby (ME)
Connecticut College
Connecticut, U. of
DePaul (IL)
Flagler (FL)
Gettysburg (PA)
George Fox (OR)
George Washington (DC)
Hobart & William Smith (NY)
Hunter (CUNY)(NY)
Johns Hopkins (MD)
Kansas, U. of
Lawrence (WI)
Loyola Marymount (CA)
Macalester (MN)
Michigan, U. of
Minnesota (Morris)
▲ Mount Holyoke (MA)

Nebraska, U. of (Omaha)
New Mexico, U. of
North Carolina
Northern Colorado
Northridge State (CA)
Northwestern (IL)
Oberlin (OH)
Ohio Wesleyan
Pennsylvania, U. of
Pomona (CA)
Puerto Rico, U. of (Mayaguez)
Redlands (CA)
Rhodes (TN)
Rice (TX)
Rollins (FL)
Rutgers (NJ)
St. Peter's (NJ)
San Francisco, U. of (CA)
San Diego State (CA)
San Francisco State (CA)
▲ Scripps (CA)
▲ Smith (MA)
Sonoma State (CA)
Stetson (FL)
Texas, U. of
Texas, U. of (El Paso)
Tulane (LA)
Virginia, U. of
Washington, U. of
Wheaton (MA)
Whittier (CA)
Willamette (OR)
Wisconsin, U. of
Wisconsin, U. of
    (Eau Claire)
Yale (CT)

■ *Men Only*
▲ *Women Only*

HORTICULTURE

Auburn (AL)
Arkansas, U. of
Berry (GA)
Brigham Young (UT)
Cal Poly (Pomona)
Cal Poly (San Luis Obispo)
California, U. of (Davis)
* California, U. of (Riverside)
Christopher Newport
Clemson (SC)
Colorado State
Connecticut, U. of
Cornell (NY)
Delaware Valley (PA)
Delaware, U. of
* Dordt (IA)
Florida, U. of
● Florida Southern
Georgia, U. of
Hawaii, U. of
Idaho, U. of
Illinois, U. of
Iowa State
Kansas State
Louisiana State
Maine, U. of
Maryland, U. of
Michigan State
Minnesota, U. of
Mississippi State
Missouri, U. of

Montana State (Bozeman)
Nebraska, U. of
New Hampshire, U. of
North Carolina State
North Dakota State
Northwest Missouri
Ohio State
Oklahoma State
Oregon State
Pennsylvania State
Puerto Rico, U. of (Mayaguez)
Purdue (IN)
Rhode Island, U. of
Rutgers (NJ)
South Dakota State
Southwest Missouri
Tarleton (TX)
Temple (PA)
Tennessee Tech
Tennessee, U. of
Texas A & M
Texas Tech
Utah State
Vermont, U. of
Virginia Poly
Washington State
Washington, U. of
Wisconsin, U. of
Wisconsin, U. of (Platteville)
Wisconsin, U. of (River Falls)

* *Plant Science*
● *And Citrus*

HOTEL AND RESTAURANT MANAGEMENT

Ashland (OH)	New Hampshire, U. of
Auburn (AL)	New Haven (CT)
Berea (KY)	New Mexico State
Bowling Green (OH)	New Orleans, U. of (LA)
Cal Poly (Pomona)	New York University
Central Florida	Niagara (NY)
Champlain (VT)	** Nicholls State (LA)
Colorado State	Northwood (MI)
Cornell (NY)	North Dakota State
Delaware	Northern Arizona
Denver, U. of (CO)	Northern Michigan
East Stroudsburg (PA)	North Texas
Endicott (MA)	Oklahoma State
Fairleigh Dickinson (NJ)	Ozarks (MO)
Findlay (OH)	π Paul Smith's (NY)
Florida International U.	Penn State
Florida State	Plattsburgh (SUNY)(NY)
Georgia Southern	Purdue (IN)
* Green Mountain (VT)	Robert Morris (PA)
Georgia State	Rochester Inst. of Tech. (NY)
Houston, U. of (TX)	Roosevelt (IL)
Illinois, U. of	Rutgers (Camden) (NJ)
Indiana (PA)	Siena Heights (MI)
Iowa State	South Carolina, U. of
π Johnson & Wales (RI)	South Dakota State U.
Johnson State (VT)	Southern Illinois
Kansas State	(Carbondale)
Lasell (MA)	Southern New Hampshire, U. of
● Lyndon State (VT)	# Texas A&M (Kingsville)
Massachusetts, U. of	Texas Tech.
Mercyhurst (PA)	Virginia Poly. Inst.
Michigan State	Washington State
Missouri, U. of	Western Illinois
Nebraska	Western Kentucky
Nevada (Las Vegas)	Widener (PA)
New Hampshire College	Wisconsin, U. of (Stout)

** *Culinary Arts*

* *Resort Management*

● *Ski Resort Management*

Restaurant and Food Management

π *Also, Culinary Arts*

HUMAN RESOURCES MANAGEMENT

American (DC)
Baylor (TX)
Birmingham-Southern (AL)
Black Hills State U. (SD)
Boston College (MA)
Bowling Green (OH)
Briar Cliff (IA)
Cabrini (PA)
Cal. Poly. State U.
   (Pomona)
Cal. State (Los Angeles)
DeSales (PA)
Duquesne (PA)
Evansville (IN)
Findlay (OH)
Florida State
George Washington (DC)
Hastings (NE)
Hawaii Pacific
Holy Names (CA)
Houston (TX)
Indiana (PA)
Loras (IA)
LeMoyne (NY)
Lesley (MA)
Lindenwood (MO)
Lipscomb (TN)
Marietta (OH)
Marquette (WI)
Michigan State
Mount Mercy (IA)

Muhlenberg (PA)
Nevada, U. of (Las Vegas)
New Mexico, U. of
North Dakota, U. of
North Dakota State
Northeastern (MA)
Oakland (MI)
Oakland City (IN)
Ohio State
Ohio University
Oklahoma, U. of
Oswego (SUNY) (NY)
Point Park (PA)
Puerto Rico, U. of (Rio Piedras)
Rider (NJ)
Rockhurst (MO)
Roosevelt (IL)
Rowan (NJ)
St. Leo (FL)
St. Mary's (TX)
Silver Lake (WI)
Southwestern (KS)
Tarleton State (TX)
Utah State
Washington U. (MO)
Western Illinois
Wichita State (KS)
Widener (PA)
Wisconsin, U. of
Wisconsin, U. of (Oshkosh)

INDUSTRIAL ARTS

Auburn (AL)
Berea (KY)
California (PA)
π California State U. (Fresno)
Cal. Poly. (Pomona)
Central Michigan
Cincinnati, U. of (OH)
Clemson (SC)
Colorado State
Ferris State (MI)
Fitchburg (MA)
Florida A & M
Idaho
Indiana State
Iowa State
Louisiana State U.
Millersville (PA)

Montclair (NJ)
Nebraska, U. of
New Mexico, U. of
North Carolina State
Northern Colorado
Northern Illinois
Oklahoma State
Oswego (SUNY) (NY)
Pittsburgh, U. of (PA)
Purdue (IN)
San Francisco State (CA)
Southern Illinois
Texas A&M
Western Michigan
Wisconsin, U. of (Stout)
Wyoming

π *Also Construction Management*

INDUSTRIAL DESIGN

Alfred (NY)
Appalachian State (NC)
Arizona State
Arts, U. of the (PA)
Auburn (AL)
Brigham Young (UT)
California College of
　　Arts & Crafts
California State U.
　　(Long Beach)
Carnegie-Mellon (PA)
Cincinnati, U of (OH)
Georgia Inst. of Tech.
Illinois, U. of (Chicago)
Illinois, U. of
Kansas, U. of
Kent State (OH)
Metropolitan State (CO)
Michigan, U. of

North Carolina State
Philadelphia U. (PA)
Pittsburgh, U. of (PA)
Pratt (NY)
Purdue (IN)
Rhode Island School
　　of Design
Rochester Inst. of Tech. (NY)
San Francisco State (CA)
San Houston State (TX)
San Jose State (CA)
Syracuse (NY)
Tufts (MA)
Virginia Poly
Washington U. (MO)
Western Michigan
Western Washington
Washington, U. of

■ *Men Only*
▲ *Women Only*

INTERIOR DESIGN

Adrian (MI)
Akron, U. of (OH)
Alabama, U. of
Arcadia (PA)
Arizona State
Arkansas, U. of
Auburn (AL)
Bayor (TX)
Boston Architectural Center (MA)
Bowling Green (OH)
Bridgeport, U. of (CT)
California State U. (Fresno)
California State U.
    (Sacramento)
Centenary (NJ)
Central Michigan
Central Washington
Chaminade (HI)
Cincinnati, U. of (OH)
Cleveland Inst. of Art (OH)
Colorado State U.
Columbia College (IL)
Columbus College of Art &
    Design (OH)
Cornell (NY)
Drexel (PA)
Eastern Kentucky
Eastern Michigan
Fairmont (WV)
Fashion Inst. of Tech. (NY)
Ferris State (MI)
Florida, U. of
Florida International
Florida State
George Washington (DC)
Georgia, U. of
Georgia Southern
High Point (NC)
Houston, U. of (TX)
Howard (DC)
Idaho, U. of
Indiana U.
Iowa State
Kansas State
Kansas, U. of

Kean (NJ)
Kent State (OH)
Kentucky, U. of
Louisiana State
Louisiana, U. of (Lafayette)
Louisville, U. of (KY)
Maryland Inst. of Art
▲ Meredith (NC)
Miami (OH)
Michigan State
Michigan, U. of
Minnesota, U. of
Mississippi, U. of
Moore (PA)
Mt. Ida (MA)
Mt. St. Joseph (OH)
Murray State (KY)
Nevada, U. of (Las Vegas)
Nevada, U. of (Reno)
New Haven, U. of (CT)
NY Sch. of Interior Design
North Carolina (Greensboro)
North Dakota State U.
Northern Iowa
Ohio State
Ohio U.
Oklahoma, U. of
Oregon, U. of
Oregon State
Parsons (NY)
Pratt Institute (NY)
Rhode Island School of
    Design
Ringling College of Art &
    Design (FL)
Rochester Inst. of Tech. (NY)
▲ Salem (NC)
San Diego State (CA)
San Jose State
School of the Art Inst.
    of Chicago (IL)

■ *Men Only*
▲ *Women Only*

INTERIOR DESIGN continues next page

INTERIOR DESIGN, continued

Seattle Pacific (WA)
South Dakota State U.
Southern Illinois (Carbondale)
Suffolk (MA)
Syracuse (NY)
Tennessee Tech. U
Tennessee, U. of
Texas A&M (Kingsville)
Texas Christian
Texas, U. of

Ursuline (OH)
Utah State
Virginia Commonwealth
Visual Arts, Sch. of (NY)
West Virginia, U. of
Western Carolina
Western Kentucky
Western Michigan
William Woods (MO)
Wisconsin, U. of

■ *Men Only*
▲ *Women Only*

INTERNATIONAL RELATIONS/STUDIES

Adelphi (NY)
▲ Agnes Scott (GA)
Alaska (Anchorage)
**Amerian International (MA)
**American U. (DC)
Aquinas (MI)
+ Arcadia (PA)
☎ Arizona State
Austin (TX)
☎ Babson (MA)
π Belmont Abbey (NC)
Beloit (WI)
● Bentley (MA)
Bethany (WV)
Bethel (IN)
☎ Bethune-Cookman (FL)
Binghamton (SUNY) (NY)
Boise State (ID)
Boston U. (MA)
Bradley (IL)
Brown (RI)
☎ Bryant (RI)
▲ Bryn Mawr (PA)
Bucknell (PA)
☎ Butler (IN)
☎ Caldwell (NJ)
California State U. (Chico)
California State U.
   (Long Beach)
California, U. of (Davis)
++ Carthage (WI)
π Central (IA)
▲ Chatham (PA)
City (CUNY) (NY)
+ Claremont McKenna (CA)
●● Clark (MA)
Colby (ME)
Colgate (NY)
Colorado
Connecticut College
☎ Cornell (IA)
Davidson (NC)
Dayton (OH)
Denison (OH)
☎ Denver, U. of (CO)
DePaul (IL)
☎ Dickinson (PA)
Dominican (CA)
☎ Drake (IA)
π D'Youville (NY)
✪ Earlham (IN)
Eckerd (FL)

☎ Elizabethtown (PA)
☎ Elmira (NY)
Emory (GA)
Evansville (IN)
Fairleigh Dickinson (NJ)
☎ Florida International
Franklin & Marshall (PA)
George Mason (VA)
+ George Washington (DC)
+ Georgetown (DC)
π Georgia
Georgia Tech.
Goucher (MD)
Grand Valley (MI)
Hamline (MN)
☎ Hawaii
+ Hawaii Pacific
☎ Hiram (OH)
☎ Hofstra (NY)
☎ Husson (ME)
Johns Hopkins (MD)
Juniata (PA)
☎ Illinois
Illinois State
Illinois Wesleyan
Indiana
Iowa, U. of
Kalamazoo (MI)
★ Kansas State
Kenyon (OH)
Knox (IL)
Lafayette (PA)
π LaSalle (PA)
Lehigh (PA)
☎ Lenoir-Rhyne (NC)
Lewis & Clark (OR)
Linfield (OR)
Loras (IA)
Macalester (MN)
Maine (Farmington)
Manhattanville (NY)
▲ Mary Baldwin (VA)
☎ Marygrove (MI)
Massachusetts, U. of
▲ Meredith (NC)
**Miami, U. of (FL)
☎ Michigan, U. of
Middlebury (VT)
++ Minnesota, U. of

■ *Men Only*
▲ *Women Only*

INTERNATIONAL RELATIONS
continues next page

INTERNATIONAL RELATIONS/STUDIES, continued

☎ Minnesota State U. (Mankato)
**Mississippi, U. of
Missouri Southern
☎ Moravian (PA)
Mt. Holyoke (MA)
Mt. Mercy (IA)
Mt. St. Mary's (MD)
Muhlenberg (PA)
Nebraska
Nebraska (Omaha)
**New Jersey, College of
North Carolina (Chapel Hill)
\# North Central (IL)
North Texas
π Northeastern (MA)
Occidental (CA)
Oglethorpe (GA)
Ohio U.
Ohio Wesleyan
π Oklahoma City U.
Pacific, U. of the (CA)
Pennsylvania, U. of
Pepperdine (CA)
Pittsburgh, U. of
Pitzer (CA)
Pomona (CA)
Princeton (NJ)
\# Providence (RI)
++ Puget Sound (WA)
Randolph College (VA)
Redlands (CA)
Reed (OR)
Richmond (VA)
Rhodes (TN)
Rochester, U. of (NY)
☎ Rochester Inst. of Tech. (NY)
** Rollins (FL)
☎ St. Andrews (NC)
▲ St. Catherine (MN)
☎ St. Louis U. (MO)
☎ St. Mary's (MN)
St. Mary's (TX)
St. Michael's (VT)
☎ St. Norbert (WI)
St. Olaf (MN)
☎ St. Peter's (NJ)
St. Thomas (TX)
San Diego, U. of (CA)

++ San Diego State (CA)
☎ San Francisco State (CA)
Scranton, U. of (PA)
▲ Scripps (CA)
Seton Hall (NJ)
☎ South Carolina, U. of
South Florida
+ Southern California, U. of
Southern Polytechnic (GA)
Southwestern (TX)
Spring Hill (AL)
Stanford (CA)
▲ Stephens (MO)
☎ Stetson (FL)
▲ Sweet Briar (VA)
Syracuse (NY)
☎ Texas A&M (Kingsville)
Trinity (CT)
▲ Trinity (DC)
Tufts (MA)
Tulane (LA)
U. S. Military Academy (NY)
Vassar (NY)
Virginia Poly. Institute
Virginia Wesleyan
Washington College (MD)
Washington, U. of
☎▲ Wesleyan (GA)
Westminster (MO)
π Westmont (CA)
☎ Westminster (UT)
Wheaton (MA)
Wheeling Jesuit (WV)
Whittier (CA)
Willamette (OR)
William & Mary (VA)
William Jewell (MO)
Wilson (PA)
Wisconsin, U. of
Wisconsin (Oshkosh)
Wyoming, U. of

\# *Global Studies*
* *International Economics*
☎ *International Business*
★ *International Marketing*
✪ *Peace & Global Studies*
* * *Also, International Business*
● *International Culture and Economy*
● ● *Also, Global Environmental Studies*
π *International Business and Global Affairs*
\+ *International Relations, also International Business*
++ *International Business, also International Political Economy*

■ *Men Only*
▲ *Women Only*

JAPANESE STUDIES

Boston U. (MA)	Linfield (OR)
Bucknell (PA)	Macalester (MN)
California, U. of (Berkeley)	Michigan, U. of
California, U. of (Irvine)	Middlebury (VT)
California, U. of (Los Angeles)	Minnesota, U. of
California, U. of (Santa Barbara)	North Central (IL)
Carnegie-Mellon (PA)	Oberlin (OH)
Case Western Reserve (OH)	Oregon, U. of
Colorado, U. of	Pacific, U. of the (CA)
Colorado State	San Diego State (CA)
Connecticut College	San Francisco State (CA)
DePaul (IL)	Sarah Lawrence (NY)
Dillard (LA)	Stanford (CA)
Earlham (IN)	Swarthmore (PA)
Florida State	Washington, U. of
George Washington (DC)	Washington U. (MO)
Georgetown (DC)	Willamette (OR)
Gettysburg (PA)	Williams (MA)
Harvard (MA)	Wisconsin, U. of
Hawaii, U. of	Yale (CT)
Lawrence (WI)	

■ *Men Only*
▲ *Women Only*

JAZZ

Alabama
Arizona State
Arizona, U. of
Arts, U. of the (PA)
Auburn (AL)
Augustana (IL)
Bellarmine (KY)
Bennington College (VT)
Berklee College of Music (MA)
Bowling Green (OH)
California Institute of the Arts
California State U. (Fullerton)
California State U. (Los Angeles)
California State U. (Northridge)
Cincinnati
Columbia College Chicago (IL)
Delaware
Denver, U. of
DePaul U. (IL)
Duquesne U. (PA)
Elmhurst (IL)
Five Towns College (NY)
Florida Atlantic
Georgia State
Hampshire College (MA)
Hartford (CT)
Idaho
Iowa
Indiana U.
Indiana U. (PA)
Jacksonville State (AL)
* Johns Hopkins (MD)
Juilliard (NY)
Knox (IL)
Long Island U. (Brooklyn)(NY)
Louisville (KY)
Loyola U. (New Orleans) (LA)
Manhattan School of
   Music (NY)
Mannes College of Music (NY)
Marlboro College (VT)
Miami (FL)
Michigan, U. of
Michigan State
Middle Tennessee
Minnesota (Duluth)
Minnesota
Nevada, U. of (Reno)

New England Conservatory
   of Music (MA)
New Orleans, U. of (LA)
New York U. (NY)
North Carolina (Asheville)
North Carolina (Greensboro)
North Carolina (Wilmington)
North Central (IL)
North Florida
North Texas
Northeastern State (OK)
Northern Illinois
Oberlin College (OH)
Ohio State U. (OH)
Oneonta (SUNY) (NY)
Oregon, U. of
Portland State (OR)
Purchase (SUNY) (NY)
Rochester (NY)
Roosevelt (IL)
Rowan (NJ)
Rutgers (NJ)
San Diego State (CA)
San Francisco State (CA)
San Jose State (CA)
Shenandoah U. (VA)
South Carolina
South Florida
Southern California
Southern Maine
Southern Mississippi
Southwest Texas State
Temple U. (PA)
Tennessee
Tennessee Tech
Truman State (MO)
Texas (Arlington)
Virginia Commonwealth
Washington, U. of
Webster U. (MO)
Western Maryland
Western Michigan U.
Western Washington
Westfield State (MA)
Whitworth (WA)
William Paterson (NJ)
Youngstown State (OH)

■ *Men Only*
▲ *Women Only*

* *Jazz Performance*

JEWISH STUDIES

Albany (SUNY) (NY)
American (DC)
Arizona, U. of
Bard (NY)
Binghamton (SUNY) (NY)
Brandeis (MA)
Brown (RI)
California, U. of (Berkeley)
California, U. of (San Diego)
California State U.
    (Northridge)
Chicago, U. of (IL)
Cincinnati, U. of (OH)
Florida, U. of
Florida Atlantic
George Washington (DC)
Georgia State
Hampshire (MA)
Harvard (MA)
Hofstra (NY)
Hunter (CUNY) (NY)
Indiana U.
Kalamazoo (MI)
Maryland, U. of
Massachusetts, U. of
Miami, U. of (FL)

Michigan, U. of
Minnesota, U. of
New York U.
Oberlin (OH)
Ohio State
Oregon. U. of
Pennsylvania, U. of
Penn State
Rutgers (NJ)
San Francisco State (CA)
▲ Scripps (CA)
Southern California
Temple (PA)
Texas, U. of
Trinity (CT)
Tufts (MA)
Tulane (LA)
Vanderbilt (TN)
Vassar (NY)
Wahington, U. of
Washington U. (MO)
Wisconsin, U. of
Wisconsin, U. of (Milwaukee)
Yale (CT)
Yeshiva (NY)

■ *Men Only*
▲ *Women Only*

LINGUISTICS

Alaska, U. of (Fairbanks)
Arizona, U. of
Beloit (WI)
Boston U. (MA)
Brown (RI)
Buffalo (SUNY) (NY)
California State U. (Fresno)
California, U. of (Berkeley)
California, U. of (Los Angeles)
California, U. of (San Diego)
California, U. of
　　　(Santa Barbara)
California, U. of (Santa Cruz)
Chicago, U. of (IL)
Clemson (SC)
Colorado, U. of
Connecticut, U. of
Cornell (NY)
Florida State
Florida, U. of
Georgetown (DC)
Georgia, U. of
Harvard (MA)
Hawaii, U. of
Illinois, U. of
Indiana U.
Iowa, U. of
Iowa State
Kansas, U. of
Kentucky, U. of
Lawrence (WI)
Macalester (MN)
Mary Washington (VA)
Maryland, U. of
Massachusetts, U. of
MIT (MA)
Michigan, U. of
Minnesota, U. of
Mississippi, U. of

Missouri, U. of
New Hampshire, U. of
New Mexico, U. of
New York U.
North Carolina, U. of
Northeastern (MA)
Northwestern (IL)
Oakland (MI)
Ohio State U.
Ohio U.
Oklahoma, U. of
Oregon, U. of
Pennsylvania, U. of
Pittsburgh, U. of (PA)
Pitzer (CA)
Pomona (CA)
Portland State (OR)
Queens (CUNY) (NY)
Reed (OR)
Rice (TX)
Rochester, U. of
Rutgers (NJ)
San Jose State (CA)
▲ Scripps (CA)
Southern California, U. of
Southern Maine, U. of
Stanford (CA)
Stony Brook (SUNY) (NY)
Swarthmore (PA)
Tennessee, U. of
Texas, U. of
Tulane (LA)
Virginia, U. of
Washington, U. of
Wayne State (MI)
▲ Wellesley (MA)
Wisconsin, U. of
Yale (CT)

■ *Men Only*
▲ *Women Only*

MARINE SCIENCE

Alaska Pacific
American (DC)
Atlantic, College of the (ME)
Barry (FL)
Brown (RI)
California State U.
   (Long Beach)
California State U. (Stanislaus)
California, U. of (San Diego)
California, U. of
   (Santa Barbara)
California, U. of (Santa Cruz)
Coastal Carolina (SC)
College of Charleston (SC)
Eckerd (FL)
Evergreen (WA)
Fairleigh Dickinson (NJ)
Florida Inst. of Technology
Hawaii Pacific
Hawaii, U. of
Hawaii, U. of (Hilo)
Idaho, U. of
Jacksonville U. (FL)
▲ Judson (AL)
Juniata (PA)
Kutztown (PA)
Maine, U. of
Maine, U. of (Machias)
Maine Maritime
★ Maritime College (SUNY)(NY)
Miami, U. of (FL)
∗∗ Nicholls State (LA)

North Carolina, U. of
   (Wilmington)
North Carolina State
Northern Michigan
∗∗ Northwest Missouri
Occidental (CA)
Rhode Island, U. of
Richard Stockton (NJ)
Roger Williams (RI)
Rollins (FL)
Rutgers (NJ)
St. Joseph's (ME)
Samford (AL)
San Diego, U. of (CA)
South Alabama
π South Carolina
South Florida
Southern Mississippi
Southwest Texas State
Spring Hill (AL)
Stetson (FL)
Stony Brook (SUNY) (NY)
Tampa, U. of (FL)
Texas A&M
Texas A&M (Corpus Christi)
Texas A&M (Galveston)
U.S. Coast Guard Academy (CT)
Unity (ME)
Washington, U. of
West Florida
∗∗ Wisconsin, U. of (Whitewater)

∗∗ *Marine Biology*

π *Also, Oceanography*

★ *and Marine Environmental Science*

■ *Men Only*
▲ *Women Only*

MEDICAL TECHNOLOGY

Woodbury (CA)
Alabama, U. of (Birmingham)
Alaska, U. of (Anchorage)
American International (MA)
Avila (MO)
Barry (FL)
Blackburn (IL)
Bowling Green (OH)
Bradley (IL)
Briar Cliff (IA)
Buffalo (SUNY) (NY)
Carroll (WI)
Cincinnati (OH)
Connecticut
East Tennessee
Edgewood (WI)
Elon (NC)
Fairmont (WV)
Florida Atlantic
Florida International
Fredonia (SUNY) (NY)
Gwynedd-Mercy (PA)
Hartwick (NY)
▲ Hood (MD)
Houston (TX)
Humboldt (CA)
Indiana Wesleyan
Kansas, U. of
King (TN)
Loma Linda (CA)
Marist (NY)
▲ Mary Baldwin (VA)
Massachusetts, U. of (Boston)

Mercy (NY)
Miami U. (OH)
Michigan
Michigan State
Midwestern State (TX)
Minnesota, U. of
Minnesota State U. (Mankato)
North Carolina (Greensboro)
Pacific U. (OR)
Pittsburgh (PA)
Plattsburgh (SUNY) (NY)
St. Francis (PA)
St. Leo (FL)
St. Mary's (NE)
▲ St. Mary's (IN)
Salisbury (MD)
Sciences, U. of the (PA)
Scranton (PA)
Sioux Falls, U. of (SD)
Springfield (MA)
Stetson (FL)
Suffolk (MA)
Texas
Texas, U. of (San Antonio Health Center)
Texas A&M (Corpus Christi)
Thomas More (KY)
Tuskegee (AL)
Virginia Commonwealth
Washington, U. of
Western Connecticut
West Virginia U.

■ *Men Only*
▲ *Women Only*

MIDDLE EASTERN STUDIES

Arizona, U. of
Arkansas, U. of
Bard (NY)
Barnard (NY)
Binghamton (SUNY) (NY)
Brandeis (MA)
Brigham Young (UT)
Brown (RI)
California, U. of (Berkeley)
California, U. of (Los Angeles)
California, U. of (Santa Barbara)
Chicago, U. of
Columbia (NY)
Connecticut, U. of
Cornell (NY)
Dickinson (PA)
Emory (GA)
Florida State
Fordham (NY)
George Washington (DC)
Hampshire (MA)

Harvard (MA)
Indiana, U. of
Johns Hopkins (MD)
Lycoming (PA)
Massachusetts, U. of
Michigan, U. of
Minnesota, U. of
New York U.
Princeton (NJ)
Rutgers (NJ)
Southwest Texas State
Texas, U. of
Toledo, U. of (OH)
U.S. Military Academy (NY)
Utah, U. of
Virginia, U. of
Washington, U. of
Washington U (MO)
William & Mary (VA)
Wooster (OH)
Yale (CT)

MORTUARY SCIENCE/FUNERAL SERVICES

Bemidji State (MN)
Central Oklahoma
Chadron State (NE)
Cincinnati Coll. of Mort. Sci.
π District of Columbia, U. of the
π Ferris State (MI)
Gannon (PA)
Lindenwood (MO)
π Lynn (FL)

Minnesota, U. of
Mount Ida (MA)
Point Park (PA)
Southern Illinois
St. John's (NY)
Thiel (PA)
Upper Iowa
Wayne State (MI)

π *Two Year Only*

MUSIC THERAPY

Alabama, U. of
Alverno (WI)
Anna Maria (MA)
Arizona State
Augsburg (MN)
Baldwin-Wallace (OH)
Berklee Coll. of Music (MA)
Charleston Southern (SC)
Colorado State
Dayton (OH)
Drury (MO)
Duquesne (PA)
East Carolina (NC)
Eastern Michigan (MI)
Elizabethtown (PA)
Evansville (IN)
Florida State
Fredonia (SUNY)(NY)
Georgia
Howard (DC)
Immaculata (PA)
Incarnate Word (TX)
Iowa
Kansas
Louisville (KY)
Loyola (LA)
Mansfield (PA)
Maryville, U. of
   (St. Louis)(MO)

Miami, U. of (FL)
Michigan State
Minnesota
Mississippi U. for Women
Missouri, U. of (Kansas City)
Molloy (NY)
Montclair (NJ)
Nazareth (NY)
New Paltz (SUNY)(NY)
North Dakota, U. of
Ohio U.
Pacific, U. of the (CA)
Queens (NC)
Radford (VA)
Seton Hill (PA)
Shenandoah (VA)
Slippery Rock (PA)
Southern Methodist (TX)
Southwestern Oklahoma
Temple (PA)
Texas Woman's
Utah State
Wartburg (IA)
Western Illinois
Western Michigan
Wisconsin, U. of (Eau Claire)
Wisconsin, U. of (Oshkosh)
Wooster (OH)

■ *Men Only*
▲ *Women Only*

MUSICAL THEATER

Adrian (MI)
American Academy of
   Dramatic Arts (NY)
American U. (DC)
Arizona, U. of
Arts, U. of the (PA)
Baldwin-Wallace (OH)
Boston Conservatory (MA)
California State (Fullerton)
Carnegie Mellon (PA)
Catholic U. (DC)
Central Florida
Central Michigan
Central Oklahoma
Cincinnati, U. of (OH)
Coastal Carolina (SC)
Columbia College Chicago (IL)
Elmhurst (IL)
Elon (NC)
Emerson (MA)
Florida
Florida State
Fredonia (SUNY)(NY)
Illinois State
Illinois Wesleyan
Ithaca (NY)
Jacksonville (FL)
James Madison (VA)
▲ Meredith (NC)
Miami, U. of (FL)
Michigan, U. of
Missouri State
Mobile, U. of (AL)
Montclair (NJ)
Muhlenberg (PA)
Nazareth (NY)
North Colorado
Northwestern (IL)
Nebraska, U. of (Kearney)

New York U.
Northeastern State (OK)
Oklahoma, U. of
Oklahoma City U.
Otterbein (OH)
Ouachita (AR)
Pacific, U. of the (CA)
Palm Beach Atlantic (FL)
Penn State
Plymouth (NH)
Point Park (PA)
Rider (NJ)
Rochester, U. of (NY)
Rockford (IL)
Roosevelt (IL)
Russell Sage (NY)
Santa Clara (CA)
Sarah Lawrence (NY)
Shenandoah (VA)
Shorter (GA)
South Dakota, U.of
Southern Illinois U.
   (Carbondale)
Southwest Missouri State
Syracuse (NY)
Texas Christian
Texas, U. of (El Paso)
Trinity (CT)
Tulsa (OK)
Viterbo (WI)
Weber State (UT)
West Virginia Wesleyan
Western Carolina (NC)
Western Illinois
Western Michigan
Wichita State (KS)
Wilkes (PA)
Wisconsin (Stevens Point)
Wright State (OH)

■ *Men Only*
▲ *Women Only*

NAVAL ARCHITECTURE

Maine Maritime Academy
Massachusetts Maritime
   Academy
Michigan, U. of
New Orleans, U. of (LA)
Stevens Institite (NJ)
SUNY Maritime College (NY)

Texas A&M (Galveston)
U.S. Coast Guard Academy (CT)
U.S. Merchant Marine
   Academy (NY)
U.S. Naval Academy (MD)
Webb Institute (NY)

NEUROSCIENCE

▲ Agnes Scott (GA)
Allegheny (PA)
Amherst (MA)
Baldwin-Wallace (OH)
▲ Barnard (NY)
Bowling Green (OH)
Bowdoin (ME)
Brown (RI)
Bucknell (PA)
California, U. of
   (Los Angeles)
Carthage (WI)
Central Michigan
Claremont McKenna (CA)
Colby (ME)
Colgate (NY)
Colorado College
Connecticut, U. of
Dickinson (PA)
Drake (IA)
Drew (NJ)
Emory (GA)
Florida State
Harvey Mudd (CA)
Kenyon (OH)
King (TN)
Lafayette (PA)
Macalester (MN)

Michigan
Middlebury (VT)
MIT (MA)
Minnesota, U. of
Montana State
Muskingum (OH)
New College (FL)
Northeastern (MA)
Northwestern (IL)
Oberlin (OH)
Pittsburgh (PA)
Pitzer (CA)
Pomona (CA)
Queens (CUNY) (NY)
Regis (CO)
Rochester, U. of (NY)
St. Lawrence (NY)
Scranton (PA)
▲ Scripps (CA)
Skidmore (NY)
Southern California
Temple (PA)
Texas, U. of (Dallas)
Union (NY)
Ursinus (PA)
Washington State
▲ Wellesley (MA)
Wesleyan (CT)

■ *Men Only*
▲ *Women Only*

NUTRITIONAL SCIENCE

Akron, U. of (OH)
Alabama, U. of
Andrews (MI)
Arizona, U. of
Auburn (AL)
Ball State (IN)
Benedictine (IL)
Boston U. (MA)
Bridgewater (VA)
Brigham Young (UT)
Cal Poly (SLO)
California, U. of (Berkeley)
California, U. of (Davis)
Case Western Reserve (OH)
Chapman (CA)
Clemson (SC)
Colorado State
Connecticut, U. of
Cornell (NY)
Delaware
Dominican (IL)
Drexel (PA)
Florida, U. of
Framingham State (MA)
✳ Gannon (PA)
Georgia, U. of
Hawaii, U. of
Illinois
Iowa State
Kansas State
LaSalle (PA)
Long Island U.
   (C.W. Post)(NY)
Maine, U. of
Marygrove (MI)
Maryland, U. of
Marywood (PA)
Massachusetts, U. of (Lowell)
Minnesota, U. of

Mississippi State
Missouri, U. of
Montclair (NJ)
Nebraska, U. of
New Hampshire, U. of
New York Inst. of Tech.
New York U.
North Carolina, U. of
North Carolina, U. of
   (Greensboro)
Ohio State
Oklahoma State
Oneonta (SUNY) (NY)
Oregon State
Ozarks, College of the (MO)
Penn State
Pittsburgh, U. of (PA)
Purdue (IN)
Rhode Island, U. of
Rutgers (NJ)
▲ Sage Colleges
   (Russell Sage)(NY)
St. John's/St. Benedict (MN)
▲ St. Joseph (CT)
St. Louis U. (MO)
San Jose State
Seattle Pacific (WA)
▲ Simmons (MA)
Syracuse (NY)
Tennessee Tech
Tennessee, U. of
Texas A&M
Texas A&M (Kingsville)
Texas Tech
Virginia Poly
Viterbo (WI)
Winthrop (SC)
Wisconsin, U. of
Wisconsin, U. of (Stout)

✳ *Nutrition and Human Performance*

■ *Men Only*
▲ *Women Only*

OCCUPATIONAL THERAPY

Wisconsin, U. of
American International (MA)
▲ Bay Path (MA)
Belmont (TN)
Boston U. (MA)
Brenau (GA)
Buffalo (SUNY) (NY)
Cleveland State (OH)
Colorado State
Dominican (CA)
Eastern Carolina
Eastern Kentucky
Elizabethtown (PA)
Findlay (OH)
Florida Gulf Coast
Florida, U. of
Gannon (PA)
Illinois (Chicago)
I.U.- P.U.- Indianapolis (IN)
Ithaca (NY)
Kansas, U. of
Lenoir-Rhyne (NC)
Long Island U. (Brooklyn)(NY)
Louisiana-Monroe
Maryville (St. Louis)(MO)
McKendree (IL)
Minnesota, U. of
Missouri
New England, U. of (ME)
New Hampshire, U. of
New Mexico, U. of
Newman (KS)
New York Inst. of Tech.
North Carolina, U. of
North Dakota, U. of
Ohio State

Penn State
Pittsburgh, U. of (PA)
Puget Sound (WA)
Quinnipiac (CT)
St. Ambrose (IA)
▲ St. Catherine (MN)
St. Francis (PA)
St. Louis U. (MO)
▲ St. Mary (NE)
St. Scholastica (MN)
Salem State (MA)
San Jose State (CA)
Sciences, U. of the (PA)
Scranton (PA)
South Dakota
Southern California
Stony Brook (SUNY)(NY)
Temple (PA)
Texas A&M (Corpus Christi)
Texas, U. of (El Paso)
▲ Texas Woman's
Texas U. of (Health Sci.Ctr.-
   San Antonio)
Towson (MD)
Tuskegee (AL)
Utica College (NY)
Washington U. (MO)
Washington, U. of
Wayne State (MI)
Western Michigan
Wisconsin, U. of
Wisconsin, U. of
   (La Crosse)
Wisconsin, U. of
   (Milwaukee)
Worcester State (MA)

ORTHOTICS / PROSTHETICS

California State
   (Dominguez Hills)
Florida International

Texas, U. of, S.W. Med Ctr.
   (Dallas)
Washington, U. of

■ *Men Only*
▲ *Women Only*

PARKS AND RECREATION SERVICES

π Alaska Pacific
Alderson-Broaddus (WV)
Appalachian State (NC)
Arizona State
Aurora (IL)
Bowling Green (OH)
Brigham Young (UT)
Cal. Poly. State U. (Pomona)
Cal. Poly. State U. (SLO)
California State U.
   (Dominguez Hills)
California State U. (Fresno)
California State U.
   (Los Angeles)
California State U.
   (Northridge)
California State U.
   (Sacramento)
Catawba (NC)
Central Michigan
Clemson (SC)
Colorado State
Connecticut
East Stroudsburg (PA)
Florida International
Florida State
Franklin (IN)
Georgia State
Georgia, U. of
Gordon (MA)
\# Green Mountain (VT)
* Houghton (NY)
Idaho
Idaho State
Illinois State
Illinois, U. of
Indiana U.
Indiana Wesleyan
Kansas State
Kean (NJ)
Lock Haven (PA)
● Lyndon (VT)
Maine, U. of
Mankato State (MN)
Maryland, U. of
Mesa State (CO)
Michigan State
Minnesota
** Minnesota (Duluth)

Minnesota State U. (Mankato)
Missouri
Montana
Montreat (NC)
Mount Marty (SD)
Nevada (Reno)
New Hampshire, U. of
New York U.
North Carolina (Greensboro)
North Carolina (Wilmington)
North Carolina State
Northern Arizona
Northern Iowa
π Northland (WI)
Ohio State
Ohio U.
Penn State
Pfeiffer (NC)
Pittsburgh (Bradford)
Purdue (IN)
San Diego State (CA)
San Jose State (CA)
Science & Arts of Oklahoma
Shepherd (WV)
Slippery Rock (PA)
Southern Conneccticut
Southeast Missouri State
Southwest Missouri
Southwestern Oklahoma State
Springfield College (MA)
Taylor (IN)
Texas A&M
\#\# Utah, U. of
Virginia Wesleyan
●● Warren Wilson (NC)
West Virginia U.
Western Carolina (NC)
Western State College of
   Colorado
Western Washington
Wingate (NC)
Winona State (MN)
Wisconsin (LaCrosse)

π *Outdoor Studies*
** *Outdoor Education*
\# *Resort Management*
●● *Outdoor Leadership*
\#\# *And Outdoor Recreation*
● *Also Ski Resort Management*
* *Also Equestrian Studies Option*

■ *Men Only*
▲ *Women Only*

PEACE AND CONFLICT STUDIES

American (DC)
Arcadia (PA)
Bethel (KS)
Bluffton (OH)
California, U. of (Berkeley)
Chapman (CA)
π Clark (MA)
Colgate (NY)
DePauw (IN)
Earlham (IN)
Eastern Mennonite (PA)
Goshen (IN)
Goucher (MD)
Guilford (NC)
Hamline (MN)
Hampshire (MA)
Juniata (PA)
Kent State (OH)
LeMoyne (NY)
Maine, U. of
Manchester (IN)

Manhattan (NY)
Missouri, U. of
Molloy (NY)
Mount St. Clair (IA)
North Carolina, U. of
Northland (WI)
North Texas
Norwich (VT)
Quincy (IL)
Regis (CO)
St. Benedict/St. John's (MN)
St. Michaels (VT)
St. Thomas (MN)
San Diego, U. of (CA)
Swarthmore (PA)
Tufts (MA)
Villanova (PA)
Washington, U. of
▲Wellesley (MA)
Whitworth (WA)
Youngstown State (OH)

Peace & Justice

π *Also Global Environmental Studies*

PHOTOJOURNALISM

Boston U. (MA)
* Columbia College Chicago (IL)
* Evergreen (WA)
Indiana U.
Missouri, U. of
Montana, U. of
Northern Illinois U.
Ohio U.

Rochester Inst. of Tech. (NY)
St. Edward's (TX)
San Jose State (CA)
South Carolina, U. of
Southern Illinois
Texas
Western Kentucky

* *Photography*
# *Photocommunications*

■ *Men Only*
▲ *Women Only*

PHYSICAL EDUCATION

Adelphi (NY)	Jamestown (ND)
Alderson-Broaddus (WV)	Johnson C. Smith (NC)
Asbury (KY)	Kansas State
Augsburg (MN)	Kansas, U. of
Azusa Pacific (CA)	Kean (NJ)
Baker (KS)	Kennesaw State (GA)
Bemidji State (MN)	Kentucky Wesleyan
Berea (KY)	King (TN)
Berry (GA)	Kutztown (PA)
Bethany (WV)	Lebanon Valley (PA)
Blackburn (IL)	LeTourneau (TX)
Bridgewater (MA)	Linfield (OR)
Brockport (SUNY) (NY)	Lock Haven (PA)
Castleton (VT)	Longwood (VA)
Chowan (NC)	Louisiana College
Coe (IA)	Luther (IA)
Colorado, U. of	Maine, U. of
Colorado State	McPherson (KS)
Cornell (IA)	Michigan State
Cortland State (NY)	Monmouth (IL)
Dana (NE)	Muskingum (OH)
Davis & Elkins (WV)	Nebraska, U. of
Denison (OH)	Nevada (Reno)
Doane (NE)	North Carolina, U. of
East Stroudsburg (PA)	North Central (IL)
Elon (NC)	North Georgia
Eureka (IL)	Northern Iowa
Faulkner (AL)	Northwestern Louisiana
Findlay (OH)	Norwich (VT)
Florida Southern	Occidental (CA)
Florida State	Ohio U.
Florida, U. of	Oregon State
Franklin (IN)	Otterbein (OH)
Georgia, U. of	Ozarks (MO)
Goshen (IN)	Pacific U. (OR)
Graceland (IA)	Pennsylvania State
Grambling (LA)	Peru State (NE)
Hamline (MN)	Plymouth State (NH)
Hanover (IN)	Puerto Rico, U. of
Hardin-Simmons (TX)	(Mayaguez)
Illinois College	Purdue (IN)
Illinois, U. of (Chicago)	Randolph College (VA)
Indiana (PA)	Rhode Island College
Iowa, U. of	Rockford (IL)
Ithaca (NY)	
Jacksonville (FL)	

■ *Men Only*
▲ *Women Only*

PHYSICAL EDUCATION continues next page

PHYSICAL EDUCATION, continued

St. Leo (FL)
Skidmore (NY)
Slippery Rock (PA)
South Florida, U. of
Springfield (MA)
Sterling (KS)
Texas, U. of
Union (TN)
Ursinus (PA)
Walsh (OH)

Washington State
Western Illinois
Western Washington
Westmont (CA)
West Virginia U.
West Virginia Wesleyan
William & Mary (VA)
Wisconsin (LaCrosse)
Wisconsin, U. of

■ *Men Only*
▲ *Women Only*

PHYSICAL THERAPY

Akron (OH)
American International (MA)
Azusa Pacific (CA)
Barry (FL)
Belmont (TN)
Boston University (MA)
Bowling Green (OH)
Bradley (IL)
Buffalo (SUNY) (NY)
California State U. (Fresno)
California State U.
   (Sacramento)
Carroll (MT)
Clarke (IA)
Clarkson (NY)
Connecticut, U. of
Dayton (OH)
D'Youville (NY)
Daemen (NY)
Duquesne (PA)
Evansville (IN)
Fairmont State (WV)
Florida Gulf Coast U.
Florida International
Florida, U. of
Grambling (LA)
Grand Valley (MI)
Hartford (CT)
Houston, U. of (TX)
Hunter (CUNY) (NY)
Huntington (AL)
Husson (ME)
Illinois (Chicago)
Indiana State
I.U.-P.U.- Indianapolis (IN)
Ithaca (NY)
Kentucky, U. of
Lebanon Valley (PA)
Louisiana-Lafayette
Louisville, U. of (KY)
Manhattan (NY)
Marquette (WI)

Maryville (St. Louis) (MO)
Miami, U. of (FL)
Midwestern State (TX)
Minnesota, U. of
Missouri, U. of
Mount St. Joseph (OH)
Mt. St. Mary's (CA)
Nazareth (NY)
Nebraska, U. of
New England, U. of (ME)
New Mexico, U. of
North Dakota, U. of
Northeastern (MA)
Northern Illinois
Ohio State U.
Ohio University
Pacific (OR)
Pittsburgh, U. of (PA)
Quinnipiac (CT)
Regis (CO)
Russell Sage (NY)
St. Francis (PA)
St. Louis U. (MO)
Saint Scholastica (MN)
San Diego State (CA)
San Francisco State (CA)
Sciences, U. of the (PA)
Scranton, U. of (PA)
Slippery Rock (PA)
Springfield College (MA)
Texas Southern
Texas U. of (Health Sci.Ctr.-
   San Antonio)
Toledo (OH)
Utah
Washington U. (MO)
Waynesburg (PA)
Wayne State (MI)
West Virginia U.
Western Carolina (NC)
Wisconsin, U. of
Wisconsin, U. of (La Crosse)

■ *Men Only*
▲ *Women Only*

PHYSICIAN ASSISTANT

Alderson-Broaddus (WV)
Augsburg (MN)
Butler (IN)
Daeman (NY)
DeSales (PA)
D'Youville (NY)
East Carolina
Findlay (OH)
Gannon (PA)
George Washington (DC)
High Point (NC)
Hofstra (NY)
Howard (DC)
Idaho State
Kentucky
King's (PA)
LeMoyne (NY)
Long Island U. (Brooklyn)(NY)
Miami, U. of (FL)

New York Inst. of Tech.
Nova Southeastern (FL)
Pace (NY)
Pacific (OR)
Philadelphia U. (PA)
Rochester Inst. of Tech. (NY)
Rocky Mountain (MT)
St. Francis (NY)
St. Francis (PA)
St. Louis (MO)
Sciences, U. of the (PA)
Seton Hill (PA)
South Dakota
Southern California
Springfield (MA)
Stony Brook (SUNY)(NY)
Union (NE)
Wichita State (KS)
Wisconsin

PRE-VETERINARY

Arkansas, U. of
Auburn (AL)
California, U. of (Davis)
Cal. Poly. State U.
    (San Luis Obispo)
Clemson (SC)
Colorado State
Delaware Valley (PA)
Elmhurst (IL)
Evansville, U. of (IN)
Findlay (OH)
Fort Lewis (CO)
Georgia, U. of
Goucher (MD)
▲Hollins (VA)
Humboldt State (CA)
Idaho, U. of
Illinois, U. of
Iowa State
Juniata (PA)
Kansas State
Lawrence (WI)
Louisiana-Lafayette
Loyola (LA)
MacMurray (IL)
Maryland, U. of
Massachusetts, U. of
Mercy (NY)
Michigan State
Minnesota, U. of
Montana, U. of
Moravian (PA)
π Mount Ida (MA)
Murray State (KY)
Muskingum (OH)

Nebraska, U. of
Nebraska, U. of (Kearney)
Nevada, U. of (Reno)
New Hampshire, U. of
New Mexico State
Northland (WI)
North Dakota State
Oklahoma State
Oregon, U. of
Purdue (IN)
Rhode Island, U. of
▲Russell Sage
    (The Sage Colleges)(NY)
St. Andrews (NC)
St. Francis (PA)
▲Salem (NC)
South Dakota State U.
Southern Mississippi, U. of
Susquehanna (PA)
Tennessee, U. of
Texas A & M
Tuskegee (AL)
Utah State
Vermont, U. of
Virginia Wesleyan
Warren Wilson (NC)
Washington & Jefferson (PA)
Washington State
West Virginia Wesleyan
Wilmington (OH)
Wingate (NC)
Winona State (MN)
Wyoming, U. of

■ *Men Only*
▲ *Women Only*

π *Veterinary Technician*

PUBLIC HEALTH

American (DC)
Baylor (TX)
Bethel (MN)
Brigham Young (UT)
Brown (RI)
Central Oklahoma
Central State (OH)
Central Washington
Columbia College Chicago (IL)
Delaware State
Dillard (LA)
Florida State
Hofstra (NY)
Holy Family (PA)
* Hunter (CUNY) (NY)
Idaho, U. of
Indiana U.
Ind. U.-Pur U.-Ind U. (IN)
Johns Hopkins(MD)
Kansas, U. of
Kent State (OH)
Moorhead State (MN)
Nevada, U. of (Reno)
New Mexico State
New Orleans, U. of (LA)
North Carolina (Greensboro)

Northern Illinois
Ohio U.
Potsdam (SUNY) (NY)
Purdue (IN)
Richard Stockton (NJ)
Rutgers (NJ)
St. Cloud (MN)
St. Joseph's (NY)
Salem-Teikyo (WV)
San Francisco State (CA)
San Jose State (CA)
▲ Simmons (MA)
Southern Connecticut State
Temple (PA)
Texas Women's
Tulane (LA)
Utah State
Virginia Commonwealth
West Chester (PA)
Western Illinois
Western Kentucky
Western Michigan
Western Washington
Wisconsin (Eau Claire)
Worcester State (MA)

* Urban Public Health
 # Health Ecology

PUBLIC RELATIONS

Alabama, U. of
American (DC)
Auburn (AL)
Boston U. (MA)
Champlain (VT)
Coe (IA)
Dayton (OH)
Drake (IA)
Duquesne (PA)
Florida, U. of
Florida State
Georgia, U. of
Hawaii Pacific
Illinois, U. of
Louisiana-Lafayette
Marietta (OH)
Marquette (WI)
Miami, U. of (FL)
Michigan State

Monmouth (IL)
Northern Arizona
Oklahoma, U. of
Oregon, U. of
Pennsylvania State
Quinnipiac (CT)
Rhode Island, U. of
St. Scholastica (MN)
San Diego State (CA)
San Jose State (CA)
Southern California, U. of
Syracuse (NY)
Tennessee, U. of
Texas Tech.
Texas, U. of
Valparaiso (IN)
Vermont, U. of
West Virginia

■ *Men Only*
▲ *Women Only*

RANGE MANAGEMENT

Brigham Young (UT)
California, U. of
   (Berkeley)
California, U. of (Davis)
Colorado State
Eastern Oregon
Humboldt State (CA)
Idaho, U. of
Montana State (Bozeman)
Nebraska, U. of
New Mexico State U.
North Dakota State U.

Oregon State U.
South Dakota State U.
Stephen F. Austin State U. (TX)
Tarleton State (TX)
Texas A&M
Texas A&M (Kingsville)
Texas Christian
Texas Tech.
Utah State
Washington State
Wyoming, U. of

ROBOTICS TECHNOLOGY

Harvard (MA)
New Mexico, U. of

Parsons School of Design (NY)
Washington U. (MO)

SIGN LANGUAGE INTERPRETATION

Arkansas, U. of
Augustana (SD)
Bethel (IN)
Gardner Webb (NC)
Goshen (IN)
IUPUI (IN)
Kent State (OH)
MacMurray (IL)
Madonna (MI)
New Hampshire, U. of

New Mexico
North Colorado
North Florida
Northeastern (MA)
Quincy (IL)
Rochester, U. of (NY)
Rochester Inst. of Tech. (NY)
Western Oregon
William Woods (MO)

SOCIAL AND REHABILITATION SERVICES

Xavier (OH)
Arizona, U. of
Assumption (MA)
Boston U. (MA)
California State U.
   (Los Angeles)
Gustavus Adolphus (MN)
Iowa, U. of
Louisiana State
Maine (Farmington)
Marshall (WV)
Marysville U.-St. Louis (MO)
Montana, U. of
Northern Colorado
North Texas
Ohio State

Penn State
Pittsburgh, U. of (PA)
Seattle (WA)
South Florida, U. of
Southern Mississippi
Springfield College (MA)
Texas, U. of (Austin)
Virginia Commonwealth
Wartburg (IA)
West Virginia Wesleyan
Wilberforce (OH)
Wisconsin
π Wisconsin (Stout)

π *Vocational Rehabilitation*
Business and Rehabilitation Services

■ *Men Only*
▲ *Women Only*

SOCIAL WORK

Abilene Christian (TX)
Adelphi (NY)
Alabama, U. of
Alaska, U. of (Anchorage)
Alaska, U. of (Fairbanks)
Albany (SUNY) (NY)
Andrews (MI)
Arizona State
Arkansas, U. of
Ashland (OH)
Augsburg (MN)
Azusa Pacific (CA)
Ball State (IN)
Barry (FL)
Baylor (TX)
Belmont (TN)
Bemidji State (MN)
▲ Bennett (NC)
Bethany (KS)
Bethany (WV)
Bethel (KS)
Boise State (ID)
Brescia (KY)
Briar Cliff (IA)
Bridgewater State (MA)
Brigham Young (UT)
Brockport (SUNY) (NY)
Buena Vista (IA)
California (PA)
California (Berkeley)
California State U. (Chico)
California State U. (Fresno)
California State U. (Fullerton)
California State U.
   (Los Angeles)
California State U.
   (Sacramento)
California State U.
   (San Bernardino)
Carroll (WI)
Castleton (VT)
Catholic (DC)
Clarke (IA)
Colorado State
Connecticut, U. of
Creighton (NE)
Cumberland (KY)

Dana (NE)
David Lipscomb (TN)
Dillard (LA)
Eastern Michigan
Eastern Nazarene (MA)
Eastern Washington
Elizabethtown (PA)
Elmira (NY)
Elms (MA)
Ferris State (MI)
Findlay (OH)
Florida Atlantic
Florida International
Florida State
Fordham (NY)
Fort Hays (KS)
Franciscan U. of Steubenville (OH)
Fredonia (SUNY) (NY)
Georgia State
Georgia U. of
Gordon (MA)
Grand Valley (MI)
Hawaii, U. of
Hawaii Pacific
Hood (MD)
Hope (MI)
Humboldt State (CA)
Illinois, U. of
Illinois, U. of (Chicago)
Illinois, U. of (Springfield)
Indiana
Indiana U.-Purdue U.-
   Indianapolis (IN)
Indiana Wesleyan
Iowa, U. of
Jacksonville State (AL)
Johnson C. Smith (NC)
Juniata (PA)
Kansas State
Kansas, U. of
Kean (NJ)
Kentucky
Lewis-Clark (ID)
Lindenwood (MO)
Lipscomb (TN)

■ *Men Only*
▲ *Women Only*

SOCIAL WORK continues next page

SOCIAL WORK, continued

Lock Haven (PA)
Longwood (VA)
Loras (IA)
Louisiana-Monroe
Lourdes (OH)
Loyola (IL)
MacMurray (IL)
Madonna (MI)
Maine, U. of
Manchester (IN)
Mansfield (PA)
Marquette (WI)
Marshall (WV)
▲ Mary Baldwin (VA)
Marygrove (MI)
Maryland (Baltimore Co.)
Marywood (PA)
McDaniel (MD)
Mercyhurst (PA)
▲ Meredith (NC)
Michigan State
Michigan, U. of
Middle Tennessee
Millersville (PA)
Minnesota (Duluth)
Minnesota State U.
　(Moorhead)
Misericordia (PA)
Missouri, U. of
Montana, U. of
Mount St. Joseph (OH)
Mount St. Mary's (NY)
Nazareth (NY)
Nevada, U. of (Las Vegas)
Nevada, U. of (Reno)
New Mexico State
New York University
Niagara (NY)
North Carolina (Greensboro)
North Carolina (Pembroke)
North Carolina State
Northeastern State (OK)
Northern Iowa
Northwestern (IA)
Northwestern State (LA)
Ohio U.
Oklahoma, U. of

Oral Roberts (OK)
Pittsburgh, U. of (PA)
Portland, U. of (OR)
Presentation (SD)
Providence (RI)
Radford (VA)
Ramapo (NJ)
Rhode Island College
Richard Stockton (NJ)
Rochester Inst. of Tech. (NY)
Rockford (IL)
Sacred Heart (CT)
Saginaw Valley (MI)
▲ St. Catherine (MN)
St. Edward's (TX)
St. Francis (IN)
St. Francis (PA)
St. Leo (FL)
St. Louis (MO)
St. Olaf (MN)
St. Scholastica (MN)
St. Thomas (MN)
Salem State (MA)
Salisbury (MD)
San Diego State (CA)
San Francisco State (CA)
San Jose State (CA)
Shaw (NC)
Shepherd (WV)
Shippensburg U. of (PA)
Siena (NY)
South Florida, U. of
Southern Connecticut
Southern Illinois (Carbondale)
Southwestern Oklahoma State U.
Stony Brook (SUNY) (NY)
Tarleton State (TX)
Tennessee, U. of
Texas A&M (Kingsville)
Texas, U. of (Arlington)
Texas, U. of (Austin)
Texas State
Texas Women's
Utah, U. of

■ *Men Only*
▲ *Women Only*

SOCIAL WORK continues next page

SOCIAL WORK, continued

Utah State
Valparaiso (IN)
Vermont, U. of
Virginia Commonwealth
Walla Walla (WA)
Warren Wilson (NC)
Wartburg (IA)
Washburn (KS)
Washington U. (MO)
Washington, U. of
Wayne State (MI)
West Florida
Western Carolina (NC)

Western Maryland
Western Michigan
Western New England (MA)
Wheelock (MA)
William Woods (MO)
Winona State (MN)
Winthrop (SC)
Wisconsin, U. of
Wisconsin, U. of (Milwaukee)
Wisconsin, U. of (Superior)
Wisconsin, U. of (Whitewater)
Wyoming, U. of
Youngstown State (OH)

SPECIAL EDUCATION

Alabama, U. of
Alderson-Broaddus (WV)
American International (MA)
Arizona State
Arizona, U. of
Arkansas
Auburn (AL)
Augustana (SD)
Bemidji State (MN)
π Bethel (IN)
Boston U. (MA)
Brenau (GA)
Bridgewater State (MA)
California State (Fresno)
π California State
    (Northridge)
Central (CT)
Clarke (IA)
Clarion (PA)
Columbia (SC)
Connecticut, U. of
▲ Converse (SC)
Culver-Stockton (MO)
Curry (MA)
Dana (NE)
Delaware State
Doane (NE)
Eastern Kentucky
Eastern Illinois
Eastern Michigan
Edinboro (PA)
Emporia State (KS)
Fitchburg (MA)
π Flagler (FL)
Florida Atlantic
Florida Gulf Coast
Florida, U. of
Fontbonne (MO)
Fort Hays (KS)
Geneseo (SUNY) (NY)
Georgia Southwestern
Georgia, U. of
Gonzaga (WA)
Grand Valley (MI)
Hartford (CT)
Hofstra (NY)
Holy Names (CA)

Hood (MD)
Idaho, U. of
Illinois State
Indiana U.
James Madison (VA)
Juniata (PA)
Kansas State
Kansas Wesleyan
Kean (NJ)
Keene (NH)
Kentucky, U. of
Kutztown (PA)
Landmark College (VT)
Lasell (MA)
Lesley (MA)
Lindenwood (MO)
Lock Haven (PA)
Longwood (VA)
Loras (IA)
Louisiana State U.
Lyndon State (VT)
MacMurray (IL)
Maine, U. of (Farmington)
Malone (OH)
Mansfield (PA)
Marygrove (MI)
Maryland, U. of
Mercyhurst (PA)
Miami, U. of (FL)
Michigan State
Michigan, U. of
Millersville (PA)
Montana State (Billings)
Mount St. Mary's (NY)
Muskingum (OH)
Nebraska, U. of
Nebraska, U. of (Omaha)
New Mexico State
Nevada, U. of (Las Vegas)
Nevada, U. of (Reno)
North Florida
North Georgia
North Texas
Northeastern Illinois

π *Also Deaf Studies*

■ *Men Only*
▲ *Women Only*

SPECIAL ED. continues next page

SPECIAL EDUCATION, continued

Northern Colorado, U. of
Northern Illinois
Northern Iowa
Northern State U. (SD)
Nyack (NY)
Oklahoma, U. of
Old Dominion (VA)
Oregon, U. of
Pennsylvania State
Peru State (NE)
Portland State (OR)
Presbyterian (SC)
Providence (RI)
Quincy (IL)
Rhode Island College
Rockford (IL)
Rowan (NJ)
St. Cloud (MN)
St. Elizabeth (NJ)
St. Francis (IN)
St. John Fisher (NY)
▲ St. Joseph (CT)
St. Louis U. (MO)
St. Martin's (WA)
Silver Lake (WI)
▲ Simmons (MA)
Slippery Rock (PA)
Southern Connecticut

South Florida
Southern Illinois U.
     (Carbondale)
Southern Utah
Temple (PA)
Tennessee, U. of
Texas, U. of
▲ Trinity (DC)
Utah State
Utah, U. of
Vanderbilt (TN)
Walsh (OH)
West Chester (PA)
West Florida
Western Carolina
Western Washington
Westfield (MA)
Wheelock (MA)
Wisconsin, U. of
Wisconsin, U. of (Eau Claire)
Wisconsin, U. of (Milwaukee)
Wisconsin, U. of (Oshkosh)
Wisconsin, U. of (Whitewater)
Winona (MN)
Wittenberg (OH)
Wyoming, U. of
Xavier (LA)

■ *Men Only*
▲ *Women Only*

SPORTS MEDICINE/ATHLETIC TRAINING

Adrian (MI)	LaSell (MA)
Alderson-Broaddus (WV)	Laverne (CA)
Alfred (NY)	Lees-McCrae (NC)
Alma (MI)	Lindenwood (MO)
Baldwin Wallace (OH)	Linfield (OR)
Ball State (IN)	Lipscomb (TN)
Boise State (ID)	Long Island U. (Brooklyn)(NY)
Brockport (SUNY) (NY)	Louisiana College
Bryan (TN)	Lynchburg (VA)
California (PA)	Manchester (IN)
California Lutheran	Manhattan (NY)
Canisius (NY)	Marietta (OH)
Carthage (WI)	McKendree (IL)
Castleton (VT)	Merrimack (MA)
Catawba (NC)	Mercyhurst (PA)
Charleston, College of (SC)	Minnesota State U. (Mankato)
Charleston, U. of (WV)	Missouri Baptist
Chowan (NC)	Mobile, U. of (AL)
Clarke (IA)	Mount Union (OH)
Coe (IA)	Neumann (PA)
Colby-Sawyer (NH)	Nevada, U. of (Las Vegas)
Colorado State	New Mexico State
Connecticut, U. of	Nicholls State (LA)
East Stroudsburg (PA)	North Dakota
Eastern Nazarene (MA)	North Florida
Elon (NC)	North Georgia
Endicott (MA)	Northeastern (MA)
Eureka (IL)	Northwestern (IA)
Evansville (IN)	Norwich (VT)
Findlay (OH)	Ohio Northern
* Florida Institute of Tech.	Ohio State
Florida Southern	Otterbein (OH)
Florida State	Palm Beach Atlantic (FL)
Gardner-Webb (NC)	Pepperdine (CA)
George Fox (OR)	Quincy (IL)
Gustavus Adolphus (MN)	Quinnipiac (CT)
Heidelberg (OH)	Roanoke (VA)
High Point (NC)	St. Andrews (NC)
Hope (MI)	Samford (AL)
Houston Baptist (TX)	Slippery Rock (PA)
Illinois (Chicago)	Southern Maine
Indiana U.	Southwest Missouri
Indiana Wesleyan	Southwest Texas State
James Madison (VA)	Springfield (MA)
Kansas Wesleyan	
King's (PA)	

* Sports Psychology

■ *Men Only*
▲ *Women Only*

SPORTS MEDICINE / ATHLETIC TRAINING continues next page

SPORTS MEDICINE/ATHLETIC TRAINING, continued

Sterling (KS)
Stony Brook (SUNY) (NY)
Taylor (IN)
Texas (Arlington)
Texas Lutheran
Toledo (OH)
Towson (MD)
Tusculum (TN)
Tulsa (OK)
Union (TN)

Waynesburg (PA)
West Virginia Wesleyan
West Chester (PA)
Whitworth (WA)
William Woods (MO)
Wilmington (OH)
Wingate (NC)
Wisconsin (La Crosse)
Xavier (OH)

SPORTS SCIENCES / MANAGEMENT

Alabama, U. of
Alderson-Broaddus (WV)
Aquinas (MI)
Arizona State
Averett (VA)
Belmont Abbey (NC)
Bemidji (MN)
Berry (GA)
Bowling Green (OH)
Briar Cliff (IA)
Brockport (SUNY) (NY)
Buena Vista (IA)
Cabrini (PA)
Carthage (WI)
Castleton (VT)
Central Washington
Chowan (NC)
* Coastal Carolina (SC)
Colby-Sawyer (NH)
Concordia (CA)
Connecticut, U. of
Dallas, U. of (TX)
Eastern Connecticut
Elon (NC)
Endicott (MA)
Faulkner (AL)
Flagler (FL)
Florida Southern
Florida, U. of
Gannon (PA)
Guilford (NC)
High Point (NC)

Husson (ME)
Idaho, U. of
Incarnate Word (TX)
Indiana U.
Ithaca (NY)
Kansas, U. of
Kentucky Wesleyan
Knox (IL)
Liberty (VA)
Lock Haven (PA)
Louisville (KY)
Lynchburg (VA)
Lynn (FL)
MacMurray (IL)
Malone (OH)
Marian (WI)
Massachusetts, U. of
Michigan, U. of
Millersville (PA)
Misericordia (PA)
Mississippi U. for Women
Missouri Baptist
Mount St. Joseph (OH)
Mount Union (OH)
Nebraska, U. of
Neumann (PA)
Nicholls State (LA)
** North Carolina State

PGA Golf Management
* Professional Golf Management
** Also, Professional Golf Management

■ *Men Only*
▲ *Women Only*

SPORTS SCIENCES / MANAGEMENT continues next page

SPORTS SCIENCES / MANAGEMENT, continued

North Florida
North Michigan
Northern State U. (SD)
Northwood (MI)
Nova Southeastern (FL)
Ohio Northern
Ohio State
Ohio U.
Oklahoma
Oregon, U. of
Pfeiffer (NC)
Principia (IL)
Richmond (VA)
Robert Morris (PA)
Rutgers (NJ)
Seton Hall (NJ)
Shepherd (WV)
Siena Heights (MI)
Simpson (IA)
South Carolina, U. of
Southern New Hampshire, U. of
Southwest Baptist (MO)
Springfield (MA)

St. Ambrose (IA)
St. John's (NY)
St. Leo (FL)
St. Olaf (MN)
St. Thomas U. (FL)
Stetson (FL)
Tampa, U. of (FL)
Tarleton State (TX)
Taylor (IN)
Temple (PA)
Tennessee
Texas Christian
Towson (MD)
Tulsa (OK)
Union (TN)
West Virginia U.
Western Carolina
Western New England (MA)
Wilson (PA)
Wingate (NC)
Wisconsin (La Crosse)

URBAN STUDIES

Akron, U. of (OH)
Albany (SUNY)(NY)
Aquinas (MI)
Augsburg (MN)
▲ Barnard (NY)
Boston U. (MA)
Brown (RI)
▲✪ Bryn Mawr (PA)
California State U. (Northridge)
California, U. of (San Diego)
★ Cal Poly State U. (SLO)
Canisius (NY)
Cincinnati, U. of (OH)
Clark (MA)
Cleveland State (OH)
College of Charleston (SC)
Columbia (NY)
Connecticut College
Connecticut, U. of
Cornell (NY)
David Lipscomb (TN)
DePaul (IL)
Eastern Washington
Elmhurst (IL)
Evergreen (WA)
Florida International
Florida, U. of
Furman (SC)
Georgia State
Grambling (LA)
Hamline (MN)
Hampshire (MA)
Harvard (MA)
Hunter (CUNY)(NY)
Illinois (Chicago)
Indiana State
Lehigh (PA)
Lipscomb (TN)
Loyola Marymount (CA)
Macalester (MN)
Malone (OH)
Manhattan (NY)
Maryland, U. of

\# Michigan State
Minnesota, U. of
π Minnesota State U. (Mankato)
■ Morehouse (GA)
Mount Mercy (IA)
Nebraska, U. of
New School U. (NY)
New York U.
Northwestern (IL)
Ohio State
Pennsylvania, U. of
Pittsburgh, U. of (PA)
** Portland State (OR)
Queens (CUNY) (NY)
Rockford (IL)
Rutgers (NJ)
Rutgers (Camden) (NJ)
St. Louis (MO)
St. Peter's (NJ)
San Francisco State U. (CA)
Shippensburg (PA)
Stanford (CA)
Tampa, U. of (FL)
Towson State (MD)
Trinity (TX)
Vanderbilt (TN)
Vassar (NY)
Virginia Commonwealth
Virginia Poly
Washington, U. of
Washington U. (MO)
Wayne State (MI)
Western Washington
π Westfield State (MA)
Wisconsin, U. of
    (Green Bay)
Wittenberg (OH)
Wooster (OH)
Worcester State (MA)
Wright State (OH)

π *Regional Planning*
\# *And Regional Planning*
★ *City & Regional Planning*
** *Community Development*
✪ *Growth and Structure of Cities*

■ *Men Only*
▲ *Women Only*

VOICE

Ball State (IN)
Bucknell (PA)
Catholic (DC)
Chapman (CA)
Cincinnati, U. of (OH)
Cleveland Inst. of Music (OH)
Columbia College Chicago (IL)
Connecticut College
Florida Southern
Florida State
Fredonia (SUNY)(NY)
Furman (SC)
Illinois, U. of
Illinois Wesleyan
Ithaca (NY)
Indiana U.
Juilliard (NY)
Kansas, U. of
Manhattan Sch. of Music (NY)
Mannes (NY)
Mercer (GA)
▲ Meredith (NC)
Miami, U. of (FL)
Michigan, U. of
Middle Tennessee
Millersville (PA)
Missouri, U. of (Kansas City)
Missouri State
Nebraska Wesleyan
New England Conservatory (MA)

New Hampshire, U. of
New York U.
North Carolina (Greensboro)
North Carolina School of the Arts
North Texas
Northwestern (IL)
Nyack (NY)
Oberlin (OH)
Ohio U.
Oklahoma City U.
Ouachita (AR)
Pacific Lutheran (WA)
Palm Beach Atlantic (FL)
Purchase (SUNY) (NY)
Rice (TX)
Rider (Westminster) (NJ)
Roosevelt (IL)
Samford (AL)
San Francisco Conserv. of
    Music (CA)
Shenandoah (VA)
Shorter (GA)
Southeast Missouri State
Southern California
Syracuse (NY)
Temple (PA)
Tennessee, U. of
Tulsa, U. of (OK)
Weber State (UT)
Wheaton (IL)

■ *Men Only*
▲ *Women Only*

WILDLIFE/WILDLANDS MANAGEMENT

Alaska (Fairbanks)
Arizona, U. of
Auburn (AL)
Ball State (IN)
Brevard (NC)
Brigham Young (UT)
California, U. of (Davis)
Clemson (SC)
Colorado State
Connecticut, U. of
Cornell (NY)
Eastern Kentucky
Eastern New Mexico
Florida, U. of
Frostburg State (MD)
Georgia, U. of
π Grand Valley (MI)
Humboldt State (CA)
Idaho, U. of
Kansas State
Louisiana State
Maine, U. of
Massachusetts, U. of
Michigan State
Michigan Tech
Michigan, U. of
Minnesota, U. of
Mississippi State
Missouri, U. of
Montana, U. of

Montana State
Nebraska, U. of
New Hampshire, U. of
New Mexico State
North Carolina State
Ohio State
Oklahoma State
Oregon State
Penn State
Purdue (IN)
Rhode Island, U. of
Rutgers (NJ)
South Dakota State
Southeastern Louisiana
Tarleton State (TX)
Tennessee Tech
Tennessee, U. of
Texas A&M
Texas Tech.
Unity (ME)
Utah State
Vermont, U. of
Virginia Poly Tech
Washington State
Washington, U. of
West Virginia U.
Wisconsin, U. of
Wisconsin, U. of
   (Stevens Point)
Wyoming, U. of

π *Natural Resources Management*

WOMEN'S STUDIES

Wright State (OH)
▲ Agnes Scott (GA)
Albion (MI)
Allegheny (PA)
Antioch (OH)
Appalachian State (NC)
Arizona State
Arizona, U. of
Augsburg (MN)
▲ Barnard (NY)
Bates (ME)
Beloit (WI)
Berea (WV)
Bowling Green (OH)
Brandeis (MA)
Brown (RI)
Cal Poly State U. (Pomona)
California State U. (Fresno)
California State U.
    (Long Beach)
California, U. of (Berkeley)
California, U. of (Davis)
California, U. of (Riverside)
California, U. of
    (Santa Barbara)
California, U. of (Santa Cruz)
Carleton (MN)
Colby (ME)
Colorado College
Colorado, U. of
Connecticut College
Connectut, U. of
Dartmouth (NH)
Delaware, U. of
Denver, U. of (CO)
DePauw (IN)
Drew (NJ)
Duke (NC)
Emory (GA)
Evergreen (WA)
Florida, U. of
Florida International
Florida State
Franklin & Marshall (PA)
Fredonia (SUNY) (NY)

Georgetown (DC)
Goucher (MD)
Harvard (MA)
Hawaii, U. of
Hobart & William Smith (NY)
▲ Hollins (VA)
Hope (MI)
Iowa, U. of
Iowa State
Kansas, U. of
Kansas State
Kalamazoo (MI)
Kenyon (OH)
\# Lawrence (WI)
Louisiana State
Louisville (KY)
π Loyola (IL)
Loyola Marymount (CA)
Macalester (MN)
Maine, U. of
Maine, U. of (Farmington)
Maryland, U. of
Massachusetts, U. of
Mercer (GA)
▲ Meredith (NC)
Michigan, U. of
Middlebury (VT)
▲ Mills (CA)
Minnesota (Duluth)
Minnesota (Morris)
Missouri, U. of
▲ Mt. Holyoke (MA)
Nebraska, U. of
Nebraska Wesleyan
Nevada, U. of (Las Vegas)
Nevada, U. of (Reno)
New College (FL)
New Hampshire, U. of
New Jersey, College of
New Mexico, U. of
Northwestern (IL)

\# *Gender Studies*
π *Must be a Second Major*

■ *Men Only*
▲ *Women Only*

WOMEN'S STUDIES continues next page

WOMEN'S STUDIES, continued

Oakland (MI)
Oberlin (OH)
Ohio State
Ohio Wesleyan
Oklahoma, U. of
Old Dominion (VA)
Oregon, U. of
Pennsylvania, U. of
Pittsburgh, U. of (PA)
Pitzer (CA)
Pomona (CA)
Portland State (OR)
Providence College (RI)
Purchase (SUNY) (NY)
Randolph College (VA)
Randolph-Macon (VA)
Regis (CO)
Rhode Island, U. of
Rhode Island College
Rice (TX)
Richmond, U. of (VA)
Rochester, U. of (NY)
▲ Rosemont (PA)
Rutgers (NJ)
St. Catherine (MN)
\# St. Michael's (VT)
San Diego State (CA)
San Francisco State (CA)
Sarah Lawrence (NY)
▲ Scripps (CA)
▲ Simmons (MA)

Skidmore (NY)
▲ Smith (MA)
Southern California
Southern Maine
✳ Southwestern (TX)
▲ Spelman (GA)
Stanford (CA)
Stony Brook (SUNY) (NY)
Syracuse (NY)
Texas, U. of
Toledo, U. of (OH)
Towson (MD)
Union (NY)
Vassar (NY)
Vermont, U. of
Washington State
Washington U. (MO)
Washington, U. of
▲ Wellesley (MA)
Wells (NY)
Wesleyan (CT)
West Chester (PA)
Wheaton (MA)
William Paterson (NJ)
Wisconsin, U. of
Wisconsin, U. of
    (Milwaukee)
Wisconsin, U. of
    (Whitewater)
Wooster (OH)
Wyoming, U. of
Yale (CT)

\# *Gender Studies*
✳ *Feminist Studies*
π *Must be a Second Major*

■ *Men Only*
▲ *Women Only*

SECTION THREE

**AVERAGE SAT-1/
EXPECTED AVERAGE (3-TESTS) SAT-1/
ACT TOTALS
RECOMMENDED MAJORS**

ABILENE CHRISTIAN UNIVERSITY (TX) .... acu.edu **1140/1710/25**
Art, Bus Admin, Chem, English, Math, Nurs, Pre-Med/Pre-Dental, Reli Stu

ADELPHI UNIVERSITY (NY) .... adelphi.edu **1100/1620/24**
Art, Bus Admin, Chem, Communic, Comp Sci, Drama, Ed, Nurs, Physics, Psych

ADRIAN COLLEGE (MI) .... adrian.edu **1040/1560/22**
Art, Bus Admin, Chem, Ed, English, Math, Poli Sci, Pre-Law, Soc

AGNES SCOTT COLLEGE (GA) .... agnesscott.edu **1200/1800/26**
Art, Bio, Bus Admin, Classics, Drama, Econ, English, For Lang, Hist, Math, Physics, Poli Sci, Pre-Law, Pre-Med/Pre-Dental, Psych, Reli Stu

AKRON, UNIVERSITY OF (OH) .... uakron.edu **1000/1500/21**
Art, Bus Admin, Chem, Communic, Drama, Ed, Engine, English, Hist, Home Ec, Nurs, Pre-Med/Pre-Dental, Psych, Soc

ALABAMA, UNIVERSITY OF (AL) .... ua.edu **1140/1710/25**
Amer St, Anthro, Art, Bot, Bus Admin, Communic, Drama, Engine, English, For Lang, Geol, Hist, Home Ec, Music, Nurs, Philo, Physics, Pre-Law, Pre-Med/Pre-Dental, Psych

ALABAMA, UNIVERSITY OF (BIRMINGHAM) .... uab.edu **1060/1600/23**
Bus Admin, Chem, Comp Sci, Drama, Engine, English, Math, Nurs, Philo, Physics, Psych

ALABAMA, UNIVERSITY OF (HUNTSVILLE) .... uah.edu **1120/1670/24**
Bus Admin, Chem, Communic, Comp Sci, Engine, English, Math, Nurs, Philo, Physics, Psych, Soc

ALASKA PACIFIC UNIVERSITY (AK) .... alaskapacific.edu **1080/1620/23**
Bus Admin, Ed, Music, Psych, Reli Stu

ALASKA, UNIVERSITY OF (ANCHORAGE) (AK) .. uaa.alaska.edu **1000/1545/21**
Art, Bio, Bus Admin, Econ, Ed, English, Nurs

ALASKA, UNIVERSITY OF (FAIRBANKS) (AK) .... uaf.edu **1050/1575/22**
Anthro, Bio, Bus Admin, Drama, Engine, Geol, Nurs, Physics

ALBANY COLL. OF PHARMACY & HEALTH SCIENCE (NY) acphs.edu **1140/1715/25**
Pharm

ALBION COLLEGE (MI) .... albion.edu **1150/1725/25**
Chem, Econ, English, Geol, Hist, Math, Philo, Physics, Poli Sci, Pre-Law, Pre-Med/Pre-Dental

ALBRIGHT COLLEGE (PA) .... albright.edu **1030/1550/22**
Art, Biochem, Bio, Bus Admin, English, Poli Sci, Pre-Law, Pre-Med/Pre-Dental, Psych, Soc

ALDERSON-BROADDUS COLLEGE (WV) .... ab.edu **1030/1545/22**
Bus Admin, Ed, Music, Nurs

ALFRED UNIVERSITY (NY) .... alfred.edu **1140/1715/25**
Art, Art Hist, Bio, Bus Admin, Chem, Communic, Ed, Engine, English, Hist, Math, Pre-Law, Pre-Med/Pre-Dental, Psych

ALLEGHENY COLLEGE (PA) .... alleg.edu **1215/1815/26**
Art, Bio, Chem, Comp Sci, Drama, Econ, English, For Lang, Geol, Hist, Math, Philo, Physics, Poli Sci, Pre-Law, Pre-Med/Pre-Dental, Psych

ALMA COLLEGE (MI) .... alma.edu **1140/1710/25**
Art, Bio, Bus Admin, Chem, Communic, Comp Sci, Drama, Ed, English, Hist,
Math, Poli Sci, Pre-Law, Pre-Med/Pre-Dental, Psych

ALVERNO COLLEGE (WI) .... alverno.edu **1000/1500/21**
Art, Bio, Communic, Bus Admin, Ed, English, Music, Nurs, Psych

AMERICAN ACADEMY OF DRAMATIC ARTS (NY) ..... aada.org **1200/1800/26**
Drama

AMERICAN INTERNATIONAL COLLEGE (MA) .... aic.edu **1000/1500/21**
Bus Admin, Pre-Med/Pre-Dental, Psych

AMERICAN UNIVERSITY (DC) .... american.edu **1260/1890/27**
Amer St, Anthro, Art, Bus Admin, Communic, Drama, Econ, Ed, English,
For Lang, Hist, Math, Poli Sci, Pre-Law, Pre-Med/Pre-Dental, Psych

AMHERST COLLEGE (MA) .... amherst.edu **1420/2130/32**
Amer St, Astro, Bio, Chem, Classics, Drama, Econ, English, Geol, Hist,
Philo, Physics, Poli Sci, Pre-Law, Pre-Med/Pre-Dental, Psych, Soc

ANDERSON UNIVERSITY (IN) .... anderson.edu **1050/1575/22**
Ed, Music

ANDREWS UNIVERSITY (MI) .... andrews.edu **1080/1620/23**
Arch, Chem, English, Music, Nurs, Physics, Reli Stu

ANNA MARIA COLLEGE (MA) .... annamaria.edu **1000/1500/21**
Art, Bus Admin, Music

APPALACHIAN STATE UNIVERSITY (NC) .... appstate.edu **1125/1690/25**
Bus Admin, Communic, Ed, English, Hist, Poli Sci, Soc

AQUINAS COLLEGE (MI) .... aquinas.edu **1060/1590/23**
Art, Bio, Bus Admin, Chem, Drama, Ed, English, Geog, Math, Music, Psych, Reli Stu, Soc

ARCADIA UNIVERSITY (PA) .... arcadia.edu **1048/1572/22**
Art, Bio, Chem, Comp Sci, Ed, English, Math, Poli Sci, Pre-Law, Psych, Soc

ARIZONA, UNIVERSITY OF (AZ) .... arizona.edu **1100/1650/24**
Ag, Amer St, Anthro, Arch, Art, Astro, Bio, Bus Admin, Chem, Communic, Drama,
Ed, Engine, English, Forest, For Lang, Geol, Hist, Math, Nurs, Pharm, Philo, Pre-Law,
Pre-Med/Pre-Dental, Psych, Soc

ARIZONA STATE UNIVERSITY (AZ) .... asu.edu **1100/1650/24**
Anthro, Arch, Art, Biochem, Bio, Bus Admin, Communic, Comp Sci,
Drama, Econ, Ed, Engine, English, For Lang, Geog, Geol, Hist, Math, Music,
Nurs, Physics, Poli Sci, Pre-Med/Pre-Dental, Psych, Reli Stu, Zoo

ARKANSAS, UNIVERSITY OF (AR) .... uark.edu **1170/1755/26**
Ag, Anthro, Arch, Bio, Bus Admin, Chem, Communic, Comp Sci, Econ, Ed,
Engine, English, Hist, Math, Music, Physics, Pre-Law, Psych

ART CENTER COLLEGE OF DESIGN (CA) .... artcenter.edu **1110/1660/24**
Art

ART INSTITUTE OF CHICAGO, SCHOOL OF THE (IL) .... saic.edu **1100/1650/24**
Art, Art Hist

ARTS, UNIVERSITY OF THE (PA) .... uarts.edu **1040/1560/22**
Art, Drama, Music

ASBURY COLLEGE (KY) .... asbury.edu **1150/1725/25**
Art, Bus Admin, Communic, Ed, Music, Philo, Reli Stu, Soc

ASHLAND UNIVERSITY (OH) .... ashland.edu **1060/1600/23**
Bus Admin, Chem, Ed, English

ASSUMPTION COLLEGE (MA) .... assumption.edu **1080/1620/23**
Bus Admin, Econ, Ed, English, Hist, Philo, Psych

AUBURN UNIVERSITY (AL) ....auburn.edu **1140/1710/25**
Ag, Arch, Art, Bio, Bus Admin, Communic, Comp Sci, Econ, Ed, Engine,
English, Forest, Hist, Home Ec, Math, Pharm, Physics, Poli Sci

AUGSBURG COLLEGE (MN) .... augsburg.edu **1080/1620/23**
Bus Admin, Communic, Comp Sci, Ed, English, Physics, Pre-Law, Reli Stu, Soc

AUGUSTA STATE UNIVERSITY (GA) .... aug.edu **1000/1500/21**
Ed, English, Soc

AUGUSTANA COLLEGE (IL) .... augustana.edu **1160/1740/25**
Art, Bio, Bus Admin, Ed, English, Hist, Music, Pre-Law

AUGUSTANA COLLEGE (SD) .... augie.edu **1120/1680/24**
Bio, Chem, Ed, English, Music, Nurs, Pre-Med/Pre-Dental, Reli Stu

AUSTIN COLLEGE (TX) .... austincollege.edu **1240/1860/28**
Biochem, Bio, Bus Admin, Chem, Econ, Ed, Hist, Philo, Poli Sci, Pre-Med/Pre-Dental, Reli Stu

AVERETT UNIVERSITY (VA) .... averett.edu **1000/1500/21**
Bus Admin, Ed, Math, Psych, Soc

AVILA UNIVERSITY (MO) ....avila.edu **1000/1500/21**
Bus Admin, Drama, Ed, Nurs

AZUSA PACIFIC (CA) .... apu.edu **1080/1620/23**
Bio, Bus Admin, English, Music, Nurs, Poli Sci, Reli Stu

BABSON COLLEGE (MA) .... babson.edu **1250/1875/28**
Bus Admin, Econ

BAKER UNIVERSITY (KS) .... bakeru.edu **1080/1620/23**
Bio, Bus Admin, Comp Sci, Ed, English, Music, Nurs, Poli Sci, Psych

BALDWIN-WALLACE COLLEGE (OH) .... bw.edu **1100/1650/24**
Bus Admin, Chem, Comp Sci, Econ, Ed, English, Hist, Math, Music, Poli Sci, Pre-Law, Psych, Soc

BALL STATE UNIVERSITY (IN) .... bsu.edu **1040/1560/22**
Anthro, Arch, Art, Bio, Botany, Communic, Comp Sci, Ed, Geog, Math, Nurs, Physics, Poli Sci, Psych

BARD COLLEGE (NY) .... bard.edu **1330/2000/30**
Amer St, Art, Art Hist, Astro, Comp Sci, Drama, English, For Lang, Hist, Music, Pre-Law, Psych, Soc

BARNARD COLLEGE (NY) .... barnard.edu **1390/2100/30**
Amer St, Anthro, Arch, Art Hist, Biochem, Bio, Chem, Classics, Drama, Econ, Engine, English, For Lang, Hist, Math, Music, Philo, Physics, Poli Sci, Pre-Law, Psych, Reli Stu, Soc

BARRY UNIVERSITY (FL) .... barry.edu **1000/1500/21**
Bio, Bus Admin, Drama, Ed, Nurs, Reli Stu

BATES COLLEGE (ME) .... bates.edu **1335/2000/30**
Amer St, Art, Bio, Chem, Econ, English, For Lang, Geol, Hist, Math, Philo, Physics, Poli Sci, Pre-Law, Pre-Med/Pre-Dental, Psych, Rel Stu

BAYLOR UNIVERSITY (TX) .... baylor.edu **1220/1830/27**
Bus Admin, Chem, Classics, Drama, Ed, Engine, English, Hist, Math, Music, Nurs, Physics, Pre-Law, Pre-Med/Pre-Dental, Reli Stu

BAY PATH COLLEGE (MA) .... baypath.edu **1000/1500/21**
Bio, Bus Admin, Psych

BELHAVEN COLLEGE (MS) .... belhaven.edu **1080/1620/23**
Art, Bus Admin, Comp Sci, Drama, Ed, Music, Reli Stu

BELLARMINE UNIVERSITY (KY) .... bellarmine.edu **1100/1650/24**
Bus Admin, Econ, Ed, English, Hist, Math, Nurs, Philo

BELMONT ABBEY COLLEGE (NC) .... belmontabbeycollege.edu **1020/1565/22**
Bus Admin, English, Poli Sci, Pre-Law, Soc

BELMONT UNIVERSITY (TN) .... belmont.edu **1170/1755/26**
Art, Bio, Bus Admin, Ed, English, Math, Music, Nurs, Philo, Poli Sci, Pre-Law, Psych, Reli Stu, Soc

BELOIT COLLEGE (WI) .... beloit.edu **1250/1875/28**
Anthro, Biochem, Bio, Classics, Drama, Econ, English, For Lang, Hist, Geol, Music, Physics, Poli Sci, Psych, Soc

BEMIDJI STATE UNIVERSITY (MN) .... bemidjistate.edu **1040/1555/22**
Chem, Communic, Comp Sci, Ed, English, Geog, Music, Psych

BENEDICTINE COLLEGE (KS) .... benedictine.edu **1070/1600/23**
Astro, Bus Admin, Chem, Comp Sci, Drama, Ed, English, Music, Philo, Reli Stu, Soc

BENEDICTINE UNIVERSITY (IL) .... ben.edu **1075/1615/23**
Bio, Bus Admin, Chem, Comp Sci, Ed, Math, Pre-Med/Pre-Dental

BENNETT COLLEGE (NC) .... bennett.edu **1000/1500/21**
Bus Admin, Comp Sci, Ed, Math, Poli Sci, Pre-Law, Pre-Med/Pre-Dental, Psych

BENNINGTON COLLEGE (VT) .... bennington.edu **1130/1770/26**
Art, Drama, English, Music, Pre-Law

BENTLEY COLLEGE (MA) .... bentley.edu **1170/1755/26**
Bus Admin, Econ, English, Math

BEREA COLLEGE (KY) .... berea.edu **1095/1645/24**
Ag, Art, Bio, Bus Admin, Chem, Econ, Ed, English, Home Ec, Music, Nurs, Reli Stu

BERKLEE COLLEGE OF MUSIC (MA) .... berklee.edu **1100/1650/24**
Music

BERRY COLLEGE (GA) .... berry.edu **1140/1710/25**
Bio, Bus Admin, Chem, Ed, English, Pre-Med/Pre-Dental, Psych

BETHANY COLLEGE (KS) .... bethanylb.edu **1020/1530/22**
Art, Chem, Ed, Music

BETHANY COLLEGE (WV) .... bethanywv.edu **1040/1560/22**
Bio, Chem, Communic, Drama, Econ, Ed, English, For Lang, Music,
Physics, Poli Sci, Pre-Law, Pre-Med/Pre-Dental, Psych, Reli Stu

BETHEL COLLEGE (IN) .... bethelcollege.edu **1040/1560/22**
Bio, Drama, Ed, English, Music, Nurs, Philo, Reli Stu

BETHEL COLLEGE (KS) .... bethelks.edu **1100/1650/24**
Ed, English, Music, Nurs

BETHEL COLLEGE (MN) .... bethel.edu **1160/1740/25**
Biochem, Bio, Bus Admin, Chem, Ed, Nurs, Philo, Psych, Reli Stu

BIOLA UNIVERSITY (CA) .... biola.edu **1115/1675/24**
Ed, Philo, Psych, Reli Stu, Soc

BIRMINGHAM-SOUTHERN COLLEGE (AL) .... bsc.edu **1160/1740/25**
Art, Bio, Bus Admin, Chem, Drama, Ed, English, Hist, Math, Music, Poli Sci,
Pre-Law, Pre-Med/Pre-Dental, Psych, Reli Stu

BLACKBURN COLLEGE (IL) .... blackburn.edu **1040/1560/22**
Bio, Bus Admin, Ed, Pre-Med/Pre-Dental, Psych

BLACK HILLS STATE UNIVERSITY (SD) .... bhsu.edu **1000/1500/21**
Ed

BLOOMSBURG UNIVERSITY (PA)............................ bloomu.edu **1010/1515/21**
Art, Bio, Bus Admin, Chem, Comp Sci, Ed, Geog, Geol, Nurs

BLUFFTON COLLEGE (OH) .... bluffton.edu **1050/1575/22**
Bus Admin, Chem, Ed, Math, Music, Reli Stu

BOISE STATE UNIVERSITY (ID) .... boisestate.edu **1120/1680/24**
Art, Bus Admin, Communic, Drama, Ed, Engine, Geol, Hist, Math, Music, Nurs

BOSTON ARCHITECTURAL CENTER (MA) .... the-bac.edu **1100/1650/24**
Arch

BOSTON COLLEGE (MA)... bc.edu **1340/2010/30**
Art, Art Hist, Bio, Bus Admin, Chem, Communic, Comp Sci, Drama, Econ, Ed, English,
For Lang, Hist, Music, Nurs, Philo, Poli Sci, Pre-Law, Pre-Med/Pre-Dental, Reli Stu, Soc

BOSTON CONSERVATORY OF MUSIC (MA).. bostonconservatory.edu **1050/1575/22**
Drama, Music

BOSTON UNIVERSITY (MA) .... bu.edu **1260/1890/28**
Anthro, Art, Art Hist, Astro, Bio, Bus Admin, Chem, Communic, Drama, Econ, Ed, Engine, For
Lang, Geog, Hist, Math, Music, Philo, Physics, Poli Sci, Pre-Law, Pre-Med/Pre-Dental, Psych

BOWDOIN COLLEGE (ME) ....bowdoin.edu **1390/2085/31**
Anthro, Art Hist, Biochem, Bio, Chem, Classics, Econ, English, For Lang, Geol,
Hist, Math, Music, Philo, Poli Sci, Pre-Law, Pre-Med/Pre-Dental, Reli Stu, Soc

BOWLING GREEN STATE UNIVERSITY (OH) .... bgsu.edu **1030/1550/22**
Amer St, Art, Bus Admin, Communic, Ed, Geol, Math, Music, Philo, Psych

BRADLEY UNIVERSITY (IL) .... bradley.edu **1160/1740/25**
Art, Bus Admin, Chem, Comp Sci, Econ, Ed, Engine, English, Nurs,
Physics, Poli Sci, Pre-Law

BRANDEIS UNIVERSITY (MA) .... brandeis.edu **1350/2020/30**
Amer St, Anthro, Biochem, Bio, Chem, Comp Sci, Drama, Econ, English, Hist, Math,
Music, Physics, Poli Sci, Pre-Law, Pre-Med/Pre-Dental, Psych

BRENAU UNIVERSITY (GA) .... brenau.edu **1020/1580/22**
Drama, Music, Nurs

BRESCIA UNIVERSITY (KY) .... brescia.edu **1020/1580/22**
Art, Bus Admin, Ed, English, Reli Stu

BRIAR CLIFF UNIVERSITY (IA) .... briarcliff.edu **1040/1550/22**
Art, Bio, Bus Admin, English, Hist, Math, Music, Nurs, Reli Stu

BRIDGEWATER COLLEGE (VA) .... bridgewater.edu **1010/1510/22**
Bio, Bus Admin, Hist, Music, Psych, Soc

BRIDGEWATER STATE COLLEGE (MA) .... bridgew.edu **1010/1515/21**
Communic, Ed, English, Geog, Hist, Poli Sci, Psych, Soc

BRIGHAM YOUNG UNIVERSITY (UT) .... byu.edu **1220/1830/27**
Art, Astro, Bus Admin, Chem, Econ, Ed, Engine, English, For Lang, Geol,
Home Ec, Music, Nurs, Pre-Law, Pre-Med, Reli Stu, Psych, Zoo

BROWN UNIVERSITY (RI) .... brown.edu **1390/2085/31**
Amer St, Anthro, Art, Art Hist, Bio, Biochem, Chem, Classics, Comp Sci, Econ, Engine, English,
For Lang, Geol, Hist, Philo, Poli Sci, Physics, Pre-Law, Pre-Med/Pre-Dental, Reli Stu, Soc

BRYAN COLLEGE (TN) .... bryan.edu **1100/1650/24**
Bio, Communic, Ed, Hist, Music, Reli Stu

BRYANT UNIVERSITY (RI) .... bryant.edu **1120/1680/24**
Bus Admin, Comp Sci, Econ, Math

BRYN ATHYN COLLEGE (PA) .... brynathyn.edu **1140/1710/25**
Bio, English, Hist, Reli Stu

BRYN MAWR COLLEGE (PA) ....brynmawr.edu **1310/1970/29**
Art, Art Hist, Astro, Bio, Chem, Classics, Comp Sci, Econ, English, For Lang,
Geol, Hist, Math, Physics, Pre-Law, Pre-Med/Pre-Dental, Psych, Soc

BUCKNELL UNIVERSITY (PA) .... bucknell.edu **1310/1970/29**
Bio, Bus Admin, Chem, Comp Sci, Drama, Econ, Ed, Engine, English, Geol,
Hist, Math, Music, Philo, Poli Sci, Pre-Law, Pre-Med/Pre-Dental, Psych, Soc

BUENA VISTA UNIVERSITY (IA) .... bvu.edu **1050/1590/23**
Bus Admin, Communic, Comp Sci, Ed, Poli Sci

BUTLER UNIVERSITY (IN) .... butler.edu   **1180/1770/26**
Art, Bus Admin, Chem, Communic, Comp Sci, Drama, Ed, Engine, English,
Music, Pharm, Pre-Law, Pre-Med/Pre-Dental

CALDWELL COLLEGE (NJ) .... caldwell.edu   **1000/1500/21**
Bus Admin, Ed, Psych

CALIFORNIA BAPTIST UNIVERSITY (CA) .... calbaptist.edu   **1030/1550/22**
Ed, Psych

CALIFORNIA COLLEGE OF THE ARTS (CA) .... cca.edu   **1060/1590/23**
Arch, Art

CALIFORNIA INSTITUTE OF TECHNOLOGY (CA) . caltech.edu   **1500/2250/33**
Astro, Bio, Chem, Engine, Geol, Math, Physics, Pre-Med/Pre-Dental

CALIFORNIA INSTITUTE OF THE ARTS (CA) .... calarts.edu   **1100/1650/24**
Art, Drama, Music

CALIFORNIA, UNIVERSITY OF, AT
   BERKELEY .... berkeley.edu   **1320/1980/30**
   Anthro, Arch, Biochem, Bio, Bot, Bus Admin, Chem, Comp Sci, Engine,
   English, For Lang, Geog, Geol, Hist, Math, Music, Philo, Poli Sci, Physics,
   Pre-Law, Pre-Med/Pre-Dental, Psych, Reli Stu, Soc, Zoo
   DAVIS .... ucdavis.edu   **1190/1790/26**
   Ag, Anthro, Art, Bio, Biochem, Bot, Chem, Econ, Engine, English, Geol,
   Hist, Math, Physics, Poli Sci, Pre-Law, Pre-Med/Pre-Dental, Zoo
   IRVINE .... uci.edu   **1230/1850/27**
   Anthro, Art, Bio, Chem, Comp Sci, Drama, Engine, English, Math, Physics, Pre-Law,
   Pre-Med/Pre-Dental, Psych
   LOS ANGELES .... ucla.edu   **1310/1965/29**
   Anthro, Art Hist, Bio, Biochem, Bus Admin, Chem, Communic, Comp Sci, Drama,
   Econ, Engine, English, For Lang, Hist, Math, Music, Philo, Poli Sci, Pre-Law,
   Pre-Med/Pre-Dental, Psych, Soc
   MERCED .... ucmerced.edu   **1150/1725/25**
   Bio, Comp Sci, Econ, Engine, Hist, Pre-Med/PreDental, Psych
   RIVERSIDE .... ucr.edu   **1100/1650/24**
   Ag, Art Hist, Biochem, Bio, Bot, Bus Admin, Drama, Ed, Engine, Hist,
   Math, Music, Poli Sci, Pre-Law, Pre-Med/Pre-Dental, Psych
   SAN DIEGO .... ucsd.eu   **1275/1915/29**
   Amer St, Biochem, Bio, Chem, Communic, Comp Sci, Drama, Econ, Engine,
   Math, Music, Physics, Poli Sci, Pre-Law, Pre-Med/Pre-Dental, Psych
   SANTA BARBARA ....ucsb.edu   **1200/1800/26**
   Art, Art Hist, Bio, Bus Admin, Chem, Classics, Comp Sci, Ed, Econ, Engine,
   For Lang, Geog, Geol, Music, Philo, Physics, Poli Sci, Pre-Law,
   Pre-Med/Pre-Dental, Psych, Reli Stu, Soc, Zoo
   SANTA CRUZ ....ucsc.edu   **1160/1740/25**
   Amer St, Anthro, Art Hist, Bio, Chem, Comp Sci, Econ, English, Hist,
   Math, Music, Philo, Physics, Pre-Med/Pre-Dental, Psych

CALIFORNIA LUTHERAN UNIVERSITY (CA) .... clunet.edu   **1090/1635/24**
Bus Admin, Communic, Ed, Psych

CALIFORNIA MARITIME ACADEMY (CA) .... csum.edu   **1030/1540/22**
Bus Admin, Engine

CALIFORNIA POLYTECHNIC U. AT POMONA (CA) csupomona.edu **1015/1520/22**
Ag, Arch, Bio, Bus Admin, Comp Sci, Engine, Physics, Zoo

CALIFORNIA POLYTECHNIC U. AT SAN LUIS OBISPO (CA) calpoly.edu **1185/1780/26**
Ag, Arch, Biochem, Bio, Bus Admin, Comp Sci, Communic, Drama, Engine,
English, Hist, Math, Music, Physics, Psych

CALIFORNIA STATE UNIVERSITY, AT:
     BAKERSFIELD .... csubak.edu **1000/1500/21**
     Bus Admin, Econ, Ed, English, Geol, Nurs, Psych
     CHANNEL ISLANDS (CAMARILLO)(CA) .... csuci.edu **1000/1500/21**
     Art, Bio, Bus Admin, Econ, Ed, English, Hist, Math, Pre-Law,
     Pre-Med/Pre-Dental, Psych
     CHICO .... csuchico.edu **1020/1530/22**
     Ag, Anthro, Bio, Chem, Comp Sci, Econ, Geog, Geol, Nurs, Poli Sci, Psych, Reli Stu
     DOMINGUEZ HILLS .... csudh.edu **1000/1500/21**
     Bus Admin, Chem, Math, Nurs, Philo, Physics, Psych
     EAST BAY .... csueb.edu **1000/1500/21**
     Art, Bus Admin, Comp Sci, Econ, English, Geol, Hist, Music, Soc
     FRESNO ....csufresno.edu **1000/1500/21**
     Ag, Amer St, Art, Bus Admin, Chem, Ed, Engine, English, Home Ec,
     Music, Nurs, Philo, Soc
     FULLERTON .... fullerton.edu **1000/1500/21**
     Amer St, Anthro, Bus Admin, Chem, Communic, Engine, English, Hist,
     Music, Nurs, Poli Sci, Pre-Med/Pre-Dental, Soc
     LONG BEACH .... csulb.edu **1020/1530/22**
     Anthro, Art, Art Hist, Chem, Classics, Communic, Drama, Econ, Hist, Music,
     Poli Sci, Pre-Law, Psych
     LOS ANGELES .... calstatela.edu **1000/1500/21**
     Art, Bus Admin, Ed, Engine, Nurs, Psych, Soc
     MONTEREY BAY .... scumb.edu **1000/1500/21**
     Art, Bio, Comp Sci, Ed, English, Math, Pre-Law, Pre-Med/Pre-Dental
     NORTHRIDGE .... csun.edu **1000/1500/21**
     Art, Art Hist, Bus Admin, Comp Sci, Communic, Drama, Econ, Engine,
     English, Geog, Music, Philo, Physics, Poli Sci, Pre-Law, Psych, Soc
     SACRAMENTO .... csus.edu **1000/1500/21**
     Anthro, Bus Admin, Communic, Comp Sci, Drama, Ed, Engine, English,
     For Lang, Geol, Home Ec, Music, Poli Sci, Psych, Soc
     SAN BERNARDINO .... csusb.edu **1000/1500/21**
     Art, Bus Admin, Communic, Comp Sci, Ed, Psych, Soc
     SAN JOSE .... sjsu.edu **1000/1500/21**
     Anthro, Art, Bus Admin, Chem, Communic, Comp Sci, Engine, Math,
     Music, Nurs, Physics, Poli Sci, Pre-Med/Pre-Dental, Zoo
     SAN MARCOS .... csusm.edu **1000/1500/21**
     Bus Admin, Chem, Comp Sci, Ed, Hist, Poli Sci, Psych, Soc
     STANISLAUS .... csustan.edu **1000/1500/21**
     Bus Admin, Comp Sci, Ed, Poli Sci, Psych

CALIFORNIA UNIVERSITY OF PENNSYLVANIA (PA). cup.edu **1000/1500/21**
Chem, Ed, English, Nurs, Psych

CALVIN COLLEGE (MI) .... calvin.edu **1190/1770/26**
Ed, Engine, English, For Lang, Hist, Nurs, Philo, Physics, Pre-Law

CAMPBELL UNIVERSITY (NC) .... campbell.edu **1060/1590/23**
Bus Admin, English, Hist, Pharm, Poli Sci, Pre-Law

CANISIUS COLLEGE (NY) .... canisius.edu **1160/1740/25**
Bio, Bus Admin, Communic, Comp Sci, Ed, English, Hist, Pre-Med/Pre-Dental, Psych

CAPITAL UNIVERSITY (OH) .... capital.edu **1080/1620/23**
Bus Admin, Chem, Communic, Comp Sci, Ed, Hist, Music, Nurs, Reli Stu

CARLETON COLLEGE (MN) .... carleton.edu **1400/2100/31**
Amer St, Bio, Chem, Classics, Comp Sci, Drama, Econ, English, For Lang, Geol, Hist, Math, Music, Philo, Physics, Poli Sci, Pre-Law, Pre-Med/Pre-Dental, Psych, Reli Stu

CARNEGIE MELLON UNIVERSITY (PA) .... cmu.edu **1360/2040/30**
Arch, Art, Bio, Bus Admin, Chem, Comp Sci, Drama, Econ, Engine, English, Hist, Math, Music, Philo, Physics, Pre-Law, Pre-Med/Pre-Dental, Psych

CARROLL COLLEGE (MT) .... carroll.edu **1080/1620/23**
Bio, Chem, Comp Sci, Econ, Ed, Engine, Hist, Math, Nurs, Philo, Pre-Med/Pre-Dental

CARROLL COLLEGE (WI) .... cc.edu **1070/1605/23**
Art, Chem, Comp Sci, Ed, Nurs, Pre-Med/Pre-Dental, Psych

CARSON-NEWMAN COLLEGE (TN) .... cn.edu **1075/1605/23**
Chem, Ed, English, Hist, Music, Nurs, Pre-Med/Pre-Dental, Psych

CARTHAGE COLLEGE (WI) .... carthage.edu **1090/1630/24**
Bus Admin, For Lang, Geog, Music, Physics, Poli Sci, Psych, Reli Stu

CASE WESTERN RESERVE UNIVERSITY (OH) .... cwru.edu **1330/2000/30**
Amer St, Anthro, Art, Art Hist, Astro, Biochem, Bio, Bus Admin, Chem, Classics, Comp Sci, Drama, Econ, Engine, Hist, Math, Music, Nurs, Physics, Pre-Law, Pre-Med/Pre-Dental, Psych, Reli Stu

CASTLETON STATE COLLEGE (VT) .... castleton.edu **1000/1500/21**
Art, Bus Admin, Communic, Ed, Psych, Soc

CATAWBA COLLEGE (NC) .... catawba.edu **1000/1500/21**
Bus Admin, Comp Sci, Drama, Ed

CATHOLIC UNIVERSITY OF AMERICA (DC) .... cua.edu **1140/1710/25**
Arch, Classics, Drama, Engine, English, For Lang, Music, Nurs, Philo, Physics, Poli Sci, Pre-Law, Psych, Reli Stu, Soc

CEDAR CREST COLLEGE (PA) .... cedarcrest.edu **1070/1610/23**
At, Bio, Nurs, Psych

CEDARVILLE UNIVERSITY (OH) .... cedarville.edu **1160/1730/25**
Bus Admin, Ed, Music, Nurs

CENTENARY COLLEGE OF LOUISIANA (LA) ...... centenary.edu **1160/1740/25**
Art, Bio, Bus Admin, Chem, Ed, English, Geol, Music, Pre-Med/Pre-Dental

CENTRAL ARKANSAS, UNIVERSITY OF (AR) .... uca.edu **1070/1600/23**
Bus Admin, Nurs

CENTRAL COLLEGE (IA) .... central.edu **1108/1660/24**
Bio, Chem, Comp Sci, Ed, English, For Lang, Music, Philo, Reli Stu

CENTRAL CONNECTICUT STATE UNIVERSITY (CT) ccsu.edu **1010/1515/21**
Bus Admin, Ed, Engine, Geog, Hist, Music, Psych, Soc

CENTRAL FLORIDA, UNIVERSITY OF (FL) .... ucf.edu **1150/1725/25**
Bus Admin, Comp Sci, Communic, Drama, Ed, Engine, English, Music, Philo, Physics, Psych

CENTRAL MICHIGAN UNIVERSITY (MI) ....cmich.edu **1050/1570/22**
Bio, Communic, Drama, Ed, English, Home Ec, Geog, Music, Psych

CENTRAL MISSOURI STATE UNIVERSITY (MO) ...... cmsu.edu **1020/1530/22**
Communic, Econ, Nurs

CENTRAL OKLAHOMA, UNIVERSITY OF (OK).......... ucok.edu **1000/1500/21**
Bus Admin, Econ, Ed, Music

CENTRAL WASHINGTON UNIVERSITY .... cwu.edu **1000/1500/21**
Anthro, Bus Admin, Chem, English, Geog, Music, Psych

CENTRE COLLEGE (KY) .... centre.edu **1240/1860/27**
*Art, Biochem, Bio, Chem, Classics, Econ, Ed, English, For Lang, Hist, Philo,
Physics, Poli Sci, Pre-Law, Pre-Med/Pre-Dental, Psych, Reli Stu*

CHAMINADE UNIVERSITY OF HONOLULU (HI) . chaminade.edu **1000/1500/21**
Bus Admin, Ed

CHAMPLAIN COLLEGE (VT) .... champlain.edu **1120/1680/24**
Bus Admin, Comp Sci

CHAPMAN UNIVERSITY (CA) .... chapman.edu **1210/1820/27**
Art Hist, Bus Admin, Communic, Econ, Music, Pre-Law, Pre-Med/Pre-Dental, Psych

CHARLESTON, COLLEGE OF (SC) .... cofc.edu **1180/1770/26**
*Bio, Bus Admin, Chem, Communic, Drama, Ed, For Lang, Geol, Math, Poli Sci,
Pre-Med/Pre-Dental, Psych, Soc*

CHARLESTON SOUTHERN UNIVERSITY (SC)....... csuniv.edu **1060/1590/23**
Comp Sci, Ed, English, Music

CHARLESTON, UNIVERSITY OF (WV).................... uchaswv.edu **1030/1545/22**
Hist, Nurs

CHATHAM COLLEGE (PA) .... chatham.edu **1040/1560/22**
Art, Bio, Bus Admin, Communic, English, Hist, Poli Sci, Pre-Law

CHESTNUT HILL COLLEGE (PA) .... chc.edu **1000/1500/21**
Ed, English, Pre-Law

CHEYNEY UNIVERSITY OF PENNSYLVANIA (PA) .. cheney.edu **1000/1500/21**
Ed

CHICAGO, UNIVERSITY OF (IL) .... uchicago.edu **1430/2145/32**
*Amer St, Anthro, Art, Art Hist, Biochem, Bio, Chem, Classics, Comp Sci,
Econ, English, For Lang, Geog, Geol, Hist, Math, Music, Philo, Physics,
Poli Sci, Pre-Law, Pre-Med/Pre-Dental, Psych, Reli Stu, Soc*

CHOWAN COLLEGE (NC) .... chowan.edu **900/1350/20**
Art, Bus Admin, Comp Sci, English

CHRISTIAN BROTHERS UNIVERSITY (TN) .... cbu.edu **1100/1650/24**
Bus Admin, Ed, Engine, Reli Stu

CHRISTENDOM COLLEGE (VA)........................ christendom.edu **1220/1830/27**
Hist, Philo, Reli Stu

CHRISTOPHER NEWPORT UNIVERSITY (VA) ....cnu.edu **1160/1740/25**
Bus Admin, Comp Sci, English, Math, Music, Philo, Physics, Poli Sci

CINCINNATI, UNIVERSITY OF (OH) .... uc.edu **1100/1650/24**
Arch, Art, Bus Admin, Classics, Ed, Engine, English, Hist, Math, Music, Nurs, Pharm, Psych, Soc

CITADEL, THE (SC) .... citadel.edu **1090/1635/24**
Bus Admin, Chem, Ed, Engine, English, Pre-Law

CLAFLIN UNIVERSITY (SC) .... claflin.edu **1000/1500/21**
Ed

CLAREMONT MCKENNA COLLEGE (CA) ....mckenna.edu **1400/2100/31**
*Bio, Bus Admin, Chem, Econ, English, Hist, Philo, Poli Sci, Pre-Law,
Pre-Med/Pre-Dental, Psych, Reli Stu*

CLARK ATLANTA UNIVERSITY (GA) ....cau.edu **1000/1500/21**
Bus Admin, Comp Sci, Ed, Math, Physics

CLARK UNIVERSITY (MA) .... clarku.edu **1210/1815/27**
*Bio, Biochem, Bus Admin, Chem, Communic, Econ, English, For Lang, Geog,
Hist, Music, Physics, Poli Sci, Pre-Law, Pre-Med/Pre-Dental, Psych, Soc*

CLARKE COLLEGE (IA) .... clarke.edu **1100/1650/24**
Art, Art Hist, Bio, Chem, Communic, Comp Sci, Drama, Ed, Music, Nurs, Philo

CLARKSON UNIVERSITY (NY) ....clarkson.edu **1170/1755/26**
Bio, Biochem, Bus Admin, Chem, Comp Sci, Engine, Math, Physics, Pre-Law, Psych, Soc

CLEMSON UNIVERSITY (SC) ....clemson.edu **1195/1785/26**
*Ag, Arch, Bio, Bus Admin, Chem, Comp Sci, Drama, Econ, Ed, Engine,
English, Forest, For Lang, Physics, Poli Sci, Soc, Zoo*

CLEVELAND INSTITUTE OF ART (OH) .... cia.edu **1040/1560/22**
Art

CLEVELAND INSTITUTE OF MUSIC (OH) ....cim.edu **1220/1840/27**
Music

COASTAL CAROLINA UNIVERSITY (SC) .... coastal.edu **1050/1575/22**
Art, Bus Admin, Comp Sci, Ed, Philo

COE COLLEGE (IA) ....coe.edu **1160/1740/25**
Art, Bio, Bus Admin, Chem, Drama, Ed, English, Hist, Music, Nurs, Physics, Psych

COGSWELL POLYTECHNIC COLLEGE (CA) ....cogswell.edu **1000/1500/21**
Comp Sci, Engine

COKER COLLEGE (SC) .... coker.edu **1000/1500/21**
Art, Bus Admin, Drama, Ed, Music, Psych, Soc

COLBY COLLEGE (ME) .... colby.edu **1340/2010/30**
Art, Bio, Chem, Econ, English, For Lang, Math, Music, Philo,
Physics, Poli Sci, Pre-Law, Pre-Med/Pre-Dental, Psych, Soc, Reli Stu

COLBY-SAWYER COLLEGE (NH) .... colby-sawyer.edu **1000/1500/21**
Bio, Ed, English, Nurs, Psych

COLGATE UNIVERSITY (NY) .... colgate.edu **1360/2040/31**
Art, Art Hist, Bio, Chem, Classics, Comp Sci, Drama, Econ, English,
For Lang, Geog, Geol, Hist, Math, Philo, Poli Sci, Pre-Law,
Pre-Med/Pre-Dental, Psych, Reli Stu

COLORADO COLLEGE (CO) .... coloradocollege.edu **1310/1965/29**
Anthro, Art, Art Hist, Bio, Chem, Drama, Econ, English, Geol, Hist,
Math, Philo, Poli Sci, Pre-Law, Pre-Med/Pre-Dental, Psych, Soc

COLORADO, UNIVERSITY OF (CO) .... colorado.edu **1170/1755/26**
Anthro, Astro, Bio, Biochem, Bus Admin, Chem, Communic, Econ, Engine, English,
Hist, Geog, Geol, Math, Music, Nurs, Physics, Pre-Med/Pre-Dental, Psych, Soc

COLORADO, UNIVERSITY OF (COLORADO SPRINGS) . uccs.edu **1090/1635/24**
Anthro, Bus Admin, Chem, Communic, Comp Sci, Ed, Engine, Geog, Nurs, Physics, Psych, Soc

COLORADO, UNIVERSITY OF (DENVER) .... cudenver.edu **1060/1590/23**
Art, Bio, Bus Admin, Comp Sci, Math, Psych

COLORADO SCHOOL OF MINES (CO) .... mines.edu **1230/1845/27**
Comp Sci, Econ, Engine, Geol, Math, Physics, Pre-Med/Pre-Dental

COLORADO STATE UNIVERSITY (CO) .... colostate.edu **1110/1660/24**
Ag, Anthro, Art, Art Hist, Bot, Bus Admin, Comp Sci, Engine, Forest, Geol, Poli Sci, Psych, Zoo

COLUMBIA COLLEGE CHICAGO (IL) .... colum.edu **1000/1500/21**
Art Hist, Communic, Drama

COLUMBIA COLLEGE (MO) .... ccis.edu **1000/1500/21**
Art, Bus Admin

COLUMBIA COLLEGE (SC) .... columbiacollegesc.edu **1020/1530/22**
Bio, Bus Admin, Drama, Ed, Music, Pre-Law, Pre-Med/Pre-Dental, Psych, Reli Stu

COLUMBIA UNIVERSITY (NY) .... columbia.edu **1430/2150/32**
Anthro, Arch, Art Hist, Biochem, Bio, Chem, Classics, Drama, Econ, Engine,
English, For Lang, Geol, Hist, Math, Music, Philo, Physics, Poli Sci, Pre-Law,
Pre-Med/Pre-Dental, Psych, Reli Stu, Soc

CONCORDIA COLLEGE-MOORHEAD (MN) .... cord.edu **1120/1680/24**
Bio, Bus Admin, Chem, Ed, English, For Lang, Math, Music,
Pre-Med/Pre-Dental, Psych, Reli Stu, Soc

CONCORDIA UNIVERSITY (CA) .... cui.edu **1020/1530/22**
Bus Admin, Music, Reli Stu

CONCORDIA UNIVERSITY (NE) .... cune.edu **1100/1650/24**
Bus Admin, Ed, Reli Stu

CONCORDIA UNIVERSITY (OR) .... cu-portland.edu **1000/1500/21**
Ed, Psych

CONCORDIA UNIVERSITY-AUSTIN (TX) ....concordia.edu   **1030/1550/22**
Bus Admin

CONNECTICUT, UNIVERSITY OF (CT) .... uconn.edu   **1197/1795/26**
Ag, Art, Biochem, Bio, Bot, Bus Admin, Communic, Econ, Ed, Engine, Forest, Hist,
Home Ec, Nurs, Poli Sci, Pharm, Pre-Law, Pre-Med/Pre-Dental, Psych, Soc, Zoo

CONNECTICUT COLLEGE (CT) .... conncoll.edu   **1310/1965/29**
Anthro, Art, Art Hist, Biochem, Bio, Bot, Chem, Classics, Drama,
Econ, Ed, English, For Lang, Hist, Math, Music, Philo, Physics,
Poli Sci, Pre-Law, Pre-Med/Pre-Dental, Psych, Soc

CONVERSE COLLEGE (SC) .... converse.edu   **1080/1620/23**
Art, Chem, Drama, Ed, Music, Poli Sci

THE COOPER UNION (NY) .... cooper.edu   **1420/2130/32**
Arch, Art, Engine

CORBAN COLLEGE (OR) .... corban.edu   **1050/1575/22**
Ed, Psych

CORNELL COLLEGE (IA) .... cornell-iowa.edu   **1210/1815/26**
Art, Bio, Econ, Ed, English, Geol, Hist, Philo, Poli Sci, Pre-Law, Pre-Med/Pre-Dental, Psych, Soc

CORNELL UNIVERSITY (NY) .... cornell.edu   **1380/2070/31**
Ag, Arch, Art, Astro, Biochem, Bio, Bot, Bus Admin, Chem, Comp Sci, Drama,
Econ, Engine, English, Hist, Math, Philo, Physics, Pre-Law, Pre-Med/Pre-Dental, Zoo

CORNISH COLLEGE OF THE ARTS (WA) .... cornish.edu   **1100/1650/24**
Art, Drama, Music

COVENANT COLLEGE (GA) .... covenant.edu   **1150/1725/25**
Hist, Music, Soc

CREIGHTON UNIVERSITY (NE) .... creighton.edu   **1210/1815/27**
Art, Bio, Bus Admin, Chem, Classics, Communic, Drama, Ed, English, Music, Nurs,
Pharm, Philo, Physics, Poli Sci, Pre-Law, Pre-Med/Pre-Dental, Psych, Reli Stu

CULVER-STOCKTON COLLEGE (MO) .... culver.edu   **1000/1500/21**
Art, Bus Admin

CUMBERLAND COLLEGE (KY) .... cumber.edu   **1050/1575/22**
Chem, Ed, Hist, Music, Reli Stu

CURTIS INSTITUTE OF MUSIC (PA) .... curtis.edu   **1100/1650/24**
Music

DAEMEN COLLEGE (NY) .... daemen.edu   **1000/1500/21**
Bio, Bus Admin, Ed, English, Nurs

DAKOTA STATE UNIVERSITY (SD) .... dsu.edu   **1040/1560/22**
Ed, Comp Sci

DALLAS, UNIVERSITY OF (TX) .... udallas.edu   **1210/1815/27**
Art, Bio, Biochem, Classics, Comp Sci, Drama, Econ, Ed, English, For Lang, Hist,
Philo, Poli Sci, Pre-Law, Pre-Med/Pre-Dental, Psych

DANA COLLEGE (NE) .... dana.edu **1020/1530/22**
Art, Communic, Drama, Ed, English, Music, Reli Stu

DARTMOUTH COLLEGE (NH) .... dartmouth.edu **1435/2150/32**
Anthro, Art, Bio, Chem, Classics, Comp Sci, Drama, Econ, Engine, English, For Lang,
Geog, Geol, Hist, Math, Physics, Poli Sci, Pre-Law, Pre-Med/Pre-Dental, Psych, Reli Stu, Soc

DAVIDSON COLLEGE (NC) .... davidson.edu **1360/2040/31**
Bio, Chem, Drama, Econ, English, Hist, Math, Philo, Poli Sci, Pre-Law, Pre-Med/Pre-Dental,
Psych, Reli Stu

DAYTON, UNIVERSITY OF (OH) .... udayton.edu **1170/1755/26**
Bus Admin, Communic, Ed, Engine, Geol, Math, Music, Philo, Poli Sci, Pre-Law,
Pre-Med/Pre-Dental, Reli Stu, Soc

DELAWARE STATE UNIVERSITY (DE) .... dsc.edu **1000/1500/21**
Hist, Psych

DELAWARE, UNIVERSITY OF (DE) .... udel.edu **1195/1790/26**
Art, Art Hist, Bio, Bot, Bus Admin, Chem, Communic, Econ, Ed, Engine,
English, Hist, Nurs, Poli Sci, Pre-Law, Pre-Med/Pre-Dental, Psych

DELAWARE VALLEY COLLEGE (PA) .... devalcol.edu **1000/1500/21**
Ag, Bio, Bus Admin, Chem, English, Pre-Med/Pre-Dental

DENISON UNIVERSITY (OH) .... denison.edu **1210/1810/27**
Art, Art Hist, Bio, Biochem, Comp Sci, Drama, Econ, English, Geol, Hist,
Music, Philo, Physics, Poli Sci, Pre-Law, Pre-Med/Pre-Dental, Psych, Soc

DENVER, UNIVERSITY OF (CO) .... du.edu **1200/1800/26**
Art, Art Hist, Bio, Bus Admin, Chem, Communic, Comp Sci, Engine, English,
Geog, Hist, Music, Physics, Pre-Law, Pre-Med/Pre-Dental, Psych, Reli Stu, Soc

DePAUL UNIVERSITY (IL) .... depaul.edu **1145/1710/25**
Amer St, Bus Admin, Chem, Communic, Comp Sci, Drama, Ed, English, Geog,
Hist, Math, Music, Philo, Poli Sci, Pre-Law, Pre-Med/Pre-Dental, Psych, Reli Stu

DePAUW UNIVERSITY (IN) .... depauw.edu **1200/1800/26**
Art, Biochem, Bio, Chem, Communic, Comp Sci, Econ, English, For Lang, Hist, Music,
Philo, Physics, Poli Sci, Pre-Law, Pre-Med/Pre-Dental, Psych, Reli Stu, Soc

DeSALES UNIVERSITY (PA) .... desales.edu **1090/1635/24**
Bio, Chem, Drama, English, Nurs, Philo, Pre-Med/Pre-Dental, Reli Stu

DETROIT MERCY, UNIVERSITY OF (MI) .... udmercy.edu **1090/1640/24**
Arch, Engine, Nurs, Philo, Reli Stu

DICKINSON COLLEGE (PA) .... dickinson.edu **1270/1805/28**
Bio, Comp Sci, Ed, English, For Lang, Hist, Math, Physics, Poli Sci, Pre-Law,
Pre-Med/Pre-Dental, Psych, Reli Stu

DILLARD UNIVERSITY (LA) .... dillard.edu **1030/1540/22**
Bio, Bus Admin, Ed, Nurs, Pre-Med/Pre-Dental

DIXIE STATE COLLEGE (UT) .... dixie.edu **1000/1500/21**
Nurs

DOANE COLLEGE (NE) .... doane.edu **1080/1620/23**
Bio, Bus Admin, Ed, English, Music, Philo, Physics, Reli Stu, Soc

DOMINICAN UNIVERSITY OF CALIFORNIA (CA) ... dominican.edu **1035/1555/22**
Ed, Nurs, Pre-Med/Pre-Dental, Psych

DOMINICAN UNIVERSITY (IL) .... dom.edu **1070/1600/23**
Bus Admin, Psych

DORDT COLLEGE (IA) .... dordt.edu **1130/1690/25**
Ag, Art, Ed, Engine, English, Reli Stu

DRAKE UNIVERSITY (IA) .... drake.edu **1190/1780/26**
Art, Astro, Bio, Bus Admin, Chem, Communic, Drama, Econ, Ed, English,
For Lang, Hist, Music, Pharm, Poli Sci, Pre-Law, Soc

DREW UNIVERSITY (NJ) .... drew.edu **1200/1800/26**
Art, Chem, Classics, Drama, Econ, English, For Lang, Hist, Poli Sci, Pre-Law,
Pre-Med/Pre-Dental, Psych, Reli Stu

DREXEL UNIVERSITY (PA) .... drexel.edu **1190/1790/26**
Arch, Comp Sci, Engine

DRURY UNIVERSITY (MO) .... drury.edu **1130/1690/25**
Arch, Bio, Ed, English, Music, Pre-Law, Reli Stu

DUBUQUE, UNIVERSITY OF (IA) .... dbq.edu **1020/1530/22**
Bus Admin, Communic, English, Ed, Psych

DUKE UNIVERSITY (NC) .... duke.edu **1450/2175/32**
Anthro, Bio, Bot, Chem, Classics, Comp Sci, Econ, Engine, English, Hist, Math,
Philo, Poli Sci, Pre-Law, Pre-Med/Pre-Dental, Psych, Reli Stu, Soc

DUQUESNE UNIVERSITY (PA) .... duq.edu **1090/1635/24**
Bio, Bus Admin, Chem, Classics, Communic, Ed, Music, Nurs, Pharm, Pre-Med/Pre-Dental, Reli Stu

D'YOUVILLE COLLEGE (NY) .... dyc.edu **1000/1500/21**
Bio, Ed, English, Nurs, Psych, Soc

EARLHAM COLLEGE (IN) .... earlham.edu **1240/1860/28**
Anthro, Astro, Bio, Chem, Ed, English, For Lang, Geol, Math, Philo, Pre-Med/Pre-Dental,
Psych, Reli Stu, Soc

EAST CAROLINA UNIVERSITY (NC) .... ecu.edu **1080/1620/23**
Art, Art Hist, Econ, Ed, Engine, Hist, Math, Music, Nurs, Pre-Med/Pre-Dental, Psych

EAST CENTRAL UNIVERSITY (OK) .... ecok.edu **1000/1500/21**
Ed, English

EAST STROUDSBURG UNIVERSITY (PA) .... esu.edu **1000/1500/21**
Bio, Chem, Comp Sci, Ed, Nurs, Physics

EAST TENNESSEE STATE UNIVERSITY (TN) .... etsu.edu **1030/1540/22**
Art, Bio, Bus Admin, Communic, Econ, English, Hist, Math, Nurs, Philo

EASTERN UNIVERSITY (PA) .... eastern.edu **1070/1600/23**
Bus Admin, Nurs, Soc

EASTERN CONNECTICUT STATE UNIVERSITY (CT) easternct.edu **1050/1575/22**
Amer St, Art Hist, Bio, Bot, Bus Admin, Communic, Comp Sci, Econ, Ed, Hist, Math, Poli Sci, Psych, Soc

EASTERN ILLINOIS UNIVERSITY (IL) .... eiu.edu **1030/1540/22**
Art, Bot, Bus Admin, Chem, Communic, Ed, English, Home Ec, Math, Poli Sci, Psych, Zoo

EASTERN KENTUCKY UNIVERSITY (KY) .... eku.edu **1000/1500/21**
Communic, Ed, Nurs, Poli Sci

EASTERN MENNONITE UNIVERSITY (VA) .... emu.edu **1070/1600/23**
Ed, Nurs, Reli Stu

EASTERN MICHIGAN UNIVERSITY (MI) .... emich.edu **1010/1510/21**
Bus Admin, Chem, Comp Sci, Ed, English, Hist, Music, Nurs, Physics, Poli Sci, Psych

EASTERN NAZARENE COLLEGE (MA) .... enc.edu **1060/1590/23**
Bus Admin, English

EASTERN NEW MEXICO UNIVERSITY (NM) .... cnmu.edu **1000/1500/21**
Bio, Communic

EASTERN OREGON UNIVERSITY (OR) .... eou.edu **1000/1500/21**
Bio, Bus Admin, Ed, English, Nurs

EASTERN WASHINGTON UNIVERSITY (WA) .... ewu.edu **1000/1500/21**
Chem, Econ, English, For Lang, Geol, Math, Nurs

ECKERD COLLEGE (FL) .... eckerd.edu **1120/1680/24**
Bio, Bus Admin, Comp Sci, English, For Lang, Pre-Med/Pre-Dental, Psych, Reli Stu

EDGEWOOD COLLEGE (WI) .... edgewood.edu **1040/1560/22**
Art, Ed, Music, Nurs

EDINBORO UNIVERSITY OF PENNSYLVANIA (PA) .... edinboro.edu **1000/1500/21**
Art, Art Hist, Ed, English, Geog, Geol, Philo, Physics

ELIZABETHTOWN COLLEGE (PA) .... etown.edu **1140/1710/25**
Bio, Bus Admin, Chem, Ed, English, Music, Pre-Law, Reli Stu

ELMHURST COLLEGE (IL) .... elmhurst.edu **1090/1635/24**
Bio, Chem, Ed, Geog, Music, Nurs, Physics, Pre-Med/Pre-Dental, Psych

ELMIRA COLLEGE (NY) .... elmira.edu **1130/1700/25**
Art, Bus Admin, Ed, Hist, Nurs, Psych

ELMS COLLEGE (MA) .... elms.edu **1000/1500/21**
Ed, Nurs

ELON UNIVERSITY (NC) .... elon.edu **1200/1800/26**
Anthro, Bio, Bus Admin, Communic, Drama, Ed, Philo, Poli Sci, Psych

EMBRY-RIDDLE AERONAUTICAL UNIVERSITY (FL) emu.edu **1100/1650/24**
Comp Sci, Engine

EMERSON COLLEGE (MA) .... emerson.edu **1220/1830/27**
Communic, Drama, English, Poli Sci, Pre-Law

EMMANUEL COLLEGE (MA) .... emmanuel/edu **1000/1500/21**
Art, Bio

EMORY & HENRY COLLEGE (VA) .... ehc.edu **1020/1530/22**
Bus Admin, For Lang

EMORY UNIVERSITY (GA) .... emory.edu **1380/2070/31**
Amer St, Anthro, Art Hist, Bio, Bus Admin, Chem, Classics, Econ, English, For Lang,
Hist, Nurs, Poli Sci, Pre-Law, Pre-Med/Pre-Dental, Psych, Reli Stu, Soc

EMPORIA STATE UNIVERSITY (KS) .... emporia.edu **1040/1560/22**
Art, Chem, Ed, Geol, Nurs

ENDICOTT COLLEGE (MA) .... endicott.edu **1070/1600/23**
Art, Bus Admin, Communic

ERSKINE COLLEGE (SC) .... erskine.edu **1100/1650/24**
Bio, Bus Admin, Ed, Hist, Pre-Med/Pre-Dental

EUREKA COLLEGE (IL) .... eureka.edu **1050/1575/22**
Bus Admin, Comp Sci, Ed, English

EVANSVILLE, UNIVERSITY OF (IN) .... evansville.edu **1130/1695/25**
Bio, Bus Admin, Chem, Comp Sci, Drama, Ed, English, Math, Music, Nurs, Physics, Pre-Med/Pre-Dental

FAIRFIELD UNIVERSITY (CT) .... fairfield.edu **1180/1770/26**
Bio, Bus Admin, Communic, Math, Nurs, Physics, Pre-Med/Pre-Dental, Psych

FAIRLEIGH DICKINSON (NJ) .... fdu.edu **1020/1530/22**
Art, Bus Admin, English, Poli Sci, Pre-Law

FAIRMONT STATE COLLEGE (WV) .... fscwv.edu **1000/1500/21**
Bus Admin, Ed, Hist, Nurs, Psych

FAULKNER UNIVERSITY (AL) .... faulkner.edu **1000/1500/21**
Bus Admin

FERRIS STATE UNIVERSITY (MI) .... ferris.edu **1010/1515/21**
Bus Admin, Comp Sci, Nurs, Pharm

FINDLAY, UNIVERSITY OF (OH) .... findlay.edu **1070/1600/23**
Bio, Bus Admin, Ed, Math, Pre-Med/Pre-Dental, Psych

FISK UNIVERSITY (TN) .... fisk.edu **1010/1510/21**
Bus Admin, Math, Physics, Pre-Law, Soc

FITCHBURG STATE COLLEGE (MA) .... fsc.edu **1000/1500/21**
Bio, Communic, Comp Sci, Ed, Hist, Math, Nurs, Psych

FIVE TOWNS COLLEGE (NY) .... ftc.edu **1000/1500/21**
Music

FLAGLER COLLEGE (FL) .... flagler.edu **1100/1650/24**
Bus Admin, Communic, Ed, English, Pre-Law, Psych

FLORIDA, UNIVERSITY OF (FL) .... ufl.edu **1270/1905/28**
Ag, Anthro, Arch, Art, Astro, Bot, Bus Admin, Classics, Communic, Drama, Engine, English, Forest, For Lang, Geol, Hist, Math, Music, Nurs, Pharm, Philo, Physics, Poli, Sci, Pre-Law, Pre-Med/Pre-Dental, Soc, Zoo

FLORIDA A&M (FL) .... famu/edu **1040/1560/22**
Arch, Bus Admin, Communic, Ed, Engine, English, Pharm, Physics, Pre-Law, Pre-Med/Pre-Dental

FLORIDA ATLANTIC UNIVERSITY (FL) .... fau.edu **1050/1575/22**
Bus Admin, Comp Sci, Econ, Ed, Engine, Hist, Math, Nurs, Psych

FLORIDA GULF COAST UNIVERSITY (FL) .... fgcu.edu **1030/1550/22**
Bus Admin, Comp Sci, Ed, English, Nurs

FLORIDA INSTITUTE OF TECHNOLOGY (FL) .... fit.edu **1150/1725/25**
Astro, Bio, Biochem, Bus Admin, Chem, Communic, Comp Sci, Engine, Physics, Pre-Law, Psych

FLORIDA INTERNATIONAL UNIVERSITY (FL) .... fiu.edu **1150/1725/25**
Arch, Art, Bio, Bus Admin, Ed, Engine, Geog, Nurs, Poli Sci, Psych, Soc

FLORIDA SOUTHERN COLLEGE (FL) .... flsouthern.edu **1070/1600/23**
Bio, Chem, Communic, Drama, Ed, Music, Pre-Med/Pre-Dental

FLORIDA STATE UNIVERSITY (FL) .... fsu.edu **1190/1785/26**
Amer St, Art, Art Hist, Bus Admin, Chem, Classics, Comp Sci, Drama, Econ, Ed, English, Hist, Home Ec, Music, Philo, Physics, Pre-Med/Pre-Dental, Psych, Reli Stu

FONTBONNE UNIVERSITY (MO) .... fontbonne.edu **1050/1575/22**
Art, Bus Admin, Communic, Drama, Ed, Math

FORDHAM UNIVERSITY (NY) .... fordham.edu **1170/1755/26**
Bus Admin, Classics, Communic, Drama, English, Philo, Pre-Law, Pre-Med/Pre-Dental, Reli Stu

FORT HAYS STATE UNIVERSITY (KS) .... fhsu.edu **1000/1500/21**
Art, Ed, English, Music, Nurs, Philo, Soc

FORT LEWIS COLLEGE (CO) .... fortlewis.edu **1000/1500/21**
Anthro, Art, Bio, English, Geol, Physics, Pre-Law, Reli Stu

FRAMINGHAM STATE COLLEGE (MA) .... framingham.edu **1050/1575/22**
Bio, Biochem, Bus Admin, Chem, Econ, Ed, Psych

FRANCISCAN UNIVERSITY OF STEUBENVILLE (OH) franuniv.edu **1150/1725/25**
English, Nurs, Philo, Psych, Reli Stu

FRANKLIN COLLEGE (IN) .... franklincollege.edu **1000/1500/21**
Communic, Drama, Ed, Pre-Med

FRANKLIN & MARSHALL COLLEGE (PA) .... fandm.edu **1295/1945/29**
Amer Stu, Astro, Bio, Bus Admin, Chem, Classics, Econ, English, For Lang, Geol, Physics, Poli Sci, Pre-Law, Pre-Med/Pre-Dental, Psych, Soc

FREED-HARDEMAN UNIVERSITY (TN) .... fhu.edu **1080/1620/23**
Bus Admin, Ed, Pre-Med/Pre-Dental, Reli Stu

FRIENDS UNIVERSITY (KS) .... friends.edu **1050/1575/22**
Ed, English, Music

FROSTBURG STATE UNIVERSITY (MD) .... frostburg.edu   **1015/1520/21**
Art, Bus Admin, Comp Sci, Ed, Geog, Philo

FULL SAIL UNIVERSITY (FL) .... fullsail.com   **1000/1500/21**
Music

FURMAN UNIVERSITY (SC) .... furman.edu   **1280/1920/29**
Art, Bio, Bus Admin, Chem, Comp Sci, Econ, Geol, Hist, Music, Physics, Poli Sci,
Pre-Law, Pre-Med/Pre-Dental, Psych, Reli Stu

GANNON UNIVERSITY (PA) .... gannon.edu   **1040/1560/22**
Bio, Bus Admin, Chem, Comp Sci, Ed, Engine, Nurs, Pre-Med/Pre-Dental, Psych, Reli Stu

GARDNER-WEBB UNIVERSITY (NC) .... gardner-webb.edu   **1020/1530/22**
Bus Admin, Comp Sci, Poli Sci, Pre-Med/Pre-Dental, Soc

GENEVA COLLEGE (PA) .... geneva.edu   **1100/1650/24**
Chem, Communic, Ed, Engine, Reli Stu

GEORGETOWN COLLEGE (KY) .... georgetowncollege.edu   **1080/1620/23**
Bio, Bus Admin, Chem, Communic, Ed, English, Hist, Pre-Law, Soc

GEORGETOWN UNIVERSITY (DC) .... georgetown.edu   **1380/2070/31**
Amer St, Anthro, Art Hist, Biochem, Bio, Bus Admin, Chem, Classics, Econ, English, For Lang,
Hist, Nurs, Philo, Physics, Poli Sci, Pre-Law, Pre-Med/Pre-Dental, Psych, Reli Stu, Soc

GEORGE FOX UNIVERSITY (OR) .... georgefox.edu   **1110/1650/24**
Art, Bio, Bus Admin, Ed, Psych, Reli Stu, Soc

GEORGE MASON UNIVERSITY (VA) .... gmu.edu   **1150/1725/25**
Amer St, Anthro, Art Hist, Bus Admin, Communic, Comp Sci, Drama,
Econ, English, Math, Nurs, Philo, Physics, Poli Sci, Psych, Pre-Law

GEORGE WASHINGTON UNIVERSITY (DC) .... gwu.edu   **1270/1905/28**
Amer St, Anthro, Art Hist, Bus Admin, Chem, Comp Sci, Drama, Econ, Engine,
Geog, Hist, Philo, Poli Sci, Pre-Law, Psych, Soc

GEORGIA, UNIVERSITY OF (GA) .... uga.edu   **1230/1845/27**
Ag, Art Hist, Astro, Bio, Biochem, Chem, Classics, Communic, Drama, Econ, Ed,
English, For Lang, Forest, Geog, Hist, Home Ec, Music, Pharm, Philo, Poli Sci, Pre-Law,
Pre-Med/Pre-Dental, Psych, Zoo

GEORGIA INSTITUTE OF TECHNOLOGY (GA) .... gatech.edu   **1330/1990/30**
Arch, Bus Admin, Chem, Comp Sci, Econ, Engine, Hist, Math, Physics, Psych

GEORGIA SOUTHERN UNIVERSITY (GA) .... gasou.edu   **1030/1550/22**
Art, Bus Admin, Ed, Hist, Home Ec, Nurs

GEORGIA SOUTHWESTERN STATE UNIVERSITY (GA) ... gsw.edu   **1000/1500/21**
Ed, English, Nurs

GEORGIA STATE UNIVERSITY (GA) .... gsu.edu   **1080/1620/23**
Astro, Bio, Bus Admin, Chem, Communic, Comp Sci, Econ, Ed, Math, Music,
Nurs, Philo, Physics, Psych, Soc

GETTYSBURG COLLEGE (PA) .... gettysburg.edu   **1280/1920/29**
Bio, Bus Admin, Drama, Econ, English, Hist, Philo, Physics, Poli Sci,
Pre-Law, Pre-Med/Pre-Dental, Psych, Soc

GONZAGA UNIVERSITY (WA) .... gonzaga.edu   **1195/1795/26**
Bio, Bus Admin, Chem, Communic, Ed, Engine, English, Hist, Philo, Poli Sci, Pre-Law, Pre-Med/Pre-Dental, Reli Stu

GORDON COLLEGE (MA) .... gordon.edu   **1199/1800/26**
Art, Bio, Ed, English, Music, Philo, Reli Stu, Soc

GOSHEN COLLEGE (IN) .... goshen.edu   **1105/1655/24**
English, Music, Nurs, Physics

GOUCHER COLLEGE (MD) .... goucher.edu   **1170/1755/26**
Art, Bus Admin, Chem, Comp Sci, Drama, Ed, English, Hist, Poli Sci, Pre-Law, Pre-Med/Pre-Dental

GRACELAND UNIVERSITY (IA) .... graceland.edu   **1001/1500/21**
Bus Admin, Ed, Hist, Nurs

GRAMBLING STATE UNIVERSITY (LA) .... gram.edu   **1000/1500/21**
Bus Admin, Ed, Nurs, Poli Sci, Soc

GREAT FALLS, UNIVERSITY OF (MT) .... ugf.edu   **1000/1500/21**
Comp Sci, Ed

GRAND VALLEY STATE UNIVERSITY (MI) .... gvsu.edu   **1120/1680/24**
Anthro, Art, Bio, Drama, Ed, Engine, English, For Lang, Math, Pre-Law, Psych

GREEN MOUNTAIN COLLEGE (VT) .... greenmtn.edu   **1000/1500/21**
Bus Admin

GREENSBORO COLLEGE (NC) .... gborocollege.edu   **1000/1500/21**
Art, Drama, Ed, Reli Stu

GRINNELL COLLEGE (IA) .... grinnell.edu   **1340/2010/30**
Anthro, Bio, Chem, Classics, Comp Sci, Econ, English, For Lang, Hist, Math, Physics, Poli Sci, Pre-Law, Pre-Med/Pre-Dental, Psych, Reli Stu, Soc

GROVE CITY COLLEGE (PA) .... gcc.edu   **1270/1900/28**
Bio, Bus Admin, Econ, Ed, Engine, English, Poli Sci, Pre-Med/Pre-Dental

GUILFORD COLLEGE (NC) .... guilford.edu   **1130/1700/25**
Art, Bio, Bus Admin, Econ, Ed, English, Geol, Hist, Physics, Poli Sci, Pre-Law, Pre-Med/Pre-Dental, Psych, Reli Stu

GUSTAVUS ADOLPHUS COLLEGE (MN) .... gustavus.edu   **1200/1800/26**
Bio, Bus Admin, Chem, Classics, Ed, English, For Lang, Geol, Hist, Music, Nurs, Physics, Pre-Med/Pre-Dental, Psych, Reli Stu

GWYNEDD-MERCY COLLEGE (PA) .... gmc.edu   **1000/1500/21**
Bio, Communic, English, Nurs, Pre-Law

HAMILTON COLLEGE (NY) .... hamilton.edu   **1360/2040/31**
Bio, Chem, Comp Sci, Drama, Econ, English, Geol, Hist, Philo, Physics, Poli Sci, Pre-Law, Pre-Med/Pre-Dental, Reli Stu

HAMLINE UNIVERSITY (MN) .... hamline.edu   **1120/1680/24**
Anthro, Art, Bio, Chem, Ed, English, Hist, Physics, Philo, Pre-Law, Pre-Med/Pre-Dental, Psych, Reli Stu, Soc

HAMPDEN-SYDNEY COLLEGE (VA) .... hsc.edu   **1120/1680/24**
Bio, Chem, Classics, Econ, English, Hist, Poli Sci, Pre-Law, Pre-Med/Pre-Dental, Reli Stu

HAMPTON UNIVERSITY (VA) .... hamptonu.edu   **1040/1560/22**
Bio, Bus Admin, Chem, Communic, English, Psych, Pre-Law

HANNIBAL-LA GRANGE COLLEGE (MO) .... hlg.edu   **1000/1500/21**
Ed, Music

HANOVER COLLEGE (IN) .... hanover.edu   **1170/1755/26**
*Bus Admin, Classics, Communic, Drama, Econ, Ed, English, Hist, Philo,
Physics, Pre-Med/Pre-Dental, Psych, Soc, Reli Stu*

HARDIN-SIMMONS UNIVERSITY (TX) .... hsutx.edu   **1020/1530/22**
Bio, Communic, Econ, Ed, Music, Nurs, Reli Stu

HARDING UNIVERSITY (AR) .... harding.edu   **1120/1680/24**
Bus Admin, Ed, Music, Nurs, Reli Stu

HARRISBURG UNIVERSITY (PA) .... harrisburgu.net   **1100/1650/24**
Bio, Chem, Comp Sci, Geog, Pre-Med/Pre-Dental

HARTFORD, UNIVERSITY OF (CT) .... hartford.edu   **1060/1590/23**
Bus Admin, Communic, Drama, Ed, Engine, Music, Soc

HARTWICK COLLEGE (NY) .... hartwick.edu   **1100/1650/24**
Bus Admin, Drama, Geol, Music, Nurs, Poli Sci, Pre-Law, Soc

HARVARD UNIVERSITY (MA) .... harvard.edu   **1485/2230/33**
*Amer St, Anthro, Art, Art Hist, Astro, Biochem, Bio, Chem, Classics, Comp Sci, Econ,
English, For Lang, Geol, Hist, Math, Music, Philo, Physics, Poli Sci, Pre-Law,
Pre-Med/Pre-Dental, Psych, Soc*

HARVEY MUDD COLLEGE (CA) .... hmc.edu   **1490/2235/33**
Bio, Chem, Comp Sci, Engine, Math, Physics, Pre-Med/Pre-Dental

HASTINGS COLLEGE (NE) .... hastings.edu   **1090/1635/24**
Art, Bus Admin, Communic, Ed, Hist, Music, Physics, Reli Stu

HAVERFORD COLLEGE (PA) .... haverford.edu   **1400/2100/31**
*Art, Astro, Bio, Chem, Classics, Econ, English, For Lang, Hist, Math, Philo,
Physics, Poli Sci, Pre-Law, Pre-Med/Pre-Dental, Psych, Reli Stu*

HAWAII, UNIVERSITY OF (HILO) (HI) .... hilo.hawaii.edu   **1000/1500/21**
Astro, Geol, Pharm, Psych

HAWAII, UNIVERSITY OF (MANOA) (HI) .... uhm.hawaii.edu   **1100/1650/24**
*Ag, Amer St, Anthro, Art, Astro, Bot, Comp Sci, Drama, English, For Lang,
Hist, Poli Sci, Pre-Law, Soc, Zoo*

HAWAII PACIFIC UNIVERSITY (HI) .... hpu.edu   **1000/1500/21**
Bus Admin, Communic, Comp Sci, Econ, English, Nurs, Pre-Law, Pre-Med/Pre-Dental

HEIDELBERG COLLEGE (OH) .... heidelberg.edu   **1050/1575/22**
Bio, Bus Admin, Comp Sci, Econ, Ed, Hist, Music, Poli Sci, Pre-Law, Pre-Med/Pre-Dental

HENDERSON STATE UNIVERSITY (AR) .... hsu.edu **1030/1545/22**
Art, Bus Admin, Chem, Ed, Nurs

HENDRIX COLLEGE (AR) .... hendrix.edu **1230/1845/27**
*Bio, Bus Admin, Chem, Comp Sci, Econ, English, Math, Physics, Poli Sci,
Pre-Law, Pre-Med/Pre-Dental, Psych, Reli Stu, Soc*

HIGH POINT UNIVERSITY (NC) .... highpoint.edu **1040/1560/22**
Chem, Comp Sci, Ed, Math, Reli Stu

HILLSDALE COLLEGE (MI) .... hillsdale.edu **1190/1790/26**
Amer St, Bio, Bus Admin, Econ, Ed, English, For Lang, Hist, Poli Sci

HIRAM COLLEGE (OH) .... hiram.edu **1100/1650/24**
Bio, Chem, Comp Sci, Ed, English, Hist, Math, Music, Pre-Law, Pre-Med/Pre-Dental, Reli Stu

HOBART & WILLIAM SMITH COLLEGE (NY) .... hws.edu **1170/1755/26**
*Amer Stu, Art, Bio, Chem, Econ, English, Hist, Philo, Poli Sci, Pre-Law,
Pre-Med/Pre-Dental, Psych, Soc*

HOFSTRA UNIVERSITY (NY) .... hofstra.edu **1170/1755/26**
*Anthro, Art, Bus Admin, Communic, Comp Sci, Drama, Ed, English, Music,
Poli Sci, Pre-Law, Pre-Med/Pre-Dental, Psych, Soc*

HOLLINS UNIVERSITY (VA) .... hollins.edu **1140/1710/25**
*Art, Art Hist, Chem, Classics, Drama, Econ, English, For Lang, Hist, Poli Sci,
Pre-Law, Pre-Med/Pre-Dental, Soc, Psych*

HOLY CROSS, COLLEGE OF THE (MA) .... holycross.edu **1285/1925/29**
*Bio, Chem, Classics, Econ, English, For Lang, Hist, Math, Philo, Physics,
Poli Sci, Pre-Law, Pre-Med/Pre-Dental, Psych, Reli Stu, Soc*

HOLY NAMES UNIVERSITY (CA) .... hnu.edu **1000/1500/21**
Bio, Ed, Hist, Music, Nurs, Psych, Reli Stu

HOOD COLLEGE (MD) .... hood.edu **1130/1700/25**
Art, Bio, Bus Admin, Ed, English, Hist, Philo, Poli Sci, Pre-Law, Pre-Med/Pre-Dental, Psych

HOPE COLLEGE (MI) .... hope.edu **1190/1790/26**
*Bio, Chem, Classics, Drama, English, For Lang, Geol, Music, Nurs,
Physics, Poli Sci, Pre-Law, Pre-Med/Pre-Dental, Psych, Reli Stu*

HOUGHTON COLLEGE (NY) .... houghton.edu **1160/1740/25**
Art, Bio, Chem, Ed, English, Hist, Music, Pre-Med/Pre-Dental, Psych, Reli Stu

HOUSTON BAPTIST UNIVERSITY (TX) .... hbu.edu **1050/1575/22**
Bio, Chem, Music, Nurs, Pre-Med/Pre-Dental

HOUSTON, UNIVERSITY OF (TX) .... uh.edu **1070/1600/23**
*Arch, Art, Bio, Bus Admin, Chem, Communic, Drama, Ed, Engine, English, Geol, Hist,
Music, Pharm, Physics, Pre-Med/Pre-Dental, Psych*

HOWARD UNIVERSITY (DC) .... howard.edu **1060/1590/23**
*Arch, Bus Admin, Chem, Classics, Communic, Engine, English, Hist, Nurs,
Pharm, Poli Sci, Pre-Law, Pre-Med/Pre-Dental, Soc, Zoo*

HUMBOLDT STATE UNIVERSITY (CA) .... humboldt.edu **1040/1560/22**
Anthro, Art, Bio, Bot, Chem, Forest, Geog, Geol, Math, Physics, Zoo

HUNTINGDON COLLEGE (AL) .... huntingdon.edu **1100/1650/24**
Chem, Ed, Music, Pre-Med/Pre-Dental, Reli Stu

HUNTINGTON UNIVERSITY (IN) .... huntcol.edu **1070/1600/23**
Art, Ed, Music

HUSSON UNIVERSITY (ME) .... husson.edu **1000/1500/21**
Bus Admin, Chem, Comp Sci, Ed, Nurs, Pharm, Pre-Law

IDAHO, COLLEGE OF (ID) .... collegeofidaho.edu **1150/1725/25**
Art, Bio, Bus Admin, Chem, Ed, English, Hist, Math, Music, Poli Sci, Pre-Law,
Pre-Med/Pre-Dental, Zoo

IDAHO, UNIVERSITY OF (ID) .... uidaho.edu **1080/1620/23**
Ag, Arch, Bus Admin, Communic, Comp Sci, Engine, Forest, Geol, Music, Physics

IDAHO STATE UNIVERSITY (ID) .... isu.edu **1010/1515/21**
Nurs, Pharm

ILLINOIS, UNIVERSITY OF, AT:
       URBANA-CHAMPAIGN .... uiuc.edu **1270/1900/28**
       Ag, Anthro, Arch, Astro, Bus Admin, Chem, Communic, Comp Sci, Drama,
       Ed, Engine,English, Forest, For Lang, Hist, Math, Music, Nurs, Pharm,
       Physics, Poli Sci, Pre-Law, Pre-Med/Pre-Dental, Psych, Soc
       CHICAGO .... uic.edu **1100/1650/24**
       Arch, Art, Art Hist, Bio, Bus Admin, Classics, Econ, Engine, English, For Lang, Hist,
       Math, Music, Nurs, Pharm, Philo, Poli Sci, Pre-law, Pre-Med/Pre-Dental, Psych
       SPRINGFIELD .... uis.edu **1100/1650/24**
       Bus Admin, Comp Sci

ILLINOIS COLLEGE (IL) .... ic.edu **1120/1680/24**
Bio, Bus Admin, Communic, Comp Sci, Econ, Ed, English, For Lang, Hist, Math,
Poli Sci, Pre-Law, Soc

ILLINOIS INSTITUTE OF TECHNOLOGY (IL) .... iit.edu **1280/1920/29**
Arch, Chem, Comp Sci, Engine, English, Math, Music, Physics, Soc

ILLINOIS STATE UNIVERSITY (IL) .... ilstu.edu **1080/1620/24**
Drama, Ed, Poli Sci, Pre-Law

ILLINOIS WESLEYAN UNIVERSITY (IL) .... iwu.edu **1270/1900/28**
Bio, Chem, Drama, Econ, English, Music, Nurs, Philo, Physics, Poli Sci,
Pre-Law, Pre-Med/Pre-Dental, Psych, Soc

IMMACULATA UNIVERSITY (PA) .... immaculata.edu **1020/1530/22**
Bio, Bus Admin, Ed, Music, Nurs

INDIANA INSTITUTE OF TECHNOLOGY (IN) ... indianatech.edu **1000/1500/21**
Bus Admin, Comp Sci

INDIANA STATE UNIVERSITY (IN) .... indstate.edu **1000/1500/21**
Art, Bus Admin, Communic, Drama, Ed, Geog, Math, Music, Physics

INDIANA UNIVERSITY (IN) .... indiana.edu **1150/1725/25**
*Bio, Bus Admin, Chem, Communic, Drama, Ed, For Lang, Geog, Geol, Hist, Music,
Nurs, Pre-Med/Pre-Dental, Psych, Soc, Zoo*

INDIANA UNIVERSITY OF PENNSYLVANIA .... iup.edu **1050/1575/22**
*Anthro, Art, Art Hist, Biochem, Bio, Bus Admin, Communic, Ed, Geog, Hist, Math,
Music, Nurs, Philo, Physics, Soc*

INDIANA U./PURDUE U./INDIANAPOLIS (IN) .... iupui.edu **1000/1500/21**
Communic, Econ, Ed, Engine, English, Hist, Math, Nurs, Soc

INDIANA WESLEYAN UNIVERSITY (IN) .... indwes.edu **1060/1590/23**
Bus Admin, Pre-Med/Pre-Dental, Reli Stu

IONA COLLEGE (NY) .... iona.edu **1070/1605/23**
Bus Admin, Communic, Comp Sci, Ed, Poli Sci

IOWA, UNIVERSITY OF .... uiowa.edu **1160/1740/25**
*Amer St, Anthro, Art, Astro, Biochem, Bus Admin, Chem, Communic,
Comp Sci, Drama, Ed, Engine, English, For Lang, Hist, Music, Nurs, Pharm,
Physics, Poli Sci, Pre-Law, Pre-Med/Pre-Dental, Psych, Reli Stu*

IOWA STATE UNIVERSITY (IA) .... iastate.edu **1160/1740/25**
*Ag, Arch, Art, Bio, Bus Admin, Chem, Comp Sci, Econ, Ed, Engine, English, Forest, Home Ec,
Music, Philo, Physics, Pre-Law, Pre-Med/Pre-Dental, Soc, Zoo*

ITHACA COLLEGE (NY) .... ithaca.edu **1170/1755/26**
Anthro, Biochem, Bio, Bus Admin, Chem, Communic, Drama, Music, Pre-Med/Pre-Dental

JACKSONVILLE STATE (AL) .... jsu.edu **1000/1500/21**
Bio, Comp Sci, Ed, Music, Nurs

JACKSONVILLE UNIVERSITY (FL) .... ju.edu **1020/1530/22**
Art, Bio, Bus Admin, Communic, Comp Sci, Drama, Ed, Music, Nurs, Physics, Pre-Med/Pre-Dental

JAMES MADISON UNIVERSITY (VA) .... jmu.edu **1170/1755/26**
*Anthro, Art, Bus Admin, Communic, Comp Sci, Drama, Ed, Engine, For Lang,
Hist, Math, Music, Poli Sci, Pre-law, Pre-Med/Pre-Dental, Psych, Soc*

JAMESTOWN COLLEGE (ND) .... jc.edu **1050/1575/22**
Bus Admin, Comp Sci, Ed, English, Nurs

JOHN BROWN UNIVERSITY (AR) .... jbu.edu **1100/1650/24**
Music, Reli Stu

JOHN CARROLL UNIVERSITY (OH) .... jcu.edu **1120/1680/24**
*Bus Admin, Chem, Communic, Econ, English, Hist, Math, Philo, Poli Sci,
Psych, Reli Stu, Soc*

JOHNS HOPKINS UNIVERSITY (MD) .... jhu.edu **1400/2100/31**
*Amer St, Anthro, Art Hist, Bio, Chem, Classics, Comp Sci, Engine, English, Geog, Hist,
Music, Nurs, Philo, Physics, Poli Sci, Pre-Law, Pre-Med/Pre-Dental, Psych, Soc*

JOHNSON C. SMITH (NC) .... jcsu.edu **1000/1500/21**
Communic, Comp Sci, Psych, Soc

JOHNSON STATE COLLEGE (VT) .... jsc.vsc.edu **1000/1500/21**
Art, Drama, Ed, English, Music

JUDSON COLLEGE (AL) .... judson.edu **1030/1540/22**
Art, Bus Admin, Communic, Ed, English, Music, Psych, Reli Stu

JUILLIARD SCHOOL(NY) .... juilliard.edu **1120/1680/24**
Drama, Music

JUNIATA COLLEGE (PA)... juniata.edu **1160/1740/25**
Art, Art Hist, Bio, Bus Admin, Chem, Communic, Comp Sci, Ed, English, Geol, Hist,
Math, Pre-Law, Pre-Med/Pre-Dental

KALAMAZOO COLLEGE (MI) .... kzoo.edu **1300/1950/28**
Amer St, Anthro, Bio, Chem, Classics, Communic, Econ, English, For Lang,
Hist, Music, Physics, Poli Sci, Pre-Law, Pre-Med/Pre-Dental, Psych, Soc

KANSAS CITY ART INSTITUTE (MO) .... kcai.edu **1080/1620/23**
Art

KANSAS, UNIVERSITY OF (KS).................................. ukans.edu **1125/1685/25**
Amer St, Anthro, Arch, Art, Art Hist, Astro, Bio, Bus Admin, Chem, Communic,
Drama, Econ, Ed, Engine, For Lang, Geog, Hist, Music, Nurs, Pharm, Physics,
Poli Sci, Pre-Med/Pre-Dental, Psych, Zoo

KANSAS STATE UNIVERSITY (KS) .... ksu.edu **1120/1680/24**
Ag, Anthro, Arch, Art, Bio, Biochem, Bus Admin, Communic, Comp Sci, Drama,
Ed, Engine, English, For Lang, Geog, Hist, Home Ec, Math, Music, Philo, Physics,
Pre-Law, Pre-Med/Pre-Dental, Psych, Soc

KANSAS WESLEYAN UNIVERSITY (KS)...................... kwu.edu **1050/1575/22**
Bus Admin, Chem, Comp Sci, Ed, Nurs

KEAN UNIVERSITY (NJ) .... kean.edu **1010/1510/21**
Art, Ed, English, Nurs, Psych, Soc

KEENE STATE COLLEGE (NH).................................. keene.edu **1000/1500/21**
Arch, Art, Communic, Drama, Ed, English, Geog, Music, Psych, Soc

KENNESAW STATE UNIVERSITY (GA) .... kennesaw.edu **1070/1605/23**
Bus Admin, Chem, Comp Sci, Ed, English, Hist, Math, Nurs, Poli Sci

KENT STATE UNIVERSITY (OH) .... kent.edu **1030/1545/22**
Arch, Art, Chem, Communic, Comp Sci, Ed, English, Music, Nurs, Philo, Physics, Poli Sci

KENTUCKY, UNIVERSITY OF (KY) .... uky.edu **1120/1680/24**
Ag, Arch, Bio, Bus Admin, Classics, Communic, Comp Sci, Ed, Engine, English,
Forest, Hist, Music, Nurs, Pharm, Pre-Med/Pre-Dental, Psych, Zoo

KENTUCKY WESLEYAN COLLEGE (KY) .... kwc.edu **1030/1540/22**
Bio, Bus Admin, Chem, Communic, Ed, English, Hist, Music, Pre-Med/Pre-Dental, Psych, Reli Stu

KENYON COLLEGE (OH) .... kenyon.edu **1290/1935/29**
Anthro, Art, Biochem, Bio, Chem, Classics, Drama, Econ, English, Hist, Math,
Music, Philo, Physics, Poli Sci, Pre-Law, Pre-Med/Pre-Dental, Psych, Reli Stu, Soc

KETTERING UNIVERSITY (MI) .... kettering.edu **1200/1800/26**
Engine, Physics

KING COLLEGE (TN) .... king.edu **1100/1650/24**
Chem, Ed, English, Nurs, Reli Stu

KING'S COLLEGE (PA) .... kings.edu **1025/1540/22**
Bio, Bus Admin, Chem, Ed, English

KNOX COLLEGE (IL) .... knox.edu **1250/1875/28**
*Amer St, Anthro, Art, Bio, Biochem, Chem, Drama, Econ, English, Hist, Math,
Music, Physics, Poli Sci, Pre-Law, Pre-Med/Pre-Dental, Soc*

KUTZTOWN UNIVERSITY (PA) .... kutztown.edu **1000/1500/21**
Art, Ed, English, Hist, Music, Philo, Poli Sci, Psych

LAFAYETTE COLLEGE (PA) .... lafayette.edu **1300/1950/29**
*Anthro, Art, Bio, Bus Admin, Chem, Comp Sci, Econ, Engine, English, Geol, Hist,
Math, Poli Sci, Pre-Law, Pre-Med/Pre-Dental, Psych*

LAKE FOREST COLLEGE (IL) .... lfc.edu **1200/1800/26**
*Art, Art Hist, Bio, Chem, Econ, Ed, English, For Lang, Hist, Music, Philo,
Poli Sci,Pre-Law, Pre-Med/Pre-Dental, Psych, Soc*

LAMAR UNIVERSITY (TX) .... lamar.edu **1000/1500/21**
Chem, Comp Sci, Ed, Engine, Geol, Nurs, Soc

LAMBUTH UNIVERSITY (TN) .... lambuth.edu **1080/1620/23**
Art, Bio, Chem, Ed, Hist, Reli Stu

LA SALLE UNIVERSITY (PA) .... lasalle.edu **1100/1650/24**
*Amer St, Bus Admin, Chem, Communic, Comp Sci, Ed, English, Math, Nurs,
Philo, Pre-Law, Pre-Med/Pre-Dental, Psych, Reli Stu*

LASELL COLLEGE (MA) .... lasell.edu **1000/1500/21**
Bus Admin, Ed

LA VERNE, UNIVERSITY OF (CA) .... ulv.edu **1000/1500/21**
Bus Admin, Comp Sci, Ed, Poli Sci, Pre-Law, Psych

LAWRENCE UNIVERSITY (WI) .... lawrence.edu **1300/1950/28**
*Anthro, Art, Art Hist, Bio, Chem, Drama, Econ, English, For Lang, Hist, Music,
Philo, Physics, Pre-Law, Pre-Med/Pre-Dental, Reli Stu*

LEBANON VALLEY COLLEGE OF PENNSYLVANIA (PA) . lvc.edu **1100/1650/24**
*Amer St, Art, Art Hist, Bus Admin, Chem, Math, Music, Nurs, Pre-Law, Pre-Med/Pre-Dental,
Psych, Soc*

LEHIGH UNIVERSITY (PA) .... lehigh.edu **1300/1950/29**
*Amer St, Arch, Biochem, Bio, Bus Admin, Chem, Comp Sci, Econ, Engine,
English, Geol, Hist, Math, Physics, Poli Sci, Pre-Med/Pre-Dental, Psych*

LEMOYNE COLLEGE (NY) .... lemoyne.edu **1100/1650/24**
Bio, Bus Admin, Chem, Communic, Drama, Ed, English, Hist, Psych, Reli Stu

LENOIR-RHYNE COLLEGE (NC) .... lrc.edu **1020/1530/22**
Bus Admin, Comp Sci, Music, Nurs, Soc

LESLEY UNIVERSITY (MA) .... lesley.edu **1000/1500/21**
Art, Bus Admin, Comp Sci, Ed

LETOURNEAU COLLEGE (TX) .... letu.edu **1180/1770/26**
Bus Admin, Comp Sci, Ed, Engine

LEWIS & CLARK COLLEGE (OR) .... lclark.edu **1280/1920/29**
Art, Bio, Biochem, Bus Admin, Chem, Communic, Drama, English, For Lang, Hist, Music, Philo, Physics, Pre-Med/Pre-Dental, Soc

LEWIS-CLARK STATE COLLEGE (ID) .... lcsc.edu **1000/1500/21**
Art, Bio, Chem, Communic, Ed, English, Math, Nurs

LIBERTY UNIVERSITY (VA) .... liberty.edu **1030/1550/22**
Communic, Comp Sci, Ed, Hist, Nurs, Psych, Reli Stu

LINDENWOOD UNIVERSITY (MO) .... lindenwood.edu **1060/1600/23**
Art, Bus Admin, Communic, Drama, Ed, English, Psych

LINFIELD COLLEGE (OR) .... linfield.edu **1110/1655/24**
Bio, Bus Admin, Chem, Comp Sci, Econ, Ed, For Lang, Hist, Math, Music, Physics

LIPSCOMB UNIVERSITY (TN) .... lipscomb.edu **1120/1680/24**
Bio, Bus Admin, Chem, Ed, Engine, English, Nurs, Poli Sci, Pre-Med/Pre-Dental, Reli Stu

LOCK HAVEN UNIVERSITY (PA) .... lhup.edu **1015/1525/22**
Art, Bio, Chem, Ed, Hist, Music, Poli Sci, Psych

LONG ISLAND UNIVERSITY (BROOKLYN) (NY) .... liu.edu **1000/1500/21**
Chem, Comp Sci, Drama, Ed, English, Pharm, Nurs

LONG ISLAND UNIVERSITY (C.W.POST) (NY) .... liu.edu **1000/1500/21**
Art, Bio, Bus Admin, Chem, Comp Sci, Drama, Ed, English, Math, Music, Psych

LONGWOOD UNIVERSITY (VA) .... lwc.edu **1080/1620/23**
Art, Bus Admin, Drama, Ed, English, Music, Pre-Law, Psych, Soc

LORAS COLLEGE (IA) .... loras.edu **1050/1575/22**
Art, Bio, Bus Admin, Chem, Communic, Comp Sci, Econ, Ed, English, Hist, Philo, Physics, Pre-Law, Psych, Reli Stu

LOUISIANA COLLEGE (LA) .... lacollege.edu **1050/1575/22**
Ed, English, Hist, Music, Nurs, Pre-Law, Pre-Med/Pre-Dental, Reli Stu

LOUISIANA-LAFAYETTE, UNIVERSITY OF (LA) . louisiana.edu **1080/1620/22**
Arch, Art, Bio, Bus Admin, Chem, Comp Sci, Econ, Ed, Engine, English, Geol, Math, Music, Nurs, Physics, Pre-Med/Pre-Dental, Zoo

LOUISIANA-MONROE, UNIVERSITY OF (LA) .... ulm.edu **1000/1500/21**
Communic, Ed, Music, Pharm

LOUISIANA STATE UNIVERSITY (LA) .... lsu.edu **1150/1725/25**
Ag, Anthro, Arch, Art, Astro, Biochem, Bot, Chem, Communic, Comp Sci, Econ, Engine, English, Geog, Geol, Hist, Math, Music, Philo, Physics, Poli Sci, Pre-Law, Pre-Med/Pre-Dental, Psych, Reli Stu, Soc, Zoo

LOUISIANA TECH UNIVERSITY (LA) .... latech.edu **1070/1605/23**
Bus Admin, Ed, Geog

LOUISVILLE, UNIVERSITY OF (KY) .... louisville.edu **1100/1650/24**
Art, Bus Admin, Chem, Engine, Music, Nurs, Poli Sci, Soc

LOYOLA COLLEGE IN MARYLAND (MD) .... loyola.edu **1210/1815/27**
*Bio, Bus Admin, Chem, Classics, Communic, Comp Sci, Ed, Engine, For Lang,
Philo, Psych, Pre-Law, Pre-Med/Pre-Dental*

LOYOLA MARYMOUNT UNIVERSITY (CA) .... lmu.edu **1170/1755/26**
Amer St, Art, Bus Admin, Classics, Communic, Econ, Engine, English, Hist, Math, Reli Stu, Soc

LOYOLA UNIVERSITY OF CHICAGO (IL) .... luc.edu **1145/1710/25**
*Anthro, Art, Bio, Communic, Classics, Drama, Hist, Math, Music, Nurs, Philo,
Physics, Pre-Med/Pre-Dental, Psych, Reli Stu*

LOYOLA UNIVERSITY OF NEW ORLEANS (LA) .... loyno.edu **1230/1840/27**
*Art, Bio, Bus Admin, Chem, Comp Sci, Communic, Econ, English, Hist,
Music, Philo, Pre-Law, Pre-Med/Pre-Dental, Reli Stu*

LUTHER COLLEGE (IA) .... luther.edu **1170/1750/26**
Anthro, Bio, Bus Admin, Drama, Ed, English, Hist, Math, Music, Nurs, Psych, Reli Stu

LYCOMING COLLEGE (PA) .... lycoming.edu **1060/1590/23**
Art, Astro, Bio, Chem, Drama, English, Philo, Pre-Med/Pre-Dental, Psych, Reli Stu

LYNCHBURG COLLEGE (VA) .... lynchburg.edu **1015/1525/22**
Bio, Communic, Comp Sci, Ed, English, Math, Music, Pre-Law, Pre-Med/Pre-Dental, Soc

LYNDON STATE COLLEGE (VT) .... lsc.vsc.edu **1000/1500/21**
Bio, Bus Admin, Communic, English, Psych

LYON COLLEGE (AR) .... lyon.edu **1160/1740/25**
Chem, Drama, Econ, Ed, English, For Lang, Math, Poli Sci, Psych

MACALESTER COLLEGE (MN) .... macalester.edu **1340/2000/30**
*Anthro, Art, Bio, Chem, Classics, Communic, Comp Sci, Drama, Econ, English, For Lang,
Geog, Hist, Math, Philo, Physics, Poli Sci, Pre-Law, Pre-Med/Pre-Dental, Psych, Reli Stu*

MacMURRAY COLLEGE (IL) .... mac.edu **1010/1515/21**
Ed, Nurs

MAINE, UNIVERSITY OF (ME) .... umaine.edu **1080/1620/24**
*Ag, Anthro, Biochem, Bot, Bus Admin, Chem, Communic, Comp Sci, Drama, Econ,
Ed, Engine, Forest, Music, Nurs, Philo, Physics, Psych*

MAINE, UNIVERSITY OF (FARMINGTON) (ME) . umf.maine.edu **1050/1575/22**
Bus Admin, Ed, English, Geog, Psych

MALONE COLLEGE (OH) .... malone.edu **1050/1575/22**
Bus Admin, Math, Music, Nurs

MANCHESTER COLLEGE (IN) .... manchester.edu **1050/1575/22**
Bus Admin, Ed, Hist, Poli Sci, Psych, Soc

MANHATTAN COLLEGE (NY) .... manhattan.edu **1090/1635/24**
Bus Admin, Chem, Comp Sci, Ed, Engine, Math, Poli Sci, Pre-Law, Pre-Med/Pre-Dental, Reli Stu

MANHATTAN SCHOOL OF MUSIC (NY).................. msmnyc.edu **1100/1650/24**
Music

MANHATTANVILLE COLLEGE (NY) .... manhattanville.edu **1060/1590/23**
*Amer St, Art, Art Hist, Bus Admin, Drama, Econ, Ed, English, Hist, Music,
Poli Sci, Psych, Reli Stu, Soc*

MANNES SCHOOL OF MUSIC (NEW SCHOOL U.) (NY) mannes.edu **1100/1650/24**
Music

MANSFIELD UNIVERSITY OF PENNSYLVANIA (PA) mnsfld.edu **1000/1500/21**
Chem, Communic, Ed, English, For Lang, Geog, Hist, Music, Philo, Physics

MARIETTA COLLEGE (OH) .... marietta.edu **1085/1625/23**
Art, Bus Admin, Chem, Communic, Ed, Engine, English, Physics, Pre-Law

MARIST COLLEGE (NY) .... marist.edu **1160/1740/25**
Bio, Bus Admin, Chem, Comp Sci, Communic, Math, Poli Sci, Psych

MARQUETTE UNIVERSITY (WI) .... marquette.edu **1180/1770/26**
*Bio, Bus Admin, Chem, Communic, Comp Sci, Ed, English, Engine, Hist,
Math, Nurs, Philo, Poli Sci, Pre-Law, Pre-Med/Pre-Dental, Psych, Reli Stu*

MARSHALL UNIVERSITY (WV) .... marshall.edu **1050/1575/22**
Bus Admin, Chem, Communic, Econ, Ed, Math, Nurs, Psych

MARY BALDWIN COLLEGE (VA) .... mbc.edu **1025/1540/22**
Art, Bus Admin, Chem, Communic, Drama, English, Hist, Physics, Poli Sci, Psych, Soc

MARYGROVE COLLEGE (MI) .... marygrove.edu **1000/1500/21**
Comp Sci, Ed, English

MARYLAND INSTITUTE-COLLEGE OF ART (MD) ...... mica.edu **1140/1710/25**
Art

MARYLAND, UNIVERSITY OF (MD) .... maryland.edu **1260/1890/27**
*Ag, Amer St, Anthro, Arch, Astro, Bot, Bus Admin, Communic, Comp Sci, Econ, Ed, Engine,
English, For Lang, Geog, Hist, Music, Pharm, Philo, Physics, Poli Sci, Pre-Law, Soc, Zoo*

MARYLAND, UNIVERSITY OF (BALTIMORE COUNTY) (MD)umbc.edu **1230/1840/27**
*Amer St, Art, Chem, Classics, Comp Sci, Drama, Econ, Ed, Hist, Math, Nurs,
Physics, Poli Sci, Pre-Law, Pre-Med/Pre-Dental*

MARYMOUNT MANHATTAN COLLEGE (NY) .... mmm.edu **1040/1560/22**
Art, Communic, Drama, Psych

MARYMOUNT UNIVERSITY (VA) ....marymount.edu **1000/1500/21**
Nurs, Psych

MARYVILLE COLLEGE (TN) .... maryvillecollege.edu **1090/1635/24**
Bio, Chem, Hist, Music, Psych, Reli Stu

MARYVILLE UNIVERSITY-ST. LOUIS (MO) .... maryville.edu **1110/1650/24**
Art, Ed, Nurs

MARY WASHINGTON, UNIVERSITY OF (VA) ....umw.edu **1225/1840/27**
Amer St, Bio, Bus Admin, Chem, Classics, Comp Sci, Econ, English, Geog, Geol, Hist,
Math, Poli Sci, Pre-Med/Pre-Dental, Psych

MARYWOOD UNIVERSITY (PA) .... marywood.edu **1030/1540/22**
Arch, Art, Ed, Home Ec, Music, Psych, Reli Stu

MASSACHUSETTS, UNIVERSITY OF (MA) .... umass.edu **1110/1665/24**
Anthro, Astro, Bus Admin, Chem, Communic, Comp Sci, Econ, Engine, English, Forest,
Geol, Hist, Music, Nurs, Poli Sci, Pre-Law, Pre-Med/Pre-Dental, Psych, Zoo

MASSACHUSETTS, UNIVERSITY OF (BOSTON) (MA). umb.edu **1060/1590/23**
Amer St, Anthro, Bus Admin, Chem, Classics, English, Geog, Hist, Music, Nurs,
Philo, Physics, Poli Sci, Pre-Law, Psych, Soc

MASSACHUSETTS, UNIV. OF (DARTMOUTH) (MA) .... umassd.edu **1070/1605/23**
Art, Bus Admin, Chem, Engine, Nurs, Psych, Soc

MASSACHUSETTS, UNIV. OF (LOWELL) (MA) .... uml.edu **1080/1620/23**
Art, Art Hist, Bus Admin, Chem, Comp Sci, Engine, Math, Music, Nurs, Physics

MASSACHUSETTS COLLEGE OF ART (MA) .... massart.edu **1100/1650/24**
Art

MASSACHUSETTS COLL. OF LIBERAL ARTS (NO. ADAMS)(MA).. mcla.edu **1030/1545/22**
Bus Admin, Communic, Ed, English, Hist, Philo, Physics, Soc

MASSACHUSETTS COLLEGE OF PHARMACY (MA) .... mcp.edu **1040/1560/22**
Pharm

MASSACHUSETTS INSTITUTE OF TECHNOLOGY (MA) ... mit.edu **1480/2215/33**
Anthro, Arch, Astro, Biochem, Bio, Bus Admin, Chem, Comp Sci, Econ, Engine,
Geol, Hist, Math, Physics, Poli Sci, Pre-Law, Pre-Med/Pre-Dental

MASSACHUSETTS MARITIME ACADEMY (MA) .... mma.edu **1040/1560/22**
Engine

MASSACHUSETTS STATE COLLEGE SYSTEM (MA) **1020/1530/22**
Ed

MASTER'S COLLEGE, THE (CA) .... masters.edu **1130/1700/25**
Bus Admin, Communic, English, Home Ec, Music, Reli Stu

McDANIEL COLLEGE (MD) .... mcdaniel.edu **1130/1700/25**
Art Hist, Bio, Bio Chem, Bus Admin, Drama, Ed, English, Music, Physics,
Poli Sci, Pre-Med/Pre-Dental, Soc

McKENDREE COLLEGE (IL) .... mckendree.edu **1120/1680/24**
Bio, Chem, Comp Sci, Ed, English, Hist, Nurs

McMURRY UNIVERSITY (TX) .... mcm.edu **1000/1500/21**
Bus Admin, Chem, Hist, Nurs, Reli Stu

McPHERSON COLLEGE (KS) .... mcpherson.edu **1020/1530/22**
Art, Drama, Ed, Hist, Music

MEMPHIS COLLEGE OF ART (TN) .... mca.edu **1000/1500/21**
Art

MEMPHIS, UNIVERSITY OF (TN) .... memphis.edu **1070/1600/23**
Art, Communic, Ed, Engine, English, Music, Nurs

MERCER UNIVERSITY (GA) .... mercer.edu **1170/1755/26**
Bus Admin, Chem, Comp Sci, Econ, Ed, Engine, English, Music, Nurs, Pharm, Psych, Reli Stu

MERCY COLLEGE (NY) .... mercy.edu **1000/1500/21**
Ed, Nurs, Psych

MERCYHURST COLLEGE (PA) .... mercyhurst.edu **1060/1590/23**
Anthro, Art, Bus Admin, Chem, Ed, English, Poli Sci, Pre-Law, Reli Stu

MEREDITH COLLEGE (NC) .... meredith.edu **1050/1575/22**
Art, Bio, Bus Admin, Drama, English, Math, Music, Psych, Reli Stu

MERRIMACK COLLEGE (MA) .... merrimack.edu **1100/1665/24**
Bio, Bus Admin, Chem, English, Philo, Poli Sci, Psych, Reli Stu, Soc

MESSIAH COLLEGE (PA) .... messiah.edu **1190/1785/26**
Art, Bio, Bus Admin, Ed, Engine, English, Math, Philo, Reli Stu

MIAMI UNIVERSITY (OH) .... muohio.edu **1210/1810/27**
*Arch, Bot, Bus Admin, Comp Sci, Econ, Ed, Engine, English, Geog, Hist, Math,
Music, Physics, Poli Sci, Pre-Law, Pre-Med/Pre-Dental, Psych, Zoo*

MIAMI, UNIVERSITY OF (FL) .... miami.edu **1260/1890/28**
*Arch, Bio, Biochem, Bus Admin, Chem, Communic, Comp Sci, Drama, Ed, English,
Hist, Music, Nurs, Pre-Law, Pre-Med/Pre-Dental, Psych*

MICHIGAN, UNIVERSITY OF (MI) .... umich.edu **1320/1980/29**
*Amer St, Anthro, Arch, Art, Art Hist, Astro, Bot, Bus Admin, Chem, Classics, Communic,
Comp Sci, Drama, Econ, Ed, Engine, English, Forest, For Lang, Geog, Geol, Hist, Math, Music,
Nurs, Pharm, Philo, Physics, Poli Sci, Pre-Law, Pre-Med/Pre-Dental, Psych, Soc, Zoo*

MICHIGAN, UNIVERSITY OF (DEARBORN) (MI) .... umd.umich.edu **1090/1635/24**
*Bus Admin, Chem, Comp Sci, Econ, Engine, Hist, Math, Philo, Physics, Pre-Law,
Pre-Med/Pre-Dental*

MICHIGAN STATE UNIVERSITY (MI) .... msu.edu **1140/1710/25**
*Ag, Anthro, Biochem, Bio, Bot, Bus Admin, Chem, Communic, Econ, Ed, Engine, English,
Forest, Geog, Geol, Hist, Home Ec, Math, Music, Nurs, Philo, Physics, Poli Sci, Pre-Law,
Pre-Med/Pre-Dental, Psych, Soc, Zoo*

MICHIGAN TECHNOLOGICAL UNIVERSITY (MI) .... mtu.edu **1170/1755/26**
Bus Admin, Comp Sci, Engine, Forest, Geol, Math, Physics

MIDDLEBURY COLLEGE (VT) .... middlebury.edu **1400/2100/32**
*Art, Art Hist, Bio, Classics, Chem, Comp Sci, Drama, Econ, English, For Lang, Geog,
Hist, Math, Physics, Poli Sci, Pre-Law, Pre-Med/Pre-Dental, Reli Stu*

MIDDLE TENNESSEE STATE UNIVERSITY (TN) .... mtsu.edu **1050/1575/22**
Bio, Bus Admin, Chem, Ed, English, Hist, Math, Music, Nurs, Psych

MIDWESTERN STATE UNIVERSITY (TX) .... mwsu.edu **1000/1500/21**
Art, Comp Sci, Math, Nurs

MILLERSVILLE UNIV. OF PENNSYLVANIA (PA) ..... millersville.edu **1060/1590/23**
*Art, Bio, Bus Admin, Chem, Comp Sci, Econ, Ed, English, Hist, Math,
Poli Sci, Physics, Pre-Law, Psych, Soc*

MILLIGAN COLLEGE (TN) .... milligan.edu **1070/1600/23**
Bio, Bus Admin, Chem, Communic, Ed, Hist, Music, Nurs, Philo, Psych, Reli Stu

MILLIKIN UNIVERSITY (IL) .... millikin.edu **1080/1620/23**
Art, Drama, Ed, English, Music, Nurs

MILLS COLLEGE (CA) .... mills.edu **1110/1665/24**
Art, Art Hist, Communic, Ed, English, For Lang, Music, Psych

MILLSAPS COLLEGE (MS) .... millsaps.edu **1185/1775/26**
*Bio, Bus Admin, Chem, Classics, Comp Sci, Drama, Ed, English, Geol, Hist,
Math, Music, Poli Sci, Pre-Law, Pre-Med/Pre-Dental*

MILWAUKEE SCHOOL OF ENGINEERING (WI) .... msoe.edu **1185/1770/26**
Arch, Bus Admin, Engine, Nurs

MINNESOTA STATE UNIVERSITY (MANKATO) (MN) ... mnsu.edu **1020/1530/22**
Astro, Comp Sci, Drama, Engine

MINNESOTA STATE UNIVERSITY (MOORHEAD) (MN) mnstate.edu **1040/1560/22**
Anthro, Art, Bio, Ed, Math, Music, Physics, Psych

MINNESOTA, UNIVERSITY OF (MN) .... umn.edu **1200/1800/26**
*Ag, Amer St, Arch, Art Hist, Biochem, Bus Admin, Classics, Communic, Drama, Econ, Ed,
Engine, English, For Lang, Forest, Geog, Geol, Hist, Music, Nurs, Pharm, Philo, Poli Sci,
Pre-Law, Psych, Soc*

MINNESOTA, UNIVERSITY OF (DULUTH) (MN) ...... d.umn.edu **1070/1600/23**
Art, Bio, Communic, Comp Sci, Ed, Engine, Geol, Music, Pharm, Psych, Soc

MINNESOTA, UNIVERSITY OF (MORRIS) (MN) .... mrs.umn.edu **1120/1680/24**
*Art, Bio, Chem, Comp Sci, Ed, English, For Lang, Geol, Hist, Philo, Poli Sci,
Pre-Law, Pre Med/Pre-Dental, Psych*

COLLEGE MISERICORDIA (PA) .... miseri.edu **1010/1515/21**
Biochem, Bio, Bus Admin, Chem, Communic, Ed, English, Hist, Nurs

MISSISSIPPI COLLEGE (MS) ....mc.edu **1095/1645/24**
Art, Bus Admin, Comp Sci, Ed, Music, Nurs, Reli Stu

MISSISSIPPI STATE UNIVERSITY (MS) .... msstate.edu **1090/1635/24**
*Ag, Arch, Art, Biochem, Bus Admin, Comp Sci, Ed, Engine, Forest, Math,
Physics, Pre-Med/Pre-Dental, Soc*

MISSISSIPPI, UNIVERSITY OF (MS) .... olemiss.edu **1080/1620/23**
*Bus Admin, Classics, Communic, Econ, Ed, Engine, English, Hist, Pharm,
Physics, Pre-Law, Pre-Med/Pre-Dental*

MISSISSIPPI UNIVERSITY FOR WOMEN (MS) .... muw.edu **1090/1635/24**
Bus Admin, Communic, Ed, English, Nurs

MISSOURI BAPTIST UNIVERSITY (MO) .... mobap.edu **1000/1500/21**
Ed, Music

MISSOURI SOUTHERN STATE UNIVERSITY (MO) ..... mssc.edu **1030/1545/22**
Art, Bio, Bus Admin, Communic, Ed, English, Nurs

MISSOURI STATE UNIVERSITY (MO) .... missouristate.edu **1095/1645/24**
Classics, Communic, Comp Sci, Drama, Ed, Math, Poli Sci, Pre-Law, Soc

MISSOURI, UNIVERSITY OF (MO) .... missouri.edu **1140/1710/25**
Ag, Art Hist, Biochem, Bus Admin, Classics, Communic, Econ, Ed, Engine, English,
Forest, Hist, Music, Nurs, Philo, Poli Sci, Pre-Law, Pre-Med/Pre-Dental, Psych

MISSOURI, UNIVERSITY OF (KANSAS CITY) (MO) ... umkc.edu **1100/1650/24**
Art, Art Hist, Bio, Bus Admin, Chem, Communic, Comp Sci, Drama, Econ,
Ed, English, Hist, Music, Pharm, Psych

MISSOURI, UNIVERSITY OF (ROLLA) (MO) .... umr.edu **1230/1840/27**
Bio, Chem, Comp Sci, Engine, Hist, Physics

MISSOURI, UNIVERSITY OF (ST. LOUIS) .... umsl.edu **1080/1620/23**
Bus Admin, Chem, Communic, Ed, Nurs, Philo, Poli Sci, Psych

MOBILE, UNIVERSITY OF (AL) .... umobile.edu **1050/1575/23**
Bio, Bus Admin, Comp Sci, Ed, Music, Nurs

MOLLOY COLLEGE (NY) .... molloy.edu **1010/1515/21**
Nurs, Philo, Pre-Law, Psych

MONMOUTH COLLEGE (IL) .... monm.edu **1050/1575/22**
Biochem, Bio, Bus Admin, Chem, Drama, Econ, Ed, Hist, Pre-Med/Pre-Dental

MONMOUTH UNIVERSITY (NJ) .... monmouth.edu **1070/1600/23**
Art, Bus Admin, Communic, Comp Sci, Math, Music, Poli Sci

MONTANA TECH OF THE UNIV. OF MONTANA (MT) ... mtech.edu **1050/1575/22**
Bio, Chem, Comp Sci, Engine, Math, Nurs

MONTANA, UNIVERSITY OF (MT) .... umt.edu **1080/1620/23**
Astro, Bot, Bus Admin, Chem, Classics, Communic, Comp Sci, Drama, Ed, English,
Forest, Geol, Math, Music, Pharm, Poli Sci, Soc, Zoo

MONTANA STATE UNIVERSITY (BILLINGS) (MT) . msubillings.edu **1000/1500/21**
Art, Bus Admin, Ed, Math, Poli Sci, Soc

MONTANA STATE UNIVERSITY (BOZEMAN) (MT) . montana.edu **1090/1630/24**
Ag, Arch, Art, Bus Admin, Chem, Comp Sci, Econ, Engine, For Lang, Math, Nurs, Physics, Poli Sci

MONTCLAIR STATE (NJ) .... montclair.edu **1015/1520/21**
Art, Bus Admin, Classics, Ed, English, Home Ec, Math, Music, Psych

MONTEVALLO, UNIVERSITY OF (AL) .... montevallo.edu **1020/1530/22**
Art, Communic, Ed, English, Hist, Home Ec, Math, Music

MONTREAT COLLEGE (NC) .... montserrat.edu **1050/1570/22**
Bus Admin, Music, Reli Stu

MONTSERRAT COLLEGE OF ART (MA) .... montreat.edu **1000/1500/21**
Art

MOORE COLLEGE OF ART (PA) .... moore.edu **1000/1500/21**
Art, Art Hist

MORAVIAN COLLEGE (PA) .... moravian.edu **1140/1710/25**
Art, Biochem, Bus Admin, Communic, Comp Sci, Econ, Ed, Math, Music, Nurs,
Pre-Med/Pre-Dental, Psych, Soc

MOREHOUSE COLLEGE (GA) .... morehouse.edu **1080/1620/23**
Bus Admin, Comp Sci, English, Hist, Math, Poli Sci, Reli Stu, Soc

MORGAN STATE UNIVERSITY (MD) .... morgan.edu **1000/1500/21**
Arch, Bio, Engine, English, Hist

MORNINGSIDE COLLEGE (IA) .... morningside.edu **1050/1575/22**
Art, Bio, Bus Admin, Chem, Communic, Ed, Music, Nurs, Pre-Med/Pre-Dental, Psych

MOUNT HOLYOKE COLLEGE (MA) .... mtholyoke.edu **1290/1935/29**
Art Hist, Astro, Biochem, Bio, Chem, Comp Sci, Drama, Econ, English, For Lang, Geol,
Hist, Math, Music, Philo, Physics, Poli Sci, Pre-Law, Pre-Med/Pre-Dental, Psych, Reli Stu

MOUNT MARTY COLLEGE (SD) .... mtmc.edu **1040/1560/22**
Bus Admin

MOUNT MERCY COLLEGE (IA) .... mtmercy.edu **1050/1575/22**
Art, Bio, Bus Admin, Ed, English, Nurs, Philo, Soc

MOUNT ST. JOSEPH, COLLEGE OF (OH) .... msj.edu **1020/1530/22**
Art, Bio, Bus Admin, Chem, Comp Sci, Ed, English, Math, Music, Nurs,
Pre-Law, Pre-Med/Pre-Dental, Psych, Reli Stu, Soc

MOUNT ST. MARY'S COLLEGE (CA) .... msmc.la.edu **1055/1580/23**
Art, Bio, Bus Admin, Music, Nurs, Reli Stu

MOUNT ST. MARY'S UNIVERSITY (MD) .... msmary.edu **1080/1620/23**
Bus Admin, Ed, Hist, Philo, Poli Sci, Pre-Law, Pre-Med/Pre-Dental

MOUNT ST. MARY COLLEGE (NY) .... msmc.edu **1010/1515/21**
Comp Sci, Ed, Nurs

MOUNT SAINT VINCENT, COLLEGE OF (NY) . mountsaintvincent.edu **1000/1500/21**
Bio, Communic, Nurs, Pre-Law

MOUNT UNION COLLEGE (OH) .... muc.edu **1050/1575/22**
Bus Admin, Comp Sci, Ed, English, Music, Poli Sci

MUHLENBERG COLLEGE (PA) .... muhlenberg.edu **1225/1840/27**
Amer St, Art, Bio, Biochem, Bus Admin, Chem, Communic, Drama, Econ, English,
Hist, Math, Philo, Poli Sci, Pre-Law, Pre-Med/Pre-Dental, Psych, Reli Stu

MURRAY STATE UNIVERSITY (KY) .... murraystate.edu **1070/1600/23**
Ag, Art, Bio, Bus Admin, Chem, Communic, Comp Sci, Ed, English, Hist, Math, Music, Nurs

MUSEUM OF FINE ARTS, SCHOOL OF THE (MA) ..... smfa.edu **1070/1600/23**
Art

MUSKINGUM COLLEGE (OH) .... muskingum.edu   **1060/1590/23**
Bus Admin, Chem, Communic, Comp Sci, Ed, English, Geol, Hist, Music,
Physics, Poli Sci, Psych, Reli Stu

NAZARETH COLLEGE OF ROCHESTER (NY) .... naz.edu   **1135/1700/25**
Art, Bio, Bus Admin, Ed, English, For Lang, Math, Music, Nurs, Philo, Reli Stu

NEBRASKA, UNIVERSITY OF (NE) .... unl.edu   **1140/1710/25**
Ag, Arch, Astro, Biochem, Bus Admin, Classics, Communic, Econ, Ed, Engine,
For Lang, Hist, Home Ec, Music, Physics, Pre-Law

NEBRASKA, UNIVERSITY OF (KEARNEY) (NE) .... unk.edu   **1040/1560/22**
Art, Bus Admin, Econ, Ed

NEBRASKA, UNIVERSITY OF (OMAHA) (NE) ...... unomaha.edu   **1070/1600/23**
Bus Admin, Comp Sci, Econ, Ed, Poli Sci

NEBRASKA WESLEYAN UNIVERSITY (NE) .... nebrwesleyan.edu   **1130/1700/25**
Bio, Chem, Drama, Pre-Med/Pre-Dental, Psych

NEVADA, UNIVERSITY OF, AT:
       LAS VEGAS .... unlv.edu   **1020/1530/22**
       Anthro, Arch, Art, Bus Admin, Drama, Ed, Engine, English, Geol, Hist,
       Music, Nurs, Poli Sci, Psych, Soc
       RENO .... unr.edu   **1050/1575/22**
       Ag, Biochem, Bus Admin, Communic, Comp Sci, Ed, Engine, English,
       Geol, Home Ec, Music, Nurs, Physics, Poli Sci, Pre-Med/Pre-Dental, Soc

NEW COLLEGE OF FLORIDA (FL) .... ncf.edu   **1330/2000/30**
Anthro, Bio, Chem, English, Hist, Math, Philo, Physics, Pre-Law,
Pre-Med/Pre-Dental, Psych, Reli Stu, Soc

NEW ENGLAND CONSERVATORY (MA) newenglandconservatory.edu   **1100/1650/24**
Music

NEW HAMPSHIRE, UNIVERSITY OF (NH) .... unh.edu   **1110/1665/24**
Ag, Bio, Bus Admin, Chem, Communic, Comp Sci, Drama, Ed, Engine, English, For Lang,
Forest, Home Ec, Hist, Music, Nurs, Philo, Physics, Pre-Law, Pre-Med/Pre-Dental, Psych, Zoo

NEW JERSEY, COLLEGE OF (NJ) .... tcnj.edu   **1240/1860/28**
Art, Bus Admin, Chem, Cmp Sci, Ed, Engine, English, Hist, Math,
Nurs, Physics, Pre-Law, Pre-Med/Pre-Dental, Psych, Soc

NEW JERSEY INSTITUTE OF TECHNOLOGY (NJ) .... njit.edu   **1150/1725/25**
Arch, Chem, Comp Sci, Engine, Math

NEWMAN UNIVERSITY (KS) .... newmanu.edu   **1060/1600/23**
Bus Admin, Math, Nurs, Psych, Reli Stu

NEW MEXICO INST. OF MINING & TECHNOLOGY (NM) .. nmt.edu   **1160/1740/25**
Chem, Comp Sci, Engine, Geol, Math, Physics

NEW MEXICO STATE UNIVERSITY (NM) .... nmsu.edu   **1000/1500/21**
Ag, Anthro, Bio, Bus Admin, Chem, Comp Sci, Ed, Engine, English, Geol,
Hist, Home Ec, Math, Music, Nurs, Poli Sci

NEW MEXICO, UNIVERSITY OF (NM) .... unm.edu **1050/1575/22**
Amer St, Anthro, Art, Bio, Bus Admin, Comp Sci, Drama, Econ, Ed, Engine,
For Lang, Geol, Hist, Nurs, Pharm, Pre-Med/Pre-Dental, Psych, Soc

NEW ORLEANS, UNIVERSITY OF (LA) .... uno.edu **1050/1575/22**
Bus Admin, Ed, English, Engine, Geog, Hist, Physics, Poli Sci, Soc

NEW SCHOOL UNIV. (EUGENE LANG COLL.) (NY) .. newschool.edu **1200/1800/26**
Drama, Ed, English, Philo, Psych

NEW YORK, CITY UNIVERSITY OF, AT
    BARUCH COLLEGE .... baruch.cuny.edu **1060/1590/23**
    Bus Admin, Comp Sci, Econ, English, Hist
    BROOKLYN COLLEGE .... brooklyn.cuny.edu **1010/1515/22**
    Bio, Chem, Classics, Comp Sci, Drama, Ed, Geol, Music, Philo,
    Physics, Pre-Med/Pre-Dental, Psych
    CITY COLLEGE .... ccny.cuny.edu **1000/1500/21**
    Anthro, Arch, Art Hist, Chem, Ed, Econ, Engine, English, Hist, Math,
    Philo, Physics, Poli Sci, Pre-Law, Pre-Med/Pre-Dental, Soc
    HERBERT LEHMAN COLLEGE .... lehmman.cuny.edu **1000/1500/21**
    Ed, English, For Lang, Math, Nurs, Philo, Psych, Soc
    HUNTER COLLEGE .... hunter.cuny.edu **1020/1530/22**
    Anthro, Art, Art Hist, Bio, Chem, Classics, Communic, Comp Sci, Drama, Ed,
    English, For Lang, Geog, Nurs, Poli Sci, Pre-Law, Psych, Soc
    JOHN JAY COLL. OF CRIMINAL JUSTICE . jjay.cuny.edu **1000/1500/21**
    Poli Sci, Psych
    QUEENS COLLEGE .... qc.edu **1040/1560/22**
    Amer St, Anthro, Art Hist, Chem, Comp Sci, Econ, Ed, English, Music,
    Philo, Poli Sci, Psych, Soc
    STATEN ISLAND .... csi.cuny.edu **1050/1575/22**
    Psych

NEW YORK INSTITUTE OF TECHNOLOGY (NY) .... nyit.edu **1130/1700/25**
Arch, Comp Sci, Engine

NEW YORK, STATE UNIVERSITY OF, AT
    ALBANY .... albany.edu **1140/1710/25**
    Anthro, Art, Art Hist, Bio, Bus Admin, Chem, Comp Sci, Econ, English, For Lang,
    Geol, Hist, Math, Philo, Physics, Poli Sci, Pre-Law, Pre-Med/Pre-Dental, Psych, Soc
    BINGHAMTON .... binghamton.edu **1270/1900/28**
    Anthro, Art, Art Hist, Bio, Biochem, Bus Admin, Chem, Comp Sci, Drama,
    Econ, Engine, English, For Lang, Geol, Hist, Math, Music, Nurs, Philo,
    Physics, Poli Sci, Pre-Law, Pre-Med/Pre-Dental, Psych, Soc
    BROCKPORT, COLLEGE AT .... brockport.edu **1080/1620/23**
    Bus Admin, Chem, Communic, Comp Sci, Drama, Ed, English, Geol,
    Hist, Nurs, Poli Sci, Pre-Law, Psych
    BUFFALO .... buffalo.edu **1170/1755/26**
    Amer St, Anthro, Arch, Art, Bio, Bus Admin, Chem, Classics, Comp Sci,
    Drama, Ed, Engine, English, Geog, Hist, Math, Music, Nurs, Pharm,
    Physics, Pre-Law, Pre-Med/Pre-Dental, Psych
    FREDONIA, COLLEGE AT .... fredonia.edu **1100/1650/24**
    Amer St, Art, Bus Admin, Communic, Drama, Ed, English, Hist, Music
    GENESEO, COLLEGE AT .... geneseo.edu **1280/1920/29**
    Bio, Biochem, Bus Admin, Ed, English, Geol, Hist, Math, Music, Philo,
    Physics, Pre-Med/Pre-Dental, Soc

NEW YORK, STATE UNIVERSITY OF, AT *(Continued)*

        MARITIME COLLEGE .... sunymaritime.edu   **1080/1620/23**
        Engine
        NEW PALTZ, COLLEGE AT .... newpaltz.edu   **1130/1700/25**
        Art Hist, Bus Admin, Communic, Ed, Engine, English, For Lang, Geog, Philo, Psych
        ONEONTA, COLLEGE AT ....oneonta.edu   **1120/1680/24**
        Econ, Ed, English, Geog, Geol, Hist, Home Ec, Music, Philo, Physics, Pre-Law
        OSWEGO, COLLEGE AT .... oswego.edu   **1090/1635/24**
        Bio, Bus Admin, Communic, Comp Sci, Ed, English, Hist, Poli Sci, Pre-Law, Psych, Zoo
        PLATTSBURGH, COLLEGE AT .... plattsburgh.edu   **1060/1590/23**
        Anthro, Art, Bus Admin, Communic, Ed, Geol, Hist, Nurs, Psych
        POTSDAM, COLLEGE AT ....potsdam.edu   **1060/1590/23**
        Anthro, Art, Bus Admin, Comp Sci, Ed, Math, Music, Psych
        PURCHASE, COLLEGE AT.......................... purchase.edu   **1090/1640/24**
        Art, Communic, Drama, English, Hist, Music, Philo, Poli Sci,
        Pre-Law, Pre-Med/Pre-Dental, Psych
        STONY BROOK .... sunysb.edu   **1150/1725/25**
        Anthro, Art Hist, Astro, Biochem, Bio, Chem, Comp Sci, Engine, English, For Lang, Geol,
        Hist, Music, Philo, Physics, Poli Sci, Pre-Law, Pre-Med/Pre-Dental, Psych, Reli Stu, Soc

NEW YORK UNIVERSITY (NY).....................................nyu.edu   **1340/2000/30**
Anthro, Art, Art Hist, Bus Admin, Classics, Communic, Comp Sci, Drama,
Econ, For Lang, Hist, Math, Music, Nurs, Philo, Physics, Pre-Med/Pre-Dental, Psych

NIAGARA UNIVERSITY (NY) .... niagara.edu   **1050/1575/22**
Bus Admin, Drama, Ed, English, Pre-Law, Reli Stu

NICHOLLS STATE UNIVERSITY (LA) .... nicholls.edu   **1000/1500/21**
Art, Bio, Bus Admin, Chem, Ed, English, Home Ec, Nurs, Pre-Med/Pre-Dental

NORTH CAROLINA SCHOOL OF THE ARTS (NC) ......ncarts.edu   **1130/1700/25**
Drama, Music

NORTH CAROLINA, UNIVERSITY OF, AT

        ASHEVILLE .... unca.edu   **1160/1740/25**
        Art, Classics, Ed, Hist, Psych, Soc
        CHAPEL HILL .... unc.edu   **1300/1950/29**
        Amer St, Anthro, Art Hist, Bio, Bot, Bus Admin, Chem, Classics, Communic, Drama, Ed,
        English, For Lang, Hist, Nurs, Pharm, Poli Sci, Pre-Law, Pre-Med/Pre-Dental, Reli Stu, Soc
        CHARLOTTE .... uncc.edu   **1060/1590/23**
        Bus Admin, Chem, Engine, For Lang, Geog, Nurs, Poli Sci, Pre-Law,
        Pre-Med/Pre-Dental, Psych, Reli Stu
        GREENSBORO .... uncg.edu   **1040/1560/22**
        Art, Bus Admin, Classics, Communic, Comp Sci, Drama, Ed, Hist,
        Home Ec, Music, Nurs, Psych
        PEMBROKE .... uncp.edu   **1000/1500/21**
        Art, Bio, Bus Admin, Communic, Soc
        WILMINGTON .... uncwil.edu   **1160/1740/25**
        Bio, Bus Admin, Chem, English, Geol, Nurs, Pre-Law, Psych, Soc

NORTH CAROLINA STATE UNIVERSITY (NC) .... ncsu.edu   **1200/1800/26**
Ag, Arch, Astro, Bot, Chem, Comp Sci, Econ, Ed, Engine, English, Forest,
Math, Physics, Pre-Law, Psych, Zoo

NORTH CENTRAL COLLEGE (IL) .... noctrl.edu   **1130/1700/25**
Bio, Bus Admin, Chem, Communic, Comp Sci, English, Poli Sci, Pre-Law,
Pre-Med/Pre-Dental, Zoo

NORTH DAKOTA STATE UNIVERSITY (ND) .... ndsu.edu **1080/1620/23**
Ag, Arch, Chem, Ed, Engine, Home Ec, Math, Pharm

NORTH DAKOTA, UNIVERSITY OF (ND) .... und.edu **1070/1600/23**
Art, Bio, Bus Admin, Chem, Communic, Comp Sci, Ed, Engine, English, Math, Nurs

NORTH FLORIDA, UNIVERSITY OF (FL) .... unf.edu **1100/1650/24**
Bus Admin, Communic, Comp Sci, Ed, Engine, Math, Music, Nurs

NORTH GEORGIA COLLEGE & STATE UNIV. (GA) .. ngcsu.edu **1080/1620/23**
Bio, Bus Admin, Ed

NORTH TEXAS, UNIVERSITY OF (TX) .... unt.edu **1110/1665/24**
Art, Bus Admin, Communic, Ed, English, Music, Poli Sci, Soc

NORTHEASTERN ILLINOIS UNIVERSITY (IL) .... neiu.edu **1000/1500/21**
Comp Sci, Ed, English, Philo

NORTHEASTERN STATE UNIVERSITY (OK) .... nsuok.edu **1000/1500/21**
Ed, English, Math, Psych

NORTHEASTERN UNIVERSITY (MA) .... neu.edu **1220/1830/27**
Arch, Bus Admin, Chem, Communic, Comp Sci, Engine, English, Hist, Math,
Pharm, Philo, Physics, Psych

NORTHERN ARIZONA (AZ) .... nau.edu **1050/1575/22**
Art, Astro, Bot, Bus Admin, Ed, Forest, Geol, Nurs, Poli Sci, Psych

NORTHERN COLORADO, UNIVERSITY OF .... unco.edu **1040/1560/22**
Bus Admin, Econ, Ed, English, Hist, Math, Music, Nurs, Psych, Soc

NORTHERN ILLINOIS UNIVERSITY (IL) .... niu.edu **1050/1575/22**
Art, Bio, Biochem, Bus Admin, Chem, Communic, Ed, Engine, Hist, Home Ec,
Geol, Math, Music, Nurs, Physics, Philo

NORTHERN IOWA, UNIVERSITY OF (IA) .... uni.edu **1080/1620/23**
Art, Bus Admin, Ed, Psych

NORTHERN KENTUCKY UNIVERSITY (KY) .... nku.edu **1000/1500/21**
Bus Admin, Chem, Communic, Drama, Ed, English, Math, Music

NORTHERN MICHIGAN UNIVERSITY (MI) .... nmu.edu **1070/1600/23**
Art, Bio, Bus Admin, Chem, Comp Sci, Econ, Ed, English, Math, Nurs, Physics, Soc

NORTHERN STATE UNIVERSITY (SD) .... northern.edu **1040/1560/22**
Ed

NORTHLAND COLLEGE (WI) ....northland.edu **1130/1695/25**
Bio, Geol, Pre-Law, Reli Stu, Soc

NORTHWEST MISSOURI STATE UNIVERSITY (MO) nwmissouri.edu **1055/1580/23**
Ag, Communic

NORTHWESTERN COLLEGE (IA) .... nwciowa.edu **1120/1680/24**
Bio, Bus Admin, Chem, Comp Sci, Drama, Ed, English, For Lang, Hist, Music, Philo,
Physics, Psych, Reli Stu

NORTHWESTERN COLLEGE (MN) .... nwc.edu **1100/1660/24**
Art, Bus Admin, Ed, English, Hist, Music, Psych, Reli Stu

NORTHWESTERN STATE UNIV. OF LOUISIANA (LA) .... nsula.edu **1000/1500/21**
Bus Admin, Comp Sci, Ed, Hist, Home Ec, Math, Music, Nurs, Pharm

NORTHWESTERN UNIVERSITY (IL) .... northwestern.edu **1430/2145/32**
Amer Stu, Anthro, Astro, Chem, Classics, Communic, Drama, Econ, Engine, English,
For Lang, Hist, Math, Music, Physics, Poli Sci, Pre-Law, Pre-Med/Pre-Dental, Psych, Reli Stu, Soc

NORTHWOOD UNIVERSITY (MI) .... northwood.edu **1000/1500/21**
Bus Admin, Econ

NORWICH UNIVERSITY (VT) .... norwich.edu **1030/1550/22**
Arch, Bio, Engine, Math

NOTRE DAME, UNIVERSITY OF (IN) .... nd.edu **1370/2055/31**
Anthro, Arch, Bio, Bus Admin, Chem, Classics, Engine, English, For Lang, Hist,
Math, Philo, Physics, Poli Sci, Pre-Med/Pre-Dental, Pre-Law, Psych, Reli Stu, Soc

NOVA SOUTHEASTERN UNIVERSITY (FL) .... nova.edu **1010/1515/21**
Bus Admin, Ed, Pharm, Pre-Med/Pre-Dental

NYACK COLLEGE (NY) .... nyackcollege.edu **1000/1500/21**
Bus Admin, Ed, English, Music, Psych, Reli Stu

OAKLAND CITY UNIVERSITY (IN) .... oak.edu **1000/1500/21**
Bus Admin, Ed, Music, Psych, Reli Stu

OAKLAND UNIVERSITY (MI) .... oakland.edu **1040/1560/22**
Art Hist, Bus Admin, Chem, Communic, Comp Sci, Econ, Ed, Engine, Math, Physics, Nurs

OBERLIN COLLEGE (OH) .... oberlin.edu **1350/2030/30**
Art Hist, Bio, Chem, Classics, Drama, Econ, English, Geol, Hist, Math, Music,
Philo, Physics, Poli Sci, Pre-Law, Pre-Med/Pre-Dental, Reli Stu, Soc

OCCIDENTAL COLLEGE (CA) .... oxy.edu **1280/1920/29**
Bio, Chem, Drama, Econ, English, Ed, Math, Physics, Poli Sci, Pre-Law,
Pre-Med/Pre-Dental, Psych, Reli Stu

OGLETHORPE UNIVERSITY (GA) .... ogelthorpe.edu **1150/1725/25**
Bio, Bus Admin, Econ, English, Hist, Poli Sci, Pre-Law, Pre-Med/Pre-Dental

OHIO NORTHERN UNIVERSITY (OH) .... onu.edu **1140/1710/25**
Bio, Biochem, Bus Admin, Chem, Ed, Engine, Math, Nurs, Pharm

OHIO STATE UNIVERSITY (OH) .... osu.edu **1200/1800/26**
Ag, Arch, Art, Astro, Biochem, Bus Admin, Chem, Classics, Communic, Comp Sci,
Drama, Econ, Ed, Engine, English, For Lang, Geog, Geol, Hist, Math, Music, Nurs,
Pharm, Philo, Physics, Poli Sci, Pre-Law, Pre-Med/Pre-Dental, Psych

OHIO UNIVERSITY (OH) .... ohio.edu **1100/1650/24**
Art, Art Hist, Bot, Bus Admin, Classics, Communic, Comp Sci, Drama, Ed,
Engine, English, Hist, Math, Music, Nurs, Physics, Pre-Law, Psych, Soc, Zoo

OHIO WESLEYAN UNIVERSITY (OH) .... owu.edu **1210/1820/27**
Bio, Bot, Chem, Communic, Econ, Ed, English, Poli Sci, Pre-Med/Pre-Dental,
Pre-Law, Psych, Zoo

OKLAHOMA BAPTIST UNIVERSITY (OK) .... okbu.edu **1120/1680/24**
Ed, English, Hist, Music, Nurs, Philo, Psych, Reli Stu

OKLAHOMA CHRISTIAN UNIVERSITY (OK) .... oc.edu **1100/1650/24**
Bio, Comp Sci, Ed, English, Reli Stu

OKLAHOMA CITY UNIVERSITY (OK) .... okcu.edu **1130/1700/25**
*Bio, Bus Admin, Communic, Comp Sci, Drama, English, Hist, Music, Nurs,
Poli Sci, Pre-Law, Psych, Reli Stu*

OKLAHOMA, UNIVERSITY OF (OK) .... ou.edu **1150/1725/25**
*Anthro, Arch, Astro, Bot, Bus Admin, Chem, Classics, Communic, Comp Sci, Drama, Econ,
Ed, Engine, English, Geog, Geol, Hist, Math, Pharm, Poli Sci, Pre-Law, Psych, Zoo*

OKLAHOMA STATE UNIVERSITY (OK) .... okstate.edu **1130/1700/25**
*Ag, Arch, Biochem, Bio, Botany, Bus Admin, Drama, Ed, Engine, English, Forest,
Geog, Geol, Hist, Home Ec, Math, Music, Physics, Poli Sci, Psych, Soc, Zoo*

OLD DOMINION UNIVERSITY (VA) .... odu.edu **1050/1575/22**
Art, Bus Admin, Comp Sci, Econ, Ed, Engine, Hist, Nurs, Physics, Soc

OLIN COLLEGE OF ENGINEERING (MA) .... olin.edu **1490/2220/34**
Engine

OLIVET NAZARENE UNIVERSITY (IL) .... olivet.edu **1100/1650/24**
Ed, English, Geol, Music, Nurs, Reli Stu

ORAL ROBERTS UNIVERSITY (OK) .... oru.edu **1060/1590/23**
Bus Admin, Chem, Ed, Music, Nurs, Reli Stu

OREGON, UNIVERSITY OF (OR) .... uoregon.edu **1105/1660/24**
*Anthro, Arch, Art, Art Hist, Bio, Bus Admin, Chem, Communic, Comp Sci, Econ, Ed,
English, For Lang, Geog, Math, Music, Poli Sci, Pre-Law, Pre-Med/Pre-Dental, Psych, Soc*

OREGON INSTITUTE OF TECHNOLOGY (OR) .... oit.edu **1030/1545/22**
Bus Admin, Engine

OREGON STATE UNIVERSITY (OR) .... orst.edu **1090/1635/24**
*Ag, Biochem, Bot, Comp Sci, Econ, Engine, Forest, Geol, Hist, Home Ec,
Math, Philo, Physics, Soc, Zoo*

OTIS ART INSTITUTE (CA) .... otis.edu **1020/1530/22**
Art

OTTERBEIN COLLEGE (OH) .... otterbein.edu **1080/1620/23**
Art, Chem, Drama, Ed, English, Math, Music, Nurs, Psych

OUACHITA BAPTIST UNIVERSITY (AR) .... obu.edu **1090/1630/24**
Chem, Ed, Music, Reli Stu

OZARKS, COLLEGE OF THE (MO) .... cofo.edu **1050/1575/22**
Ag, Art, Bus Admin, Comp Sci, Ed, Hist, Math, Philo, Physics, Psych

PACE UNIVERSITY (NY) .... pace.edu **1080/1620/23**
Bus Admin, Comp Sci, Drama, Ed, English, Nurs, Poli Sci, Psych, Soc

PACIFIC LUTHERAN UNIVERSITY (WA) .... plu.edu   **1110/1665/24**
Anthro, Bio, Bus Admin, Chem, Comp Sci, Ed, English, Music, Nurs, Pre-Med/Pre-Dental, Reli Stu

PACIFIC UNIVERSITY (OR) .... pacificu.edu   **1100/1650/24**
Art, Bio, Bus Admin, Comp Sci, English, For Lang, Physics, Pre-Med/Pre-Dental

PACIFIC, UNIVERSITY OF THE (CA) .... uop.edu   **1170/1755/26**
Art, Bus Admin, Chem, Ed, Engine, Math, Music, Pharm, Poli Sci, Pre-Med/Pre-Dental

PALM BEACH ATLANTIC UNIVERSITY (FL) .... pba.edu   **1070/1610/23**
Bus Admin, Ed, Pharm, Psych, Reli Stu

PARSONS SCHOOL OF DESIGN (NY) .... parsons.edu   **1080/1620/23**
Arch, Art

PAUL SMITH'S COLLEGE (NY) .... paulsmiths.edu   **1000/1500/21**
Forest

PENNSYLVANIA ACAD. OF THE FINE ARTS (PA) ..... pafa.edu   **1000/1500/21**
Art

PENNSYLVANIA, UNIVERSITY OF (PA) .... upenn.edu   **1410/2115/32**
Amer St, Anthro, Art, Art Hist, Astro, Biochem, Bus Admin, Classics, Econ, Engine, English, For Lang, Geol, Hist, Math, Nurs, Philo, Physics, Poli Sci, Pre-Law, Psych, Reli Stu, Soc

PENNSYLVANIA STATE UNIV. (ERIE)(PA) .... pserie.psu.edu   **1080/1620/23**
Bio, Bus Admin, Chem, English, Math, Physics

PENNSYLVANIA STATE UNIV. (HARRISBURG)(PA) hbg.psu.edu   **1060/1590/23**
Comp Sci, Engine, Psych

PENNSYLVANIA STATE UNIVERSITY (PA) .... psu.edu   **1200/1800/26**
Ag, Arch, Astro, Biochem, Bot, Bus Admin, Chem, Communic, Comp Sci, Drama, Econ, Ed, Engine, Forest, Geog, Geol, Hist, Home Ec, Music, Nurs, Physics, Poli Sci, Pre-Law, Pre-Med/Pre-Dental, Psych, Soc, Zoo

PEPPERDINE UNIVERSITY (CA) .... pepperdine.edu   **1240/1860/28**
Art, Bio, Bus Admin, Communic, Comp Sci, For Lang

PERU STATE COLLEGE (NE) .... peru.edu   **1000/1500/21**
Art, Bus Admin, Ed, Music, Psych

PHILADELPHIA BIBLICAL UNIVERSITY (PA) .... pbu.edu   **1070/1600/23**
Ed, Music, Reli Stu

PHILADELPHIA UNIVERSITY (PA) .... philau.edu   **1070/1600/23**
Arch, Bus Admin

PIEDMONT COLLEGE (GA) .... piedmont.edu   **1100/1650/24**
Ed, Soc

PINE MANOR COLLEGE (MA) .... pmc.edu   **1000/1500/21**
Amer St, Art, Bio, Bus Admin, Communic, Poli Sci, Psych

PITTSBURG STATE UNIVERSITY (KS) .... pittstate.edu   **1030/1550/22**
Bio, Bus Admin, Ed, English, Music, Nurs

PITTSBURGH, UNIVERSITY OF (PA) .... pitt.edu **1250/1875/28**
Anthro, Art Hist, Astro, Biochem, Bus Admin, Chem, Classics, Communic, Comp Sci,
Econ, Ed, Engine, English, For Lang, Hist, Math, Nurs, Pharm, Philo, Physics, Poli Sci,
Pre-Law, Pre-Med/Pre-Dental, Psych, Reli Stu

PITTSBURGH, UNIV. OF (BRADFORD) (PA) ....upb.pitt.edu **1000/1500/21**
Bio, Comp Sci, Math, Nurs, Soc

PITTSBURGH, UNIV. OF (GREENSBURG) (PA) ...... upg.pitt.edu **1030/1545/22**
Anthro, Bus Admin, English, Hist, Poli Sci, Psych

PITTSBURGH, UNIV. OF (JOHNSTOWN) (PA) .... upj.pitt.edu **1030/1545/22**
Bus Admin, Chem, Comp Sci, Ed, Engine, Math

PITZER COLLEGE (CA) .... pitzer.edu **1260/1890/28**
Anthro, Bio, Chem, English, Hist, Pre-Law, Pre-Med/Pre-Dental, Psych, Soc

PLYMOUTH STATE COLLEGE (NH) .... plymouth.edu **1000/1500/21**
Art, Comp Sci, Drama, Ed, English, Math

POINT LOMA NAZARENE UNIVERSITY (CA) ....ptloma.edu **1130/1700/25**
Bus Admin, Ed, Home Ec, Music, Nurs, Pre-Med/Pre-Dental

POINT PARK UNIVERSITY (PA) ....pointpark.edu **1020/1530/22**
Bio, Communic, Drama, Ed, English, Psych

POLYTECHNIC UNIVERSITY OF NEW YORK (NY) ...... poly.edu **1200/1800/26**
Comp Sci, Engine

POMONA COLLEGE (CA) ....pomona.edu **1450/2175/32**
Amer St, Anthro, Art Hist, Bio, Chem, Communic, Drama, Econ, English, For Lang, Geol, Hist,
Math, Music, Philo, Physics, Poli Sci, Pre-Law, Pre-Med/Pre-Dental, Psych, Reli Stu, Soc

PORTLAND STATE UNIVERSITY (OR) .... pdx.edu **1030/1550/22**
Art, Bus Admin, Comp Sci, Engine, English, For Lang, Music, Pre-Law, Psych, Soc

PORTLAND, UNIVERSITY OF (OR) .... up.edu **1180/1770/26**
Bus Admin, Chem, Ed, Engine, Hist, Math, Nurs, Philo, Poli Sci, Reli Stu

PRATT INSTITUTE (NY) .... pratt.edu **1130/1700/25**
Arch, Art

PRESBYTERIAN COLLEGE (SC) .... presby.edu **1140/1710/25**
Bio, Bus Admin, English, Hist, Physics, Poli Sci, Pre-Law, Pre-Med/Pre-Dental, Reli Stu

PRESENTATION COLLEGE (SD) .... presentation.edu **1000/1500/21**
Bus Admin, Nurs

PRINCETON UNIVERSITY (NJ) ....princeton.edu **1460/2190/33**
Anthro, Arch, Art Hist, Bio, Biochem, Chem, Classics, Comp Sci, Drama, Econ,
Engine, English, For Lang, Geol, Hist, Math, Music, Philo, Physics, Poli Sci,
Pre-Law, Pre-Med/Pre-Dental, Psych, Reli Stu, Soc

PRINCIPIA COLLEGE (IL) .... prin.edu/college **1160/1740/25**
Art, Bus Admin, Comp Sci, Ed, English, Math, Philo, Pre-Law, Soc

PROVIDENCE COLLEGE (RI) .... providence.edu **1210/1815/27**
Bio, Bus Admin, Chem, Econ, Ed, English, Hist, Math, Philo, Poli Sci, Pre-Law, Pre-Med/Pre-Dental, Reli Stu

PUERTO RICO, UNIV. OF (PR) .... upr.clu.edu **1100/1650/24**
Bus Admin, Econ, Ed, Psych

PUERTO RICO, UNIV. OF (CAYEY) (PR) ..... wwwcuc.upr.clu.edu **1000/1500/21**
Bio, Bus Admin, Chem, Ed

PUERTO RICO, UNIV. OF (MAYAGUEZ) (PR) .... uprm.edu **1170/1750/26**
Ag, Chem, Engine, For Lang, Math, Physics

PUGET SOUND, UNIVERSITY OF (WA) .... ups.edu **1250/1875/28**
Art, Bio, Bus Admin, Chem, Classics, Econ, English, Music, Poli Sci, Pre-Law, Pre-Med/Pre-Dental, Soc

PURDUE UNIVERSITY (IN) .... purdue.edu **1140/1710/25**
Ag, Biochem, Bot, Bus Admin, Chem, Comp Sci, Engine, Forest, Geol, Home Ec, Math, Nurs, Pharm, Soc

QUEENS UNIVERSITY OF CHARLOTTE (NC) .... queens.edu **1100/1650/24**
Amer St, Bus Admin, English, Hist, Music, Pre-Law

QUINCY UNIVERSITY (IL) .... quincy.edu **1050/1575/22**
Bus Admin, Hist, Nurs, Reli Stu

QUINNIPIAC UNIVERSITY (CT) .... quinnipiac.edu **1160/1740/25**
Bus Admin, Communic, Comp Sci, Nurs, Psych, Soc

RADFORD UNIVERSITY (VA) .... radford.edu **1000/1500/21**
Art Hist, Bus Admin, Ed, English, Geog, Math, Pre-Law, Psych

RAMAPO COLLEGE OF NEW JERSEY (NJ) .... ramapo.edu **1180/1770/26**
Amer St, Biochem, Bus Admin, Communic, Comp Sci, English, Hist, Math, Physics, Poli Sci, Psych

RANDOLPH COLLEGE (VA) .... randolphcollege.edu **1170/1755/26**
Amer St, Art, Bio, Chem, Classics, Communic, English, Poli Sci, Pre-Law, Pre-Med/Pre-Dental, Psych

RANDOLPH-MACON COLLEGE (VA) .... rmc.edu **1115/1675/24**
Bio, Classics, Econ, English, For Lang, Hist, Pre-Law, Pre-Med/Pre-Dental, Psych, Soc

REDLANDS, UNIVERSITY OF (CA) .... redlands.edu **1180/1770/26**
Art, Bus Admin, Econ, Ed, English, Music, Philo, Poli Sci, Pre-Law, Pre-Med/Pre-Dental

REED COLLEGE (OR) .... reed.edu **1380/2070/31**
Amer St, Anthro, Art Hist, Bio, Chem, Classics, Econ, English, For Lang, Hist, Math, Philo, Physics, Pre-Law, Pre-Med/Pre-Dental, Psych

REGIS COLLEGE (MA) .... regiscollege.edu **1000/1500/21**
Biochem, Communic, English, Nurs, Poli Sci

REGIS UNIVERSITY (CO) .... regis.edu **1080/1620/23**
Bus Admin, Communic, Comp Sci, Ed, Hist, Nurs, Philo, Poli Sci, Pre-Med/Pre-Dental, Psych, Reli Stu, Soc

REINHARDT COLLEGE (GA) .... reinhardt.edu **1000/1500/21**
Bio, Bus Admin, Communic, Ed, Hist, Music

RENSSELAER POLYTECHNIC INSTITUTE (NY) .... rpi.edu **1335/2005/30**
Arch, Bio, Bus Admin, Chem, Communic, Comp Sci, Econ, Engine, Geol, Math, Physics

RHODE ISLAND COLLEGE (RI) .... ric.edu **1000/1500/21**
Bio, Econ, Ed, Hist, Math, Music, Nurs, Philo, Psych

RHODE ISLAND SCHOOL OF DESIGN (RI) .... risd.edu **1190/1785/26**
Arch, Art

RHODE ISLAND, UNIVERSITY OF (RI) .... uri.edu **1100/1650/24**
*Anthro, Bio, Bus Admin, Communic, Comp Sci, Econ, Engine, English, Geol,
Home Ec, Math, Music, Nurs, Pharm, Physics, Poli Sci, Pre-Law, Psych*

RHODES COLLEGE (TN) .... rhodes.edu **1280/1920/28**
*Art, Bio, Bus Admin, Chem, Classics, Econ, English, For Lang, Hist, Math,
Music, Philo, Physics, Poli Sci, Pre-Law, Pre-Med/Pre-Dental, Psych, Reli Stu*

RICE UNIVERSITY (TX) .... rice.edu **1430/2145/32**
*Anthro, Arch, Biochem, Bio, Chem, Comp Sci, Econ, Engine, English, Hist,
Math, Music, Physics, Poli Sci, Pre-Law, Pre-Med/Pre-Dental*

RICHARD STOCKTON COLL. OF NEW JERSEY (NJ) .. stockton.edu **1132/1700/25**
*Bus Admin, Chem, Comp Sci, Econ, Hist, Math, Philo, Physics, Poli Sci,
Pre-Med/Pre-Dental, Psych*

RICHMOND, UNIVERSITY OF (VA) .... richmond.edu **1300/1950/29**
*Bio, Bus Admin, Chem, Comp Sci, English, Hist, Math, Philo, Poli Sci,
Pre-Law, Pre-Med/Pre-Dental, Reli Stu*

RIDER UNIVERSITY (NJ) .... rider.edu **1040/1560/22**
*Amer St, Bio, Bus Admin, Chem, Communic, Comp Sci, Ed, Hist, Math,
Music, Poli Sci, Pre-Med/Pre-Dental*

RIPON COLLEGE (WI) .... ripon.edu **1120/1680/24**
*Anthro, Bio, Biochem, Bus Admin, Chem, Econ, Ed, English, Hist, Math,
Poli Sci, Pre-Law, Pre-Med/Pre-Dental*

ROANOKE COLLEGE (VA) .... roanoke.edu **1130/1700/25**
Art, Bio, Bus Admin, Chem, Comp Sci, English, Hist, Math, Music, Poli Sci, Pre-Law, Psych, Reli Stu, Soc

ROBERT MORRIS UNIVERSITY (PA) .... rmu.edu **1020/1530/22**
Bus Admin, Comp Sci, Communic, Econ, Ed, English, Nurs

ROCHESTER, UNIVERSITY OF (NY) .... rochester.edu **1320/1980/30**
*Art, Art Hist, Biochem, Bio, Chem, Comp Sci, Econ, Engine, English, For Lang, Geol,
Hist, Math, Music, Philo, Physics, Poli Sci, Pre-Law, Pre-Med/Pre-Dental, Psych*

ROCHESTER INSTITUTE OF TECHNOLOGY (NY) .... rit.edu **1220/1830/27**
Bio, Bus Admin, Chem, Comp Sci, Econ, Engine, Math, Physics

ROCKFORD COLLEGE (IL) .... rockford.edu **1050/1575/22**
Art, Bio, Bus Admin, Drama, English, Nurs, Pre-Law, Psych

ROCKHURST UNIVERSITY (MO)........................... rockhurst.edu **1140/1710/25**
Bus Admin, Chem, Ed, Math, Nurs, Philo, Psych, Reli Stu

ROCKY MOUNTAIN COLLEGE (MT)........................ rocky.edu **1060/1590/22**
Art, Bio, Bus Admin, Chem, Drama, Ed, English, Music

ROGER WILLIAMS UNIVERSITY (RI) .... rwu.edu **1080/1620/23**
Arch, Bio, Bus Admin, Communic, Drama, Ed, Engine, Psych

ROLLINS COLLEGE (FL) .... rollins.edu **1190/1785/26**
Bio, Chem, Classics, Drama, Ed, Econ, English, Philo, Physics, Psych, Reli Stu

ROOSEVELT UNIVERSITY (IL) .... roosevelt.edu **1050/1575/22**
Bus Admin, Communic, Comp Sci, Ed, Music, Psych

ROSE-HULMAN INST. OF TECHNOLOGY (IN) . rose-hulman.edu **1300/1950/29**
Chem, Comp Sci, Econ, Engine, Math, Physics

ROSEMONT COLLEGE (PA) .... rosemont.edu **1000/1500/21**
Art, Art Hist, English, For Lang, Hist, Pre-Law, Psych, Reli Stu, Soc

ROWAN UNIVERSITY (NJ) .... rowan.edu **1130/1700/25**
*Art, Bio, Bus Admin, Communic, Comp Sci, Ed, Engine, Hist, Math, Music
Philo, Physics, Pre-Law, Pre-Med/Pre-Dental, Psych, Reli Stu*

RUSSELL SAGE COLL. (THE SAGE COLLEGES) (NY) ...... sage.edu **1065/1600/23**
Ed, Nurs, Psych

RUTGERS UNIVERSITY (NJ) .... rutgers.edu **1220/1830/27**
*Ag, Amer St, Anthro, Art, Art Hist, Biochem, Bio, Bus Admin, Chem, Comp Sci, Drama,
Econ, Ed, Engine, English, For Lang, Hist, Math, Music, Nurs, Pharm, Philo, Physics,
Poli Sci, Pre-Law, Pre-Med/Pre-Dental, Psych, Reli Stu, Soc*

RUTGERS UNIVERSITY (CAMDEN) (NJ) .... rutgers.edu **1120/1680/24**
Comp Sci, Ed, English, Hist, Math, Pre-Law, Soc

RUTGERS-NEWARK (NJ) .... rutgers-newark.rutgers.edu **1110/1650/24**
Bus Admin, Nurs, Psych

SACRED HEART UNIVERSITY (CT) .... sacredheart.edu **1070/1600/23**
Biochem, Bus Admin, Chem, Ed, Nurs, Psych, Reli Stu

SAGINAW VALLEY STATE UNIVERSITY (MI) .... svsu.edu **1000/1500/21**
Ed, Engish, Math, Nurs

ST. AMBROSE UNIVERSITY (IA) .... sau.edu **1030/1545/22**
Bus Admin, Chem, Communic, Comp Sci, Ed, English, Hist, Music, Nurs, Philo, Psych, Reli Stu

ST. ANDREWS PRESBYTERIAN COLLEGE (NC) .... sapc.edu **1000/1500/21**
Art, Biochem, Bus Admin, Ed, Philo

ST. ANSELM COLLEGE (NH) .... anselm.edu **1120/1680/24**
Classics, Econ, English, For Lang, Nurs, Philo, Poli Sci, Pre-Law, Psych, Reli Stu, Soc

ST. BONAVENTURE UNIVERSITY (NY) .... sbu.edu **1060/1590/23**
*Art Hist, Bus Admin, Communic, Comp Sci, Drama, Ed, English, Math, Philo,
Poli Sci, Pre-Law, Reli Stu*

ST. CATHERINE, COLLEGE OF (MN) .... stkate.edu **1130/1700/25**
Bio, Bus Admin, Econ, Ed, English, Music, Nurs, Philo, Reli Stu, Soc

ST. CLOUD STATE UNIVERSITY (MN) .... stcloudstate.edu **1020/1530/22**
Bus Admin, Communic, Comp Sci, Econ, Ed, English, Math, Philo, Poli Sci, Pre-Law

ST. EDWARD'S UNIVERSITY (TX) .... stedwards.edu **1130/1700/25**
Art, Bus Admin, Chem, Communic, Comp Sci, Drama, Ed, English, Math, Philo, Psych, Reli Stu

ST. FRANCIS COLLEGE (NY) .... stfranciscollege.edu **1000/1500/21**
Bus Admin, Econ, English, Psych

ST. FRANCIS, UNIVERSITY OF (IN) .... sf.edu **1020/1530/22**
Art, Ed, Nurs, Reli Stu

ST. FRANCIS UNIVERSITY (PA) .... francis.edu **1040/1560/22**
Bio, Chem, Nurs, Philo, Pre-Law, Pre-Med/Pre-Dental, Reli Stu, Soc

ST. JOHN FISHER COLLEGE (NY) .... sjfc.edu **1070/1605/23**
Bus Admin, Communic, Ed, English

ST. JOHN'S UNIVERSITY (NY) .... stjohns.edu **1080/1620/23**
Bus Admin, Chem, Communic, Econ, Ed, Math, Pharm, Philo, Poli Sci, Psych, Reli Stu, Soc

SAINT JOHN'S UNIV./COLL. OF SAINT BENEDICT (MN) .... csbsju.edu **1150/1725/25**
Biochem, Bio, Bus Admin, Chem, Classics, Comp Sci, Econ, Ed, Hist, Music,
Nurs, Philo, Physics, Poli Sci, Pre-Law, Pre-Med/Pre-Dental, Reli Stu

SAINT JOSEPH COLLEGE (CT) .... sjc.edu **1000/1500/21**
Bus Admin, Ed, Home Ec, Nurs

ST. JOSEPH'S COLLEGE (IN) .... saintjoe.edu **1020/1530/22**
Bio, Bus Admin, Ed, Psych

ST. JOSEPH'S COLLEGE (ME) .... sjcme.edu **1000/1500/21**
Chem, Ed, Hist, Nurs

ST. JOSEPH'S COLLEGE (NY) .... sjcny.edu **1060/1600/23**
Bio, Bus Admin, Comp Sci, Ed, Hist, Math, Psych

SAINT JOSEPH'S UNIVERSITY (PA) .... sju.edu **1220/1830/27**
Bus Admin, Ed, English, Hist, Math, Philo, Poli Sci, Pre-Med/Pre-Dental, Reli Stu

ST. LAWRENCE UNIVERSITY (NY) .... stlawu.edu **1160/1740/25**
Econ, Ed, English, Geol, Hist, Math, Poli Sci, Pre-Law, Psych, Soc

ST. LOUIS COLLEGE OF PHARMACY (MO) .... stlcop.edu **1180/1770/26**
Pharm, Pre-Med/Pre-Dental

SAINT LOUIS UNIVERSITY (MO) .... slu.edu **1195/1795/26**
Bio, Bus Admin, Chem, Communic, Comp Sci, Ed, Engine, English, Math, Nurs,
Philo, Pre-Law, Pre-Med/Pre-Dental, Psych, Reli Stu

SAINT MARTIN'S UNIVERSITY (WA) .... stmartin.edu **1000/1500/21**
Bus Admin, Ed, Engine, Psych, Reli Stu

SAINT MARY, COLLEGE OF (NE) .... csm.edu   **1000/1500/21**
Comp Sci, Ed, Nurs, Psych, Reli Stu

SAINT MARY, UNIVERSITY OF (KS) .... stmary.edu   **1010/1515/21**
Bus Admin, Comp Sci, Ed, English, Psych

SAINT MARY'S COLLEGE (IN) .... saintmarys.edu   **1140/1710/25**
Art, Bio, Bus Admin, Chem, Communic, Ed, English, Nurs, Philo, Pre-Law, Reli Stu

SAINT MARY'S COLLEGE OF CALIFORNIA (CA) .. stmarys-ca.edu   **1080/1620/23**
Bus Admin, Ed, English, Psych, Reli Stu, Soc

ST. MARY'S COLLEGE OF MARYLAND (MD) .... smcm.edu   **1230/1845/27**
Anthro, Bio, Drama, Econ, English, Hist, Math, Music, Philo, Poli Sci, Pre-Med/Pre-Dental, Psych, Reli Stu

ST. MARY'S UNIVERSITY OF MINNESOTA (MN) .... smumn.edu   **1050/1575/22**
Bio, Bus Admin, Chem, Communic, Comp Sci, Drama, Ed, English, Hist, Philo, Reli Stu

ST. MARY'S UNIVERSITY (TX) .... stmarytx.edu   **1060/1590/23**
Bus Admin, Chem, English, Math, Philo, Poli Sci, Pre-Law, Pre-Med/Pre-Dental, Reli Stu, Soc

SAINT MICHAEL'S COLLEGE (VT) .... smcvt.edu   **1115/1670/24**
Bio, Bus Admin, Chem, Communic, Econ, Ed, Hist, Psych, Reli Stu

SAINT NORBERT COLLEGE (WI) .... snc.edu   **1130/1700/25**
Bio, Bus Admin, Communic, Comp Sci, Ed, English, Hist, Math, Philo, Reli Stu

SAINT OLAF COLLEGE (MN) .... stolaf.edu   **1240/1860/28**
Amer St, Art, Bio, Chem, Classics, Comp Sci, Drama, Econ, English, Hist, Math, Music, Nurs, Philo, Physics, Pre-Law, Pre-Med/Pre-Dental, Psych, Reli Stu

SAINT PETER'S COLLEGE (NJ) .... spc.edu   **1000/1500/21**
Bus Admin, Comp Sci, Ed, English, Math, Philo, Reli Stu

SAINT ROSE, COLLEGE OF (NY) .... strose.edu   **1040/1560/22**
Art, Bus Admin, Ed, English, Soc

ST. SCHOLASTICA, COLLEGE OF (MN) .... css.edu   **1100/1650/24**
Bio, Bus Admin, Chem, Comp Sci, Ed, English, Hist, Nurs, Pre-Med/Pre-Dental, Psych, Reli Stu

SAINT THOMAS AQUINAS COLLEGE (NY) .... stac.edu   **1060/1600/23**
Bus Admin, Ed, Psych

SAINT THOMAS, UNIVERSITY OF (MN) .... stthomas.edu   **1145/1720/25**
Bus Admin, Chem, Communic, Comp Sci, Econ, Ed, English, Geol, Philo, Reli Stu

SAINT THOMAS, UNIVERSITY OF (TX) .... stthom.edu   **1140/1710/25**
Chem, Hist, Philo, Poli Sci, Pre-Med/Pre-Dental, Psych, Reli Stu

ST. VINCENT COLLEGE (PA) .... stvincent.edu   **1100/1650/24**
Bio, Bus Admin, Chem, Econ, English, Poli Sci, Pre-Med/Pre-Dental, Psych, Reli Stu

SALEM COLLEGE (NC) .... salem.edu   **1120/1680/24**
Art, Art Hist, Bus Admin, Econ, Ed, English, Music, Pre-Law, Soc

SALEM STATE COLLEGE (MA) .... salemstate.edu **1000/1500/21**
Art, Bio, Chem, Comp Sci, Drama, Ed, English, Geog, Geol, Hist, Nurs, Psych, Soc

SALISBURY UNIVERSITY (MD) .... ssu.edu **1140/1710/25**
Art, Bio, Bus Admin, Ed, English, Geog, Math, Philo, Pre-Law, Psych

SAMFORD UNIVERSITY (AL) .... samford.edu **1140/1700/25**
Bio, Bus Admin, Classics, Communic, English, Math, Music, Nurs, Pharm, Reli Stu

SAN DIEGO STATE UNIVERSITY (CA) .... sdsu.edu **1120/1680/24**
*Art, Art Hist, Astro, Bio, Bus Admin, Chem, Communic, Drama, Econ, Ed, Engine, English,
Geog, Geol, Hist, Math, Nurs, Poli Sci, Pre-Law, Pre-Med/Pre-Dental, Psych, Soc*

SAN DIEGO, UNIVERSITY OF (CA) .... sandiego.edu **1180/1780/26**
Bus Admin, Chem, Math, Nurs, Philo, Poli Sci, Pre-Law, Pre-Med/Pre-Dental, Reli Stu

SAN FRANCISCO ART INSTITUTE (CA) .... sfai.edu **1000/1510/21**
Art

SAN FRANCISCO CONSERVATORY OF MUSIC (CA) .. sfcm.edu **1170/1760/26**
Music

SAN FRANCISCO, UNIVERSITY OF (CA) .... usfca.edu **1130/1700/25**
Bus Admin, Comp Sci, Econ, Nurs, Poli Sci, Pre-Law, Pre-Med/Pre-Dental, Psych, Soc

SAN FRANCISCO STATE UNIVERSITY (CA) .... sfsu.edu **1010/1515/21**
Anthro, Astro, Bot, Bus Admin, Communic, Drama, English, Hist, Music, Pre-Law, Zoo

SAN JOSE STATE UNIVERSITY (CA) .... sjsu.edu **1000/1500/21**
*Anthro, Art, Bus Admin, Chem, Communic, Comp Sci, Engine, Math, Music,
Nurs, Physics, Poli Sci, Pre-Med/Pre-Dental, Zoo*

SANTA CLARA UNIVERSITY (CA) .... scu.edu **1205/1810/27**
*Anthro, Bus Admin, Chem, Communic, Comp Sci, Drama, Econ, Engine, English, Hist,
Music, Philo, Physics, Poli Sci, Pre-Law, Pre-Med/Pre-Dental, Psych, Reli Stu*

SANTA FE, COLLEGE OF (NM) .... csf.edu **1115/1675/24**
Art, Drama, Ed

SARAH LAWRENCE COLLEGE (NY) .... slc.edu **1260/1890/28**
Amer St, Anthro, Art, Art Hist, Drama, English, Geog, Hist, Music, Pre-Law

SCHOOL OF THE ART INSTITUTE OF CHICAGO (IL) .. saic.ed **1100/1660/24**
Arch, Art

SCHREINER UNIVERSITY (TX) .... schreiner.edu **1020/1530/22**
Art, Bus Admin, Ed, English, Math, Poli Sci, Pre-Law

SCIENCES IN PHILADELPHIA, UNIV. OF THE (PA) ...... usip.edu **1120/1680/24**
Bio, Biochem, Bus Admin, Chem, Comp Sci, Pharm

SCRANTON, UNIVERSITY OF (PA) .... scranton.edu **1120/1680/24**
Bio, Bus Admin, Communic, Ed, Math, Nurs, Philo, Pre-Med/Pre-Dental, Reli Stu

SCRIPPS COLLEGE (CA) .... scrippscol.edu **1350/2035/30**
*Art, Art Hist, Bio, Chem, Classics, Communic, Drama, Econ, English, For Lang,
Music, Poli Sci, Pre-Law, Pre-Med/Pre-Dental, Psych*

SEATTLE PACIFIC UNIVERSITY (WA)..........................spu.edu   **1150/1725/25**
Art, Bio, Chem, Drama, Ed, Engine, English, Nurs, Physics, Psych, Reli Stu

SEATTLE UNIVERSITY (WA) ....seattleu.edu   **1150/1725/25**
Bus Admin, Chem, Drama, Econ, Engine, English, Hist, Math, Nurs, Philo, Pre-Law, Reli Stu

SETON HALL UNIVERSITY (NJ) ....shu.edu   **1120/1680/24**
*Bus Admin, Communic, Ed, English, Nurs, Philo, Poli Sci, Pre-Law,
Pre-Med/Pre-Dental, Psych, Reli Stu*

SETON HILL COLLEGE (PA) ....setonhill.edu   **1000/1500/21**
Art, Drama, Ed, Music

SHAW UNIVERSITY (NC) ....shawuniversity.edu   **1010/1510/21**
Bus Admin, Ed, Soc

SHAWNEE STATE UNIVERSITY (OH) ....shawnee.edu   **1000/1500/21**
Art, Ed, Math, Nurs

SHENANDOAH UNIVERSITY (VA) ....su.edu   **1010/1510/21**
Hist, Music, Nurs

SHEPHERD UNIVERSITY (WV) .... shepherd.edu   **1020/1530/22**
Art, Bus Admin, Chem, Econ, Ed, English, Hist, Music, Nurs, Poli Sci, Psych

SHIPPENSBURG UNIVERSITY (PA) ....ship.edu   **1060/1590/23**
Bio, Bus Admin, Chem, Comp Sci, Econ, Ed, English, Geog, Hist, Math, Physics, Psych, Soc

SHORTER COLLEGE (GA) ....shorter.edu   **1050/1575/22**
Bio, Chem, Ed, Music

SIENA COLLEGE (NY) ....siena.edu   **1125/1690/24**
*Bio, Biochem, Bus Admin, Chem, English, Philo, Poli Sci, Pre-Law, Pre-Med/Pre-Dental,
Psych, Reli Stu*

SIENA HEIGHTS UNIVERSITY (MI).................. sienaheights.edu   **1000/1500/21**
Art, Bus Admin, Ed, English, Psych

SILVER LAKE COLLEGE (WI) .... sl.edu   **1000/1500/21**
Art, Bus Admin, Ed, Music, Reli Stu

SIMMONS COLLEGE (MA) .... simmons.edu   **1110/1660/24**
Art, Bus Admin, Communic, Ed, English, Math, Nurs, Psych, Soc

SIMPSON COLLEGE (IA) .... simpson.edu   **1120/1680/24**
Bus Admin, Comp Sci, Ed, Hist, Math, Music, Psych, Reli Stu, Soc

SIOUX FALLS, UNIVERSITY OF (SD) .... usiouxfalls.edu   **1040/1560/22**
Bus Admin, Poli Sci

SKIDMORE COLLEGE (NY) .... skidmore.edu   **1260/1890/28**
*Amer St, Anthro, Art, Art Hist, Bio, Biochem, Bus Admin, Chem, Classics, Drama, Econ, Ed,
English, For Lang, Geol, Math, Music, Philo, Poli Sci, Pre-Law, Pre-Med/Pre-Dental, Psych*

SLIPPERY ROCK UNIVERSITY (PA) ....sru.edu   **1000/1500/21**
Communic, Comp Sci, Drama, Ed, English, For Lang, Geog, Music

SMITH COLLEGE (MA) .... smith.edu **1280/1920/29**
Amer St, Anthro, Art, Art Hist, Biochem, Bio, Econ, Engine, English, For Lang, Geol, Hist, Math, Music, Philo, Physics, Poli Sci, Pre-Law, Pre-Med/Pre-Dental, Psych

SONOMA STATE UNIVERSITY (CA) .... sonoma.edu **1040/1560/22**
Anthro, Art Hist, Bus Admin, Chem, Comp Sci, Ed, English, Geog, Music, Nurs, Physics, Psych, Soc

SOUTH, UNIVERSITY OF THE (TN) .... sewanee.edu **1230/1845/27**
Amer St, Anthro, Bio, Chem, Classics, Econ, Drama, English, Forest, For Lang, Geol, Hist, Math, Poli Sci, Physics, Pre-Law, Pre-Med/Pre-Dental, Reli Stu

SOUTH ALABAMA, UNIVERSITY OF (AL) .... usouthal.edu **1060/1590/23**
Bio, Bus Admin, Chem, Communic, Comp Sci, Ed, Engine, English, For Lang, Nurs, Philo, Soc

SOUTH CAROLINA, UNIVERSITY OF (SC) .... sc.edu **1150/1725/25**
Bio, Bus Admin, Chem, Communic, Comp Sci, Drama, Ed, Engine, English, For Lang, Geog, Geol, Hist, Math, Music, Nurs, Pharm, Physics, Poli Sci, Pre-Law

SOUTH DAKOTA, UNIVERSITY OF (SD) .... usd.edu **1050/1575/22**
Art, Bio, Bus Admin, Chem, Comp Sci, Ed, English, Hist, Math, Music, Nurs, Poli Sci, Pre-Law, Pre-Med/Pre-Dental, Psych

SOUTH DAKOTA SCHOOL OF MINES AND TECH. (SD) .... sdsmt.edu **1140/1710/25**
Chem, Comp Sci, Engine, Geol, Math, Physics

SOUTH DAKOTA STATE UNIVERSITY (SD) .... sdstate.edu **1060/1590/23**
Bio, Chem, Econ, Engine, Geog, Math, Nurs, Pharm, Soc

SOUTH FLORIDA, UNIVERSITY OF (FL) .... usf.edu **1130/1700/25**
Amer St, Anthro, Bio, Bus Admin, Chem, Drama, Ed, Engine, For Lang, Hist, Music, Nurs, Philo, Physics

SOUTHEAST MISSOURI STATE UNIV. (MO) .... semo.edu **1040/1560/22**
Bus Admin, Communic, Ed, English, Music

SOUTHEASTERN LOUISIANA STATE UNIV. (LA) .... selu.edu **1000/1500/21**
Art, Bio, Communic, Comp Sci, Ed, English, Music, Nurs

SOUTHEASTERN OKLAHOMA STATE UNIV. (OK) ..... sosu.edu **1000/1500/21**
Bot, Bus Admin, Ed, Zoo

SOUTHERN CALIFORNIA, UNIVERSITY OF (CA) .... usc.edu **1370/2000/31**
Astro, Arch, Bio, Bus Admin, Communic, Drama, Ed, Engine, English, Math, Music, Pharm, Philo, Psych

SOUTHERN CONNECTICUT STATE UNIV. (CT) .... southernct.edu **1000/1500/21**
Chem, Communic, Comp Sci, Econ, Ed, English, Geog, Hist, Math, Physics, Poli Sci, Psych, Soc

SOUTHERN ILLINOIS UNIV. (CARBONDALE) (IL) .... siuc.edu **1030/1545/22**
Bot, Bus Admin, Chem, Communic, Ed, Engine, English, Forestry, Geog, Hist, Music, Poli Sci, Psych, Zoo

SOUTHERN ILLINOIS UNIV. (EDWARDSVILLE) (IL) .... siue.edu **1060/1590/23**
Bio, Chem, Ed, Engine, Nurs, Pharm, Philo, Poli Sci

SOUTHERN MAINE, UNIVERSITY OF (ME) .... usm.maine.edu **1030/1550/22**
Art, Bus Admin, Chem, Communic, Comp Sci, Drama, Engine, English, Music, Nurs, Philo

SOUTHERN METHODIST UNIVERSITY (TX) .... smu.edu **1220/1830/27**
*Anthro, Art, Art Hist, Bus Admin, Communic, Drama, Econ, Engine, English,
Hist, Music, Reli Stu*

SOUTHERN MISSISSIPPI, UNIVERSITY OF (MS) .... usm.edu **1010/1515/21**
Bio, Bus Admin, Drama, Ed, Hist, Math, Music, Nurs

SOUTHERN NAZARENE UNIVERSITY (OK) ....snu.edu **1050/1575/22**
Ed, English, Music, Nurs, Reli Stu

SOUTHERN OREGON UNIVERSITY (OR) .... sou.edu **1030/1550/22**
Art, Bio, Bus Admin, Chem, Ed, For Lang, Geol, Math, Music, Psych, Soc

SOUTHERN POLYTECHNIC UNIVERSITY (GA) .... spsu.edu **1100/1650/24**
Arch, Comp Sci, Engine, Math

SOUTHERN UTAH UNIVERSITY (UT) .... suu.edu **1000/1500/21**
Bus Admin, Communic, Drama, Econ, Ed, English, Math, Music, Nurs

SOUTHWEST BAPTIST UNIVERSITY (MO) .... sbuniv.edu **1060/1590/23**
Ed, Music, Nurs, Psych, Reli Stu

SOUTHWESTERN COLLEGE (KS) .... sckans.edu **1040/1560/22**
Bio, English, Music, Nurs, Physics

SOUTHWESTERN OKLAHOMA STATE UNIV. (OK) .. swosu.edu **1000/1500/21**
Bus Admin, Chem, Ed, Music, Nurs, Pharm

SOUTHWESTERN UNIVERSITY (TX) .... southwestern.edu **1230/1845/27**
*Art, Bio, Bus Admin, Chem, Classics, Communic, Drama, Econ, Ed, English, For Lang,
Hist, Music, Philo, Poli Sci, Pre-Law, Pre-Med/Pre-Dental, Psych, Reli Stu, Soc*

SPELMAN COLLEGE (GA) .... spelman.edu **1080/1630/24**
Bio, Chem, Comp Sci, Econ, English, Math, Poli Sci, Pre-Law, Pre-Med/Pre-Dental, Soc

SPRING HILL COLLEGE (AL) .... shc.edu **1100/1650/24**
*Bio, Bus Admin, Chem, Communic, English, Hist, Nurs, Poli Sci, Pre-Law,
Pre-Med/Pre-Dental, Reli Stu*

SPRINGFIELD COLLEGE (MA) .... spfldcol.edu **1030/1545/22**
Bio, Drama, Ed, English, Psych, Soc

STANFORD UNIVERSITY (CA) .... stanford.edu **1450/2175/32**
*Amer St, Anthro, Art, Art Hist, Bio, Chem, Classics, Communic, Comp Sci, Drama,
Econ, Ed, Engine, English, For Lang, Math, Music, Philo, Physics, Poli Sci, Pre-Law,
Pre-Med/Pre-Dental, Psych, Reli Stu, Soc*

STEPHEN F. AUSTIN STATE UNIVERSITY (TX) .... sfasu.edu **1010/1515/21**
Ed, Forest, Hist, Music

STEPHENS (MO) .... stephens.edu **1090/1640/24**
Bus Admin, Communic, Drama, Ed, Pre-Law, Psych

STERLING COLLEGE (KS) .... sterling.edu **1000/1500/21**
Drama, Ed, Music

STETSON UNIVERSITY (FL) .... stetson.edu **1130/1700/25**
Bus Admin, Chem, Comp Sci, Ed, English, Hist, Math, Music, Physics, Poli Sci, Pre-Law, Pre-Med/Pre-Dental, Psych, Reli Stu

STEVENS INSTITUTE OF TECHNOLOGY (NJ) .... stevens.edu **1330/2000/30**
Comp Sci, Engine, Math, Physics

STEVENSON UNIVERSITY (MD) .... stevenson.edu **1050/1575/22**
Nurs

STONEHILL COLLEGE (MA) .... stonehill.edu **1160/1740/25**
Bio, Bus Admin, Chem, Comp Sci, Philo, Poli Sci, Pre-Law, Pre-Med/Pre-Dental, Psych, Reli Stu

SUFFOLK UNIVERSITY (MA) .... suffolk.edu **1020/1530/22**
Bus Admin, Communic, Econ, English, Physics, Poli Sci, Psych, Soc

SUNY COLL. OF ENVIRONMENTAL SCIENCE & FORESTRY (NY) esf.edu **1160/1740/25**
Forest

SUSQUEHANNA UNIVERSITY (PA) .... susqu.edu **1140/1710/23**
Bio, Biochem, Bus Admin, Chem, Communic, Drama, Econ, Ed, English, Hist, Music, Poli Sci, Pre-Med/Pre-Dental, Psych

SWARTHMORE COLLEGE (PA) .... swarthmore.edu **1420/2130/32**
Art Hist, Biochem, Bio, Classics, Drama, Econ, Ed, Engine, English, For Lang, Hist, Math, Music, Philo, Physics, Poli Sci, Pre-Law, Pre-Med/Pre-Dental, Psych

SWEET BRIAR COLLEGE (VA) .... sbc.edu **1140/1710/25**
Anthro, Art Hist, Chem, Drama, Engine, English, For Lang, Math, Poli Sci, Pre-Law, Psych

SYRACUSE UNIVERSITY (NY) .... syracuse.edu **1200/1800/26**
Anthro, Arch, Art, Art Hist, Biochem, Bus Admin, Chem, Communic, Comp Sci, Drama, Econ, Engine, Forest, Geog, Math, Music, Philo, Physics, Poli Sci, Pre-Law, Psych, Reli Stu, Soc

TABOR COLLEGE (KS) .... tabor.edu **1060/1600/23**
Ed, Reli Stu

TAMPA, UNIVERSITY OF (FL) .... utampa.edu **1080/1620/23**
Bus Admin, Communic, English, Music, Nurs, Poli Sci

TARLETON STATE UNIVERSITY (TX) .... tarleton.edu **1000/1500/21**
Ag, Drama, Ed, English, Hist, Math, Music, Soc

TAYLOR UNIVERSITY (IN) .... taylor.edu **1150/1725/25**
Bus Admin, Comp Sci, Ed, English, Math, Music, Psych, Reli Stu

TEMPLE UNIVERSITY (PA) .... temple.edu **1100/1650/24**
Arch, Art, Biochem, Bio, Bus Admin, Chem, Communic, Comp Sci, Drama, Econ, Ed, English, For Lang, Hist, Math, Music, Pharm, Poli Sci, Pre-Law, Pre-Med/Pre-Dental, Psych, Soc

TENNESSEE TECHNOLOGICAL UNIVERSITY (TN) .. tntech.edu **1060/1590/23**
Ed, Engine, Math, Music

TENNESSEE, UNIVERSITY OF
    CHATTANOOGA .... utc.edu **1020/1530/22**
    Chem, Engine, English, Math, Music, Nurs, Psych
    KNOXVILLE .... utk.edu **1130/1700/25**
    Ag, Anthro, Arch, Art, Bot, Bus Admin, Chem, Classics, Communic, Ed, Engine,
    English, Forest, Hist, Nurs, Physics, Poli Sci, Pre-Law, Pre-Med/Pre-Dental, Reli Stu, Zoo
    MARTIN .... utm.edu **1030/1550/22**
    Ag, Bus Admin, Ed, English, Math, Nurs

TEXAS, UNIVERSITY OF, AT
    ARLINGTON .... uta.edu **1050/1575/22**
    Arch, Bio, Bus Admin, Communic, Comp Sci, Engine, Hist, Math, Nurs, Poli Sci
    AUSTIN .... utexas.edu **1230/1845/27**
    Amer St, Arch, Art, Astro, Bio, Bot, Bus Admin, Classics, Communic, Comp Sci,
    Drama, Econ, Ed, Engine, English, For Lang, Geog, Geol, Hist, Math, Music,
    Pharm, Philo, Physics, Poli Sci, Pre-Med/Pre-Dental, Psych, Reli Stu, Zoo
    DALLAS .... utdallas.edu **1250/1875/28**
    Bus Admin, Comp Sci, Econ, Engine, Geog, Hist, Physics, Poli Sci
    EL PASO .... utep.edu **1000/1500/21**
    Art, Bus Admin, Communic, Drama, Ed, Engine, English, Math, Music, Nurs, Psych
    SAN ANTONIO .... utsa.edu **1000/1500/21**
    Arch, Art, Bio, Bus Admin, Comp Sci, Econ, Engine, English, Hist, Math,
    Music, Poli Sci, Pre-Med/Pre-Dental, Psych
    SAN ANTONIO (HEALTH SCIENCE CENTER) .. uthscsa.edu **1100/1650/24**
    Nurs (No Frosh - Transfers Only)
    TYLER ....uttyler.edu **1030/1545/22**
    Art, Bio, Bus Admin, Comp Sci, Engine, English, Math, Nurs, Psych

TEXAS A&M (TX) .... tamu.edu **1200/1800/26**
Ag, Anthro, Arch, Bus Admin, Chem, Communic, Comp Sci, Econ, Ed, Engine,
English, Forest, Geol, Hist, Philo, Poli Sci, Pre-Med/Pre-Dental, Soc, Zoo

TEXAS A&M - COMMERCE (TX) .... tamu-commerce.edu **1020/1530/22**
Bus Admin

TEXAS A&M - CORPUS CHRISTI (TX) .... tamucc.edu **1000/1500/21**
Art, Bio, Bus Admin, Chem, Comp Sci, Ed, English, Geog, Geol, Hist, Math, Nurs, Psych

TEXAS A&M - KINGSVILLE (TX) .... tamuk.edu **1000/1500/21**
Chem, Engine, Math

TEXAS CHRISTIAN UNIVERSITY (TX) .... tcu.edu **1160/1740/25**
Bio, Bus Admin, Chem, Communic, Drama, Ed, Geol, Hist, Music, Nurs, Reli Stu

TEXAS LUTHERAN UNIVERSITY (TX) .... tlu.edu **1040/1560/22**
Bio, Bus Admin, Chem, Ed, Hist, Music, Reli Stu

TEXAS STATE UNIVERSITY - SAN MARCOS (TX) .... txstate.edu **1050/1575/22**
Ag, Anthro, Bio, Bus Admin, Comp Sci, Drama, Ed, Geog, Hist, Math, Music, Poli Sci

TEXAS TECH UNIVERSITY (TX) .... ttu.edu **1110/1665/24**
Ag, Arch, Art, Bio, Bus Admin, Ed, Engine, English, Hist, Home Ec, Math, Music

TEXAS WESLEYAN UNIVERSITY (TX) .... txwesleyan.edu **1000/1500/21**
Bus Admin, Communic, Ed, Psych, Reli Stu

THOMAS MORE COLLEGE (KY) .... thomasmore.edu **1040/1560/22**
Bio, Bus Admin, Chem, Ed, Nurs, Physics, Pre-Med/Pre-Dental

TOLEDO, UNIVERSITY OF (OH) .... utoledo.edu **1040/1560/22**
Bus Admin, Chem, Econ, Engine, Hist, Nurs, Pharm, Pre-Med/Pre-Dental

TOUGALOO COLLEGE (MS) .... tougaloo.edu **1000/1500/21**
Bio, Chem, Ed, English

TOWSON UNIVERSITY (MD) .... towson.edu **1095/1645/24**
Anthro, Art, Bus Admin, Chem, Communic, Comp Sci, Drama, Ed, Math,
Music, Nurs, Poli Sci, Psych, Soc

TRANSYLVANIA UNIVERSITY (KY) .... transy.edu **1200/1800/26**
Bio, Bus Admin, Chem, Comp Sci, Ed, Math, Music, Philo, Pre-Med/Pre-Dental, Psych

TRINITY COLLEGE (CT) .... trincoll.edu **1290/1935/29**
Amer St, Art Hist, Bio, Chem, Econ, Engine, English, Hist, Math, Philo,
Physics, Poli Sci, Pre-Law, Pre-Med/Pre-Dental, Reli Stu

TRINITY UNIVERSITY WASHINGTON (DC) .... trinitydc.edu **1000/1500/21**
Bus Admin, Ed, English, For Lang, Math, Poli Sci, Pre-Law, Soc

TRINITY UNIVERSITY (TX) .... trinity.edu **1290/1935/29**
Art, Art Hist, Bio, Bus Admin, Chem, Classics, Communic, Comp Sci, Econ, Ed,
English, For Lang, Hist, Philo, Physics, Poli Sci, Pre-Law, Pre-Med/Pre-Dental, Soc

TRI-STATE UNIVERSITY (IN) .... tristate.edu **1060/1590/23**
Engine

TROY STATE UNIVERSITY (AL) .... troy.edu **1000/1500/21**
Bio, Bus Admin, Communic, Ed, English, Nurs

TRUMAN STATE UNIVERSITY (MO) .... truman.edu **1220/1830/27**
Bio, Bus Admin, Chem, Econ, Ed, English, For Lang, Math, Music, Nurs, Pre-Med/Pre-Dental

TUFTS UNIVERSITY (MA) .... tufts.edu **1400/2100/31**
Bio, Chem, Classics, Drama, Econ, Engine, English, Hist, Math, Philo,
Poli Sci, Pre-Law, Pre-Med/Pre-Dental, Psych

TULANE UNIVERSITY (LA) .... tulane.edu **1270/1900/28**
Amer St, Anthro, Arch, Art, Bio, Biochem, Bus Admin, Drama, Econ, Engine,
For Lang, Hist, Math, Philo, Poli Sci, Pre-Law, Pre-Med/Pre-Dental, Psych

TULSA, UNIVERSITY OF (OK) .... utulsa.edu **1230/1850/27**
Anthro, Art, Bio, Bus Admin, Communic, Comp Sci, Engine, English, Geol, Hist, Music,
Physics, Psych

TUSKEGEE UNIVERSITY (AL) .... tuskegee.edu **1000/1500/21**
Ag, Arch, Engine, Math, Nurs, Physics, Pre-Law, Pre-Med/Pre-Dental

UNION COLLEGE (NE) .... ucollege.edu **1060/1600/23**
Nurs, Reli Stu

UNION COLLEGE (NY) .... union.edu **1310/1965/30**
Astro, Biochem, Bio, Chem, Comp Sci, Econ, Engine, English, Geol, Hist,
Math, Physics, Poli Sci, Pre-Law, Pre-Med/Pre-Dental, Psych, Soc

UNION UNIVERSITY (TN) .... uu.edu **1100/1650/24**
Art, Chem, Ed, Music, Nurs, Physics, Reli Stu

U. S. AIR FORCE ACADEMY (CO) .... usafa.edu **1290/1935/29**
Bus Admin, Chem, Comp Sci, Engine, Hist, Math, Physics, Poli Sci

U. S. COAST GUARD ACADEMY (CT) .... cga.edu **1270/1905/28**
Engine, Poli Sci

U. S. MILITARY ACADEMY (NY) .... usma.edu **1280/1920/29**
Comp Sci, Econ, Engine, Hist, Math, Poli Sci

U. S. NAVAL ACADEMY (MD) .... usna.edu **1325/1980/30**
Chem, Engine, Math, Physics, Poli Sci

URSINUS COLLEGE (PA) .... ursinus.edu **1225/1840/27**
*Bio, Bus Admin, Chem, Drama, Econ, Ed, Math, Philo, Physics, Poli Sci, Pre-Law,
Pre-Med/Pre-Dental*

UTAH, UNIVERSITY OF (UT) .... utah.edu **1100/1650/24**
*Art, Art Hist, Bio, Bus Admin, Chem, Comp Sci, Drama, Engine, English, For Lang, Geol,
Hist, Home Ec, Math, Music, Pharm, Philo, Physics, Poli Sci, Pre-Law, Pre-Med/Pre-Dental*

UTAH STATE UNIVERSITY (UT) .... usu.edu **1100/1650/24**
Ag, Bio, Chem, Drama, Econ, Ed, Engine, English, Forest, Home Ec, Math, Music, Poli Sci

UTICA COLLEGE (NY) .... utica.edu **1010/1510/22**
Bus Admin

VALPARAISO UNIVERSITY (IN) .... valpo.edu **1160/1740/26**
*Bio, Bus Admin, Chem, Ed, Engine, For Lang, Math, Music, Nurs, Physics,
Pre-Med/Pre-Dental, Psych, Reli Stu*

VANDERBILT UNIVERSITY (TN) .... vanderbilt.edu **1370/2055/31**
*Anthro, Art Hist, Bio, Chem, Classics, Econ, Ed, Engine, English, Geol, Hist, Music,
Nurs, Philo, Physics, Poli Sci, Pre-Law, Pre-Med/Pre-Dental, Psych*

VASSAR COLLEGE (NY) .... vassar.edu **1350/2025/30**
*Art, Art Hist, Astro, Bio, Chem, Comp Sci, Drama, Econ, English, For Lang, Hist,
Math, Music, Philo, Poli Sci, Pre-Law, Pre-Med/Pre-Dental, Psych*

VERMONT, UNIVERSITY OF (VT) .... uvm.edu **1160/1740/25**
*Ag, Bio, Bot, Bus Admin, Chem, Classics, Econ, For Lang, Geog, Geol, Hist, Math,
Nurs, Physics, Poli Sci, Pre-Law, Pre-Med/Pre-Dental, Psych, Reli Stu, Soc, Zoo*

VILLANOVA UNIVERSITY (PA) .... villanova.edu **1260/1890/28**
*Astro, Bio, Bus Admin, Chem, Communic, Econ, Engine, Math, Nurs, Philo,
Poli Sci, Pre-Law, Pre-Med/Pre-Dental, Reli Stu*

VIRGINIA, UNIVERSITY OF (VA) .... virginia.edu **1320/1980/30**
*Amer St, Anthro, Arch, Art, Astro, Bio, Biochem, Bus Admin, Chem, Classics,
Econ, Engine, English, For Lang, Hist, Math, Music, Nurs, Physics, Poli Sci,
Pre-Law, Pre-Med/Pre-Dental, Psych, Reli Stu, Soc*

VIRGINIA COMMONWEALTH UNIVERSITY (VA) .... vcu.edu **1070/1605/23**
*Art, Bio, Bus Admin, Drama, Engine, For Lang, Music, Nurs, Pharm,
Pre-Law, Pre-Med/Pre-Dental, Psych, Reli Stu*

VIRGINIA MILITARY INSTITUTE (VA) .... vmi.edu **1140/1710/25**
Bus Admin, Chem, Econ, Engine, Hist, Math, Pre-Law

VIRGINIA POLYTECHNIC INSTITUTE (VA) .... vt.edu **1230/1845/26**
Ag, Arch, Bio, Biochem, Bus Admin, Chem, Communic, Comp Sci, Engine, English, Forest, Hist, Math, Physics, Pre-Med/Pre-Dental, Psych

VIRGINIA WESLEYAN UNIVERSITY (VA) .... vwc.edu **1030/1545/22**
Bio, Bus Admin, Communic, Hist, Philo, Poli Sci, Pre-Law, Pre-Med/Pre-Dental, Psych, Reli Stu, Soc

VISUAL ARTS, SCHOOL OF (NY) .... schoolofvisualarts.edu **1050/1575/22**
Art, Bus Admin

VITERBO UNIVERSITY (WI) ....viterbo.edu **1055/1590/23**
Art, Chem, Drama, Music, Nurs

WABASH COLLEGE (IN) ....wabash.edu **1190/1790/26**
Bio, Chem, Classics, Econ, English, Hist, Math, Philo, Poli Sci, Pre-Law, Pre-Med/Pre-Dental, Psych, Reli Stu

WAGNER COLLEGE (NY) .... wagner.edu **1130/1695/25**
Amer St, Bus Admin, Drama, Ed, Nurs, Soc

WAKE FOREST UNIVERSITY (NC) .... wfu.edu **1310/1965/29**
Biochem, Bio, Bus Admin, Chem, Drama, Econ, English, For Lang, Hist, Math, Physics, Poli Sci, Pre-Law, Pre-Med/Pre-Dental, Psych, Reli Stu, Soc

WALLA WALLA UNIVERSITY (WA) .... wallawalla.edu **1060/1600/23**
Communic, Comp Sci, Engine, English, Nurs, Pre-Med/Pre-Dental

WALSH UNIVERSITY (OH) .... walsh.edu **1020/1530/22**
Ed, English, Nurs, Reli Stu

WARREN WILSON COLLEGE (NC) .... warren-wilson.edu **1150/1725/25**
Art, English, Hist, Pre-Law

WARTBURG COLLEGE (IA) .... wartburg.edu **1110/1665/24**
Bio, Bus Admin, Communic, Drama, Ed, English, Hist, Music, Pre-Med/Pre-Dental, Reli Stu

WASHBURN UNIVERSITY (KS) .... washburn.edu **1030/1545/22**
Ed, Math, Nurs, Physics

WASHINGTON COLLEGE (MD) ....washcoll.edu **1155/1715/25**
Amer St, Bio, Bus Admin, Hist, Poli Sci, Pre-Law, Pre-Med/Pre-Dental, Psych

WASHINGTON & JEFFERSON COLLEGE (PA) ..... washjeff.edu **1130/1695/25**
Art, Bio, Bus Admin, Chem, Econ, Ed, English, Hist, Poli Sci, Pre-Law, Pre-Med/Pre-Dental, Psych

WASHINGTON & LEE UNIVERSITY (VA) .... wlu.edu **1370/2055/31**
Art, Bio, Bus Admin, Chem, Communic, Econ, English, For Lang, Geol, Hist, Math, Philo, Physics, Poli Sci, Pre-Law, Pre-Med/Pre-Dental

WASHINGTON UNIVERSITY IN ST. LOUIS (MO) .... wustl.edu **1380/2070/31**
Anthro, Arch, Art, Art Hist, Bio, Bus Admin, Chem, Comp Sci, Econ, Engine, English, For Lang, Geol, Math, Philo, Physics, Pre-Law, Pre-Med/Pre-Dental, Psych

WASHINGTON STATE UNIVERSITY (WA) .... wsu.edu **1105/1660/24**
Amer St, Ag, Anthro, Arch, Biochem, Bus Admin, Communic, Econ, Ed, Engine, English,
Hist, Home Ec, Nurs, Pharm, Physics, Soc, Zoo

WASHINGTON, UNIVERSITY OF (WA) .... washington.edu **1195/1795/26**
Anthro, Arch, Art, Art Hist, Astro, Biochem, Bio, Bot, Bus Admin, Chem, Classics, Comp
Sci, Drama, Econ, Ed, Engine, English, Forest, Geog, Geol, Hist, Math, Music, Nurs, Philo,
Physics, Poli Sci, Pre-Law, Pre-Med/Pre-Dental, Psych, Soc, Zoo

WAYNE STATE COLLEGE (NE) .... wsc.edu **1000/1500/21**
Art, Chem, Ed, Psych

WAYNE STATE UNIVERSITY (MI) .... wayne.edu **1000/1500/21**
Art, Art Hist, Bio, Bus Admin, Chem, Comp Sci, Drama, Ed, Engine, For Lang,
Music, Nurs, Pharm, Physics, Pre-Med/Pre-Dental, Psych

WAYNESBURG UNIVERSITY (PA) .... waynesburg.edu **1000/1500/21**
Communic, Ed, Nurs, Psych

WEBER STATE UNIVERSITY (UT) .... weber.edu **1020/1530/22**
Art, Bus Admin, Communic, Comp Sci, Drama, Econ, Ed, English, Math,
Music, Nurs, Physics, Zoo

WEBSTER UNIVERSITY (MO) .... webster.edu **1120/1680/24**
Communic, Comp Sci, Drama, Hist, Music, Nurs, Philo, Poli Sci, Psych

WELLESLEY COLLEGE (MA) .... wellesley.edu **1355/2030/30**
Art, Art Hist, Bio, Chem, Econ, Ed, English, For Lang, Hist, Math, Philo,
Physics, Poli Sci, Pre-Law, Pre-Med/Pre-Dental, Reli Stu

WELLS COLLEGE (NY) .... wells. edu **1115/1675/24**
Amer St, Bio, Bus Admin, Chem, Drama, Ed, English, For Lang, Hist, Math,
Music, Pre-Law, Pre-Med/Pre-Dental, Psych, Soc

WESLEYAN COLLEGE (GA) .... wesleyancollege.edu **1100/1650/24**
Amer St, Art, Bio, Bus Admin, Chem

WESLEYAN UNIVERSITY (CT) .... wesleyan.edu **1400/2100/31**
Amer St, Art, Art Hist, Astro, Bio, Chem, Classics, Drama, Econ, English, Hist,
Math, Poli Sci, Pre-Law, Pre-Med/Pre-Dental, Psych, Reli Stu

WEST CHESTER UNIVERSITY (PA) .... wcupa.edu **1070/1600/23**
Art, Bio, Bus Admin, Chem, Communic, Comp Sci, Ed, English, For Lang,
Music, Philo, Poli Sci, Pre-Law, Soc

WEST FLORIDA, UNIVERSITY OF (FL) .... uwf.edu **1100/1650/24**
Bio, Bus Admin, Chem, Communic, Comp Sci, Ed, Poli Sci, Pre-Med/Pre-Dental, Psych

WEST VIRGINIA UNIVERSITY (WV) .... wvu.edu **1060/1600/23**
Arch, Art, Bio, Bus Admin, Chem, Communic, Comp Sci, Drama, Engine, English,
Forest, Geol, Music, Nurs, Physics, Poli Sci, Pre-Law, Pre-Med/Pre-Dental, Psych, Soc

WEST VIRGINIA WESLEYAN COLLEGE (WV) .... wvwc.edu **1040/1560/22**
Art, Bio, Comp Sci, Drama, Ed, English, Hist, Physics

WESTERN CAROLINA UNIVERSITY (NC) .... wcu.edu **1030/1545/22**
Art, Bus Admin, Chem, Comp Sci, Ed, English, Hist, Math, Music, Nurs

WESTERN CONNECTICUT STATE UNIV. (CT) .... wcsu.edu　**1000/1500/21**
Amer St, Anthro, Art, Astro, Bus Admin, Ed, English, Music, Nurs, Soc

WESTERN ILLINOIS UNIVERSITY (IL) .... wiu.edu　**1010/1515/21**
Ag, Chem, Communic, Ed, English, Geog, Music, Soc

WESTERN KENTUCKY UNIVERSITY (KY) ....wku.edu　**1040/1560/22**
Ag, Bio, Comp Sci, Ed, Hist, Nurs, Physics, Psych, Soc

WESTERN MICHIGAN UNIVERSITY (MI) ....wmich.edu　**1060/1590/22**
*Art, Bus Admin, Chem, Communic, Comp Sci, Drama, Ed, English, Engine,
For Lang, Hist, Home Ec, Music, Nurs, Physics, Psych*

WESTERN NEW ENGLAND COLLEGE (MA)...............wnec.edu　**1060/1590/23**
Bus Admin, Communic, Comp Sci, Ed, Engine, Hist, Math, Pre-Law, Psych

WESTERN STATE COLLEGE OF COLORADO ....western.edu　**1000/1500/21**
Art, Bio, Bus Admin, Drama, English, Hist, Geol, Music

WESTERN WASHINGTON UNIVERSITY (WA) ....wwu.edu　**1105/1660/24**
Anthro, Art, Communic, Econ, Ed, English, Geog, Poli Sci, Pre-Law, Psych, Soc

WESTFIELD STATE COLLEGE (MA).....................wsc.mass.edu　**1020/1530/22**
Communic, Ed, English, Music, Poli Sci, Psych

WESTMINSTER COLLEGE (MO).................................wcmo.edu　**1120/1680/24**
Bio, Bus Admin, Econ, Ed, English, Hist, Poli Sci, Pre-Law, Pre-Med/Pre-Dental, Psych

WESTMINSTER COLLEGE (PA).........................westminster.edu　**1070/1605/23**
Bio, Chem, Comp Sci, Pre-Med/Pre-Dental, Soc

WESTMINSTER COLLEGE (UT)...............westminstercollege.edu　**1100/1650/24**
*Art, Bio, Bus Admin, Chem, Communic, Comp Sci, Ed, Engine, English, Hist, Nurs,
Philo, Physics, Poli Sci, Psych*

WESTMONT COLLEGE (CA) ....westmont.edu　**1210/1815/27**
Art, Bio, Chem, Econ, Hist, Pre-Law, Pre-Med/Pre-Dental, Psych, Reli Stu

WHEATON COLLEGE (IL) ....wheaton.edu　**1330/2000/30**
*Art, Bio, Chem, Communic, Ed, English, Hist, Math, Music, Philo, Physics,
Poli Sci, Pre-Law, Pre-Med/Pre-Dental, Psych, Reli Stu, Soc*

WHEATON COLLEGE (MA) ....wheatonma.edu　**1200/1800/26**
*Art, Art Hist, Astro, Bio, Chem, Drama, Econ, English, For Lang, Hist, Math,
Poli Sci, Pre-Law, Pre-Med/Pre-Dental, Psych, Soc*

WHEELING JESUIT (WV) ....wju.edu　**1045/1570/22**
Bio, Bus Admin, Chem, English, Hist, Math, Nurs, Philo, Physics, Psych, Reli Stu

WHEELOCK COLLEGE (MA) ....wheelock.edu　**1020/1530/22**
Ed

WHITMAN COLLEGE (WA) ....whitman.edu　**1330/2000/30**
*Art, Astro, Bio, Chem, Classics, Drama, Econ, English, For Lang, Geol, Hist, Math, Music,
Philo, Physics, Poli Sci, Pre-Law, Pre-Med/Pre-Dental, Psych, Reli Stu, Soc*

WHITTIER COLLEGE (CA) .... whittier.edu **1080/1620/23**
Bus Admin, Chem, Econ, Ed, English, Hist, Poli Sci, Pre-Law

WHITWORTH COLLEGE (WA) ....whitworth.edu **1180/1770/26**
Art, Bus Admin, Chem, Communic, Ed, English, Hist, Music, Physics, Psych, Reli Stu

WICHITA STATE UNIVERSITY (KS) ....wichita.edu **1080/1620/23**
Bus Admin, Communic, Drama, English, Philo

WIDENER UNIVERSITY (PA) ....widener.edu **1140/1710/25**
Bus Admin, Chem, Ed, Engine, Nurs

WILBERFORCE UNIVERSITY (OH) ....wilberforce.edu **1000/1500/21**
Bus Admin, Poli Sci, Pre-Law

WILKES UNIVERSITY (PA) .... wilkes.edu **1080/1620/23**
Bio, Chem, Comp Sci, Engine, English, Hist, Math, Nurs, Pharm, Pre-Med/Pre-Dental, Psych

WILLAMETTE UNIVERSITY (OR) .... willamette.edu **1230/1845/27**
Amer St, Art Hist, Bio, Chem, Classics, Econ, English, Hist, Math, Music, Philo,
Poli Sci, Pre-Law, Pre-Med/Pre-Dental, Psych, Reli Stu, Soc

WILLIAM JEWELL COLLEGE (MO) .... jewell.edu **1160/1740/25**
Bio, Bus Admin, Chem, Comp Sci, Ed, English, Music, Nurs, Philo, Physics

WILLIAM & MARY, COLLEGE OF (VA) .... wm.edu **1350/2030/30**
Amer St, Anthro, Bio, Bus Admin, Classics, Comp Sci, Drama, Econ, Ed, English,
For Lang, Geol, Hist, Philo, Physics, Poli Sci, Pre-Med/Pre-Dental, Reli Stu

WILLIAM PATERSON UNIVERSITY (NJ) .... wpunj.edu **1030/1545/22**
Anthro, Art, Bus Admin, Comp Sci, English, Hist, Music, Nurs, Soc

WILLIAMS COLLEGE (MA) .... williams.edu **1420/2130/32**
Amer St, Art, Art Hist, Astro, Bio, Chem, Classics, Comp Sci, Drama, Econ,
English, Geol, Hist, Poli Sci, Pre-Law, Pre-Med/Pre-Dental, Psych

WILMINGTON COLLEGE (OH) ....wilmington.edu **1000/1500/21**
Ag, Ed, English, Hist

WILSON COLLEGE (PA) .... wilson.edu **1040/1560/22**
Communic, Econ, Pre-Law, Psych, Soc

WINGATE UNIVERSITY (NC) .... wingate.edu **1000/1500/21**
Art, Communic, Ed, Hist, Music

WINONA STATE UNIVERSITY (MN) .... winona.edu **1090/1635/24**
Bio, Bus Admin, Chem, Communic, Comp Sci, Ed, English, Hist, Nurs, Pre-Med/Pre-Dental, Soc

WINTHROP UNIVERSITY (SC) .... winthrop.edu **1055/1585/22**
Art, Bio, Bus Admin, Chem, Comp Sci, Drama, Ed, English, Hist, Math, Poli Sci, Psych

WISCONSIN LUTHERAN COLLEGE (WI) .... wlc.edu **1100/1650/24**
Art, Biochem, Chem, Communic, Ed, Math, Music, Psych, Reli Stu

WISCONSIN, UNIVERSITY OF, AT

EAU CLAIRE .... uwec.edu **1090/1635/24**
Bio, Bus Admin, Chem, English, For Lang, Geol, Math, Nurs

GREEN BAY .... uwgb.edu **1060/1590/23**
Art, Bio, Bus Admin, Hist, Psych

LA CROSSE .... uwlax.edu **1130/1700/25**
Astro, Bus Admin, Chem, Communic, Comp Sci, Ed, Geog, Soc

MADISON .... wisc.edu **1250/1875/28**
Ag, Anthro, Art, Art Hist, Astro, Biochem, Bot, Bus Admin, Chem, Classics,
Communic,Comp Sci, Drama, Econ, Ed, Engine, English, For Lang, Forest,
Geog, Geol, Hist, Home Ec, Math, Music, Nurs, Pharm, Philo, Physics,
Poli Sci, Pre-Law, Pre-Med/Pre-Dental, Psych, Soc, Zoo

MILWAUKEE .... uwm.edu **1050/1575/22**
Anthro, Arch, Bio, Bus Admin, Chem, Drama, Econ, Ed, Engine, English,
For Lang, Hist, Nurs, Physics, Poli Sci, Pre-Law

OSHKOSH .... uwosh.edu **1060/1600/23**
Ed, Nurs

PLATTEVILLE .... uwplatt.edu **1050/1575/22**
Ag, Bio, Chem, Ed, Engine, English

RIVER FALLS .... uwrf.edu **1040/1560/22**
Ag, Ed, Geol

STEVENS POINT .... uwsp.edu **1100/1650/24**
Art, Bio, Bus Admin, Chem, Communic, Drama, Ed, Forest, Home Ec,
Math, Music, Pre-Med/Pre-Dental, Soc

STOUT .... uwstout.edu **1000/1500/21**
Bus Admin, Home Ec, Psych

SUPERIOR .... uwsuper.edu **1000/1500/21**
Art, Ed, Music, Soc

WHITEWATER .... uww.edu **1000/1500/21**
Bus Admin, Communic, Soc

WITTENBERG UNIVERSITY (OH) .... wittenberg.edu **1150/1725/25**
Art, Bio, Bus Admin, Chem, Ed, English, For Lang, Geog, Hist, Music, Poli Sci,
Pre-Law, Pre-Med/Pre-Dental, Psych, Reli Stu

WOFFORD COLLEGE (SC) .... wofford.edu **1210/1815/27**
Bio, Chem, Comp Sci, Econ, Ed, English, For Lang, Hist, Math, Philo,
Pre-Law, Pre-Med/Pre-Dental, Psych, Reli Stu, Soc

WOODBURY UNIVERSITY (CA) .... woodbury.edu **1000/1500/21**
Arch, Bus Admin

WOOSTER, COLLEGE OF (OH) .... wooster.edu **1190/1785/26**
Art Hist, Bio, Chem, Classics, Drama, Econ, English, For Lang, Geol, Hist, Math,
Music, Poli Sci, Pre-Law, Pre-Med/Pre-Dental, Reli Stu, Soc

WORCESTER POLYTECHNIC INSTITUTE (MA) .... wpi.edu **1290/1935/29**
Bio, Biochem, Bus Admin, Chem, Comp Sci, Econ, Engine, Math, Physics, Pre-Law

WORCESTER STATE COLLEGE (MA) .... worcester.edu **1015/1525/22**
Bus Admin, Chem, Communic, Ed, Nurs, Philo, Psych

WRIGHT STATE UNIVERSITY (OH) .... wright.edu **1010/1515/21**
Bus Admin, Econ, Engine, Geol, Nurs

WYOMING, UNIVERSITY OF (WY) .... uwyo.edu   **1080/1620/24**
*Ag, Amer St, Anthro, Astro, Bio, Bot, Bus Admin, Chem, Econ, Ed, Engine,
English, Geog, Geol, Nurs, Pharm, Pre-Law, Pre-Med/Pre-Dental, Psych, Zoo*

XAVIER UNIVERSITY (OH) .... xavier.edu   **1170/1755/26**
*Bio, Bus Admin, Chem, Classics, Communic, Econ, Hist, Nurs, Philo, Physics,
Psych, Reli Stu*

XAVIER UNIVERSITY OF LOUISIANA (LA) .... xula.edu   **1040/1560/22**
Bio, Bus Admin, Chem, Ed, Music, Pharm, Pre-Med/Pre-Dental, Psych, Soc

YALE UNIVERSITY (CT) .... yale.edu   **1500/2250/33**
*Amer St, Anthro, Arch, Art, Art Hist, Bio, Biochem, Chem, Classics, Drama,
Econ, English, For Lang, Geol, Hist, Math, Music, Philo, Physics, Poli Sci,
Pre-Law, Pre-Med/Pre-Dental, Psych, Reli Stu, Soc*

YESHIVA UNIVERSITY (NY) .... yu.edu   **1190/1785/26**
Bio, Bus Admin, Chem, Comp Sci, Hist, Physics, Poli Sci, Pre-Med/Pre-Dental, Psych

YORK COLLEGE (NE) .... york.edu   **1050/1575/22**
Bus Admin, Ed, Psych, Reli Stu

YORK COLLEGE OF PENNSYLVANIA (PA) .... ycp.edu   **1090/1635/24**
Bus Admin, Communic, Ed, Nurs, Poli Sci

YOUNGSTOWN STATE UNIVERSITY (OH) .... ysu.edu   **1000/1500/21**
Art, Bus Admin, English, Nurs

SECTION FOUR

APPENDICES

APPENDIX A
The 1115 Colleges Used In This Study

A

Abilene Christian University
Abilene, Texas 79699

Adelphi University
Garden City, NY 11530

Adrian College
Adrian, Michigan 49221

◆ **Agnes Scott College**
Decatur, Georgia 30030

Akron, University of
Akron, Ohio 44325

◆ **Alabama, University of**
Tuscaloosa, Alabama 35487

Alaska Pacific University
Anchorage, Alaska 99508

Alaska, University of
Anchorage, Alaska 99508

Alaska, University of
Fairbanks, Alaska 99775

Albany Coll. of Pharm. & Health Science
Albany, New York 12208

◆ **Albion College**
Albion, Michigan 49224

Albright College
Reading, Pennsylvania 19612

Alderson-Broaddus College
Phillipi, West Virginia 26416

◆ **Alfred University**
Alfred, New York 14802

◆ **Allegheny College**
Meadville, Pennsylvania 16335

◆ **Alma College**
Alma, Michigan 48801

Alverno College
Milwaukee, Wisconsin 53234

American Academy of Dramatic Arts
New York, New York 10016

American International College
Springfield, Massachusetts 01109

◆ **American University**
Washington, DC 20016

◆ **Amherst College**
Amherst, Massachusetts 01002

Anderson University
Anderson, Indiana 46012

Andrews University
Berrien Springs, Michigan 49104

Anna Maria College
Paxton, Massachusetts 01612

Appalachian State University
Boone, North Carolina 28608

Aquinas College
Grand Rapids, Michigan 49506

Arcadia University
Glenside, Pennsylvania 19038

◆ **Arizona, University of**
Tucson, Arizona 85721

◆ **Arizona State University**
Tempe, Arizona 85287

◆ **Arkansas, University of**
Fayetteville, Arkansas 72701

Art Center College of Design
Pasadena, California 91103

Art Institute of Chicago, School of the
Chicago, Illinois 60603

Arts, University of the
Philadelphia, Pennsylvania 19102

Asbury College
Wilmore, Kentucky 40390

Ashland University
Ashland, Ohio 44805

Assumption College
Worcester, Massachusetts 01609

◆ **Auburn University**
Auburn University, Alabama 36849

Augsburg College
Minneapolis, Minnesota 55454

Augusta State University
Augusta, Georgia 30964

◆ **Augustana College**
Rock Island, Illinois 61201

Augustana College
Sioux Falls, South Dakota 57197

◆ **Austin College**
Sherman, Texas 75091

Averett University
Danville, Virginia 24541

Avila University
Kansas City, Missouri 64145

Azusa Pacific University
Azusa, California 91702

◆ Phi Beta Kappa Schools   ▮ Predominantly African-American Institutions

B

Babson College
Wellesley, Massachusetts 02157

Baker University
Baldwin City, Kansas 66006

Baldwin-Wallace College
Berea, Ohio 44017

Ball State University
Muncie, Indiana 47306

Bard College,
Annandale-on-Hudson, New York 12504

Barry University
Miami Shores, Florida 33161

◆ **Bates College**
Lewiston, Maine 04240

Bay Path College
Longmeadow, MA 01106

◆ **Baylor University**
Waco, Texas 76798

Belhaven College
Jackson, Mississippi 39202

Bellarmine University
Louisville, Kentucky 40205

Belmont Abbey College
Belmont, North Carolina 28012

Belmont University
Nashville, Tennessee 37212

◆ **Beloit College**
Beloit, Wisconsin 53511

Bemidji State University
Bemidji, Minnesota 56601

Benedictine College
Atchison, Kansas 66002

Benedictine University
Lisle, Illinois 60532

▮ **Bennett College**
Greensboro, North Carolina 27401

Bennington College
Bennington, Vermont 05201

Bentley College
Waltham, Massachusetts 02154

Berea College
Berea, Kentucky 40404

Berklee College of Music
Boston, Massachusetts 02215

Berry College
Rome, Georgia 30149

Bethany College
Lindsborg, Kansas 67456

Bethany College
Bethany, West Virginia 26032

Bethany College
North Newton, Kansas 67117

Bethel College
Mishawaka, Indiana 46545

Bethel College
St. Paul, Minnesota 55112

Biola University
La Mirada, California 90639

◆ **Birmingham-Southern College**
Birmingham, Alabama 35254

Blackburn College
Carlinville, Illinois 62626

Black Hills State University
Spearfish, South Dakota 57799

Bloomsburg University
Bloomsburg, Pennsylvania 17815

Bluffton College
Bluffton, Ohio 45817

Boise State University
Boise, Idaho 83725

Boston Architectural Center
Boston, Massachusetts 02115

◆ **Boston College**
Chestnut Hill, Massachusetts 02167

Boston Conservatory
Boston, Massachusetts 02215

◆ **Boston University**
Boston, Massachusetts 02215

◆ **Bowdoin College**
Brunswick, Maine 04011

◆ **Bowling Green State University**
Bowling Green, Ohio 43403

Bradley University
Peoria, Illinois 61625

◆ **Brandeis University**
Waltham, Massachusetts 02254

Brescia University
Owensboro, Kentucky 42301

Briar Cliff University
Sioux City, Iowa 51104

Bridgewater College
Bridgewater, Virginia 22812

Bridgewater State College
Bridgewater, Massachusetts 02325

Brigham Young University
Provo, Utah 84602

◆ **Brown University**
Providence, Rhode Island 02912

Bryan College
Dayton, Tennessee 37321

Bryant University
Smithfield, Rhode Island 02917

Bryn Athyn College of the New Church
Bryn Athyn, Pennsylvania 19009

Bryn Mawr College
Bryn Mawr, Pennsylvania 19010

◆ **Bucknell University**
Lewisburg, Pennsylvania 17837

Buena Vista University
Storm Lake, Iowa 50588

Butler University
Indianapolis, Indiana 46208

C **Caldwell College**
Caldwell, New Jersey 07006

California Baptist University
Riverside, California 92504

California College of the Arts
San Francisco, California 94107

California Institute of the Arts
Valencia, California 91355

California Institute of Technology
Pasadena, California 91125

California, University of, at
◆ **Berkeley,** California 94720
◆ **Davis,** California 95616
◆ **Irvine,** California 92717
◆ **Los Angeles,** California 90024
   Merced, California 95344
◆ **Riverside,** California 92521
◆ **San Diego,** California 92093
◆ **Santa Barbara,** California 93106
◆ **Santa Cruz,** California 95064

California Lutheran University
Thousand Oaks, California 91360

California Maritime Academy
Vallejo, California 94590

California Polytechnic State University
Pomona, California 91768

California Polytechnic State University
San Luis Obispo, California 93407

California, State University of, at
Bakersfield, California 93311
Camarillo, California 93012
◆ **Chico,** California 95929

Dominguez Hills, Carson, California 90747
East Bay, California 94542
Fresno, California 93740
California, State University of, at (Cont.)
Fullerton, California 92834
◆ **Long Beach,** California 90840
Los Angeles, California 90032
Monterey Bay, California 93955
Northridge, California 91330
Sacramento, California 95819
San Bernardino, California 92407
San Jose, California 95192
San Marcos, California 92096
Stanislaus, California 95382

Calvin College
Grand Rapids, Michigan 49456

Campbell University
Buies Creek, North Carolina 27506

Capital University
Columbus, Ohio 43209

◆ **Carleton College**
Northfield, Minnesota 55057

◆ **Carnegie Mellon University**
Pittsburgh, Pennsylvania 15213

Carroll College
Helena, Montana 59625

Carroll College
Waukesha, Wisconsin 53186

Carson-Newman College
Jefferson City, Tennessee 37760

Carthage College
Kenosha, Wisconsin 53140

◆ **Case Western Reserve University**
Cleveland, Ohio 44106

Catawba College
Salisbury, North Carolina 28144

◆ **Catholic University of America**
Washington, DC 20064

Cedar Crest College
Allentown, Pennsylvania 18104

Cedarville University
Cedarville, Ohio 45314

Centenary College of Louisiana
Shreveport, Louisiana 71104

Central Arkansas, University of
Conway, Arkansas 72035

Central College
Pella, Iowa 50219

Central Connecticut State University
New Britain, Connecticut 06050

Central Florida, University of
Orlando, Florida 32816

Central Michigan University
Mount Pleasant, Michigan 48859

Central Missouri State University
Warrensburg, Missouri 64093

Central Oklahoma, University of
Edmond, Oklahoma 73034

◆ **Centre College**
Danville, Kentucky 40422

Chaminade University
Honolulu, Hawaii 96816

Champlain College
Burlington, Vermont 05402

Chapman College
Orange, California 92866

Coastal Carolina University
Conway, South Carolina 29528

College of Charleston
Charleston, South Carolina 29424

Charleston Southern University
Charleston, South Carolina 29423

Charleston, University of
Charleston, West Virginia 25304

◆ **Chatham College**
Pittsburgh, Pennsylvania 15232

Chestnut Hill College
Philadelphia, Pennsylvania 19118

Cheyney University of Pennsylvania
Cheyney, Pennsylvania 19319

◆ **Chicago, University of**
Chicago, Illinois 60637

Chowan College
Murfreesboro, North Carolina 27855

Christian Brothers University
Memphis, Tennessee 38104

Christopher Newport University
Newport News, Virginia 23606

Christendom College
Front Royal, Virginia 22630

◆ **Cincinnati, University of**
Cincinnati, Ohio 45221

Citadel, The
Charleston, South Carolina 29409

▮ **Claflin University**
Orangeburg, South Carolina 29115

◆ **Claremont McKenna College**
Claremont, California 91711

▮ **Clark Atlanta University**
Atlanta, Georgia 30314

◆ **Clark University**
Worcester, Massachusetts 01610

Clarke College
Dubuque, Iowa 52001

Clarkson University
Potsdam, New York 13676

◆ **Clemson University**
Clemson, South Carolina 29634

Cleveland Institute of Art
Cleveland, Ohio 44106

Cleveland Institute of Music
Cleveland, Ohio 44106

◆ **Coe College**
Cedar Rapids, Iowa 52402

Cogswell Polytechnic College
Sunnyvale, California 94089

Coker College
Hartsdale, South Carolina 29550

◆ **Colby College**
Waterville, Maine 04901

Colby-Sawyer College
New London, New Hampshire 03257

◆ **Colgate University**
Hamilton, New York 13346

◆ **Colorado College**
Colorado Springs, Colorado 80903

◆ **Colorado, University of**
Boulder, Colorado 80309

Colorado, University of
Colorado Springs, Colorado 80933

Colorado, University of
Denver, Colorado 80217

Colorado School of Mines
Golden, Colorado 80401

◆ **Colorado State University**
Fort Collins, Colorado 80523

Columbia College Chicago
Chicago, Illinois 60605

Columbia College
Columbia, Missouri 65216

Columbia College
Columbia, South Carolina 29203

◆ Phi Beta Kappa Schools   ▮ Predominantly African-American Institutions

◆ **Columbia University**
New York, New York 10027
   ◆ **Barnard College,** New York, NY 10027
Concordia University
Irvine, California 92612

Concordia College
Moorhead, Minnesota 56560

Concordia University
Seward, Nebraska 68434

Concordia University
Portland, Oregon 97211

Concordia University-Austin
Austin, Texas 78705

◆ **Connecticut, University of**
Storrs, Connecticut 06269

◆ **Connecticut College**
New London, Connecticut 06320

Converse College
Spartanburg, South Carolina 29302

Cooper Union College, The
New York, New York 10003

Corban College
Salem, Oregon 97317

◆ **Cornell College**
Mount Vernon, Iowa 52314

◆ **Cornell University**
Ithaca, New York 14853

Cornish College of the Arts
Seattle, Washington 98102

Covenant College
Lookout Mountain, Georgia 30750

Creighton University
Omaha, Nebraska 68178

Culver-Stockton College
Canton, Missouri 63435

Cumberland College
Williamsburg, Kentucky 40769

Curtis Institute of Music
Philadelphia, Pennsylvania 19103

D **Daemen College**
Amherst, New York 14226

Dakota State University
Madison, South Dakota 57042

◆ **Dallas, University of**
Irving, Texas 75062

Dana College
Blair, Nebraska 68008

◆ **Dartmouth College**
Hanover, New Hampshire 03755

◆ **Davidson College**
Davidson, North Carolina 28036

Dayton, University of
Dayton, Ohio 45469

■ **Delaware State University**
Dover, Delaware 19901

◆ **Delaware, University of**
Newark, Delaware 19716

Delaware Valley College of Pennsylvania
Doylestown, Pennsylvania 18901

◆ **Denison University**
Granville, Ohio 43023

◆ **Denver, University of**
Denver, Colorado 80208

DePaul University
Chicago, Illinois 60604

◆ **DePauw University**
Greencastle, Indiana 46135

DeSales University
Center Valley, Pennsylvania 18034

Detroit Mercy, University of
Detroit, Michigan 48221

◆ **Dickinson College**
Carlisle, Pennsylvania 17013

■ **Dillard University**
New Orleans, Louisiana 70122

Dixie State College
Saint George, Utah 84770

Doane College
Crete, Nebraska 68333

Dominican University
River Forest, Illinois 60305

Dominican University of California
San Rafael, California 94901

Dordt College
Sioux Center, Iowa 51250

◆ **Drake University**
Des Moines, Iowa 50311

◆ **Drew University**
Madison, New Jersey 07940

Drexel University
Philadelphia, Pennsylvania 19104

Drury University
Springfield, Missouri 65802

Dubuque, University of
Dubuque, Iowa 52001

◆ Phi Beta Kappa Schools   ■ Predominantly African-American Institutions

◆ **Duke University**
Durham, North Carolina 27706

Duquesne University
Pittsburgh, Pennsylvania 15282

D'Youville College
Buffalo, New York 14201

E.◆ **Earlham College**
Richmond, Indiana 47374

East Carolina University
Greenville, North Carolina 27858

East Central University
Ada, Oklahoma 74820

East Stroudsburg University
East Stroudsburg, Pennsylvania 18301

East Tennessee State University
Johnson City, Tennessee 37614

Eastern University
St. Davids, Pennsylvania 19087

Eastern Connecticut State University
Willimantic, Connecticut 06226

Eastern Kentucky University
Richmond, Kentucky 40475

Eastern Illinois University
Charleston, Illinois 61920

Eastern Mennonite University
Harrisonburg, Virginia 22802

Eastern Michigan University
Ypsilanti, Michigan 48197

Eastern Nazarene College
Quincy, Massachusetts 02170

Eastern New Mexico University
Portales, New Mexico 88130

Eastern Oregon University
La Grande, Oregon 97850

Eastern Washington University
Cheney, Washington 99034

◆ **Eckerd College**
St. Petersburg, Florida 33733

Edgewood College
Madison, Wisconsin 53711

Edinboro University of Pennsylvania
Edinboro, Pennsylvania 16444

Elizabethtown College
Elizabethtown, Pennsylvania 17022

Elon University
Elon University, North Carolina 27244

Elmhurst College
Elmhurst, Illinois 60126

◆ **Elmira College**
Elmira, New York 14901

Elms College
Chicopee, Massachusetts 01013

Embry-Riddle Aeronautical University
Daytona Beach, Florida 32114

Emerson College
Boston, Massachusetts 02116

Emmanuel College
Boston, Massachusetts 02115

Emory and Henry College
Emory, Virginia 24327

◆ **Emory University**
Atlanta, Georgia 30322

Endicott College
Beverly, MA 01915

Erskine College
Due West, South Carolina 29639

Eureka College
Eureka, Illinois 61530

Evansville, University of
Evansville, Indiana 47722

F◆ **Fairfield University**
Fairfield, Connecticut 06430

Fairleigh Dickinson University
Teaneck, New Jersey 07666

Fairmont State University
Fairmont, West Virginia 26554

Faulkner University
Montgomery, Alabama 36109

Ferris State University
Big Rapids, Michigan 49307

Findlay, University of
Findlay, Ohio 45840

◆▌**Fisk University**
Nashville, Tennessee 37208

Fitchburg State College
Fitchburg, Massachusetts 01420

Five Towns College
Dix Hills, New York 11746

Flagler College
St. Augustine, Florida 32085

◆ **Florida, University of**
Gainesville, Florida 32611

▌ **Florida A&M University**
Tallahassee, FL 32307

Florida Atlantic University
Boca Raton, Florida 33431

Florida Gulf Coast University
Fort Myers, Georgia 33965

Florida Institute of Technology
Melbourne, Florida 32901

◆ **Florida International University**
Miami, Florida 33199

Florida Southern College
Lakeland, Florida 33801

◆ **Florida State University**
Tallahassee, Florida 32306

Fontbonne University
St. Louis, Missouri 63105

◆ **Fordham University**
Bronx, New York 10458

Fort Hays State University
Hays, Kansas 67601

Fort Lewis College
Durango, Colorado 81301

Framingham State College
Framingham, Massachusetts 01701

Franciscan University of Steubenville
Steubenville, Ohio 43952

Franklin College
Franklin, Indiana 46131

◆ **Franklin & Marshall College**
Lancaster, Pennsylvania 17604

Freed-Hardeman University
Henderson, Tennessee 38340

Friends University
Wichita, Kansas 67213

Frostburg State University
Frostburg, Maryland 21532

Full Sail University
Winter Park, Florida 32792

◆ **Furman University**
Greenville, South Carolina 29613

G

Gannon University
Erie, Pennsylvania 16541

Gardner-Webb University
Boiling Springs, North Carolina 28017

Geneva College
Beaver Falls, Pennsylvania 15010

Georgetown College
Georgetown, Kentucky 40324

◆ **Georgetown University**
Washington, DC 20057

George Fox University
Newberg, Oregon 97132

George Mason University
Fairfax, Virginia 22030

◆ **George Washington University**
Washington, DC 20052

◆ **Georgia, University of**
Athens, Georgia 30602

Georgia Institute of Technology
Atlanta, Georgia 30332

Georgia Southern University
Statesboro, Georgia 30460

Georgia Southwestern University
Americus, Georgia 31704

Georgia State University
Atlanta, Georgia 30303

◆ **Gettysburg College**
Gettysburg, Pennsylvania 17325

Gonzaga University
Spokane, Washington 99258

Gordon College
Wenham, Massachusetts 01984

Goshen College
Goshen, Indiana 46526

◆ **Goucher College**
Towson, Maryland 21204

Graceland University
Lamoni, Iowa 50140

Grambling State University
Grambling, Louisiana 71245

Grand Valley State University
Allendale, Michigan 49401

Great Falls, University of
Great Falls, Montana 59405

Greensboro College
Greensboro, North Carolina 27401

◆ **Grinnell College**
Grinnell, Iowa 50112

Grove City College
Grove City, Pennsylvania 16127

Guilford College
Greensboro, North Carolina 27410

◆ **Gustavus Adolphus College**
St. Peter, Minnesota 56082

Gwynedd-Mercy College
Gwnedd Valley, Pennsylvania 19437

◆ Phi Beta Kappa Schools   ▌Predominantly African-American Institutions

H ◆ **Hamilton College**
Clinton, New York 13323

◆ **Hamline University**
St. Paul, Minnesota 55104

◆ **Hampden-Sydney College**
Hampden-Sydney, Virginia 23943

◆ **Hampton University**
Hampton, Virginia 23668

Hannibal-La Grange College
Hannibal, Missouri 63401

Hanover College
Hanover, Indiana 47243

Harding University
Searcy, Arkansas 72149

Hardin-Simmons University
Abilene, Texas 79698

Harrisburg University
Harrisburg, Pennsylvania 17101

Hartford, University of
Hartford, Connecticut 06117

Hartwick College
Oneonta, New York 13820

◆ **Harvard University**
Cambridge, Massachusetts 02138

Harvey Mudd College
Claremont, California 91711

Hastings College
Hastings, Nebraska 68901

◆ **Haverford College**
Haverford, Pennsylvania 19041

Hawaii Pacific University
Honolulu, Hawaii 96813

Hawaii, University of
Hilo, Hawaii 96720

◆ **Hawaii, University of**
Manoa, Honolulu, Hawaii 96822

Heidelberg College
Tiffin, Ohio 44883

Henderson State University
Arkadelphia, Arkansas 71999

◆ **Hendrix College**
Conway, Arkansas 72032

High Point University
High Point, North Carolina 27262

Hillsdale College
Hillsdale, Michigan 49242

◆ **Hiram College**
Hiram, Ohio 44234

◆ **Hobart & William Smith Colleges**
Geneva, New York 14456

◆ **Hofstra University**
Hempstead, New York 11550

◆ **Hollins University**
Roanoke, Virginia 24020

◆ **Holy Cross, College of the**
Worcester, Massachusetts 01610

Holy Names University
Oakland, California 94619

Hood College
Frederick, Maryland 21701

◆ **Hope College**
Holland, Michigan 49423

Houghton College
Houghton, New York 14744

Houston Baptist University
Houston, Texas 77074

Houston, University of
Houston, Texas 77004

◆■ **Howard University**
Washington, DC 20059

Humboldt State University
Arcata, California 95521

Huntingdon College
Montgomery, Alabama 36106

Huntington University
Huntington, Indiana 46750

Husson University
Bangor, Maine 04401

I **Idaho, College of**
Caldwell, Idaho 83605

◆ **Idaho, University of**
Moscow, Idaho 83844

Idaho State University
Pocatello, Idaho 83209

Illinois, University of, at
◆ **Urbana-Champaign,** Illinois 61801
◆ **Chicago,** Illinois 60680

◆ **Illinois College**
Jacksonville, Illinois 62650

Illinois Institute of Technology
Chicago, Illinois 60616

Illinois State University
Normal, Illinois 61761

◆ **Illinois Wesleyan University**
Bloomington, Illinois 61702

Immaculata University
Immaculata, Pennsylvania 19345

Indiana State University
Terre Haute, Indiana 47809

◆ **Indiana University**
Bloomington, Indiana 47405

Indiana University of Pennsylvania
Indiana, Pennsylvania 15705

I.U. - P.U. - Indianapolis University
Indianapolis, Indiana 46202

Indiana University of Technology
Fort Wayne, Indiana 46803

Indiana Wesleyan University
Marion, Indiana 46953

Iona College
New Rochelle, New York 10801

◆ **Iowa, University of**
Iowa City, Iowa 52242

◆ **Iowa State University of Science & Technology**
Ames, Iowa 50011

Ithaca College
Ithaca, New York 14850

J **Jacksonville State University**
Jacksonville, Alabama 36265

Jacksonville University
Jacksonville, Florida 32211

James Madison University
Harrisonburg, Virginia 22807

Jamestown College
Jamestown, North Dakota 58405

John Brown University
Siloam Springs, Arkansas 72761

John Carroll University
Cleveland, Ohio 44118

◆ **Johns Hopkins University**
Baltimore, Maryland 21218

Johnson State College
Johnson, Vermont 05656

Johnson C. Smith University
Charlotte, North Carolina 28216

Judson College
Marion, Alabama 36756

Juilliard School
New York, New York 10023

Juniata College
Huntingdon, Pennsylvania 16652

K ◆ **Kalamazoo College**
Kalamazoo, Michigan 49006

Kansas City Art Institute
Kansas City, Missouri 64111

◆ **Kansas, University of**
Lawrence, Kansas 66045

◆ **Kansas State University**
Manhattan, Kansas 66506

Kean University of New Jersey
Union, New Jersey 07083

Keene State College
Keene, New Hampshire 03435

Kennesaw State College
Marietta, Georgia 30144

◆ **Kent State University**
Kent, Ohio 44242

◆ **Kentucky, University of**
Lexington, Kentucky 40506

Kentucky Wesleyan College
Owensboro, Kentucky 42301

◆ **Kenyon College**
Gambier, Ohio 43022

Kettering University
Flint, Michigan 48504

King College
Bristol, Tennessee 37620

King's College
Wilkes-Barre, Pennsylvania 18711

◆ **Knox College**
Galesburg, Illinois 61401

Kutztown University
Kutztown, Pennsylvania 19530

L ◆ **Lafayette College**
Easton, Pennsylvania 18042

◆ **Lake Forest College**
Lake Forest, Illinois 60045

Lamar University
Beaumont, Texas 77710

Lambuth University
Jackson, Tennessee 38301

LaSalle University
Philadelphia, Pennsylvania 19141

Lasell College
Newton, Massachusetts 02466

La Verne, University of
La Verne, California 91750

◆ **Lawrence University**
Appleton, Wisconsin 54912

Lebanon Valley College
Annville, Pennsylvania 17003

◆ **Lehigh University**
Bethlehem, Pennsylvania 18015

LeMoyne College
Syracuse, New York 13214

Lenoir Rhyne College
Hickory, North Carolina 28603

Lesley University
Cambridge, Massachusetts 02138

LeTourneau College
Longview, Texas 75607

◆ **Lewis & Clark College**
Portland, Oregon 97219

Lewis-Clark State College
Lewiston, Idaho 83501

Liberty University
Lynchburg, Virginia 24502

Lindenwood University
St. Charles, Missouri 63301

Linfield College
McMinnville, Oregon 97128

Lipscomb University
Nashville, Tennessee 37204

Lock Haven University of Pennsylvania
Lock Haven, Pennsylvania 17745

Long Island University-Brooklyn
Brooklyn, New York 11201

Long Island University-C.W. Post
Brookville, New York 11548

Longwood University
Farmville, Virginia 23909

Loras College
Dubuque, Iowa 52001

Louisiana College
Pineville, Louisiana 71360

Louisiana-Lafayette, University of
Lafayette, Louisiana 70504

Louisiana-Monroe, University of
Monroe, Louisiana 71209

◆ **Louisiana State University**
Baton Rouge, Louisiana 70803

Louisiana Tech University
Ruston, Louisiana 71272

Louisville, University of
Louisville, Kentucky 40292

Lowell, University of
Lowell, Massachusetts 01854

◆ **Loyola College in Maryland**
Baltimore, Maryland 21210

Loyola Marymount University
Los Angeles, California 90045

◆ **Loyola University of Chicago**
Chicago, Illinois 60611

Loyola University
New Orleans, Louisiana 70118

◆ **Luther College**
Decorah, Iowa 52101

Lycoming College
Williamsport, Pennsylvania 17701

Lynchburg College
Lynchburg, Virginia 24501

Lyndon State College
Lyndonville, Vermont 05851

Lyon College
Batesville, Arkansas 72503

M ◆ **Macalester College**
St. Paul, Minnesota 55105

MacMurray College
Jacksonville, Illinois 62650

Maine, University of
Farmington, Maine 04938

◆ **Maine, University of**
Orono, Maine 04469

Malone College
Canton, Ohio 44709

Manchester College
North Manchester, Indiana 46962

◆ **Manhattan College**
Riverdale, New York 10471

Manhattan School of Music
New York, New York 10027

Manhattanville College
Purchase, New York 10577

Mannes School of Music
New York, New York 10024

Mansfield University of Pennsylvania
Mansfield, Pennsylvania 16933

◆ **Marietta College**
Marietta, Ohio 45750

◆ Phi Beta Kappa Schools ▮ Predominantly African-American Institutions

Marist College
Poughkeepsie, NY 12601

◆ **Marquette University**
Milwaukee, Wisconsin 53201

Marshall University
Huntington, West Virginia 25755

◆ **Mary Baldwin College**
Staunton, Virginia 24401

▌ **Marygrove College**
Detroit, Michigan 48221

Maryland Institute-College of Art
Baltimore, Maryland 21217

◆ **Maryland, University of Baltimore County**
Baltimore, Maryland 21250

◆ **Maryland, University of**
College Park, Maryland 20742

Marymount Manhattan College
New York, New York 10021

Marymount University
Arlington, Virginia 22207

Maryville College
Maryville, Tennessee 37804

Maryville University-Saint Louis
St. Louis, Missouri 63141

◆ **Mary Washington, University of**
Fredericksburg, Virginia 22401

Marywood University
Scranton, Pennsylvania 18509

Massachusetts College of Art
Boston Massachusetts 02215

Massachusetts College of Liberal Arts
North Adams, Massachusetts 01247

Massachusetts College of Pharmacy
Boston, Massachusetts 02115

◆ **Massachusetts, University of**
Amherst, Massachusetts 01003

Massachusetts, University of
Boston, Massachusetts 02125

Massachusetts, University of
Lowell, Massachusetts 01854

Massachusetts, University of
North Dartmouth, Massachusetts 02747

◆ **Massachusetts Institute of Technology**
Cambridge, Massachusetts 02139

Massachusetts Maritime Academy
Buzzards Bay, Massachusetts 02532

Master's College, The
Santa Clarita, California 91321

◆ **McDaniel College**
Westminster, Maryland 21157

◆ **McKendree College**
LeBaron, Illinois 62254

McMurry University
Abilene, Texas 79697

McPherson College
McPherson, Kansas 67460

Memphis College of Art
Memphis, Tennessee 38112

Memphis, University of
Memphis, Tennessee 38152

Mercer University
Macon, Georgia 31207

Mercy College
Dobbs Ferry, New York 10522

Mercyhurst College
Erie, Pennsylvania 16546

Meredith College
Raleigh, North Carolina 27607

Merrimack College
No. Andover, Massachusetts 01845

Messiah College
Grantham, Pennsylvania 17027

◆ **Miami University**
Oxford, Ohio 45056

◆ **Miami, University of**
Coral Gables, Florida 33124

◆ **Michigan, University of**
Ann Arbor, Michigan 48109

Michigan, University of
Dearborn, Michigan 48128

◆ **Michigan State University**
East Lansing, Michigan 48824

Michigan Technological University
Houghton, Michigan 49931

◆ **Middlebury College**
Middlebury, Vermont 05753

Middle Tennessee State University
Murfreesboro, Tennessee 37132

Midwestern State University
Wichita Falls, Texas 76308

Millersville University of Pennsylvania
Millersville, Pennsylvania 17551

Milligan College
Milligan College, Tennessee 37682

Millikin University
Decatur, Illinois 62522

◆ **Mills College**
Oakland, California 94613

◆ **Millsaps College**
Jackson, Mississippi 39210

Milwaukee School of Engineering
Milwaukee, Wisconsin 53201

Minnesota State University - Mankato
Mankato, Minnesota 56001

Minnesota State University - Moorhead
Moorhead, Minnesota 56563

Minnesota, University of
Duluth, Minnesota 55812

◆ **Minnesota, University of**
Minneapolis, Minnesota 55455

Minnesota, University of
Morris, Minnesota 56267

Misericordia, College
Dallas, Pennsylvania 18612

Mississippi College
Clinton, Mississippi 39058

Mississippi State University
Mississippi State, Mississippi 39762

◆ **Mississippi, University of**
University, Mississippi 38677

Mississippi University for Women
Columbus, Mississippi 39701

Missouri Baptist University
St. Louis, Missouri 63141

Missouri Southern State University
Joplin, Missouri 64801

Missouri State University
Springfield, Missouri 65897

◆ **Missouri, University of**
Columbia, Missouri 65211

Missouri, University of
Kansas City, Missouri 64110

Missouri, University of
Rolla, Missouri 65401

Missouri, University of
St. Louis, Missouri 63121

Mobile, University of
Mobile, Alabama 36663

Molloy College
Rockville Centre, New York 11571

Monmouth College
Monmouth, Illinois 61462

Monmouth University
West Long Branch, New Jersey 07764

Montana Tech. of the U. of Montana
Butte, Montana 59701

Montana, University of
Missoula, Montana 59812

Montana State University
Billings, Montana 59101

Montana State University
Bozeman, Montana 59717

Montevallo, University of
Montevallo, Alabama 35115

Montclair State College
Upper Montclair, New Jersey 07043

Montreat College
Montreat, North Carolina 28757

Montserrat College of Art
Beverly, Massachusetts 01915

Moore College of Art
Philadelphia, Pennsylvania 19103

Moravian College
Bethlehem, Pennsylvania 18018

◆■ **Morehouse College**
Atlanta, Georgia 30314

■ **Morgan State University**
Baltimore, Maryland 21257

Morningside College
Sioux City, Iowa 51106

◆ **Mount Holyoke College**
South Hadley, Massachusetts 01075

Mount Marty College
Yankton, South Dakota 57078

Mount Mercy College
Cedar Rapids, Iowa 52402

Mount St. Joseph, College of
Cincinnati, Ohio 45233

Mount St. Mary's University
Emmitsburg, Maryland 21727

Mount St. Mary's College
Los Angeles, California 90049

Mount St. Mary College
Newburgh, New York, 12550

Mount Saint Vincent, College of
Riverdale, New York, 10471

Mount Union College
Alliance, Ohio 44601

◆ **Muhlenberg College**
Allentown, Pennsylvania 18104

Murray State University
Murray, Kentucky 42071

Museum of Fine Arts, School of the
Boston, Massachusetts 02115

Muskingum College
New Concord, Ohio 43762

N **Nazareth College of Rochester**
Rochester, New York 14618

Nebraska, University of
Kearney, Nebraska 68849

◆ **Nebraska, University of**
Lincoln, Nebraska 68588

Nebraska, University of
Omaha, Nebraska 68182

Nebraska Wesleyan University
Lincoln, Nebraska 68504

Nevada, University of, at
Las Vegas, Nevada 89154
Reno, Nevada 89557

New College of Florida
Sarasota, Florida 34243

New England Conservatory of Music
Boston, Massachusetts 02115

◆ **New Hampshire, University of**
Durham, New Hampshire 03824

◆ **New Jersey, College of**
Ewing, New Jersey 08628

New Jersey Institute of Technology
Newark, New Jersey 07102

Newman University
Wichita, Kansas 67213

**New Mexico Institute of Mining
and Technology**
Socorro, New Mexico 87801

New Mexico State University
Las Cruces, New Mexico 88003

◆ **New Mexico, University of**
Albuquerque, New Mexico 87131

New Orleans, University of
New Orleans, Louisiana 70148

**New School University -
Eugene Lang College**
New York, New York 10011

New York, City University of, at

◆ **Baruch College,** New York, NY 10010
◆ **Brooklyn College,** Brooklyn, NY 11210
◆ **City College,** New York, New York 10031
◆ **Herbert H. Lehman Coll.,** Bronx, NY 10468
◆ **Hunter College,** New York, NY 10021
John Jay College, New York, NY 10019
◆ **Queens College,** Flushing, NY 11367

New York Institute of Techology
Old Westbury, New York 11568

New York, State University of, at
◆ **Albany,** New York 12222
◆ **Binghamton,** New York 13902
Brockport, New York 14420
◆ **Buffalo,** New York 14214
Fredonia, New York 14063
◆ **Geneseo,** New York 14454
Maritime College (TNS), New York 10465
New Paltz, New York 12561
Oneonta, New York 13820
Oswego, New York 13126
Plattsburgh, New York 12901
Potsdam, New York 13676
Purchase, New York 10577
Staten Island, New York 10314
◆ **Stony Brook,** New York 11794

◆ **New York University**
New York, New York 10011

Niagara University
Niagara Falls, New York, 14109

Nicholls State University
Thibodaux, Louisiana 70310

North Carolina School of the Arts
Winston-Salem, North Carolina 27117

North Carolina, University of, at
Asheville, North Carolina 28804
◆ **Chapel Hill,** North Carolina 27599
Charlotte, North Carolina 28223
◆ **Greensboro,** North Carolina 27412
Pembroke, North Carolina 28372
Wilmington, North Carolina 28403

◆ **North Carolina State University**
Raleigh, North Carolina 27695

North Central College
Naperville, Illinois 60566

North Dakota State University
Fargo, North Dakota 58105

◆ **North Dakota, University of**
Grand Forks, North Dakota 58202

North Florida, University of
Jacksonville, Florida 32216

North Georgia College & State Univ.
Dahlonega, Georgia 30597

North Texas, University of
Denton, Texas 76203

Northeastern Illinois University
Chicago, Illinois 60625

Northeastern State University
Tahlequah, Oklahoma 74464

Northeastern University
Boston, Massachusetts 02115

Northern Arizona University
Flagstaff, Arizona 86011

Northern Colorado University
Greeley, Colorado 80639

Northern Illinois University
DeKalb, Illinois 60115

Northern Iowa, University of
Cedar Falls, Iowa 50614

Northern Kentucky University
Highland Heights, Kentucky 41099

Northern Michigan University
Marquette, Michigan 49855

Northern State University
Aberdeen, South Dakota 57401

Northwest Missouri State University
Maryville, Missouri 64468

Northwestern College
Orange City, Iowa 51041

Northwestern College
St. Paul, Minnesota 55113

◆ **Northwestern University**
Evanston, Illinois 60204

Northwestern University of Louisiana
Natchitoches, Louisiana 71497

Northwood University
Midland, Michigan 48640

Norwich University
Northfield, Vermont 05663

◆ **Notre Dame, University of**
Notre Dame, Indiana 46556

Nova Southeastern University
Ft. Lauderdale, Florida 33314

Nyack College
Nyack, New York 10960

O **Oakland City University**
Oakland City, Indiana 47660

Oakland University
Rochester, Michigan 48309

◆ **Oberlin College**
Oberlin, Ohio 44074

◆ **Occidental College**
Los Angeles, California 90041

Oglethorpe University
Atlanta, Georgia 30319

Ohio Northern University
Ada, Ohio 45810

◆ **Ohio State University**
Columbus, Ohio 43210

◆ **Ohio University**
Athens, Ohio 45701

◆ **Ohio Wesleyan University**
Delaware, Ohio 43015

Oklahoma Baptist University
Shawnee, Oklahoma 74801

Oklahoma Christian University
Olahoma, City, Oklahoma 73136

Oklahoma City University
Oklahoma City, Oklahoma 73106

◆ **Oklahoma, University of**
Norman, Oklahoma 73069

Oklahoma State University
Stillwater, Oklahoma 74078

Old Dominion University
Norfolk, Virginia 23529

Olivet Nazarene University
Bourbonnais, Illinois 60914

Olin College of Engineering
Needham, Massachusetts 02492

Oral Roberts University
Tulsa, Oklahoma 74171

Oregon Institute of Technology
Klamath Falls, Oregon 97601

◆ **Oregon, University of**
Eugene, Oregon 97403

Oregon State University
Corvallis, Oregon 97331

Otis College of Art and Design
Los Angeles, California 90045

Otterbein College
Westerville, Ohio 43081

Ouachita Baptist University
Arkadelphia, Arkansas 71998

Ozarks, College of the
Point Lookout, Missouri 65726

P **Pace University**
New York, New York 10038

◆ Phi Beta Kappa Schools ▌ Predominantly African-American Institutions

Pacific Lutheran University
Tacoma, Washington 984473

◆ **Pacific, U. of the**
Stockton, California 95211

Pacific University
Forest Grove, Oregon 97116

Palm Beach Atlantic University
West Palm Beach, Florida 33416

Parsons School of Design
New York, New York 10011

Paul Smith's College
Paul Smiths, New York 12970

Pennsylvania Academy of the Fine Arts
Philadelphia, Pennsylvania 19102

Pennsylvania State University at Erie
Erie, Pennsylvania 16563

Pennsylvania State University at Harrisburg
Harrisburg, Pennsylvania 17057

◆ **Pennsylvania State University**
University Park, Pennsylvania 16802

◆ **Pennsylvania, University of**
Philadelphia, Pennsylvania 19104

Pepperdine University
Malibu, California 90263

Philadelphia Biblical University
Langhorne, Pennsylvania 19047

Philadelphia University
Philadelphia, Pennsylvania 19144

Piedmont College
Demorest, Georgia 30535

Pine Manor College
Chestnut Hill, Massachusetts 02167

Pittsburg State University
Pittsburg, Kansas 66762

Pittsburgh, University of
Bradford, Pennsylvania 16701

Pittsburgh, University of
Greensburg, Pennsylvania 15601

Pittsburgh, University of
Johnstown, Pennsylvania 15904

◆ **Pittsburgh, University of**
Pittsburgh, Pennsylvania 15260

Pitzer College
Claremont, California 91711

Plymouth State College
Plymouth, New Hampshire 03264

Point Loma Nazarene University
San Diego, California 92106

Point Park University
Pittsburgh, Pennsylvania 15222

Polytechnic Institute of New York
Brooklyn, New York 11201

◆ **Pomona College**
Claremont, California 91711

Portland State University
Portland, Oregon 97200

Portland, University of
Portland, Oregon 97203

Pratt Institute
Brooklyn, New York 11205

Presbyterian College
Clinton, South Carolina 29325

Presentation College
Aberdeen, South Dakota 57401

◆ **Princeton University**
Princeton, New Jersey 08544

Principia College
Elsah, Illinois 62028

Providence College
Providence, Rhode Island 02918

Puerto Rico, University of
Cayey, Puerto Rico 00736

Puerto Rico, University of
Mayaguez, Puerto Rico 00680

Puerto Rico, University of
Rio Piedras, Puerto Rico 00931

◆ **Puget Sound, University of**
Tacoma, Washington 98416

◆ **Purdue University**
W. Lafayette, Indiana 47907

Q **Queens University of Charlotte**
Charlotte, North Carolina 28274

Quincy University
Quincy, Illinois 62301

Quinnipiac University
Hamden, Connecticut 06518

R **Radford University**
Radford, Virginia 24142

Ramapo College
Mahwah, New Jersey 07430

◆ **Randolph College**
Lynchburg, Virginia 24503

◆ **Randolph-Macon College**
Ashland, Virginia 23005

◆ **Redlands, University of**
Redlands, California 92373

◆ **Reed College**
Portland, Oregon 97202

Regis College
Weston, Massachusetts 02193

Regis University
Denver, Colorado 80221

Reinhardt College
Waleska, Georgia 30183

Rensselaer Polytechnic Institute
Troy, New York 12180

Rhode Island College
Providence, Rhode Island 02908

Rhode Island School of Design
Providence, Rhode Island 02903

◆ **Rhode Island, University of**
Kingston, Rhode Island 02881

◆ **Rhodes College**
Memphis, Tennessee 38112

◆ **Rice University**
Houston, Texas 77251

Richard Stockton College of New Jersey
Pomona, New Jersey 08240

◆ **Richmond, University of**
Richmond, Virginia 23173

Rider University
Lawrenceville, New Jersey 08648

◆ **Ripon College**
Ripon, Wisconsin 54971

◆ **Roanoke College**
Salem, Virginia 24153

Robert Morris University
Moon Township, Pennsylvania 15108

◆ **Rochester, University of**
Rochester, New York 14627

Rochester Institute of Technology
Rochester, New York 14623

◆ **Rockford College**
Rockford, Illinois 61108

Rockhurst University
Kansas City, Missouri 64110

Rocky Mountain College
Billings, Montana 59102

Roger Williams University
Bristol, Rhode Island 02809

Rollins College
Winter Park, Florida 32789

Roosevelt University
Chicago, Illinois 60605

Rose-Hulman Institute of Technology
Terre Haute, Indiana 47803

Rosemont College
Rosemont, Pennsylvania 19010

Rowan University
Mahwah, New Jersey 08028

◆ **Rutgers University**
New Brunswick, New Jersey 08854

Rutgers University
Camden, New Jersey 08101

Rutgers-Newark
Newark, New Jersey 07102

S **Sacred Heart University**
Fairfield, Connecticut 06432

Sage Colleges
Troy, New York 12180

Saginaw Valley State University
University Center, Michigan 48710

St. Ambrose University
Davenport, Iowa 52803

St. Andrews Presbyterian College
Laurinburg, North Carolina 28352

St. Anselm College
Manchester, New Hampshire 03102

St. Bonaventure University
St. Bonaventure, New York 14778

◆ **St. Catherine, College of**
St. Paul, Minnesota 55105

St. Cloud University
St. Cloud, Minnesota 56301

St. Edward's University
Austin, Texas 78704

St. Francis College
Brooklyn, New York 11201

St. Francis, University of
Fort Wayne, Indiana 46808

St. Francis University
Loretto, Pennsylvania 15940

St. John Fisher College
Rochester, New, York 14618

St. John's University
Jamaica, New York 11439

**Saint John's University/College
of Saint Benedict**
Collegeville, Minnesota 56321

◆ Phi Beta Kappa Schools ■ Predominantly African-American Institutions

Saint Joseph College
W. Hartford, Connecticut 06117

St. Joseph's College
Rensselaer, Indiana 47978

St. Joseph's College
Standish, Maine 04084

St. Joseph's College
Patchogue, New York 11772

◆ **Saint Joseph's University**
Philadelphia, Pennsylvania 19131

◆ **St. Lawrence University**
Canton, New York 13617

St. Louis College of Pharmacy
St. Louis, Missouri 63110

◆ **Saint Louis University**
St. Louis, Missouri 63103

Saint Martin's University
Lacey, Washington 98503

Saint Mary, College of
Omaha, Nebraska 68124

Saint Mary's College
Notre Dame, Indiana 46556

Saint Mary's College of California
Moraga, California 94575

Saint Mary, University of
Leavenworth, Kansas 66048

◆ **St. Mary's College of Maryland**
St. Mary's City, Maryland 20686

St. Mary's University of Minnesota
Winona, Minnesota 55987

St. Mary's University
San Antonio, Texas 78228

◆ **Saint Michael's College**
Colchester, Vermont 05439

St. Norbert College
DePere, Wisconsin 54115

◆ **St. Olaf College**
Northfield, Minnesota 55057

St. Peter's College
Jersey City, New Jersey 07306

Saint Rose, College of
Albany, New York 12203

St. Scholastica, College of
Duluth, Minnesota 55811

St. Thomas Aquinas College
Sparkhill, New York 10976

Saint Thomas, University of
St. Paul, Minnesota 55105

St. Thomas, University of
Houston, Texas 77006

St. Vincent College
Latrobe, Pennsylvania 15650

Salem College
Winston-Salem, North Carolina 27108

Salem State College
Salem, Massachusetts 01970

Salisbury University
Salisbury, Maryland 21801

Samford University
Birmingham, Alabama 35229

◆ **San Diego State University**
San Diego, California 92182

◆ **San Diego, University of**
San Diego, California 92110

San Francisco Art Institute
San Francisco, California 94133

San Francisco Conservatory of Music
San Francisco, California 94122

San Francisco, University of
San Francisco, California 94117

◆ **San Francisco State University**
San Francisco, California 94132

San Jose State University
San Jose, California 95192

◆ **Santa Clara University**
Santa Clara, California 95053

Santa Fe, College of
Santa Fe, New Mexico 87501

Sarah Lawrence College
Bronxville, New York 10708

School of the Art Institute of Chicago
Chicago, Illinois 60603

Schreiner University
Kerrville, Texas 78028

Sciences in Philadelphia, University of the
Philadelphia, Pennsylvania 19104

Scranton, University of
Scranton, Pennsylvania 18510

◆ **Scripps College**
Claremont, California 91711

Seattle Pacific University
Seattle, Washington 98119

Seattle University
Seattle, Washington 98122

◆ Phi Beta Kappa Schools   ▮ Predominantly African-American Institutions

Seton Hall University
South Orange, New Jersey 07079

Seton Hill College
Greensburg, Pennsylvania 15601

▪ **Shaw University**
Raleigh, North Carolina 27601

Shawnee State University
Portsmouth, Ohio 45662

Shenandoah University
Winchester, Virginia 22601

Shepherd University
Shepherdstown, West Virginia 25443

Shippensburg University
Shippensburg, Pennsylvania 17257

Shorter College
Rome, Georgia 30165

Siena College
Loudonville, New York 12211

Siena Heights University
Adrian, Michigan 49221

Silver Lake College
Mantiowoc, Wisconsin 54220

Simmons College
Boston, Massachusetts 02115

Simpson College
Indianola, Iowa 50125

Sioux Falls, University of
Sioux Falls, South Dakota 57105

◆ **Skidmore College**
Saratoga Springs, New York 12866

Slippery Rock University
Slippery Rock, Pennsylvania 16057

◆ **Smith College**
Northampton, Massachusetts 01063

◆ **South, University of the**
Sewanee, Tennessee 37383

South Alabama, University of
Mobile, Alabama 36688

◆ **South Carolina, University of**
Columbia, South Carolina 29208

◆ **South Dakota, University of**
Vermillion, South Dakota 57069

South Dakota School of Mines and Technology
Rapid City, South Dakota 57701

South Dakota State University
Brookings, South Dakota 57006

South Florida, University of
Tampa, Florida 33620

Southeast Missouri State University
Cape Girardeau, Missouri 63701

Southeastern Louisiana State
Hammond, Louisiana 70402

Southeastern Oklahoma State University
Durant, Oklahoma 74701

◆ **Southern California, University of**
Los Angeles, California 90089

Southern Connecticut State University
New Haven, Connecticut 06515

Southern Illinois University
Carbondale, Illinois 62901

Southern Illinois University
Edwardsville, Illinois 62026

Southern Maine, University of
Portland, Maine 04103

◆ **Southern Methodist University**
Dallas, Texas 75275

Southern Mississippi, University of
Hattiesburg, Mississippi 39406

Southern Nazarene University
Bethany, Oklahoma 73008

Southern Oregon University
Ashland, Oregon 97520

Southern Polytechnic University
Marietta, Georgia 30060

Southern Utah University
Cedar City, Utah 84720

Southwest Baptist University
Bolivar, Missouri 65613

Southwestern College
Winfield, Kansas 67156

◆ **Southwestern University**
Georgetown, Texas 78627

Southwestern Oklahoma State Univ.
Weatherford, Oklahoma 73096

◆▪ **Spelman College**
Atlanta, Georgia 30314

Spring Hill College
Mobile, Alabama 36608

◆ **Stanford University**
Stanford, California 94305

Stephen F. Austin State University
Nagogdoches, Texas 75962

◆ Phi Beta Kappa Schools ▪ Predominantly African-American Institutions

Stephens College
Columbia, Missouri 65215

Sterling College
Sterling, Kansas 67579

◆ **Stetson University**
Deland, Florida 32720

Stevens Institute of Technology
Hoboken, New Jersey 07030

Stevenson University
Stevenson, Maryland 21153

Stonehill College
North Easton, Massachusetts 02357

Suffolk University
Boston, Massachusetts 02108

Susquehanna University
Selinsgrove, Pennsylvania 17870

◆ **Swarthmore College**
Swarthmore, Pennsylvania 19081

◆ **Sweet Briar College**
Sweet Briar, Virginia 24595

◆ **Syracuse University**
Syracuse, New York 13210

T **Tabor College**
Hillsboro, Kansas 67063

Tampa, University of
Tampa, Florida 33606

Tarleton State University
Stephenville, Texas 76402

Taylor University
Upland, Indiana 46989

◆ **Temple University**
Philadelphia, Pennsylvania 19122

Tennessee Tech University
Cookeville, Tennessee 38505

Tennessee, University of, at
  Chattanooga, Tennessee 37403
  ◆ **Knoxville,** Tennessee 37996
  Martin, Tennessee 38238

Texas, University of, at
  Arlington, Texas 76019
  ◆ **Austin,** Texas 78712
  Dallas, Richardson, Texas 75083
  Health Science Center
    San Antonio, Texas 78284
  San Antonio, Texas 78249
  Tyler, Texas 75799

◆ **Texas A & M**
College Station, Texas 77843

Texas A & M - Commerce
Commerce, Texas 75429

Texas A & M - Corpus Christi
Corpus Christi, Texas 78412

Texas A & M - Kingsville
Kingsville, Texas 78363

◆ **Texas Christian University**
Fort Worth, Texas 76129

Texas Lutheran University
Seguin, Texas 78155

Texas State University-San Marcos
San Marcos, Texas 78666

◆ **Texas Tech University**
Lubbock, Texas 79409

Texas Wesleyan University
Fort Worth, Texas 76105

Thomas College
Waterville, Maine 04901

Thomas More College
Crestview Hills, Kentucky 41017

Toledo, University of
Toledo, Ohio 43606

■ **Tougaloo College**
Tougaloo, Mississippi 39174

Towson University
Towson, Maryland 21204

Transylvania University
Lexington, Kentucky 40508

◆ **Trinity College**
Hartford, Connecticut 06106

◆ **Trinity Washington University**
Washington, DC 20017

◆ **Trinity University**
San Antonio, Texas 78212

Tri-State University
Angola, Indiana 46703

Troy State University
Troy, Alabama 36082

◆ **Truman State University**
Kirksville, Missouri 63501

◆ **Tufts University**
Medford, Massachusetts 02155

◆ **Tulane University**
New Orleans, Louisiana 70118

◆ **Tulsa, University of**
Tulsa, Oklahoma 74104

■ **Tuskegee University**
Tuskegee, Alabama 36088

U **Union College**
Lincoln, Nebraska 68506

◆ **Union College**
Schenectady, New York 12308

Union University
Jackson, Tennessee 38305

U.S. Air Force Academy
Colorado Springs, Colorado 80840

U.S. Coast Guard Academy
New London, Connecticut 06320

U.S. Military Academy
West Point, New York 10996

U.S. Naval Academy
Annapolis, Maryland 21402

◆ **Ursinus College**
Collegeville, Pennsylvania 19426

◆ **Utah, University of**
Salt Lake City, Utah 84112

Utah State University
Logan, Utah 84322

Utica College
Utica, New York 13502

V ◆ **Valparaiso University**
Valparaiso, Indiana 46383

◆ **Vanderbilt University**
Nashville, Tennessee 37240

◆ **Vassar College**
Poughkeepsie, New York 12601

◆ **Vermont, University of**
Burlington, Vermont 05401

◆ **Villanova University**
Villanova, Pennsylvania 19085

◆ **Virginia, University of**
Charlottesville, Virginia 22904

Virginia Commonwealth University
Richmond, Virginia 23284

Virginia Military Institute
Lexington, Virginia 24450

◆ **Virginia Polytechnic Institute**
Blacksburg, Virginia 24061

Virginia Wesleyan College
Norfolk, Virginia 23502

Visual Arts, School of
New York, New York 10010

Viterbo University
La Crosse, Wisconsin 54601

W ◆ **Wabash College**
Crawfordsville, Indiana 47933

Wagner College
Staten Island, New York 10301

◆ **Wake Forest University**
Winston-Salem, North Carolina 27109

Walla Walla University
College Place, Washington 99324

Walsh University
North Canton, Ohio, 44720

Warren Wilson College
Asheville, North Carolina 28815

Wartburg College
Waverly, Iowa 50677

Washburn University
Topeka, Kansas 66621

◆ **Washington College**
Chestertown, Maryland 21620

◆ **Washington & Jefferson College**
Washington, Pennsylvania 15301

◆ **Washington & Lee University**
Lexington, Virginia 24450

◆ **Washington University in St. Louis**
St. Louis, Missouri 63130

◆ **Washington, University of**
Seattle, Washington 98195

◆ **Washington State University**
Pullman, Washington 99164

◆ **Wayne State College**
Wayne, Nebraska 68787

Wayne State University
Detroit, Michigan 48202

Waynesburg University
Waynesburg, Pennsylvania 15370

Weber State University
Ogden, Utah 84408

Webster University
St. Louis, Missouri 63119

◆ **Wellesley College**
Wellesley, Massachusetts 02481

◆ **Wells College**
Aurora, New York 13026

Wesleyan College
Macon, Georgia 31210

◆ **Wesleyan University**
Middletown, Connecticut 06457

◆ Phi Beta Kappa Schools ■ Predominantly African-American Institutions

West Chester University
West Chester, Pennsylvania 19383

West Florida, University of
Pensacola, FL 32514

◆ **West Virginia University**
Morgantown, West Virginia 26506

West Virginia Wesleyan College
Buckhannon, West Virginia 26201

Western Carolina University
Cullowhee, North Carolina 28723

Western Connecticut State University
Danbury, Connecticut 06810

Western Illinois University
Marcomb, Illinois 61455

Western Kentucky University
Bowling Green, Kentucky 42101

◆ **Western Michigan University**
Kalamazoo, Michigan 49008

Western New England College
Springfield, Massachusetts 01119

Western State College of Colorado
Gunnison, Colorado 81231

Western Washington University
Bellingham, Washington 98225

Westfield State College
Westfield, Massachusetts 01086

Westminster College
Fulton, Missouri 65251

Westminster College
Wilmington, Pennsylvania 16172

Westminster College
Salt Lake City, Utah 84105

Westmont College
Santa Barbara, California 93108

Wheaton College
Wheaton, Illinois 60187

◆ **Wheaton College**
Norton, Massachusetts 02766

Wheeling Jesuit University
Wheeling, West Virginia 26003

Wheelock College
Boston, Massachusetts 02215

◆ **Whitman College**
Walla Walla, Washington 99362

Whittier College
Whittier, California 90608

Whitworth College
Spokane, Washington 99251

Wichita State University
Wichita, Kansas 67260

Widener University
Chester, Pennsylvania 19013

■ **Wilberforce University**
Wilberforce, Ohio 45384

Wilkes University
Wilkes-Barre, Pennsylvania 18766

◆ **Willamette University**
Salem, Oregon 97301

William Jewell College
Liberty, Missouri 64068

◆ **William & Mary, College of**
Williamsburg, Virginia 23187

William Paterson University
Wayne, New Jersey 07470

◆ **Williams College**
Williamstown, Massachusetts 01267

Wilmington College
Wilmington, Ohio 45177

◆ **Wilson College**
Chambersburg, Pennsylvania 17201

Wingate University
Wingate, North Carolina 28174

Winona State University
Winona, Minnesota 55987

Winthrop University
Rock Hill, South Carolina 29733

Wisconsin Lutheran College
Milwaukee, Wisconsin 53226

◆ **Wisconsin, University of, at**
 Eau Claire, Wisconsin 54701
 Green Bay, Wisconsin 54311
 LaCrosse, Wisconsin 54601
 ◆ **Madison,** Wisconsin 53706
 ◆ **Milwaukee,** Wisconsin 53201
 Platteville, Wisconsin 53818
 River Falls, Wisconsin 54022
 Stevens Point, Wisconsin 54481
 Stout, Menomonie, Wisconsin 54751
 Superior, Wisconsin 54880
 Whitewater, Wisconsin 53190

◆ **Wittenberg University**
Springfield, Ohio 45501

◆ **Wofford College**
Spartanburg, South Carolina 29303

Woodbury University
Burbank, California 91510

◆ Phi Beta Kappa Schools   ■ Predominantly African-American Institutions

◆ **Wooster, College of**
Wooster, Ohio 44691

Worcester Polytechnic Institute
Worcester, Massachusetts 01609

Worcester State College
Worcester, Massachusetts 01602

Wright State University
Dayton, Ohio 45435

◆ **Wyoming, University of**
Laramie, Wyoming 82071

X ◆ **Xavier University**
Cincinnati, Ohio 45207

▌ **Xavier University of Louisiana**
New Orleans, Louisiana 70125

Y ◆ **Yale University**
New Haven, Connecticut 06520

✡ **Yeshiva University**
New York, New York 10033

York College
York, Nebraska 68467

York College of Pennsylvania
York, Pennsylvania 17403

Youngstown State University
Youngstown, Ohio 44555

APPENDIX B

The Miscellaneous Majors Colleges Used In This Study

Aeronautics, College of
Flushing, NY 11369

Andrews University
Berrien Springs, MI 49104

Arkansas, U. of
Pine Bluff, AR 71601

Atlantic, College of the
Bar Harbor, ME 04609

Aurora University
Aurora, Il 60506

Bellevue University
Bellevue, NE 68005

■ **Bethune-Cookman College**
Daytona Beach, FL 32114

Bridgeport, University of
Bridgeport,, Connecticut 06604

Brooks Institute of Photography
Santa Barbara, CA 93108

Cabrini College
Radnor, PA 19087

Carlow College
Pittsburgh, PA 15213

Central Oklahoma University
Edmond, OK 73034

■ **Central State University**
Wilberforce, OH 45384

Centenary College
Hackettstown, NJ 07840

Chadron State University
Chadron, Nebraska 69337

Cincinnati College of Mortuary Science
Cincinnati, OH 45224

Clarion University of Pennsylvania
Clarion, PA 16214

Cleveland State University
Cleveland, OH 44115

Columbia College - Hollywood
Tarzana, CA 91356

Columbus College of Art & Design
Columbus, OH 43215

Cortland State College
Cortland, NY 13045

Curry College
Milton, MA 02186

Daniel Webster College
Nashua, NH 03063

Davis & Elkins College
Elkins, WV 26241

Deep Springs College
Deep Springs Via Dyer, NV 89010

Defiance College, The
Defiance, OH 43512

Eastern Montana College
Billings, MT 59101

Eastern New Mexico University
Portales, NM 88130

Eugene Lang College
(New School Social Research)
New York, NY 11743

Evergreen State College
Olympia, WA 98505

Fashion Institute of Technology
New York, NY 10001

Hampshire College
Amherst, MA 01002

Holy Family College
Philadelphia, PA 19114

Johnson & Wales University
Providence , Rhode Island 02903

Kendall College of Art and Design
Grand Rapids, MI 49503

Lake Erie College
Painesville, OH 44077

Landmark College
Putney, VT 05346

Langston University
Langston, OK 73050

Lees-McRae College
Banner Elk, NC 28604

Loma Linda University
Loma Linda, CA 92350

Lourdes College
Sylvania, OH 43560

Madonna University
Livonia, MI 48150

Maine Maritime
Castine, Maine 04420

Maine, University of
Machias, Maine 04654

Marian College of Fond du Lac
Fond du Lac, WI 54935

APPENDIX B (Continued)
The Miscellaneous Majors Colleges Used In This Study

Mesa State College
Grand Junction, CO 81502

Metropolitan State College
Denver, CO 80204

Midwestern State University
Wichita Falls, TX 76308

Mitchell College
New London, CT 06320

Mount Ida College
Newton Centre, Massachusetts 02459

Mt. St. Claire
Clinton, IA 52732

Neumann College
Aston, PA 19014

University of New England
Biddeford, ME 04005

New Haven, University of
New Haven, CT 06516

New School for Social Research
New York, NY 11743

New York School of Interior Design
New York, NY 10021

North Carolina Wesleyan College
Rocky Mount, NC 27804

Northeastern Louisiana University
Monroe, LA 71209

Northwestern Oklahoma State University
Alva, OK 73717

Park University
Cahokia, IL 62206

Pfeiffer College
Misenheimer, NC 28109

Prescott College
Prescott, AZ 86301

Ringling College of Art & Design
Sarasota, FL 34234

St. Elizabeth, College of
Convent Station, NJ 07960

Saint John's College
Annapolis, MD 21404

Saint Leo College
Saint Leo, FL 33574

Saint Thomas University
Miami, FL 33054

Salem International University
Salem, WV 26426

Salve Regina-The Newport College
Newport, RI 02840

Sam Houston State University
Huntsville, TX 77341

Science and Arts of Oklahoma
Chickasha, Oklahoma 73018

Simon's Rock College of Bard
Great Barrington, MA 01230

Southern Illinois, U. of
Edwardsville, IL 62026

Southern New Hampshire, University of
Manchester, NH 03106

Spring Arbor College
Spring Arbor, MI 49283

SUNY-Farmingdale
Farmingdale, NY 11735

■ **Texas Southern University**
Houston, TX 77004

Texas Woman's University
Denton, TX 76204

Thomas Aquinas College
Santa Paula, CA 93060

Tusculum College
Greenville, TN 37743

United States Merchant Marine Academy
Kings Point, NY 11024

Unity College
Unity, ME 04988

Upper iowa University
Fayette, IA 52142

Virginia Intermont College
Bristol, VA 24201

Webb Institute
Glen Cove, NY 11542

APPENDIX C

Single Sex Colleges Included In This Study

WOMEN'S COLLEGES

Agnes Scott College (GA)
Alverno (WI)
Bay Path College (MA)
Bennett College (NC)
Bryn Mawr College (PA)
Cedar Crest College (PA)
Chatham College (PA)
Converse College(SC)
Hollins College (VA)
Judson College (AL)
Mary Baldwin College (VA)
Meredith College (NC)

Mills College (CA)
Mount Holyoke College (MA)
Pine Manor College (MA)
Rosemont College (PA)
St. Catherine, College of (MN)
Saint Joseph's (CT)
Saint Mary's College (IN)
Salem College (NC)
Scripps College (CA)
Simmons College (MA)
Smith College (MA)
Spelman College (GA)

Stephens College (MO)
Sweet Briar College (VA)
Texas Woman's College
Trinity University (DC)
Wellesley College (MA)
Wesleyan College (GA)

MEN'S COLLEGES

Hampden-Sydney College (VA)
Morehouse College (GA)
Wabash College (IN)

APPENDIX D

Anyone who has been touched by the problem of alcohol or substance abuse, or who has worked with those struggling in recovery, knows that higher education will increasingly have to meet the needs of these persons. Several colleges are trying to address the needs of these students, and The Wellness Institute at Ball State has published a list of wellness dorms. Unfortunately, the grant for this no longer exists, but Ball State in Muncie, Indiana has done a fine job with young people in this area. You might call them at 765-285-8259.

Respectfully submitted,
Joseph W. Streit
Long-time Secondary School Counselor in New Jersey

APPENDIX E

A Simplified Timetable and Checklist for Seniors Planning on College*

SEPTEMBER - OCTOBER	Write for college catalogs, applications, financial aid information and pick up a financial aid booklet, continuing from your junior year.
	Keep up with your volunteer activities and extracurricula.
SEPTEMBER - OCTOBER	Inquire at your high school Guidance Office about upcoming college nights.
SEPTEMBER - NOVEMBER	Continue campus visits as senior year academic commitments permit.
SEPTEMBER	Deadline for mailing in the late October or early November National College Exam Forms.
OCTOBER	Think about which two teachers you will ask to write college recommendations for you.
LATE OCTOBER	Deadline for mailing in the December National College Exam Forms.
NOVEMBER	Prepare a final list of colleges. Talk to your counselor about need-based funds. And look into merit-based money awarded by the colleges themselves.
	Talk to your counselor and/or a favorite teacher - show them your completed college essay, if your colleges require one.
NOVEMBER 1-15	Many early applications due.
NOVEMBER OR DECEMBER	Attend, with your parents, a local financial aid night given by an area high school.
NOVEMBER - DECEMBER	Apply to colleges. But always check deadlines. Some may be earlier.
DECEMBER 1	ROTC Scholarship applications to be in.
EARLY DECEMBER	Last call for mailing in the National College Exam Forms (SAT/ACT).
DECEMBER 15	Profile of Financial Aid Form (Step 1) due to College Scholarship Service (CSS).
JANUARY	Fill out the Financial Aid Form (FAF/FAFSA/PROFILE) or Family Financial Statement. Your counselor has it, and has advice for filling it out. This form will probably help you get a good deal of your total scholarships, jobs, and loans. It is the big one. Apply. Apply. Apply. Even if your family earns over $250,000. Everything flows from these federal forms.
JANUARY - FEBRUARY	Send mid-year reports to colleges.
FEBRUARY 1	Profile application (Step 2) to College Scholarship Service (CSS).
MARCH	Local scholarship forms available in the guidance office.
EARLY APRIL	All colleges will notify you by this time if they will accept you or not. The more competitive colleges usually deliberate longer and many of these top schools wait until the first week of April to notify you.
MID-APRIL	If unhappy with the financial aid package at any of the colleges where you have been accepted, you, the student, call that office and discuss it.
LATE APRIL	Send deposit to selected college.
MAY 1	Inform all colleges which accepted you whether or not you plan to attend.
MAY 1	Notify Guidance Office of your choice of college.
MAY - JUNE	Apply for summer jobs so that you can meet summer earnings expectations.
	Don't forget to graduate from high school!
SUMMER	Attend college orientation.
LATE SUMMER	Write Thank You notes to organizations that awarded you money.

*NOTE: Before your senior year, prepare preliminary list of colleges you're interested in and those you would like to visit. Spring visits in the junior year are advised.

APPENDIX F

The Get-Going Form

A simple, useful form to use with the college-bound to get them started applying to colleges. The student and/or counselor and/or parent should fill in four colleges below, complete with address and zip codes.

Dear Student:

Within the next two weeks, please write to the Director of Admissions at the schools listed below, requesting information. A sample letter is included at the bottom of the page.

1. _____

_____

_____

2. _____

_____

_____

3. _____

_____

_____

4. _____

_____

_____

SAMPLE LETTER

Date

Director of Admissions
Name of College
Address of College and Zip Code

Dear Director:

I am a student of Northampton High School in Northampton, Massachusetts and expect to graduate in June, 2012.

I am interested in your school and would appreciate your sending me an application for admission and information concerning your financial aid program, and your _____ program of studies. Thank you.

Very truly yours,

Your signature
Your Name
Your Address and Zip Code

COUNSELOR'S NOTES

COUNSELOR'S NOTES

ABOUT THE AUTHOR

Fred Rugg

Raised by an older sister, FRED RUGG was one of a handful of "Huckleberry Finn" cases that the top universities accepted in the mid-1960's. He is a writer, speaker, workshop presenter, and author. Unlike virtually all other college guidebook people, Rugg is one of the true professionals, having directed secondary college counseling programs for 20 years in all types of communities. A 1967 Applied Math graduate from Brown, Rugg is the holder of advanced degrees in secondary school guidance and administration. Early in his career he was employed as a statistician for two New England companies and worked his way through Ivy League Brown - the only member of his class to enter public school teaching. Offering dozens of workshops yearly from coast to coast, Fred is an often animated, charismatic and humorous speaker, and has become well known for his evening speaking engagements for parents and students, which are informative and fun. He has lived and worked just about everywhere in America, has been married for over 40 years, and has two daughters. Beginning with his first volunteer assignment (Brown Youth Guidance), Rugg has been a perennial volunteer, and he's taught courses at four colleges. A native of New England, he has been based in Colorado and Florida, and now resides in California. As always, he is totally independent of the four-year colleges.

✂ **PLEASE CLIP AND MAIL TO:** ✂

Rugg's Recommendations • P.O. Box 417 • Fallbrook, CA 92088

Please send me _____ copies of *Rugg's Recommendations on the Colleges* at $25.95 (plus shipping/see page 300) each.

I have enclosed my check in the amount of $ _____   VISA   MasterCard

Name _____

Address _____

City _____ State _____ Zip _____

For additional information call 760-728-4467 or 760-728-4558.
Other products and resources from Rugg's appear on pages 298-299.

FROM RUGG'S RECOMMENDATIONS...

INFORMATION THAT IS TO THE POINT, THAT YOU CAN USE IMMEDIATELY

Saving the college counselor enormous time with lists and answers found nowhere else - presented from the secondary school point of view!

FROM RUGG, YOU ALWAYS GET A NEW SLANT ON THE COLLEGES

---

1. *THE NEW BOOK: RUGG'S RECOMMENDATIONS ON THE COLLEGES 27th Ed.*
Locating Quality Undergraduate Colleges For Counselors, Parents & Students.
ISBN #978-1-883062-76-7 • LC89-062896 • $25.95 • © 2010 by Frederick E. Rugg

★ **Over 800 Entry Changes in the New LAVENDER Book** ★

Rugg's Recommendations on the Colleges recommends quality departments at quality colleges. It is the primary brainstorming source for secondary public school counselors in creating a student's initial college list. Three new majors have been added and there are wholesale changes on over 38 others. Rugg's 27th edition is available listing 14,000 quality departments at 1115 quality colleges. The guidebook has been designated nationally as "a revered staple, the book parents and students must start with" in the search for a college to attend. The 27th edition is the accumulation of 40 years of work in the undergraduate college admissions process, and as always, ***Rugg's*** is independent of the colleges. There are over 800 entry changes since the 26th edition, 119 majors, 190 recommended departments per major.

"You make it too easy for the 21st - century guidance counselor. So much information, yet so easy to use. Great job!"

—Ralph Strycharz
Long-time teacher and counselor
Hampshire Reg. H.S. (MA)

"A Revered Staple."

—West Coast Library Reviewer

"I love your book!"

—Carol Gill, Educational Consultants
Dobbs Ferry, NY

"I am having great success with your (book) help every year."

—Bobbi Pickett, Pickett College Counseling
Middletown, CT

---

2. *THE SPECIAL REPORT: TWENTY MORE TIPS ON THE COLLEGES, Revised*
Twenty new behind the scenes tips. Ideal for counselors, parents, and students. 16th Edition.
$8.95 • © 2010

Brutally honest information about colleges and the application process. This Special Report, ***Twenty More Tips on the Colleges,*** offers important insights into assessing a college or university. Author Rugg succinctly presents 20 key tips to assist counselors, parents and students in selecting the best college for a student. Tips include colleges with high success rates for medical school acceptance, hot Canadian colleges, Rugg's "Book of the Year", and observations from top counselors around the U.S.A. Overlooked state institutions, as well as other important and helpful comments, are included. The college search and selection process is incomplete without reading the valuable information contained within this Special Report.

"I have known Fred Rugg for nearly forty years, since we were on the staff together at Bristol (RI) High School. Fred has developed an uncanny insight and he is able to ask the right questions of both student and admission officer. Always up-to-date; never disappointing. Read his material; attend the seminars. They are great!"

—Robert Jeffrey, Independent Consultant
Orlando, FL

"I have used your information for years. It is a wonderful resource."

—Harriet Gershman, Academic
Counseling Services, Evanston, IL

---

3. *FORTY TIPS ON THE COLLEGES:* **THE REVISED SPECIAL REPORT 16th edition**
For all college bound students, parents, and their counselors. 21 pages. Over 40 college entry changes for 2010.
$11.95 (money back guarantee) • Revised 2010

Get the "insider's" advice on college admissions. In ***Forty Tips on the Colleges,*** author Rugg shares with the reader 40 key tips on the college admissions process. Rugg spent in excess of 3000 hours visiting with over 9000 secondary school counselors in 48 states, to compile the information contained in this transcript. These insightful suggestions provide the reader with some of the unwritten do's and don'ts in the college admissions process. Rugg presents his 40 tips, accompanied by his personal observations of the campuses, with honesty and a sense of humor. ***Forty Tips on the Colleges*** offers straight talk about selecting a college and gaining admission. The special report contains helpful advice for the student, parent and school counselor alike. Topics include previously unpublished tips on which colleges care the most about their students; colleges with good learning disabilities programs; and how to choose a college where the student "fits in." The tips also contain helpful information concerning financial aid, college applications and SAT/ACT scores. This **must read** is our most popular special report, and includes the revised "Financial Aid in 3000 Words."

"Your book is an incredible resource. Every counselor should have a copy close at hand as a tool to help guide our youth on their academic journeys. Thanks for all you do!"

—Wendy Andreen, PhD.
College Counselor,
Memorial Private School
Houston, TX

"Rugg has implemented a comprehensive system of researching that combines statistical analysis with direct communication with hundreds of counselors and teachers around the country. He is able to sift and sort the objective with the subjective."

—New England
Independant College Counselor

4. THE SPECIAL REPORT: *THIRTY QUESTIONS ON THE COLLEGES,*
Revised 16th Edition

For all college bound students, parents and their counselors. 21 pages.

$9.95 • Revised 2010 • Over 50 college entry changes

Thirty frequently asked questions with some answers even Deans of Admissions can't give you. This Special Report includes: 200 recommended colleges where black youngsters will maximize their education • What makes individuals maximize college? • Community college graduates – how do top colleges really view them at transfer time? • The best of the best journalism schools, computer schools and architecture schools • Understanding student body make-up. And 23 other topics based on over 425 counselor meetings across the country. Counselors and parents find this transcript form extremely useful (yes, it's O.K. to copy it with appropriate acknowledgement).

> *"Your college guide is my #1 book when I visit junior classes every spring."*
> —Dr. Jim Burke
> East Brunswick H.S. (NJ)

> *"I have used Rugg's Recommendations on the Colleges for many years, as a Guidance Counselor and School Administrator. The research is excellent, up-to-date, and a most wonderful resource."*
> —Helen Unger
> Long-time N.J. Director of Pupil Personnel Services and College Counselor Consultant

5. *THIRTY SEMINAR SHEETS* $25

Our most popular lists are now available separately. Includes all of the rankings in #6 below, plus colleges where the following youngsters maximize their education: Jewish (120), Hispanic (150), Asian (130), and Black (170). Plus Dream (Magic) Colleges, and best colleges for helping and advising athletes.

> *"I rely on your seminar sheets and book constantly."*
> —Sharon Barkins-Wasson
> Director of Counseling
> Crespi Carmelite HS, Encino, CA

6. *THE COLLEGE SEMINAR SUBSTITUTE*

For Secondary School Counselors, public and private • $55 (lists updated monthly)

Can't make it to a college seminar? Do the next best thing: Order this special package. *The College Seminar Substitute* provides you with 90% of the 60 items covered in our seminar agenda. In this package you receive Rugg's three Special Reports, *Twenty More Tips on the Colleges,* *Forty Tips on the Colleges,* *Thirty Questions and Answers,* plus 30 seminar handouts. These handouts contain over 3000 entries—a wealth of information. Topics covered include: a listing of quiet and safe campuses, snob schools; prestigious school rankings; underrated schools, best undergraduate schools for Pre-Med (not Ivyish), the top 250 schools for the learning disabled, the most generous schools, new information on financial aid; advice on school recommendations; a listing of colleges for the overachiever; big colleges that play small; rated Catholic colleges; and four minority lists. This package gives the counselor a foundation in understanding and navigating the admission game. See why over 9000 secondary school counselors attended Rugg's College Admission Seminars.

> *"It is the best single source of information that we have. It answers the questions most frequently asked by parents. Your college materials help both the beginning and experienced counselor. The various ratings and lists inspire both students and their parents to further research the college scene. When parents and students are clueless, your information provides direction and humor in beginning the college selection process."*
> —Ira Lipton, Counselor, E. Hampton (NY)

7. *SPECIAL! SEND IT ALL!* $75

Includes 1 book, 3 special reports, 30 seminar sheets—all our products.

> *"As always, I find your reports and book invaluable."*
> —Michelle Koetke, Ind. College Counselor
> Newbury Park, CA

➡ *ORDER FORM ON REVERSE*

Rugg's advice and comments have appeared in such diverse publications as USA TODAY, ROLLING STONE, COLLEGE BOUND, THE BOSTON GLOBE, THE CLEVELAND PLAIN DEALER, NEW JERSEY MONTHLY, THE WASHINGTON POST and BUSINESS WEEK.

2010 PRODUCT ORDER FORM

ITEM #	TITLE OR DESCRIPTION	PRICE	QTY	AMOUNT
1	*Rugg's Recommendations on the Colleges:* The Book (27th ed.)	$25.95		
2	*20 More Tips on the Colleges:* Revised Special Report (16th ed.)	$ 8.95		
3	*Forty Tips on the Colleges:* Revised Special Report (16th ed.)	$11.95		
4	*Thirty Questions & Answers:* Revised Special Report (16th ed.)	$ 9.95		
5	*Thirty Seminar Sheets: Colleges*	$25.00		
6	*College Seminar Substitute:* Includes 2 thru 5	$55.00		
7	**SEND IT ALL!!!** Send one of each (Items 1-5)	$75.00		

Order 5 or more books:	Only $23.00 each! Discount price available only on the book.	
Prepaid Orders over $89:	Subtract $4 from total.	
International Orders:	Shipping and handling cost: Actual Cost.	
California Residents:	Please add 8.75% sales tax.	
SHIPPING CHARGES: (all orders mailed first class)	Postage $6.00	

SUBTOTAL	
Less $4 for prepaid orders over $89	
Sales Tax (CA only) 8.75%	
Shipping	
TOTAL ENCLOSED	

Name _____

Address _____

City _____ State _____ Zip _____

Send to:

RUGG'S RECOMMENDATIONS

P.O. Box 417 • Fallbrook, CA 92088

**For further information, call us at 760-728-4558 or fax 760-728-4467
OR visit our Website at http://www.ruggsrecs.com**